C++ for Fortran Programmers

C++ for Fortran Programmers

Ira Pohl

University of California
Santa Cruz

ADDISON-WESLEY

An Imprint of Addison Wesley Longman, Inc.
Reading, Massachusetts • Harlow, England • Menlo Park, California
Berkeley, California • Don Mills, Ontario • Sydney
Bonn • Amsterdam • Tokyo • Mexico City

Many of the designations used by manufacturers and sellers to distinguish their products are claimed as trademarks. Where those designations appear in this book, and Addison Wesley Longman, Inc. was aware of a trademark claim, the designations have been printed in initial capital letters or all capital letters.

The author and publisher have taken care in preparation of this book, but make no expressed or implied warranty of any kind and assume no responsibility for errors or omissions. No liability is assumed for incidental or consequential damages in connection with or arising out of the use of the information or programs contained herein.

The publisher offer discounts on this book when ordered in quantity for special sales. For more information, please contact:
    Corporate & Professional Publishing Group
    Addison Wesley Longman, Inc.
    One Jacob Way
    Reading, Massachusetts 01867

Library of Congress Cataloging-in-Publication Data
Pohl, Ira
   C++ for Fortran Programmers / Ira Pohl.
     p. cm.
   Includes bibliographical references and index.
   ISBN 0-201-92483-8
   1. C++ (Computer program language) I. Title.
QA76.73.C153P644   1997
005.13'3–dc21   97-13771
                                                                                             CIP

Copyright © 1997 by Addison Wesley Longman, Inc.

All rights reserved. No part of this publication may be reproduced, stored in a retrieval system, or transmitted, in any form or by any means, electronic, mechanical, photocopying, recording, or otherwise, without the prior written permission of the publisher. Printed in the United States of America. Published simultaneously in Canada.

0-201-92483-8

1 2 3 4 5 6 7 8 9 -MA- 0100999897
First printing, June 1997

Contents

Preface xv

1 An Overview of C++ and Object-Oriented Programming 1
    1.1   Object-Oriented Programming 2
    1.2   Why Learn C++? 4
    1.3   Fortran as a Starting Point 4
    1.4   Classes and Abstract Data Types 7
    1.5   Constructors and Destructors 9
    1.6   Overloading 10
    1.7   Inheritance 13
    1.8   Polymorphism 15
    1.9   Templates 17
    1.10 The Standard Template Library (STL) 19
    1.11 C++ Exceptions 20
    1.12 Benefits of Object-Oriented Programming 21

2 Native Types and Statements 23
    2.1   Program Elements 24
           2.1.1 Comments 24
           2.1.2 Keywords 25
           2.1.3 Identifiers 26
           2.1.4 Literals 26
           2.1.5 Operators and Punctuators 28
    2.2   Input/Output 30
    2.3   Program Structure 31
    2.4   Simple Types 34
           2.4.1 Initialization 36
    2.5   The Traditional Conversions 37
    2.6   Enumeration Types 41
    2.7   Expressions 42
    2.8   Statements 47
           2.8.1 Assignment and Expressions 47
           2.8.2 The Compound Statement 48
           2.8.3 The `if` and `if-else` Statements 48
           2.8.4 The `while` Statement 50
           2.8.5 The `for` Statement 51
           2.8.6 The `do` Statement 53
           2.8.7 The `break` and `continue` Statements 54

		2.8.8 The `switch` Statement	56
		2.8.9 The `goto` Statement	58
	Summary		58
	Exercises		60

3 Functions, Pointers, and Arrays ... 65

3.1	Functions		65
		3.1.1 Function Invocation	66
3.2	Function Definition		66
3.3	The `return` Statement		68
3.4	Function Prototypes		70
		3.4.1 Recursion	73
3.5	Default Arguments		74
3.6	Functions as Arguments		75
3.7	Overloading Functions		76
3.8	Inlining		77
3.9	Scope and Storage Class		78
		3.9.1 The Storage Class `auto`	80
		3.9.2 The Storage Class `register`	80
		3.9.3 The Storage Class `extern`	81
		3.9.4 The Storage Class `static`	82
		3.9.5 Linkage Mysteries	84
3.10	Namespaces		84
3.11	Pointer Types		85
		3.11.1 Addressing and Dereferencing	86
		3.11.2 Pointer-Based Call-by-Reference	87
3.12	Reference Declarations and Call-by-Reference		89
3.13	The Uses of `void`		93
3.14	Arrays and Pointers		95
		3.14.1 Subscripting	96
		3.14.2 Initialization	97
3.15	The Relationship Between Arrays and Pointers		97
3.16	Passing Arrays to Functions		99
3.17	Strings: A Kernel-Language ADT		100
3.18	Multidimensional Arrays		101
3.19	Assertions and Program Correctness		102
3.20	Free-Store Operators `new` and `delete`		104
	Summary		107
	Exercises		109

4 Classes ... 117

4.1	The Aggregate Type `struct` and `class`		118
4.2	Structure Pointer Operator		119
		4.2.1 `typedef` Declarations	120
4.3	Member Functions		120

	4.4	Access: Private and Public	123
	4.5	Classes	124
	4.6	Class Scope	125
		4.6.1 Scope Resolution Operator ::	125
		4.6.2 Nested Classes	126
	4.7	An Example: Flushing	128
	4.8	`static` Member	130
	4.9	The `this` Pointer	132
	4.10	`static` and `const` Members	133
		4.10.1 Mutable	137
	4.11	Unions	137
	4.12	Bit Fields	139
	4.13	A Container Class Example: `ch_stack`	140
	4.14	Fortran 90 Equivalence	142
	4.15	Pragmatics	144
		Summary	145
		Exercises	146
5	**Constructors and Destructors**		**151**
	5.1	Classes with Constructors	152
		5.1.1 The Default Constructor	153
		5.1.2 Constructor Initializer	154
		5.1.3 Constructors as Conversions	154
		5.1.4 Improving the `point` Class	155
	5.2	Constructing a Dynamically Sized Stack	157
		5.2.1 The Copy Constructor	159
	5.3	Classes with Destructors	160
	5.4	An Example: Dynamically Allocated Strings	161
	5.5	The Class `functor`	166
	5.6	The Class `dbl_vect`	167
		5.6.1 `dbl_vect` as a Linear Vector Type	169
	5.7	Members that Are Class Types	170
	5.8	Example: A Singly Linked List	171
	5.9	Two-Dimensional Arrays	176
	5.10	Polynomials as a Linked List	177
	5.11	Strings Using Reference Semantics	184
	5.12	No Constructor, Copy Constructor, and Other Mysteries	186
		5.12.1 Destructor Details	188
	5.13	Pragmatics	188
		Summary	189
		Exercises	190

6 Operator Overloading and Conversions 199
- 6.1 ADT Conversions 200
- 6.2 Overloading and Function Selection. 201
- 6.3 Friend Functions. 204
- 6.4 Overloading Operators. 207
- 6.5 Unary Operator Overloading 208
- 6.6 Binary Operator Overloading 211
- 6.7 Overloading Assignment and Subscripting Operators 213
- 6.8 Polynomial: Type and Language Expectations. 216
- 6.9 Overloading I/O Operators << and >> 218
- 6.10 Overloading Operator () for Indexing. 219
- 6.11 Pointer Operators. 222
  - 6.11.1 Pointer to Class Member 224
- 6.12 Overloading `new` and `delete`........................ 226
- 6.13 Pragmatics 229
  - 6.13.1 Signature Matching 230
  - Summary. 232
  - Exercises. 233

7 Visitation: Iterators and Containers. 245
- 7.1 Visitation 245
- 7.2 Iterators 247
- 7.3 An Example: `quicksort()`. 248
- 7.4 Friendly Classes and Iterators 251
- 7.5 Generic Programming with `void*` 254
- 7.6 List and List Iterator. 257
- 7.7 Using Vectors for Numerical Processing 261
- 7.8 Pragmatics 264
  - Summary. 265
  - Exercises. 265

8 Templates, Generic Programming, and STL 269
- 8.1 Template Class `stack` 270
- 8.2 Function Templates 272
  - 8.2.1 Signature Matching and Overloading 274
- 8.3 Class Templates 275
  - 8.3.1 Friends. 275
  - 8.3.2 Static Members 276
  - 8.3.3 Class Template Arguments 276
- 8.4 Parameterizing the Class `vector`. 277
- 8.5 Parameterizing `quicksort()` 281
- 8.6 Parameterized Binary Search Tree 283
- 8.7 STL 287

	8.8	Containers	288
		8.8.1 Sequence Containers	290
		8.8.2 Associative Containers	293
		8.8.3 Container Adaptors	295
	8.9	Iterators	296
		8.9.1 The `istream_iterator` and `ostream_iterator`	297
		8.9.2 Iterator Adaptors	298
	8.10	Algorithms	299
		8.10.1 Sorting Algorithms	300
		8.10.2 Nonmutating Sequence Algorithms	301
		8.10.3 Mutating Sequence Algorithms	302
		8.10.4 Numerical Algorithms	303
	8.11	Functions	304
	8.12	Function Adaptors	306
	8.13	Numerical Integration Made Easy	307
	8.14	Pragmatics	309
		Summary	310
		Exercises	311
9	**Inheritance**		315
	9.1	A Derived Class	316
	9.2	Typing Conversions and Visibility	318
	9.3	Code Reuse: A Binary Tree Class	321
	9.4	Virtual Functions	324
	9.5	Abstract Base Classes	328
	9.6	Templates and Inheritance	334
	9.7	Multiple Inheritance	336
	9.8	Inheritance and Design	339
		9.8.1 Subtyping Form	340
	9.9	Run-Time Type Identification	341
	9.10	Pragmatics	342
		Summary	344
		Exercises	346
10	**Exceptions**		351
	10.1	Using *assert.h*	351
	10.2	C++ Exceptions	352
	10.3	Throwing Exceptions	354
		10.3.1 Rethrown Exceptions	355
		10.3.2 Exception Expressions	356
	10.4	Try Blocks	357
	10.5	Handlers	358
	10.6	Exception Specification	359
	10.7	`terminate()` and `unexpected()`	359
	10.8	Example Exception Code	360

	10.9 Standard Exceptions and Their Uses	362
	10.10 Pragmatics	364
	Summary	365
	Exercises	367

11 OOP Using C++ . . . 369
    11.1 OOP Language Requirements . . . 369
    11.2 ADTs in Non-OOP Languages . . . 370
    11.3 Clients and Manufacturers . . . 372
    11.4 Reuse and Inheritance . . . 373
    11.5 Polymorphism . . . 374
    11.6 Language Complexity . . . 375
    11.7 C++ OOP Bandwagon . . . 376
    11.8 Platonism: Tabula Rasa Design . . . 377
    11.9 Design Principles . . . 378
    11.10 Schema, Diagrams, and Tools . . . 379
    11.11 Design Patterns . . . 382
    11.12 C++: A Critique . . . 383
    Summary . . . 385
    Exercises . . . 386

A ASCII Character Codes . . . 389

B Operator Precedence and Associativity . . . 391

C Fortran 90 and C++ . . . 393
    C.1 Program Structure . . . 393
    C.2 Identifiers . . . 396
    C.3 Simple Data Types . . . 397
    C.4 Statements . . . 398

D Language Guide . . . 403
    D.1 Program Structure . . . 403
    D.2 Lexical Elements . . . 404
        D.2.1 Comments . . . 404
        D.2.2 Identifiers . . . 405
        D.2.3 Keywords . . . 405
    D.3 Constants . . . 406
    D.4 Declarations and Scope Rules . . . 409
    D.5 Namespaces . . . 411
    D.6 Linkage Rules . . . 413
    D.7 Types . . . 414
    D.8 Conversion Rules and Casts . . . 417

D.9	Expressions and Operators		420
	D.9.1	`sizeof` Expressions	421
	D.9.2	Autoincrement and Autodecrement Expressions	422
	D.9.3	Arithmetic Expressions	422
	D.9.4	Relational, Equality, and Logical Expressions	423
	D.9.5	Assignment Expressions	424
	D.9.6	Comma Expressions	425
	D.9.7	Conditional Expressions	425
	D.9.8	Bit-Manipulation Expressions	426
	D.9.9	Address and Indirection Expressions	427
	D.9.10	`new` and `delete` Expressions	427
	D.9.11	Other Expressions	430
D.10	Statements		431
	D.10.1	Expression Statements	433
	D.10.2	The Compound Statement	433
	D.10.3	The `if` and `if-else` Statements	433
	D.10.4	The `while` Statement	434
	D.10.5	The `for` Statement	434
	D.10.6	The `do` Statement	435
	D.10.7	The `break` and `continue` Statements	436
	D.10.8	The `switch` Statement	436
	D.10.9	The `goto` Statement	437
	D.10.10	The `return` Statement	438
	D.10.11	The Declaration Statement	438
D.11	Functions		439
	D.11.1	Prototypes	440
	D.11.2	Call-by-Reference	440
	D.11.3	Inline Functions	441
	D.11.4	Default Arguments	441
	D.11.5	Overloading	441
	D.11.6	Type-Safe Linkage for Functions	443
D.12	Classes		444
	D.12.1	Constructors and Destructors	444
	D.12.2	Member Functions	446
	D.12.3	Friend Functions	446
	D.12.4	The `this` Pointer	447
	D.12.5	Operator Overloading	447
	D.12.6	`static` and `const` Member Functions	449
	D.12.7	Mutable	450
	D.12.8	Class Design	450

- D.13 Inheritance 451
  - D.13.1 Multiple Inheritance 452
  - D.13.2 Constructor Invocation 453
  - D.13.3 Abstract Base Classes 454
  - D.13.4 Pointer to Class Member 454
  - D.13.5 Run-Time Type Identification 454
  - D.13.6 Virtual Functions 455
- D.14 Templates 456
  - D.14.1 Template Parameters 458
  - D.14.2 Function Template 459
  - D.14.3 Friends 460
  - D.14.4 Static Members 460
  - D.14.5 Specialization 461
- D.15 Exceptions 461
  - D.15.1 Throwing Exceptions 462
  - D.15.2 Try Blocks 463
  - D.15.3 Handlers 464
  - D.15.4 Exception Specification 465
  - D.15.5 `terminate()` and `unexpected()` 465
  - D.15.6 Standard Library Exceptions 466
- D.16 Caution and Compatibility 466
  - D.16.1 Nested Class Declarations 466
  - D.16.2 Type Compatibilities 467
  - D.16.3 Miscellaneous 467
- D.17 New Features in C++ 468

E Input/Output 469
- E.1 The Output Class `ostream` 469
- E.2 Formatted Output and *iomanip.h* 470
- E.3 User-Defined Types: Output 473
- E.4 The Input Class `istream` 475
- E.5 Files 477
- E.6 Using Strings as Streams 480
- E.7 The Functions and Macros in *ctype.h* 481
- E.8 Using Stream States 482
- E.9 Mixing I/O Libraries 484

F STL and String Libraries 487
- F.1 Containers 487
  - F.1.1 Sequence Containers 489
  - F.1.2 Associative Containers 490
  - F.1.3 Container Adaptors 491

F.2	Iterators	493
	F.2.1 Iterator Categories	493
	F.2.2 The `Istream_iterator`	494
	F.2.3 The `Ostream_iterator`	494
	F.2.4 Iterator Adaptors	494
F.3	Algorithms	496
	F.3.1 Sorting Algorithms	496
	F.3.2 Nonmutating Sequence Algorithms	499
	F.3.3 Mutating Sequence Algorithms	500
	F.3.4 Numerical Algorithms	503
F.4	Functions	504
	F.4.1 Function Adaptors	506
F.5	Allocators	507
F.6	String Library	507
	F.6.1 Constructors	509
	F.6.2 Member Functions	510
	F.6.3 Global Operators	514

References 517

Index 519

About the Author 541

Preface

This book is intended as an introduction to programming in C++ for the programmer or student already familiar with Fortran. It uses an evolutionary teaching process, with Fortran as a starting point and C++ as a destination. The book is written to allow the reader to stop and use the language facilities at various points in the text.

This book will get the Fortran programmer up and running in C++ in the shortest possible time. It uses a teaching-by-equivalency method that allows the Fortran programmer the ability to immediately convert existing code over to C++. It emphasizes working code. A program particularly illustrative of the chapter's themes is analyzed by dissection, which is similar to a structured walk-through of the code. Dissection explains to the reader newly encountered programming elements and idioms.

Fortran is the major teaching language for beginning engineering students. It was designed by John Backus at IBM in the 1950s, and many efficient and fast compilers exist for it. Fortran is tailored to numerical scientific programming, and is the leading language for that use. For nonnumerical domains, Fortran lacks key features that limit its use in the software community, where C and C++ are the dominant languages.

C++, invented at Bell Labs by Bjarne Stroustrup in the mid-1980s, is a powerful modern successor language to C. C++ adds to C the concept of *class*, a mechanism for providing user-defined types also called *abstract data types*. It supports *object-oriented* programming by these means and by providing inheritance and run-time type binding. C++ is increasingly the choice of scientists and engineers in developing scientific software.

This book is intended for use in a first course in programming in C++. The reader is expected to know Fortran or have enough programming experience to follow this tutorial. It can be used as a supplementary text in an advanced programming, data structures, software methodology, comparative language, or other course in which the instructor wants C++ to be the language of choice. Each chapter presents a number of carefully explained programs.

All the major pieces of code were tested. A consistent and proper coding style is adopted from the beginning and is one chosen by professionals in the C++ community. The code is available at the Addison Wesley Longman Web site (*www.aw.com*).

For the Fortran programmer who wants C experience, this book could be used in conjunction with *A Book on C, Third Edition* by Al Kelley and Ira Pohl (Addison-Wesley, 1995). As a package, the two books offer an integrated treatment of the C and C++ programming languages and their use that is unavailable elsewhere. This book incorporates:

An Evolutionary Approach. The Fortran programmer is introduced to equivalent concepts in the C++ programming language. By learning how individual elements of a Fortran program translate into C++, the Fortran programmer can immediately gain a facility with C++. Chapter 1, "An Overview of C++ and Object-Oriented Programming," provides an introduction to C++'s use as an object-oriented programming language. Chapter 2, "Native Types and Statements," shows the parallels between programming in Fortran and C++ with regard to data types, expressions, and simple statements. Chapter 3, "Functions, Pointers, and Arrays," continues with similarities between functions and complex data types. The middle chapters show how to use classes, which are the basis for abstract data types and object-oriented programming (OOP). The later chapters give advanced details of the use of inheritance, templates, and exceptions. At any point in the text the programmer can stop and use the new material.

Teaching by Example. The book is a tutorial that stresses examples of working code. Right from the start the student is introduced to full working programs. An interactive environment is assumed. Exercises are integrated with the examples to encourage experimentation. Excessive detail is avoided in explaining the larger elements of writing working code. Each chapter has several important example programs. Major elements of these programs are explained by dissection.

Data Structures in C++. The text emphasizes many of the standard data structures from computer science. Stacks, safe arrays, dynamically allocated multidimensional arrays, lists, trees, and strings are all implemented. Exercises extend the student's understanding of how to implement and use these structures. Implementation is consistent with an abstract data type approach to software.

Object-Oriented Programming. The reader is led gradually to the object-oriented style. Chapter 1, "An Overview of C++ and Object-Oriented Programming," discusses how the Fortran programmer can benefit in important ways from a switch to C++ and object-oriented programming. Object-oriented concepts are defined, and the way in which these concepts are supported by C++ is introduced. Chapter 4, "Classes," introduces classes, which are the basic mechanism for producing modular programs and implementing abstract data types. Class variables are the objects being manipulated. Chapter 9, "Inheritance," develops inheritance and virtual functions, two key elements in this paradigm. Chapter 11, "OOP Using C++," discusses OOP and the Platonic programming philosophy. This book develops in the programmer an appreciation of this point of view.

Fortran Equivalence. Where appropriate, C++ code is given with equivalent FORTRAN 77 code. This gives the experienced Fortran programmer immediate access to idiomatic C++ code. FORTRAN 77 has been augmented by other versions of Fortran, the primary one being Fortran 90. Fortran 90 has many additional features, such as modules, recursion, a free-form style, pointers and structured data, and better flow of control statements.

ANSI C++ Language and *iostream.h*. For an existing, widely used language, C++ continues to change at a rapid pace. This book is based on the most recent standard: the ANSI C++ Committee language documents. A succinct informal language reference is provided in Appendix D, "Language Guide." Use of the *iostream.h* library is featured in Appendix E, "Input/Output," and STL is featured in Appendix F, "STL and String Libraries."

Standard Template Library (STL). STL is explained and used in Chapter 8, "Templates, Generic Programming, and STL," and in Appendix F, "STL and String Libraries." Many of the data structure examples foreshadow its explanation and use. There is a strong emphasis on the template mechanism required for STL and the iterator idiom that STL exploits. The numerical examples stressed are important to scientific computation.

Industry- and Course-Tested. This book is the basis of many on-site professional training courses given by the author, who has used its contents to train professionals and students in various forums since 1986. The various changes are course-tested, and reflect the author's considerable teaching and consulting experience.

Exercises. The exercises test and often advance the student's knowledge of the language. Many are intended to be done interactively while reading the text, encouraging self-paced instruction. Others test standard scientific concepts, such as the use of vectors, pseudorandom computations, numerical methods for evaluating integrals, conversion of units, and the use of complex numbers.

Engineering and Scientific Computations. Scientific and engineering computations are featured throughout. Important scientific types such as complex numbers, vectors, and polynomials are implemented. Modern simulation technique is featured through an ecological simulation that is implemented using object-oriented techniques. Numerical methods such as root finding and integration are featured.

Web site. The examples both within the book and at Addison-Wesley's Web site are intended to exhibit good programming style. The Addison-Wesley Web site for this book contains the programs in the book as well as adjunct programs that illustrate points made in the book or flesh out short pieces of programs. The programs available at the Web site are introduced by their *.cpp* or *.h* names and can be obtained by referencing:

www.aw.com/cseng/pohl/c++4f/program_name.cpp

My special thanks go to my wife, Debra Dolsberry, who encouraged me throughout this project. She acted as book designer and technical editor for this edition. She developed appropriate formats and style sheets in FrameMaker 5.0 and guided the transition process from my other books on C++. She also implemented and tested all major pieces of code.

This book was developed with the support of my editor, J. Carter Shanklin, and editorial assistant, Angela Buenning.

Ira Pohl
University of California, Santa Cruz

Chapter 1

An Overview of C++ and Object-Oriented Programming

This chapter gives an overview of C++ and provides an introduction to C++'s use as an object-oriented programming (OOP) language. Like the rest of the book, it assumes a knowledge of Fortran. It presents a series of programs of increasing complexity, and carefully explains the elements of each; examples in the later sections illustrate some of the concepts of object-oriented programming. This approach should give the student or professional Fortran programmer a sense of how C++ works. As an overview, this chapter makes use of advanced material that can be skimmed or skipped by readers who wish to begin with the elementary concepts found in the next chapter.

Each feature of C++ is explained briefly. The examples in this chapter give simple, immediate, hands-on experience with key features of the C++ language. The chapter introduces stream I/O, operator and function overloading, reference parameters, classes, constructors, destructors, and inheritance. It gives a programmer the flavor of writing C++. Mastery of individual topics requires a thorough reading of the later chapters.

Object-oriented programming is the programming methodology of choice in the 1990s. It is the product of 30 years of programming practice and experience that goes back to Simula 67 and continues with Smalltalk, LISP, Clu, and more recently Actor, Eiffel, Java, and C++. It is a programming style that captures the behavior of the real world in a way that hides detailed implementation. When successful it allows the problem solver to think in terms of the problem domain.

C++ was created by Bjarne Stroustrup in the early 1980s. Stroustrup had two main goals: (1) to make C++ compatible with ordinary C, and (2) to extend C with OOP constructs based on the class construct of Simula 67. C was developed by Dennis Ritchie in the early 1970s as a system implementation language to build UNIX. Gradually it gained popularity not only as a system-implementation language, but also as a general-purpose language.

Fortran was developed by John Backus at IBM in the 1950s. It was designed as a language to be used by engineers and scientists, and is an acronym for FORmula TRANslation. Fortran has been expanded over the years, and the main version of the language in use is FORTRAN 77. Most examples in this book use FORTRAN 77, unless otherwise noted. There is also a newer standard, called Fortran 90, which has added features such as free-form structure, better variable naming conventions, user-defined types, and pointers. Appendix C, "Fortran 90 and C++," compares the two languages.

This book teaches C++ to programmers already familiar with Fortran by transitioning the reader from Fortran to C++. It can also be used by those already familiar with other similar programming languages, such as PL/1 or Basic.

Fortran programmers can readily use structured programming methodology. This involves writing large programs as a series of procedure calls on properly structured data. Fortran 90 has a limited form of data abstraction. Fortran 90 TYPE declaration allows the programmer to extend the named types available to the program. This improves on strong typing and provides user-defined aggregates with understandable names. The C++ `class` declaration is a powerful extension of these concepts. As we shall see, it provides strong typing, data hiding, and code reuse through inheritance. Also, C++ allows programming teams to program in the large using file encapsulation, function encapsulation, and class encapsulation techniques. As a consequence, C++ can be used to teach modular programming habits within the object-oriented paradigm.

1.1 Object-Oriented Programming

Object-oriented programming (OOP) is a data-centered view of programming, in which data and behavior are strongly linked. Data and behavior are conceived of as classes whose instances are objects. For example, a polynomial can have a range of legal values, which are affected by such operations as addition and multiplication.

OOP also views computation as simulating behavior. What is simulated are objects represented by a computational abstraction. Suppose we wish to improve our poker play, and to do so we must better understand the odds of obtaining different poker hands. We need to simulate shuffling and must have appropriate ways to speak about cards and suits. Publicly we use the suit names: spades, hearts, diamonds, and clubs. Privately these suits are internally represented as integers. This internal choice is hidden and consequently should not affect our computation. Just as decks of cards can have many physical compositions and still properly behave as cards, so can computational card decks.

We will be using the terms *abstract data type (ADT)* and *object-oriented programming (OOP)* to refer to a powerful new programming approach. An ADT is a user-defined extension to the existing types available in the language. It consists of a set of values and a collection of operations that can act on those values. For example, C++ does not have a native complex number type, but uses the class construct to define such a type in the header file *complex.h*.

Objects are class variables. Object-oriented programming allows ADTs to be easily created and used. OOP uses the mechanism of inheritance to conveniently derive a new type from an existing user-defined type. Biological taxonomies are akin to this mechanism: Both rodents and cats are mammals; if the category mammal is an encoding of the information and behavior that is true for all objects in this class, then creating both the category cat and the category rodent from the category mammal is an enormous saving.

In OOP, objects are responsible for their behavior. For example, polynomial objects, complex number objects, integer objects, and floating-point number objects can all be added. Each type has code for executing addition. The compiler provides the right code for integers and floating-point numbers. The polynomial ADT has a function defining addition specific to its implementation. The ADT provider should include code for any behavior the object can be commonly expected to understand. Making an object responsible for its behavior eases the coding task for the user of that object.

Consider a class of objects called shapes. If we want a shape to draw on a screen, we need to know where the shape is to be centered and how to draw it. Some shapes, such as polygons, are relatively easy to draw. A general shape-drawing routine can be very expensive, requiring storage for a large number of individual boundary points. Avoiding this in the polygon case is clearly beneficial. If the individual shape object knows best how to draw itself, the programmer using such shapes needs only to give the object the message *draw*.

The new class construct in C++ provides the *encapsulation* mechanism to implement ADTs. Encapsulation includes both the internal implementation details of a specific type and the externally available operations and functions that can act on objects of that type. The implementation details can be made inaccessible to code that uses the type. For example, a stack might be implemented as a fixed-length array, while the publicly available operations would include push and pop. Changing the internal implementation to a linked list should not affect how push and pop are used externally. Code that uses the ADT is called *client* code for the ADT. The implementation of a stack is hidden from its clients. The details of how to provide *data hiding* in classes are introduced here and developed thoroughly in Chapter 4, "Classes," and Chapter 9, "Inheritance."

1.2 Why Learn C++?

C++ supports the object-oriented programming style. This is a major advance over the structured programming style supported by languages such as C, Pascal, and Fortran. A chief cost is the increased complexity of the language. C++ is a more complex language, but better suited to developing large software projects that include nonnumerical types.

Fortran is a procedural, imperative language. It has a small set of built-in types and limited forms of type extensibility. These types are well suited to numerically oriented scientific programming. However, for nonnumerical problems, Fortran's usefulness is hampered by its lack of type extensibility.

C++ remedies these limitations by allowing arbitrary user-defined types. A chief cost is the increased complexity of the language. This complexity is one of C++'s biggest drawbacks, for though it reflects the large number of necessary new ideas, it makes mastery more difficult. To overcome this problem, this book approaches the learning process by gradually transforming the Fortran programmer into a practiced C++ programmer. Each chapter extends from the previous chapter the range of ideas the programmer may use. At any point, the reader can stop and still be partly proficient in C++. In effect, the reader evolves into an object-oriented C++ programmer.

1.3 Fortran as a Starting Point

Fortran is an effective starting point for C++ because it is strongly typed. The Fortran programmer understands that a properly modular program is a better program. This modularity is achieved by defining subprograms that encapsulate the functionality the programmer needs. Modularity is also enhanced by Fortran block structure. Some Fortran systems, such as Fortran 90, allow file-level modularity like that in C++. Fortran programmers also have access to well-supported libraries, such as numerical packages, that extend the benefits of the language by allowing code reuse and enhanced portability.

The following Fortran program uses a SUBROUTINE to perform simple output:

1.3 ▼ Fortran as a Starting Point

In file hello.f

```
*       Hello World in Fortran
        PROGRAM WORLD
*
*       A simple main program that calls PRMSG()
*
        PRMSG('')
        END


*       If no str, then output Hello World!

        SUBROUTINE PRMSG (STR)

        CHARACTER * (*) STR
        IF LEN(STR) .LT. 1 THEN
            PRINT *, 'Hello World!'
        ELSE
            PRINT *, STR
        END IF
        END
```

Here is the equivalent C++ program:

In file hello1.cpp

```cpp
//Hello world in C++
#include <iostream>      //IO library
#include <string>        //string type
using namespace std;

inline void pr_message(string s = "Hello world!")
{ cout << s << endl;}

int main()
{
    pr_message();
}
```

When executed, this program prints the message

```
Hello world!
```

A C++ program is a collection of declarations and functions that begin executing with the function `main()`. The C++ program is compiled after the preprocessor executes #-designated directives. The *preprocessor* precedes the phase during which the compiler translates the resulting program into machine code. The `#include` directive found in the example program *hello1.cpp* imports any needed files, usually library definitions. In this case, the IO library for a typical compiler system is found in the file *iostream*. The string type is found in the standard library defined in the file *string*. On new C++ systems, these files are wrapped in the `namespace std`. The `using` declaration allows such names to be used without `std::` prepended to each name.

The `//` symbol is used as a rest-of-line comment symbol. Also, the program text can be placed in any position on the page, with white space between tokens being ignored. White space, comments, and indentation of text are all used to create a humanly readable, well-documented program, but do not affect program semantics.

The `inline` modifier of the function `pr_message()` is used to tell the compiler to compile this function without resort to function call and return instructions, if possible. It is an efficiency concern available to the C++ programmer. As written, the `pr_message()` function had a string parameter s, whose default value was "Hello world!". What this means is that when passed an empty or void parameter list, `pr_message("Hello world!")` is executed.

The identifier `cout` is defined in *iostream* as the standard output stream connected by most C++ systems to the screen for output. The identifier `endl` is a standard *manipulator* that flushes the output buffer, printing everything to that point while going to a new line. The operator `<<` is the put to output operator, which writes out what comes after it to `cout`.

A function in C++ has a return type that can be `void`, indicating no value is to be returned, as is the case with `pr_message()`. The special function `main()` returns an integer value to the run-time system—which, in the implicit case found here, is zero, meaning termination was normal.

In the following variation to `main()`:

In file hello2.cpp

```
int main()
{
   pr_message();
   pr_message("Laura Pohl");
   pr_message("It is dinner time.");
}
```

When executed, the program prints the message

```
Hello world!
Laura Pohl
It is dinner time.
```

1.4 Classes and Abstract Data Types

OOP is a balanced approach to writing software. Data and behavior are packaged together. This encapsulation creates user-defined types, which extend and interact with the native types of the language. *Type-extensibility* is the ability to add user-defined types to the language such that they are as easy to use as native types.

An abstract data type such as a complex number is a description of the ideal public behavior of the type. The user of a complex number knows that operations, such as add or print, result in certain public behaviors. Operations add and print are called *methods*. A concrete implementation of the ADT also has implementation limits; for example, complex numbers are limited in precision. These limits affect public behavior. Also, internal or private details of the implementation do not directly affect the user's understanding. For example, a complex number is frequently implemented as a set of two floating-point variables, the names of which should be of no direct consequence to the user.

Encapsulation is the ability to hide internal detail while providing a public interface to a user-defined type. C++ uses `class` and `struct` declarations in conjunction with the access keywords `private`, `protected`, and `public` to provide encapsulation. FORTRAN 77 does not include any type of class or structure to facilitate encapsulation. Fortran 90 has the TYPE addition, which provides for only a limited form of data encapsulation.

OOP terminology is strongly influenced by Smalltalk programming. The Smalltalk designers wanted programmers to break with their past habits and embrace a new programming methodology. They invented terms such as *message* and *method* to replace the traditional terms *function invocation* and *member function*.

Public members are available to any function within the scope of the class declaration. Public members provide the type's interface. Private members are available for use only by other member functions of the class. Privacy allows the implementation of a class type to be hidden, which prevents unanticipated modifications to the data structure. Restricted access, or data hiding, is a feature of object-oriented programming. Let us write a class called `complex` that will implement a restricted form of complex number.

In file complex1.cpp

```
//An elementary implementation of type complex.
class complex {
public:                        //universal access to interface
   void re_assign(double r) { real = r; }
   void im_assign(double im) { imaginary = im; }
   void print() const
      { cout << "(" << real << ","
             << imaginary << "i)" << endl; }
   friend complex operator+(complex, complex);
private:                       //restricted access to implementation
   double real, imaginary;
};
```

The hidden representation is two variables of type `double`.

The declaration of member functions allows the ADT to have particular functions act on its private representation. For example, the member function `print()` outputs a complex number as a comma-separated pair of `double`s. The imaginary part of the number has the suffix `i`. The member function `re_assign()` stores the real part of a complex number into the hidden variable `real`, and the member function `im_assign()` stores the imaginary part of a complex number into the hidden variable `imaginary`. Member functions such as `print()` that do not modify member variables values are declared `const`. The `friend` function `operator+()` declaration will be used later to implement the definition of the addition of two complex numbers. The `friend` designation means that the function, while not a member of class `complex`, has access to all its members.

We can now use the data type `complex` as if it were a basic type of the language. Code that uses this type is its *client*. The client can use only the public members to act on variables of type `complex`.

```
//Test of the class complex.
int main()
{
   complex x, y, z;

   x.re_assign(9.5);
   x.im_assign(-4.5);
   y.re_assign(4.2);
   y.im_assign(6.0);
   z = x + y;                    //uses operator+()
   x.print();
   y.print();
   z.print();
}
```

Variables x, y, and z are of type complex. The member functions are called using the dot, or *structure member*, operator. As is seen from their definitions, these member functions act on the hidden private-member fields of the named variables. The output of this example program is:

```
(9.5,-4.5i)
(4.2,6i)
(13.7,1.5i)
```

1.5 Constructors and Destructors

In OOP terminology, a variable is called an *object*. A *constructor* is a member function whose job is to initialize an object of its class. In many cases this involves dynamic storage allocation. Constructors are invoked whenever an object of a particular class is created. A *destructor* is a member function whose job is to *finalize* a variable of its class. As we shall see later, in many cases this involves dynamic storage deallocation. The programmer's explicitly allocating and deallocating memory from a pool of available memory called *free store* is not needed in most Fortran programs. If you are not familiar with these concepts, you may want to skip this material for now and wait until the later chapters, where they are explained in detail.

Let's change our complex example by adding a constructor to initialize its value. We will also add a destructor to provide debugging output when a complex object is destroyed.

In file complex1.cpp

```
class complex {
public:
//constructor
complex(double r = 0, double im = 0): real(r), imaginary(im) { }
//destructor
~complex() { cout << "destructor "; print(); }
    .....
};
```

A constructor's name is the same as the class name. It is invoked when declaring variables, as in:

```
complex  x(5.5, 1.0), y;
```

Here the variables are declared and initialized. `x.real` is initialized as 5.5 and `x.imaginary` as 1.0; `y.real` is initialized as 0 and `y.imaginary` as 0. These are the default values of the arguments passed to the constructor.

A destructor is written as a member function whose name is the class name preceded by the tilde symbol ~. The destructor written in `complex` is used for debugging. It calls `print()` to write out the value of the `complex` object being destroyed. For example, if x is not changed during execution, the destructor prints upon exit from x's scope:

```
destructor (5.5,1i)
```

1.6 Overloading

Overloading is the practice of giving several meanings to an operator or a function. The meaning selected depends on the types of arguments used by the operator or function. Let us overload the function `print` in the previous example. This will be a second definition of the `print` function.

In file complex1.cpp

```
class complex {
public:                         //universal access
   .....
   void  print(string var_name) const
      { cout << var_name << " = "; print(); }
   .....
}
```

This version of `print()` takes a single argument of type `string`. It is used to print the complex number's variable name and value.

```
complex x(1.5,2);
x.print("x");              //print: x = (1.5,2i)
x.print();                 //print: (1.5,2i)
```

It is possible to overload most of the C++ operators. For example, we will overload + to mean complex addition. To do this we need two new keywords: `friend` and `operator`. The keyword `operator` precedes the operator token, and replaces what would otherwise be a function name in a function declaration. The keyword `friend` gives a function access to the private members of a class variable. A `friend` function is not a member of the class, but has the privileges of a member function in the class in which it is declared.

In file complex1.cpp

```
//overload +
complex operator+(complex x, complex y)
{
   complex t;

   t.real = x.real + y.real;
   t.imaginary = x.imaginary + y.imaginary;
   return t;
}
```

```
int main()
{
    complex x(9.5, -4.5), y(4.2,6.0), z;

    z = x + y;
    x.print("x");
    y.print("y");
    z.print("z");
}
```

Dissection of the operator+() Function

- `complex operator+(complex x, complex y)`

Plus is overloaded. Both of its arguments are of type `complex`. The return type is `complex`, as expected.

- `complex t;`

The function needs to return a value of type `complex`. This local variable is initialized to (0,0i) by the constructor.

- ```
  t.real = x.real + y.real;
  t.imaginary = x.imaginary + y.imaginary;
  return t;
  ```

The definition adds both the real and imaginary parts of the complex numbers and returns them as the `complex` variable `t`.

Our original class definition, in Section 1.5, "Constructors and Destructors," on page 10, declared the `operator+()` function be a friend function of the class in order to access the private variables `imaginary` and `real`.
  ```

1.7 Inheritance

A singular concept in OOP is the promotion of code reuse through the *inheritance* mechanism. A new class is derived from an existing, or *base*, class. The derived class reuses the base class members and can add to or alter them.

Many types are variants of one another, and it is frequently tedious and error prone to develop new code for each. A derived class inherits the description of the base class, thus avoiding redevelopment and testing of the existing code. The inheritance relationship is hierarchical. Hierarchy is a method for coping with complexity. It imposes classifications on objects. For example, the periodic table of elements has elements that are gasses. These have properties that are shared by all elements in that classification. The inert gasses are an important subclassification. The hierarchy is that an inert gas, such as argon, is a gas, which in turn is an element. This provides a convenient way to understand the behavior of inert gasses. We know they are composed of protons and electrons, as this is shared description with all elements. We know they are in a gaseous state at room temperature, as this behavior is shared with all gasses. We know they do not combine in ordinary chemical reactions with other elements, as this is shared behavior of all inert gasses.

Consider designing a database for a college. The registrar must track various types of students. The base class we need to develop captures a description of student. Two main categories of student are graduate and undergraduate.

OOP Design Methodology

1. Decide on an appropriate set of types.

2. Design their relatedness into the code, using inheritance.

An example of deriving a class is:

In file student1.cpp

```
enum support { ta, ra, fellowship, other };
enum year { fresh, soph, junior, senior, grad };
```

```
class student {
public:
   student(char* nm, int id, double g, year x);
   void  print() const;
private:
   int      student_id;
   double   gpa;
   year     y;
   char     name[30];
};

class grad_student : public student {
public:
   grad_student(char* nm, int id, double g,
             year x, support t, char* d, char* th);
   void print() const;
private:
   support  s;
   char     dept[10];
   char     thesis[80];
};
```

In this example, grad_student is the derived class, and student is the base class. The use of the keyword public following the colon in the derived class header means that the public members of student are to be inherited as public members of grad_student. Private members of the base class cannot be accessed in the derived class. Public inheritance also means that the derived class grad_student is a subtype of student.

An inheritance structure provides a design for the overall system. For example, a database that contained all the people at a college could be derived from the base class person. The student base class could be used to derive law students as a further significant category of objects. Similarly, person could be the base class for a variety of employee categories. The hierarchical inheritance structure is illustrated below:

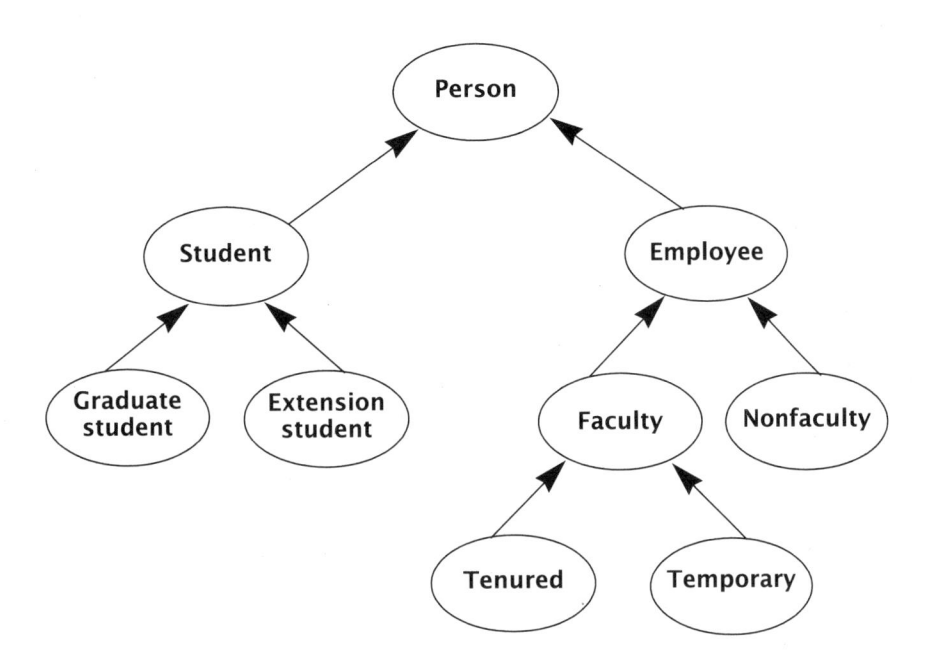

1.8 Polymorphism

A *polymorphic* function or operator has many forms. For example, in C++ the division operator is polymorphic. If the arguments to the division operator are integral, then integer division is used. However, if one or both arguments are floating-point, then floating-point division is used.

In C++, a function name or operator is overloadable. A function is called based on its *signature*, or the list of argument types in its parameter list.

For example, in the division expression

```
a / b            //type is determined by native coercions
```

the result depends on the arguments being automatically coerced to the widest type. So if both arguments are integer the result is an integer division. But if one or both arguments are floating-point, the result is floating-point.

Another example is the output statement

```
cout << a;       //polymorphism via function overloading
```

where the shift operator << is invoking a function that is able to output an object of type a. So if a is an integer, the output is integer. But if a is floating-point, the output is floating-point.

Polymorphism localizes responsibility for behavior. The client code frequently requires no revision when additional functionality is added to the system through ADT-provided code improvements. In the revision process, improvements to code are provided in a new derived class, so that additional description is localized.

Consider developing a system for drawing and manipulating shapes. New subtypes are added as derived classes. The programmer overrides the meaning of any changed routines in the derived class. Client code that does not use the new type is unaffected. Client code that is improved by the new type is typically minimally changed. C++ code following this design uses shape as an *abstract base class*. This is a class containing one or more pure virtual functions:

In file shape1.cpp

```
//shape is an abstract base class.
class shape {
public:
   virtual double  area() = 0;            //pure virtual function
};

class rectangle : public shape {
public:
   rectangle(double h, double w) :height(h), width(w) { }
   double area() { return (height * width); }      //override
private:
   double  height, width;
};

class circle : public shape {
public:
   circle(double r) : radius(r) { }
   double  area() { return(3.14159 * radius * radius); }
private:
   double  radius;
};
```

Client code for computing an arbitrary area is polymorphic. The appropriate area() function is selected at run time:

```
shape*   ptr_shape;
   .....
   cout << " area = " << ptr_shape -> area();
   .....
```

Now let us add a square class:

```
class square : public rectangle {
public:
   square(double h) : rectangle(h,h) { }
   double  area() { return (rectangle::area()); }
};
```

The client code remains unchanged.

1.9 Templates

C++ uses the keyword template to provide *parametric polymorphism*, which allows the same code to be used with respect to different types where the type is a parameter of the code body. The code is written generically. An especially important use for this technique is in writing generic *container classes*. A container class is used to contain data of a particular type. Stacks, vectors, trees, and lists are all examples of standard container classes. We shall develop a stack container class as a parameterized type.

In file tstack1.cpp

```
//template stack implementation
template <class TYPE>
class stack {
public:
   stack(int size = 1000) : max_len(size)
      { s = new TYPE[size]; top = EMPTY; }
   ~stack() { delete []s; }
   void  reset() { top = EMPTY; }
   void  push(TYPE c) { s[++top] = c; }
   TYPE  pop() { return s[top--]; }
   TYPE  top_of() { return s[top]; }
   bool  empty() { return (top == EMPTY); }
   bool  full() { return (top == max_len-1); }
```

```
    private:
        enum    {EMPTY = -1};
        TYPE*   s;
        int     max_len;
        int     top;
};
```

The syntax of the class declaration is prefaced by:

```
template <class identifier>
```

This identifier is a template argument that essentially stands for an arbitrary type. Throughout the class definition, the template argument can be used as a type name. This argument is instantiated in the actual declarations. An example of a stack declaration using this is:

```
stack<char>     stk_ch;             //1000 char stack
stack<char*>    stk_str(200);       //200 char* stack
stack<complex>  stk_cmplx(500);     //500 complex stack
```

This mechanism saves us rewriting class declarations in which the only variation would be type declarations.

When processing such a type, the code must always use the angle brackets as part of the declaration. Here are two functions using the stack template:

```
//Reversing a series of char* represented strings
void reverse(char* str[], int n)
{
    stack<char*>  stk(n);           //this stack holds char*

    for (int i = 0; i < n; ++i)
        stk.push(str[i]);
    for (i = 0; i < n; ++i)
        str[i] = stk.pop();
}
```

In the function reverse(), a stack<char*> is used to insert n strings and then pop them in reverse order.

```
//Initializing stack of complex numbers from an array
void init(complex c[], stack<complex>& stk, n)
{
   for (int i = 0; i < n; ++i)
      stk.push(c[i]);
}
```

In the function `init()`, a `stack<complex>` variable is passed by reference, and `n` complex numbers are pushed onto this stack.

1.10 The Standard Template Library (STL)

The Standard Template Library (STL) is the C++ standard library providing generic programming for many standard data structures and algorithms. The library provides container classes, such as vectors, queues, and maps; navigation over these containers using iterator classes; and algorithms for their use such as sorting and searching functions. Below is a brief description emphasizing these three legs, namely containers, iterators, and algorithms, that support a standard for generic programming.

The library is built using templates, and is highly orthogonal in design. Components can be used with one another on native and user-provided types through proper instantiation of the different elements of the STL library.

In file stl_list.cpp

```
//Using the list container.
#include <list>                //list container
#include <numerical>           //algorithm library
using namespace std;

void print(const list<double> &lst)
{ //using an iterator to traverse lst
   list<double>::const_iterator where;

   for (where = lst.begin();
        where !=lst.end(); ++where)
      cout << *where << '\t';
   cout << endl;
}
```

```
int main()
{
   double w[4] = { 0.9, 0.8, 88, -99.99 };
   list<double> z;

   for (int i = 0; i < 4; ++i)
      z.push_front(w[i]);
   print(z);
   z.sort();
   print(z);
   cout << "sum is "
        << accumulate(z.begin(), z.end(), 0.0) << endl;
}
```

In this example, a list container is instantiated to hold `doubles`. An array of doubles is pushed into the list. The `print()` function uses an iterator to print each element of the list in turn. Iterators have standard interfaces that include `begin()` and `end()` member functions for starting and ending locations of the container. The list interface also includes a stable sorting algorithm, the `sort()` member function. The `accumulate()` function is a generic function in the algorithms package that uses 0.0 as an initial value and computes the sum of the list container elements by going from the starting location `z.begin()` to the ending location `z.end()`.

1.11 C++ Exceptions

C++ introduces an exception-handling mechanism that is sensitive to context. The context for raising an exception is a try block. Handlers declared using the keyword `catch` are found at the end of a try block.

An exception is raised by using the `throw` expression. The exception will be handled by invoking an appropriate handler selected from a list of handlers found immediately after the handler's try block. A simple example of all this is:

In file stackex.cpp

```
//stack constructor with exceptions
stack::stack(int n)
{
   if (n < 1)
      throw (n);                   //want a positive value
   p = new char[n];                //create a stack of characters
   if (p == 0)                     //new returns 0 when it fails
      throw ("FREE STORE EXHAUSTED");
   top = EMPTY;
   max_len = n;
}

void g()
{
   try {
      stack   a(n), b(n);
      .....

   }
   catch (int n) {·····}           //an incorrect size
   catch (char* error) {·····}     //free store exhausted
}
```

The first throw() has an integer argument, and matches the catch(int n) signature. This handler is expected to perform an appropriate action when an incorrect array size has been passed as an argument to the constructor. For example, printing an error message and aborting are appropriate handler actions. The second throw() has a pointer-to-character argument and matches the catch(char* error) signature.

1.12 Benefits of Object-Oriented Programming

The central element of OOP is the encapsulation of an appropriate set of data types and its operations. The class construct with its member functions and data members provides an appropriate coding tool. Class variables are the objects to be manipulated.

Classes also provide data hiding. Access privileges can be managed and limited to whatever group of functions needs access to implementation details. This promotes modularity and robustness.

Another important concept in OOP is the promotion of code reuse through the inheritance mechanism. This is the mechanism of deriving a new class from an existing one called the base class. The base class can be added to or altered to create the derived class. In this way a hierarchy of related data types can be created that share code.

The OOP programming task is frequently more difficult than normal procedural programming as found in C or Fortran. There is at least one extra design step before one gets to the coding of algorithms. This involves the design of types that are appropriate for the problem at hand. Frequently one is solving the problem more generally than is strictly necessary.

The belief is that this will pay dividends in several ways. The solution will be more encapsulated and thus more robust and easier to maintain and change. It will also be more reusable. For example, where the code needs a stack, that stack is easily borrowed from existing code. In an ordinary procedural language, such a data structure is frequently "wired into" the algorithm and cannot be exported.

OOP is many things to many people. Attempts at defining it are reminiscent of the blind sages' attempts at describing the elephant. I will offer one more equation:

OOP = type extensibility + polymorphism

Chapter 2

Native Types and Statements

This chapter, together with Chapter 3, "Functions, Pointers, and Arrays," will provide an introduction to programming in C++ using its *native types* and its non-OOP features. A native type is a type provided by the language directly. In C++, this includes the simple types, such as character types, integer types, floating-point types, and the boolean type. It also includes derived types, such as array types, pointer types, and structure types, that are aggregates of the simple types. This chapter focuses on the native simple data types and statements.

The intent of this chapter, Chapter 3, "Functions, Pointers, and Arrays," and parts of Chapter 4, "Classes," is to give the programmer the ability to program in that subset of C++ that approximates a traditional imperative language such as C, Pascal, or Fortran. This is what we are calling the *kernel language*. These chapters also contain examples that will be used throughout the book.

An important feature of OOP is type extensibility, or the ability within the programming language to develop new types suitable to a problem domain. For this to work properly, the new type should work like the native types of the language. Object-oriented design of user-defined types should mimic the look and feel of the native types.

2.1 Program Elements

A program is composed of elements called *tokens*, which are collections of characters that form the basic vocabulary the compiler recognizes. The C++ character set includes:

```
a b c d e f g h i j k l m n o p q r s t u v w x y z
A B C D E F G H I J K L M N O P Q R S T U V W X Y Z
0 1 2 3 4 5 6 7 8 9
+ = _ - ( ) * & % $ # ! | <> . , ; : " ' / ? { } ~ \ [ ] ^
```
white space and nonprinting characters, such as newline, tab, and blank

In C++, tokens can be interspersed with white space and with comment text that is inserted for readability and documentation. There are five kinds of tokens: keywords, identifiers, literals, operators, and punctuators. See Section D.2, "Lexical Elements," on page 404.

The FORTRAN 77 character set is roughly equivalent. Some FORTRAN 77 compilers do not distinguish between upper- and lowercase, and it is normal to use uppercase only. Fortran 90 also allows additional character sets, such as math symbols and character sets for other languages.

C++ distinguishes between upper- and lowercase. As we shall see, C++ uses lowercase in its keyword list.

2.1.1 Comments

In FORTRAN 77, a comment line starts in column 1 with either an asterisk or a C, and the entire line is a comment. In Fortran 90, the comment style is extended to include the exclamation point as a rest-of-line comment, which may follow a statement.

```
* This is a Fortran comment line
C This is also a comment line though it is best
* To pick one style and stay with it

      I = 1           ! Fortran 90 rest of line comment
```

In C++, a multiline comment is written as /* *possibly multiline* */. Everything between the /* and */ is a comment. Comments do not nest. C++ also has a single-line comment written as // *rest of line*.

```
/*  Multiline Comments are Frequently Introductory
    Programmer:   Laura Pohl
    Date:         January 1, 1989
    Version:      DJD v4.2
*/

#include   <iostream>        //I/O library C++
```

2.1.2 Keywords

Keywords in C++ are explicitly reserved words that have a strict meaning and may not be used in any other way. They include words used for type declarations, such as int, char, and float; words used for statement syntax, such as do, for, and if; and words used for access control, such as public, protected, and private. The following table shows the keywords in use in most current C++ systems.

Keywords			
asm	else	operator	throw
auto	enum	private	true
bool	explicit	protected	try
break	extern	public	typedef
case	false	register	typeid
catch	float	reinterpret_cast	typename
char	for	return	union
class	friend	short	unsigned
const	goto	signed	using
const_cast	if	sizeof	virtual
continue	inline	static	void
default	int	static_cast	volatile
delete	long	struct	wchar_t
do	mutable	switch	while
double	namespace	template	
dynamic_cast	new	this	

2.1.3 Identifiers

An *identifier* in Fortran is a sequence of letters and digits. Fortran compilers generally do not distinguish between upper- and lowercase, and it is the standard to use only uppercase, except within strings. Many Fortran systems restrict identifiers to a maximum of six characters. Some Fortran compilers allow the use of longer names, but require the first six characters to uniquely determine the identifier. Fortran 90, like C++, allows identifiers to be up to 31 characters long, with underscore as a valid character.

An identifier in C++ is a sequence of letters, digits, and underscores. An identifier cannot begin with a digit. Upper- and lowercase letters are treated as distinct. It is bad practice and confusing to use identifiers that are distinguished only by case differences. Though in principle, identifiers can be arbitrarily long, many systems will distinguish only up to the first 31 characters. Some examples are:

```
n           //typically an integer variable
count       //meaningful as documentation
buff_size   //C++ style - underscore separates words
buffSize    //Pascal style - capital separates words
q2345       //obscure
cout        //used in the standard library iostream.h
_foo        //avoid underscore as a first letter
```

but not

```
for         //keyword
3q          //cannot start with digit
-count      //do not mistake - for _
too__bad    //double underscore is for system use
_Sysfoo     //underscore capital is for system use
```

In Fortran, unless explicitly typed, identifiers that start with the letters I though N are typed as integers and all others are implicitly real numbers. C++ identifiers must all be explicitly typed.

2.1.4 Literals

Literals are constant values, such as 1 or 3.14159. In Fortran, numeric constants may contain plus or minus signs, numbers, decimals, and Es (if scientific notation is being used). Character values in Fortran can contain single or multiple characters between single quote marks. Similar constants are available in C++.

There are literals for each C++ data type. String literals are also allowed. Some examples are:

```
5                    //an integer literal
5u                   //u or U specifies unsigned
5L                   //l or L specifies long
05                   //an integer literal written as octal
0x5                  //an integer literal written as hexadecimal
true                 //a bool literal
5.0                  //a floating-point literal treated as double
5.0F                 //f or F float - typically single precision
5.0L                 //l or L specifies long double
'5'                  //a character literal - ASCII value 53
'A'                  //letter capital A - ASCII value 65
'a'                  //letter small a - ASCII value 97
'\0'                 //the null character - terminates strings
'\t'                 //the character printing a tab space
'\n'                 //the character printing a new line
"5"                  //the string consisting of the character '5'
"a string with newline\n"
5555555555555555     //integer too large on most machines
```

String literals are stored as a series of characters that is terminated with the null character, whose value is zero. String literals are `static char[]` constants. Special characters can be represented inside strings by escaping them with the backslash character \.

```
"a"           //two bytes storing 'a' '\0'
"a\tb\n"      //five bytes 'a' '\t' 'b' '\n' '\0'
"1 \\"        //four bytes '1' ' ' '\\' '\0'
"\""          //two bytes '"' '\0'
```

When printed, these strings would produce effects required by the special characters. Thus the second string would print an a followed by a number of white-space characters as determined by the tab setting, then a b followed by a newline.

String literals that are separated only by white space are implicitly concatenated into a single string.

```
"This is a single string, "
"since it is separated only "
"by white space."
```

The character literals are usually given as '*symbol*'. Some nonprinting and special characters require an escape sequence.

Character Constants	
'\a'	alert
'\\'	backslash
'\b'	backspace
'\r'	carriage return
'\"'	double quote
'\f'	formfeed
'\t'	tab
'\n'	newline
'\0'	null character
'\''	single quote
'\v'	vertical tab
'\101'	octal 101 in ASCII 'A'
'\x041'	hexadecimal ASCII 'A'
L'oop'	wchar_t constant

Floating-point literals can be specified with or without signed integer exponents.

```
0.1234567           //double constant - the default
3.14f  1.234F       //float constant - smallest fp type
0.123456789L        //long double - either l or L
3.   3.0  0.3E1     //all express double 3.0
300e-2              //also 3.0
```

2.1.5 Operators and Punctuators

C++ gives special meaning to many characters and character sequences. Examples of C++ operators include:

```
+ - * / %           //arithmetic operators
->   ->*            //pointer & pointer-to-member operators
&&   ||             //logical operators
=  +=  *=           //assignment operators
```

The following table compares the C++ and Fortran operators.

Type	FORTRAN 77	Fortran 90	C++		Comment
Arithmetic	+ - * / **		+ - * / %		C++ has a library function pow(x, y) Fortran has a library function MOD(a1,a2)
Logical bool(C++)	.AND. .OR. .NOT.		&& || !		
Assignment	=		= += -= = *= /= etc.		C++ combines arithmetic operators with assignment
Comparison	.EQ. .EQV. .NE. .NEQ. .LT. .LE. .GT. .GE.	== /= < <= > >=	== != < <= > >=		Fortran uses .EQV. and .NEQV. for comparison of two logical variables
Bitwise			~ & ^ | << >>		Fortran has no bitwise operators
Pointers		=>	-> ->*		Fortran 90 only

Operators are used in expressions and are meaningful when given appropriate arguments. There are many operators in C++ (see Appendix B, "Operator Precedence and Associativity"). Certain symbols stand for different operators depending on context; for instance, "-" can be either unary or binary minus.

Punctuators include parentheses, braces, commas, and colons, and are used to structure elements of a program. For example, in C++:

```
foo(a, 7, b + 8)          //comma-separated argument list
{ a = b; c = d; }         //{ starts statement list or block
```

C++, like Fortran, allows operators, punctuators, and white space to separate language elements.

2.2 Input/Output

Unlike Fortran, C++ input/output is not directly part of the language. It is added as a set of types and routines found in a standard library. The C++ standard I/O library is *iostream* or *iostream.h*. The file name without the *.h* extension is the official ANSI standard name and is used with the `namespace std`. The ANSI C standard library *stdio.h* or *cstdio* is also in widespread use. The ANSI standard libraries that are C libraries are officially *c* followed by their name without a *.h* extension. We will use *iostream.h* because we are illustrating current practice. We leave to Appendix E, "Input/Output," a more complete description of this and other I/O issues. This section is introductory, and is intended to give the bare minimum of detail so as to get the reader up and running.

The *iostream.h* library overloads the two bit-shift operators.

```
<<          //"put to" output stream, normally left shift
>>          //"get from" input stream, normally right shift
```

It also declares three standard streams:

```
cout        //standard out
cin         //standard in
cerr        //standard error
```

Their use in conjunction with values and variables is analogous to assignment.

In file io.cpp

```
cout << "\nEnter a double: ";
cin >> x;
cout << "\nEnter a positive integer: ";
cin >> i;
if (i < 1)
   cerr << "error i = " << i << endl;
cout << "i * x = " << i * x;
```

The first output statement places a string on the screen. The second statement expects the double variable x to get a value converted from string input typed at the keyboard. The string represents a value that is either a double or assignment-convertible to a double. Other typed input will fail. Notice how the last two statements above allow multiple assignments to their output streams. The statements are executed left to right. For example, if i had received a value of -1, then the error message on the screen would be:

    error i = -1

The endl is a specially recognized identifier, called a *manipulator*, that flushes the cerr output stream and adds a newline. The last statement prints the string i * x = , followed by the double value of the expression i * x.

Fortran uses the built-in list-directed or formatted I/O functions PRINT *, READ *, and FORMAT to perform I/O. C++ uses libraries. This is a more powerful and flexible approach. Libraries are readily customized to new machines and easily extended to new applications.

2.3 Program Structure

A *program* in C++ is a collection of functions and declarations. The language is block structured, and variables declared within blocks are allocated automatically upon block entry. Unless otherwise specified, parameters are call-by-value. The following Fortran program, which computes the greatest common divisor of two integers, will be rewritten as a C++ program.

In file gcd.f

```
*         Greatest common divisor program.
          PROGRAM GCDPRG

          INTEGER  X, Y, GCD
          PRINT *, 'PROGRAM GCD FORTRAN'
   10     PRINT *, 'Enter two integers: '
          READ *, X, Y
          IF (X .NE. 0) THEN
             PRINT *, 'GCD(', X, ', ', Y, ') = ',
         +           GCD (X, Y)
           GO TO 10
           END IF
           END
```

```
          INTEGER FUNCTION GCD (M, N)
          INTEGER M, N, R
*         R is Remainder
          DO WHILE (N .NE. 0)
             R = MOD(M, N)
             M = N
             N = R
          END DO
          GCD = M
          END
```

In Fortran a program starts with the keyword PROGRAM, followed by an identifier naming the program. The program may contain a series of declarations and statements. FORTRAN 77 has a rigid structure that reserves columns 1 through 5 for comment symbols and line numbers, column 6 for continuation, and columns 7 through 72 for statements. Fortran generally allows only one statement per line, though Fortran 90 allows multiple statements separated by semicolons.

The corresponding program in C++ is:

In file gcd.cpp

```cpp
//Greatest common divisor program.
#include <iostream.h>
#include <assert.h>

int gcd(int m, int n)          //function definition
{                              //block
   int  r;                     //declaration of remainder

   while (n != 0) {            //not equal
      r = m % n;               //modulos operator
      m = n;                   //assignment
      n = r;
   }                           //end while loop
   return m;                   //exit gcd with value m
}
```

```
int main()
{
   int  x, y, g;

   cout << "\nPROGRAM Gcd C++";
   do {
      cout << "\nEnter two integers: ";
      cin >> x >> y;
      assert(x * y != 0);                       //precondition on gcd
      cout << "\nGCD(" << x << ", " << y << ") = "
           << (g = gcd(x, y)) << endl;
      assert(x % g == 0 && y % g == 0);   //postcondition
   } while (x != y);
}
```

As you can see, C++ is very terse. C++ compilers can compile multifile programs. Large C++ programs are prepared as separate files. Each file is conceptually a module that contains related program declarations and definitions. On many systems C++ source files have the suffix *.c*. The GNU C++ translator command is *g++*. So,

g++ module1.c module2.c my_main.c

is the Unix C++ compile command *g++*, acting on the three files *module1.c*, *module2.c*, and *my_main.c*. If compilation shows no errors, then an executable *a.out* is produced.

Some minor differences are easily seen in these two versions of the greatest common divisor program.

Some Differences Between C++ and Fortran

- The C++ comment symbols are either // or /* */.

- C++ uses braces for compound statements and function definitions. Fortran has an implied beginning for these statements and an explicit END statement.

- The Fortran keyword FUNCTION is omitted in the C++ function declaration.

Some major differences involve program organization.

C++ Program Organization

- C++ relies on an external standard library to provide input/output. The information the program needs to use this library resides in the file *iostream.h*.

- C++ relies on an external standard library to provide assertion testing. The information the program needs to use this library resides in the file *assert.h*.

- C++ uses a preprocessor to handle a set of directives, such as the `include` directive, to convert the program from its preprocessing form to pure C++ syntax. These directives are introduced by the symbol #.

- A C++ program consists of declarations that may be in different files. Each ordinary function definition is on the external or global level and may not be nested. The files act as modules and may be separately compiled.

- The function `main()` is used as the starting point for the program's execution. It obeys the C++ rules for function declaration. It is ANSI C++ for `main()` to implicitly return the integer value zero, indicating that the program completed normally. Other return values would indicate an error condition.

- The `assert` macro tests a condition for correctness and terminates the program if the test fails.

2.4 Simple Types

The *simple native types* in C++ are `bool`, `int`, `double`, `char`, and `wchar_t`. These types have a set of values and representation that is tied to the underlying machine architecture on which the compiler is running. The data types in Fortran are LOGICAL, INTEGER, REAL, DOUBLE PRECISION, COMPLEX, and CHARACTER. The Fortran and C++ types are for most practical purposes equivalent, and usually each has a set of values and representation that is tied to the underlying machine architecture on which the compiler is running. On older C++ systems there is no native boolean type. They use the value zero to mean false and nonzero values to mean true.

The complex number type in C++ is provided by including the library *complex.h*. This library provides a nonnative type `complex`, which can be used with the various ordinary arithmetic operators and mixed in expression with other arithmetic types.

Two important differences exist between C++ and Fortran simple types. First, C++ simple types can often be modified by the keywords `short`, `long`, `signed`, and `unsigned` to yield further simple types. Second, C++ allows a far wider range of automatic conversions.

The following table lists these types shortest to longest. Length here refers to the number of bytes used to store the type.

Fundamental Data Types		
bool		
char	signed char	unsigned char
wchar_t		
short	int	long
unsigned short	unsigned	unsigned long
float	double	long double

This list runs from the conceptually shortest type `bool` to the conceptually longest type `long double`. There is a requirement that each longer type be at least as long as its predecessor type. On most machines a `bool` or `char` is stored in a single byte. On many PCs `short` and `int` are stored in two bytes, while `long`, `float`, and `double` are each stored in four bytes. The `wchar_t`, or wide character type, can represent distinct codes for any element of the largest extended character set in any language's alphabet, such as Katana used in Japanese. A `wchar_t` type is the same size as an `int` type.

C++ also has the `sizeof` operator. This is used to determine the number of bytes a particular object or type requires for storage.

```
//determine how many bytes it takes to store type long
cout << sizeof(int) << " <= " << sizeof(long) << endl;
```

The range of integral values representable on your system is defined in the standard header file *limits.h*. Some examples from our system are:

```
#define CHAR_BIT 8                  //bits per char
#define SCHAR_MIN (-128)            //signed char minimum
#define SCHAR_MAX 127               //signed char maximum
#define UCHAR_MAX 255               //unsigned char maximum
#define INT_MAX 2147483647          //int maximum
#define INT_MIN (-2147483648)       //int minimum
#define UINT_MAX 4294967295U        //unsigned int maximum
```

The range of floating-point values representable on your system is defined in the standard header file *float.h*. Some examples from our system are:

```
#define FLT_EPSILON ((float)1.19209290e-07)    //single
#define FLT_MIN ((float)1.17549435e-38)        //float min
#define FLT_MAX ((float)3.40282347e+38)        //float max
#define DBL_EPSILON 2.2204460492503131e-16     //double
#define DBL_MIN 2.2250738585072014e-308        //double min
#define DBL_MAX 1.7976931348623157e+308        //double max
```

On newer systems, the file *limits* contains the template `numeric_limits`, which allows, for example:

```
numeric_limits<type>::max()              //maximum value for type
```

2.4.1 Initialization

A variable declaration associates a type with the variable name. A declaration of a variable constitutes a definition, if storage is allocated for it. Informally, we think of the definition as creating the object.

A definition can also initialize the value of the variable. Syntactically, initialization is expressed by following the identifier name with an initializer. For simple variables, this is usually:

type id = expression

Some examples are:

```
{
    int     i = 5;                    //i is initialized to 5
    char    c1, c2 = 'B';             //c1 is uninitialized
    double  x = 0.777, y = x + i;

    cout << x << '\t' << y;           //print 0.777 5.777
    cout << c2;                       //print 'B'
    cout << c1;                       //system-dependent
    .....
}
```

Initialization can involve an arbitrary expression provided all the variables and functions used in the expression are defined. In the example above, y is initialized in terms of the just-defined x. The uninitialized variable c1 cannot be relied on to have any particular value associated with it. Using it in the computation before a well-defined value is assigned to it is a mistake. As a rule of thumb, when there is a choice, it is preferable to initialize a variable than to define it as uninitialized and subsequently assign it a value. Initialization makes the code more readable, less error prone, and more efficient.

Note that C++ declarations are themselves statements and can occur throughout a block. In the above code, we could have placed the `char` declarations after the first `cout` statement without affecting the output.

```
  . . . . .
  cout << x << '\t' << y;      //print 0.777 5.777
  char    c1, c2 = 'B';        //declaration statement
  cout << c2;                  //print 'B'
  . . . . .
```

2.5 The Traditional Conversions

An expression such as x + y has both a value and a type. For example, if x and y are both variables of type `int`, then x + y is also an `int`. However, if x and y are of different types, then x + y is a *mixed expression*. Suppose x is a `short` and y is an `int`. Then the value of x is converted or *coerced* to an `int`, and the expression x + y has type `int`. Note that the value of x as stored in memory is unchanged. It is only a temporary copy of x that is converted during the computation of the value of the expression. Now suppose that both x and y are of type `short`. Even though x + y is not a mixed expression, automatic conversions again take place; both x and y are promoted to `int`, and the expression is of type `int`. The general rules are straightforward.

Automatic Expression Conversion x op y

1. Any `bool`, `char`, `short`, or `enum` is promoted to `int`. Integral values unrepresentable as `int` are promoted to `unsigned`.

2. If, after the first step, the expression is of mixed type, then, according to the hierarchy of types,

   ```
   int <  unsigned <  long    <  unsigned long
        <  float     <  double <  long double
   ```

   the operand of the lower type is promoted to that of the higher type, and the value of the expression has that type.

To illustrate implicit conversion, we make the following declarations and list a variety of mixed expressions along with their corresponding types:

Declarations			
char c;	long lg;	double d;	
short s;	float f;	unsigned u;	int i;

Expression	Type	Expression	Type
c - s / i	int	u * 3 - i	unsigned
u * 3.0 - i	double	f * 3 - i	float
c + 1	int	3 * s * lg	long
c + 1.0	double	d + s	double

Also, an automatic conversion can occur with an assignment. For example,

```
d = i
```

causes the value of i, which is an int, to be converted to a double and then assigned to d; double is the type of the expression as a whole. A promotion, or *widening*, such as d = i will usually be well behaved, but a demotion, or *narrowing*, such as i = d can lose information. Here, the fractional part of d will be discarded.

In addition to implicit conversions, which can occur across assignments and in mixed expressions, there are explicit conversions called *casts*. If i is an int, then

```
static_cast<double>(i)
```

will cast the value of i so that the expression has type double. The variable i itself remains unchanged. The static_cast is available for a conversion that is well defined, portable, and invertible. Some more examples are:

```
static_cast<char>('A' + 1.0)
x = static_cast<double>(static_cast<int>(y) + 1)
```

Casts that are representation- or system-dependent use reinterpret_cast.

```
i = reinterpret_cast<int>(&x)   //system dependent
```

These casts are undesirable and generally should be avoided.

Two other special casts exist in C++: const_cast and dynamic_cast. A useful discussion of dynamic_cast requires understanding inheritance (see Section 9.9, "Run-Time Type Identification," on page 341). The const modifier means a variable's value is nonmodifiable. Very occasionally it is convenient to remove this

2.5 ▼ The Traditional Conversions

restriction. This is known as *casting away constness*, and it is done with the const_cast, as in:

```
foo(const_cast<int>(c_var));     //used to invoke foo
```

Older C++ systems allow an unrestricted form of cast with the following forms:

    (*type*) *expression*   or   *type*(*expression*)

Some examples are:

```
y = i/double(7);              //would do division in double
ptr = (char*)(i + 88);        //int to pointer value
```

These older forms are considered obsolete and will not be used in the text, but many older compilers and older source code still use them. The older casts do not differentiate among relatively safe casts, such as static_cast, and system-dependent unsafe casts, such as reinterpret_cast. The newer casts also are self-documenting; for example, a const_cast suggests its intent through its name.

The next program is a Fortran program that converts miles to kilometers. Miles will be kept as an integer value, and kilometers will be computed in floating point.

In file milestok.f

```
*       Miles are converted to kilometers.
        PROGRAM MITOK

        REAL MTOK
        PARAMETER (MTOK = 1.609)
        INTEGER  MILES, M
        REAL     CONVRT
*         Use statement function for computation
        CONVRT(M) = (M * MTOK)

    10  PRINT *, 'Input distance in miles: '
        READ *, MILES
        PRINT *, 'This distance is ', CONVRT(MILES),
       +          'km.'
        IF (MILES .GT. 0) GO TO 10
        END
```

This program uses INTEGER and REAL variables. The mixed-type expression

```
            CONVRT = MILES * MTOK
```

is automatically promoted to REAL.
In C++ this program can be written as follows:

In file mi_to_k.cpp

```cpp
//Miles are converted to kilometers.
#include <iostream.h>
const double  m_to_k = 1.609;    //conversion constant

inline double  mi_to_km(int miles)
{
    return miles * m_to_k;
}

int main()
{
   int  miles;
   double kilometers;

   do {
      cout << "\nEnter distance in miles: ";
      cin >> miles;
      kilometers = mi_to_km(miles);
      cout << "\nThis is approximately " <<
         static_cast<int>(kilometers) << "km." << endl;
   } while (miles > 0);
}
```

This program consists of two functions, each of which has its own local scope in which variables are declared. Each variable has a type. The variable m_to_k, above, is initialized to the value 1.609, and the `const` modifier insures that this value is nonmodifiable. This is good programming practice in that the identifier is mnemonic and provides useful documentation. Notice that such a `const` variable must be initialized upon definition.

```
     *       Fortran Constants
             REAL PI
             INTEGER N
             PARAMETER (PI = 3.14159, N = 100)
```

is equivalent in C++ to

```
const double pi = 3.14159;
const int N = 100;
```

Both are methods of naming literals.

Where the `inline` keyword modifies a function definition, it suggests to the compiler that when invoked, the code defining it avoid function call by being compiled inline.

The expression `miles * m_to_k` is widened to a `double`. Conceptually, the integer valued `miles` is a narrower type than a `double`. The input statement `cin >> miles` expects keyboard input in the form of a string convertible to an integer. For example, the input 5.45 will be converted and assigned to `miles` as the integer value 5.

The safe cast `static_cast<int>(kilometers)` truncates the double value to an `int` value. Without this explicit cast the variable `kilometers` would have printed as a `double`.

2.6 Enumeration Types

The keyword `enum` is used to declare a distinct integer type with a set of named integer constants called *enumerators*. There is no equivalent to enumerators in Fortran. Consider the declaration

```
enum suit { clubs, diamonds, hearts, spades };
```

This creates an integer type with the four suit names as named integer constants. The enumerators are the identifiers `clubs`, `diamonds`, `hearts`, and `spades`, whose values are 0, 1, 2, and 3, respectively. These values are assigned by default, with the first enumerator being given the constant integer value zero. Each subsequent member of the list is one more than its left neighbor. In C++, the identifier `suit` is now its own unique type distinct from other integer types. This identifier is called *tag name*.

Enumerators can be defined and initialized to arbitrary integer constants.

```
enum ages { laura = 7, ira, harold = 59, philip = harold + 7 };
```

The enumerators can be initialized to constant expressions. Note that the default rule applies when there is no explicit initializer; therefore, in the example, `ira` is 8.

The tag name and the enumerators must be distinct identifiers within scope. The values of enumerators need not be distinct. Enumerations can be implicitly converted to ordinary integer types, but not vice versa.

In file enum_tst.cpp

```
enum signal { off, on } a = on;   //a initialized to on
enum answer { no, yes, maybe = -1 } b;
enum neg { no, off} c;            //illegal no and off redeclared
int  i, j = on;                   //legal on is converted to 1

a = off;                          //legal
i = a;                            //legal i becomes 1
b = a;                            //illegal two distinct types
b = static_cast<answer>(a);       //legal explicit cast
b = (a ? no : yes);               //legal enumerators type answers
```

Enumerators can be declared *anonymously*, without a tag name. Some examples are:

```
enum { LB = 0, UB = 99 };
enum { lazy, hazy, crazy } why;
```

The first declaration is a common means of declaring mnemonic integer constants. The second declares a variable why of enumerated type with `lazy`, `hazy`, and `crazy` as its allowable values.

2.7 Expressions

C++ has a greater variety of operators and expression forms than Fortran (see Appendix B, "Operator Precedence and Associativity"). For example, in C++, assignment is an operator. The following is legal C++:

```
a = b + (c = d + 3);
```

The equivalent Fortran code would be:

```
c = d + 3
a = b + c
```

Arithmetic expressions in C++ are consistent with expected practice. In both C++ and Fortran the results of the division operator / depend on its argument types.

```
a = 3 / 2 ;          //evaluates to integer value 1;
a = 3 / 2.0;         //evaluates to double value 1.5
```

C++ has a tolerant attitude toward mixing types and automatic conversions. C++ allows widening conversion, so an `int` may be widened when assigned to a `double`. But C++ also allows assignment conversions that narrow type, so a `double` may be assigned to an `int` or even a `char`.

```
int     i;
char    ch;
double  b = 1.9

i = b / 2.0;         //i is assigned 0
ch = 'A' + 1.0;      //not allowed in Fortran
```

The more liberal attitude taken in C++ invites bad programming practice and should not be encouraged. Narrowing conversions and mixing types can affect program correctness and should be used carefully.

In contemporary C++ systems the `bool` values `true` and `false` are used to direct the flow of control in the various statement types. These are equivalent to the `LOGICAL` values `.TRUE.` and `.FALSE.` in Fortran. The following table contains the C++ operators that are most often used to affect flow of control.

C++ Relational, Equality, and Logical Operators		
Relational operators	less than	<
	greater than	>
	less than or equal to	<=
	greater than or equal to	>=
Equality operators	equal	==
	not equal	!=
Logical operators	(unary) negation	!
	logical and	&&
	logical or	||

Just as with other operators, the relational, equality, and logical operators have rules of precedence and associativity that determine precisely how expressions involving these operators are evaluated. (See Appendix B, "Operator Precedence and Associativity.") The negation operator ! is unary. All the other relational, equality, and logical operators are binary. They operate on expressions and yield either the `bool` value `false` or the `bool` value `true`. This replaces the earlier C++ convention of treating zero as false and nonzero as true when no `bool` type existed in the language. Where a boolean value is expected, an arithmetic expression is automatically converted following this convention of treating zero as false and nonzero as true. This means that older code still works correctly.

One pitfall in C++ is that the equality operator and the assignment operator are visually similar. The expression `a == b` is a test for equality, whereas `a = b` is an assignment expression. One of the more common C++ programming mistakes is to code something like

```
if (i = 1)
    //do something
```

intending

```
if (i == 1)
    //do something
```

The first `if` statement assigns one to `i` and evaluates to one, so it is always true. This error can be very difficult to find.

The logical operators `!`, `&&`, and `||`, when applied to expressions, yield the `bool` value `true` or `false`. Logical negation can be applied to an arbitrary expression. If an expression has value `false`, then its negation will yield `true`.

The precedence of `&&` is higher than `||`, but both operators are of lower precedence than all unary, arithmetic, and relational operators. Their associativity is left to right.

In the evaluation of expressions that are the operands of `&&` and `||`, the evaluation process stops as soon as the outcome true or false is known. This is called *short-circuit* evaluation. Suppose that *expr1* and *expr2* are expressions. If *expr1* has value false, then in

expr1 && *expr2*

expr2 will not be evaluated because the value of the logical expression is already determined to be false. Similarly, if *expr1* is true, then in

expr1 || *expr2*

expr2 will not be evaluated because the value of the logical expression is already determined to be 1.

The following table shows examples in C++ and Fortran.

C++	Parenthesized Equivalent	Fortran
a + 5 && b	((a + 5) && b)	(a + 5 .NE. 0) .AND. (b .NE. 0)
!(a < b) && c	((!(a < b)) && c)	(.NOT. (a .LT. b)) .AND. (c .NE. 0)
1 || (a != 7)	(1 || (a != 7))	.TRUE.

Of all the operators in C++, the comma operator has the lowest precedence. It is a binary operator with expressions as operands. In a comma expression of the form

   expr1 , *expr2*

expr1 is evaluated first, then *expr2*. The comma expression as a whole has the value and type of its right operand. An example would be

   sum = 0, i = 1

If i has been declared an int, then this comma expression has value 1 and type int. The comma operator typically is used in the control expression part of an iterative statement, when more than one action is required. The comma operator associates from left to right.

The conditional operator ?: is unusual in that it is a ternary operator. Thus, it takes as operands three expressions. In a construct such as

   expr1 ? *expr2* : *expr3*

expr1 is evaluated first. If it is true, then *expr2* is evaluated and that is the value of the conditional expression as a whole. If *expr1* is false, then *expr3* is evaluated and that is the value of the conditional expression as a whole. The following example uses a conditional operator to assign the smaller of two values to the variable x:

   x = (y < z) ? y : z;

The parentheses are not necessary because the conditional operator has precedence over the assignment operator. However, parentheses are good style because they make clear what is being tested for.

The type of the conditional expression

expr1 ? *expr2* : *expr3*

is determined by *expr2* and *expr3*. If they are different types, then the usual conversion rules apply. The conditional expression's type cannot depend on which of the two expressions *expr2* or *expr3* is evaluated. The conditional operator ?: associates right to left.

C++ provides bit-manipulation operators unavailable in Fortran. They operate on the machine-dependent bit representation of integral operands. For example, the operand ~ changes an integral operand bit representation into its one's complement. These operators can be ignored by programmers not interested in manipulating the underlying bit representation of integral values.

Bitwise Operators	Meaning
~	unary one's complement
<<	left shift
>>	right shift
&	and
^	exclusive or
|	or

It is customary to overload the shift operators to perform I/O.

C++ considers *function call* () and *indexing* or *subscripting* [] to be operators. It also has an *address* & operation and an *indirection* * or *dereferencing* operation. The address operator is a unary operator that yields the address or location where an object is stored. The indirection operator is a unary operator that is applied to a pointer. It retrieves the value from the location being pointed at. This is also known as dereferencing (see Section 3.11.1, "Addressing and Dereferencing," on page 86).

C++ also has a `sizeof` operator, which is used to determine the number of bytes a particular object or type requires for storage; it is important for obtaining an appropriate amount of storage for dynamically allocated objects.

2.8 Statements

C++ uses the semicolon as a statement terminator. It has a large variety of statement types, including an expression statement. For example, the assignment statement in C++ is syntactically an assignment expression followed by a semicolon. C++ and Fortran both have assignment statements, procedure statements, transfer statements, conditional statements, selection statements, and iterative statements.

2.8.1 Assignment and Expressions

In C++, assignment occurs as part of an assignment expression, which can occur in several forms. An ordinary assignment is much the same as in Fortran.

    a = b + 1;   Fortran equivalent is   a = b + 1

This expression evaluates the right-hand side of the assignment and converts it to a value compatible with the left-hand side variable. This value is assigned to the left-hand side. The left-hand side must be an *lvalue*. An lvalue is a location in memory where a value can be stored or retrieved. Simple variables are lvalues.

C++ allows multiple assignment in a single statement.

    a = b + (c = 3);

is equivalent in Fortran to

    c = 3
    a = b + c

C++ provides assignment operators that combine an assignment and some other operator.

    a += b;   Fortran equivalent is   a = a + b;
    a *= a + b;   Fortran equivalent is   a = a * (a + b);

C++ also provides autoincrement (++) and autodecrement (--) operators in both prefix and postfix form. In prefix form, the autoincrement operator adds 1 to the value stored at the lvalue it acts upon. Similarly, the autodecrement operator subtracts 1 from the value stored at the lvalue it acts upon.

    ++i;   is equivalent to   i = i + 1;
    --x;   is equivalent to   x = x - 1;

The postfix form behaves differently than the prefix form by changing the affected lvalue after the rest of the expression is evaluated.

```
j = ++i;        is equivalent to      i = i + 1; j = i;
j = i++;        is equivalent to      j = i; i = i + 1;
i = ++i + i++;                        //awful practice is system-dependent
```

Note: These are not exact equivalencies. The compound assignment operators evaluate their left-hand side expression once. Therefore, for complicated expressions with side effects, results of the two forms can be different.

The null statement is written as a single semicolon. It causes no action to take place. Usually a null statement is used where a statement is required syntactically, but no action is desired. This situation sometimes occurs in statements that affect the flow of control.

2.8.2 The Compound Statement

A compound statement in C++ is a series of statements surrounded by the braces { and }. The chief use of the compound statement is to group statements into an executable unit. The body of a C++ function is always a compound statement. In C, when declarations come at the beginning of a compound statement, the statement is called a block. This rule is relaxed in C++ and declaration statements may occur throughout the statement list. Wherever it is possible to place a statement, it is also possible to place a compound statement.

2.8.3 The `if` and `if-else` Statements

The general form of an `if` statement is

>   if (*condition*)
>   *statement*

If *condition* is true, then *statement* is executed; otherwise, *statement* is skipped. After the `if` statement has been executed, control passes to the next statement. A *condition* is an expression or a declaration with initialization that selects flow of control. In the example

In file if_test.cpp

```
if (temperature >= 32)
    cout << "Above Freezing!\n";
cout << "Fahrenheit is " << temperature << endl;
```

the Fortran equivalent is

```
IF (TEMP .GE. 32) PRINT *, 'Above Freezing!'
PRINT *, 'Fahrenheit is ', TEMP, '.'
```

Above Freezing! is printed only when temperature is greater than or equal to 32. The second statement is always executed. Usually the expression in an if statement is a relational, equality, or logical expression.

The equivalent to the Fortran block if statement is the C++ if controlling a C++ compound statement. For example:

In file if_test.cpp

```
if (grade > 70 && grade < 80) {
   cout << " you passed ";
   letter_gr = 'C';
}
```

The Fortran equivalent is

```
IF ((GRADE .GT. 70) .AND. (GRADE .LT. 80)) THEN
    PRINT *, 'You Passed!'
    LETGR = 'C'
END IF
```

Closely related to the if statement is the if-else statement. It has the general form

```
if (condition)
    statement1
else
    statement2
```

If *condition* is true, then *statement1* is executed and *statement2* is skipped; if *condition* is false, then *statement1* is skipped and *statement2* is executed. After the if-else statement has been executed, control passes to the next statement. Consider the following code:

In file if_test.cpp

```
if (x < y)
    min = x;
else
    min = y;
cout << "min = " << min;
```

The Fortran equivalent is

```
IF (X .LT. Y) THEN
    MIN = X
ELSE
    MIN = Y
END IF
PRINT *, 'MIN = ', MIN
```

If `x < y` is true, then `min` will be assigned the value of x; if it is false, then `min` will be assigned the value of y. After the `if-else` statement is executed, `min` is printed.

2.8.4 The `while` Statement

The general form of a `while` statement is

> while (*condition*)
>   *statement*

First *condition* is evaluated. If it is true, then *statement* is executed and control passes back to the beginning of the `while` loop. The effect of this is that the body of the `while` loop, namely *statement*, is executed repeatedly until *condition* is false. At that point control passes to the next statement. The effect of this is that *statement* can be executed zero or more times.

An example of a `while` statement is the following:

In file while_t.cpp

```
while (i <= 10) {
    sum += i;
    ++i;
}
```

is equivalent in Fortran compilers that support WHILE to

```
DO WHILE (I .LE. 10)
   SUM = SUM + I
   I = I + 1
END DO
```

When a Fortran compiler does not support the DO WHILE statement, it is implemented using a block IF statement:

```
10   IF (I .LE. 10) THEN
        SUM = SUM + I
        I = I + 1
        GO TO 10
     END IF
```

Assume initially the value of i is one, and the value of sum is zero. The while loop increments the value of sum by the current value of i, and then increments i by one. After the body of the loop has been executed 10 times, the value of i is 11 and the value of the condition i <= 10 is false. Thus the body of the loop is not executed, and control passes to the next statement. When the while loop is exited, the value of sum is 55.

2.8.5 The for Statement

The general form of a for statement

> for (*for-init-statement*; *condition*; *expression*)
>   *statement*
> *next statement*

is equivalent using the while in C++ to

> *for-init-statement*;
> while (*condition*) {
>   *statement*
>   *expression*;
> }
> *next statement*

provided that *condition* is nonempty, and provided that a continue statement is not in the body of the for loop. From our understanding of the while statement, we can deduce the semantics of the for statement. First the *for-init-statement* is evaluated, and is used to initialize a variable used in the loop. Then *condition* is evaluated. If it is true, then *statement* is executed, *expression* is evaluated, and control passes back to the beginning of the `for` loop again, except that evaluation of *for-init-statement* is skipped. This iteration continues until *condition* is false, at which point control passes to *next statement*.

The *for-init-statement* can be an expression statement or a simple declaration. Where it is a declaration the declared variable has the scope of the `for` statement.

The `for` statement is an iterative statement typically used with a variable that is incremented or decremented. As an example, the following code uses a `for` statement to sum the integers from 1 to 10:

In file for_test.cpp

```
sum = 0;
for (i = 1; i <= 10; ++i)
   sum += i;
```

Another example shows how comma expressions can be used to initialize more than one variable.

In file for_test.cpp

```
for (factorial = n, i = n - 1; i >= 1; --i)
   factorial *= i;
```

is equivalent to

```
        FACTOR = N
        DO 10 I = N - 1, 1, -1
           FACTOR = FACTOR * I;
   10   CONTINUE
```

Any or all of the expressions in a `for` statement can be missing, but the two semicolons must remain. If *for-init-statement* is missing, then no initialization step is performed as part of the `for` loop. If *expression* is missing, then no incrementation step is performed as part of the `for` loop. If *condition* is missing, then no testing step is performed as part of the `for` loop. The special rule for when *condition* is missing is that the test is always true. Thus the `for` loop in the code

In file for_test.cpp

```
for (i = 1, sum = 0 ; ; sum += i++ )
   cout << sum << endl;
```

is an infinite loop.

The for statement is one common case in which a local declaration is used to provide the loop control variable, as in:

```
for (int i = 0; i < N; ++i)
    sum += a[i];    //sum array a[0] + ... + a[N - 1]
```

The semantics are that the int variable i is local to the given loop.

2.8.6 The do Statement

The do statement can be considered a variant of the while statement. However, instead of making its test at the top of the loop, it makes it at the bottom. An example is the following:

```
do {
    sum += i;
    cin >> i;
} while (i > 0);
```

This is equivalent to

```
10   SUM = SUM + I
     READ *, I
     IF (I .GT. 0) GO TO 10
```

Consider a construction of the form

```
do
    statement
while (condition);
next statement
```

First, *statement* is executed, then *condition* is evaluated. If it is true, then control passes back to the beginning of the do statement and the process repeats itself. When the value of *condition* is false, then control passes to *next statement*. As an example, suppose we want to read in an integer, and we want to insist that the integer be positive. The following code will accomplish this:

In file do_test.cpp

```
do {
   cout << "\nEnter a positive integer: ";
   cin >> n;
} while (n <= 0);
```

The user will be prompted for a positive integer. A negative or zero value will cause the loop to be executed again, asking for another value. Control will exit the loop only after a positive integer has been entered.

2.8.7 The break and continue Statements

In C++, the `break` and `continue` statements are used to interrupt ordinary iterative flow of control in loops. In addition, the `break` statement is used within a `switch` statement, which can select among several different cases. To interrupt the normal flow of control within a loop, the programmer can use the two special statements

    break;   and   continue;

The `break` statement, in addition to its use in loops, can be used in a `switch` statement. It causes an exit from the innermost enclosing loop or `switch` statement.

In Fortran, the `CONTINUE` statement is used to indicate the end of a `DO` loop by convention, and though its use is not required, it is good style. In this case, using a `GO TO` *label-on-continue* statement is equivalent to using the C++ `break` statement. In Fortran 90, the `END DO`, `EXIT`, and `CYCLE` statements are added. `EXIT` will give control to the statement following the `END DO` statement, and is thus equivalent to the C++ `break` statement. The `CYCLE` statement inside a `DO` loop will transfer control to the top of the `DO` statement for the next cycle and is thus equivalent to the C++ `continue` statement.

The following example illustrates the use of a `break` statement. A test for a negative value is made, and if the test is true, the `break` statement causes the `for` loop to be exited. Program control jumps to the statement immediately following the loop.

In file for_test.cpp

```
for (i = 0; i < 10; ++i) {
   cin >> x;
   if (x < 0.0) {
      cout << "All done" << endl;
      break;         //exit loop if value is negative
   }
   cout << sqrt(x) << endl;
}

//break jumps to here
.....
```

This is a typical use of a break statement. When a special condition is met, an appropriate action is taken and the loop is exited.

The continue statement causes the current iteration of a loop to stop, and causes the next iteration of the loop to begin immediately. The following code processes all characters except digits.

In file for_test.cpp

```
for (i = 0; i < MAX; ++i) {
   cin.get(c);
   if (isdigit(c))
      continue;
   .....    //process other characters
//continue jumps to here
}
```

When the continue statement is executed, control jumps to just before the closing brace, causing the loop to begin execution at the top again. Notice that the continue statement ends the current iteration, whereas a break statement would end the loop.

A break statement can occur only inside the body of a for, while, do, or switch statement. The continue statement can occur only inside the body of a for, while, or do statement.

2.8.8 The switch Statement

The `switch` statement is a multiway conditional statement generalizing the `if-else` statement. Its general form is given by

> switch (*condition*)
>   *statement*

where *statement* is typically a compound statement containing `case` labels and optionally a `default` label. In FORTRAN 77, the switch statement is simulated by using the `IF` and `ELSE IF` statements. In Fortran 90, a `CASE` construct was added. Typically, a `switch` is composed of many cases, and the *condition* in parentheses following the keyword `switch` determines which, if any, of the cases are executed.

The following `switch` statement and its Fortran equivalent count the number of test scores by category.

In file switch_t.cpp

```
switch (score) {
case 9: case 10:
    ++a_grades; break;
case 8:
    ++b_grades; break;
case 7:
    ++c_grades; break;
default:
    ++fails;
}
```

is equivalent in FORTRAN 77 to

```
IF ( (SCORE .EQ. 9) .OR. (SCORE .EQ. 10) ) THEN
    AGRADE = AGRADE + 1
ELSE IF (SCORE .EQ. 8) THEN
    BGRADE = BGRADE + 1
ELSE IF (SCORE .EQ. 7) THEN
    CGRADE = CGRADE + 1
ELSE
    FAILS = FAILS + 1
END IF
```

and is equivalent to Fortran 90 to

```
SELECT CASE (SCORE)
CASE (9, 10)
   A_GRADES = A_GRADES + 1
CASE (8)
   B_GRADES = B_GRADES + 1
CASE (7)
   C_GRADES = C_GRADES + 1
CASE DEFAULT
   FAILS = FAILS + 1
END SELECT
```

A case label is of the form

  case *constant integral expression*:

In a switch statement, each case label must be unique. Typically, the action taken after each case label ends with a break statement. If there is no break statement, then execution "falls through" to the next statement in the succeeding case or default.

If no case label is selected, then control passes to the default label, if there is one. No default label is required, but including one is good practice. If no case label is selected, and there is no default label, then the switch statement is exited. To detect errors, programmers frequently include a default even when all the expected cases have been accounted for.

The keywords case and default cannot occur outside a switch.

The Effect of a switch

1. Evaluate the integral expression in the parentheses following switch.

2. Execute the case label having a constant value that matches the value of the expression found in Step 1; if no match is found, execute the default label; if there is no default label, terminate the switch.

3. Terminate the switch when a break statement is encountered, or by "falling off the end."

2.8.9 The goto Statement

The `goto` statement is the most primitive method of interrupting ordinary control flow. It is an unconditional branch to an arbitrary labeled statement in the function. The `goto` statement is considered a harmful construct in most accounts of modern programming methodology. Thus, it can undermine all the useful structure provided by other flow-of-control mechanisms (`for`, `while`, `do`, `if`, and `switch`).

A label is an identifier. By executing a `goto` statement of the form

```
goto label;
```

control is unconditionally transferred to a labeled statement. An example would be

In file goto_tst.cpp

```
if (d == 0.0)
   goto error;
else
   ratio = n / d;
.....
error:  cerr << "ERROR:  division by zero" << endl;
```

Both the `goto` statement and its corresponding labeled statement must be in the body of the same function. In general, `goto` should be avoided.

Summary

1. A C++ program consists of declarations that may be in different files. Ordinary functions are on the external, or global, level and may not be declared in a nested manner. The files act as modules and may be separately compiled. Later we will discuss member functions that have class scope.

2. The function `main()` is used as the starting point for execution of the program. It obeys the C++ rules for function declaration.

3. C++ uses a preprocessor to handle a set of directives, such as the `include` directive, to convert the program from its preprocessing form to pure C++ syntax. These directives are introduced by the symbol #.

4. C++ relies on an external standard library to provide input/output. The information the program needs to use this library resides in the file *iostream.h* or *iostream*.

5. The required simple types in C++ are `bool`, `double`, `int`, `char`, and `wchar_t`. These are similar to the types in Fortran, which are LOGICAL, REAL, INTEGER, and CHARACTER.

6. Both C++ and Fortran have assignment, procedure, transfer, conditional, selection, and iterative statements. Three important differences are: (1) C++ has the semicolon as a statement terminator, but standard Fortran allows only one statement per line and thus does not need a terminator; (2) Fortran has no empty statements and relies heavily on the GO TO for flow-of-control statements; and (3) C++ is more expression oriented.

7. The general form of an `if` statement is

    `if` (*condition*)
       statement

    If *condition* is true, then *statement* is executed; otherwise, *statement* is skipped. After the `if` statement has been executed, control passes to the next statement.

8. The general form of a `while` statement is

    `while` (*condition*)
       statement

    First, *condition* is evaluated. If it is true, then *statement* is executed and control passes back to the beginning of the `while` loop. The effect of this is that the body of the `while` loop, namely *statement*, is executed repeatedly until *condition* is false. At that point, control passes to the next statement.

9. To interrupt normal flow of control within a loop, the programmer can use the special statements

    `break;`   and   `continue;`

    The `break` statement, in addition to its use in loops, can also be used in a `switch` statement. It causes an exit from the innermost enclosing loop or `switch` statement.

10. The `goto` statement is the most primitive method of interrupting ordinary control flow. It is an unconditional branch to an arbitrary labeled statement in the function. The `goto` statement is considered a harmful construct and should be avoided.

Exercises

1. Rewrite the `gcd()` function with a `for` loop replacing the `while` loop.

2. Write a `main()` function calling `gcd()`. Ask the user to input two integers, and compute and print the result. Have the program exit after computing five greatest common divisors.

3. Rewrite the *gcd* program to read a value for `how_many` greatest common divisors will be computed. The variable `how_many` will be used to exit the `for` loop.

4. On most systems, input can be *redirected* from a file. Assume that the *gcd* program has been compiled into an executable file called *gcd*. The command

    gcd < gcd.dat

   will take its input from the file *gcd.dat*, and write the answers to the screen. Test this with a file containing:

    4   4 6   6 21   8 20   15 20

   On most systems, output can also be redirected to a file. The command

    gcd > gcd.ans

   will place its output in the file *gcd.ans*, taking its input from the keyboard. Enter the same data as above and check the file *gcd.ans* to see that it has the four correct answers. The two redirections can be combined as follows:

    gcd < gcd.dat > gcd.ans

   This will take its input from the file *gcd.dat* and will place its output in the file *gcd.ans*. Test this on your system.

5. Short-circuit evaluation is an important feature. The following code illustrates its importance in a typical situation:

   ```
   //Compute the roots of: a * x * x + b * x + c
   cin >> a >> b >> c;
   discr = b * b - 4 * a * c;
   if ((discr > 0) && (sq_disc = sqrt(discr))) {
      root1 = (-b + sq_disc) / (2 * a);
      root2 = (-b - sq_disc) / (2 * a);
   }
   else if (discr < 0) {          //complex roots
      .....
   }
   else
      root1 = root2 = -b / (2 * a);
   ```

   The sqrt() function would fail on negative values, and short-circuit evaluation protects the program from this error. Complete this program by having it compute roots and print them out for the following values:

   ```
   a = 1.0, b = 4.0, c = 3.0
   a = 1.0, b = 2.0, c = 1.0
   a = 1.0, b = 1.0, c = 1.0
   ```

6. Use #include <complex.h> to provide the C++ complex number type and rewrite the above root-finding program to print out roots as complex numbers when appropriate. Compare this to a Fortran implementation.

7. What will the following program print?

   ```
   //What is printed.
   #include  <iostream.h>

   int main()
   {
      char   c = 'A';
      int    i = 3, j = 1, k = -2, m = 0;
      bool   p = false, q = true;
   ```

```
         cout << c << " is integer value " << int(c)
              << "   and !'A' is " << !c << endl;
         cout << "i = " << i << ", !i = " << !i << endl;
         cout << "!!i = " << !!i << ", !m = " << !m
              << endl;
         cout << "p = " << p << ", q = " << q << endl;
         cout << "!p = " << !p << ", !q = " << !q << endl;
         cout << "!(i + j) || m = " << (!(i + j) || m)
              << endl;
         cout << "q || (j / m) = " << (q || (j / m))
              << endl;
         cout << "(j / m) || q = " << ((j / m) || q)
              << endl;
      }
```

8. The C++ `switch` statement, unlike the Fortran 90 CASE statement, allows two or more cases to be executed for the same value by allowing the code to "fall through."

```
switch (i) {
case 0: case 1:
   ++hopeless;             // fall through
case 2: case 3:
   ++weak;
case 4: case 5:
   ++fails; break;
case 6: case 7:
   ++c_grades; break;
case 8:
   ++b_grades; break;
case 9:
   ++a_grades; break;
default:
   cout << "incorrect grade " << i << endl;
}
```

Hand simulate this statement for i equals 1. Write the equivalent Fortran 90 CASE statement.

9. Use `sizeof` to determine the number of bytes each of the following requires on your local system: `bool`, `char`, `short`, `int`, `long`, `float`, `double`, and `long double`. Also do this for the enumerated types:

    ```
    enum bounds { lb = -1, ub = 511 };
    enum suit { clubs, diamonds, hearts, spades };
    ```

10. Write a program to convert from Celsius to Fahrenheit. The program should use integer values and print integer values that are rounded. Recall that zero Celsius is 32 degrees Fahrenheit and that each degree Celsius is 1.8 degrees Fahrenheit.

11. Write a program that, given a temperature in Fahrenheit, prints whether water at that temperature would be solid, liquid, or gas. Use an enumerated type:

    ```
    enum state { solid = STMP, liquid = LTMP, gas = GTMP };
    ```

    in the computation.

12. Write a program that accepts either Celcius or Fahrenheit and produces the other value as output. For example, input: 0C, output: 32F; input: 212F, output: 100C.

13. Simplify the following code:

    ```
    for (sum =i = 0, j = 2, k = i + j; i < 10 || k < 15;
            ++i, ++j, ++k)
        sum += (i < j)? k : i;
    ```

    Remember that comma expressions are sequences of left-to-right evaluations, with each comma-separated subexpression evaluated in strict order.

14. In the C world, more flexible file I/O is available using the `FILE` declaration and file operations found in *stdio.h*. The C++ community uses *fstream.h*, as discussed in Appendix E, "Input/Output." Familiarize yourself with this library and convert the program in exercise 5 to use *fstreams*. The program should get its arguments from the command line, as in:

    gcd   gcd.dat   gcd.ans

15. The following code prints 100 random numbers:

    ```
    #include <stdlib.h>
    #include <iostream.h>
    int main()
    {
       int how_many = 100;

       cout << "Print " << how_many
            << "   random integers.\n";
       for (int i = 0; i < how_many; ++i)
          cout << rand() << '\t';
    }
    ```

    Add code that determines average, maximum, and minimum values generated.

16. Alter the previous program to ask the user for how many numbers should be generated. Have this be an outer loop. Exit this program when the user answers with zero or a negative number.

17. The constant RAND_MAX is the largest integer that rand() generates. Use RAND_MAX/2 to decide whether a random number is to be heads or tails. Generate 1,000 randomly generated heads and tails. Print out the ratio of heads to tails. Is this a reasonable test to see if rand() works correctly? Print out the size of the longest number of heads thrown in a row.

Chapter 3

Functions, Pointers, and Arrays

This chapter continues the discussion of the analogs between Fortran and the C++ kernel language, focusing on functions, pointers, and arrays. In C++, a primary unit for structuring a program is the function. Aggregate data in C++ are either arrays or structures. In both cases, a pointer type is used as a mechanism for accessing such data. In Fortran 90 there are derived data types analogous to C++ structures and pointers. FORTRAN 77 has arrays, but not structures or pointers.

3.1 Functions

A problem in C++ or Fortran can be decomposed into subproblems, each of which can be either coded directly or further decomposed. This method is called *stepwise refinement*. The *function* construct in C++ is used to write code for these directly solvable subproblems. These functions are combined into other functions, and ultimately used in `main()` to solve the original problem. The function mechanism is provided in C++ to perform distinct programming tasks. Some functions, such as `strcpy()`, `exit()`, and `rand()`, are provided by libraries. Others can be written by the programmer.

3.1.1 Function Invocation

A C++ program is made up of one or more functions, one of which is main(). Program execution always begins with main(). When program control encounters a function name, the function is called, or *invoked*. This means that program control passes to the function. After the function does its work, program control is passed back to the calling environment, which then continues with its work. As a simple example, consider the following program *bell*, which rings a bell:

In file bell.cpp

```cpp
//Ring my bell using '\a' literal  for the alarm.

#include   <iostream.h>
const char   BELL = '\a';

void ring()
{
   cout << BELL ;
}

int main()
{
   ring();
}
```

3.2 Function Definition

The C++ code that describes what a function does is called the *function definition*. Its form is:

function header
{
    statements
}

Everything before the first brace comprises the *header* of the function definition, and everything between the braces comprises the *body* of the function definition.
The function header is:

type name(parameter-declaration-list)

The *type* specification that precedes the function name is the *return type*. It determines the type of the value that the function returns, if any. The return mechanism is explained below.

In the function definition for `ring()` above, the parameter list is empty, so there are no declarations of parameters. The body of the function consists of a single statement. Since the function does not return a value, its return type is `void`. In Fortran such code is done with SUBROUTINE.

Parameters are syntactically identifiers, and they can be used within the body of the function. Sometimes the parameters in a function definition are called *formal parameters* to emphasize their role as placeholders for actual values that are passed to the function when it is called. Upon function invocation, the value of the argument corresponding to a formal parameter is used within the body of the executing function. Such parameters in C++ are *call-by-value*.

To illustrate these ideas, let us rewrite the above program so that `ring()` has a formal parameter, which will be used to specify how many times the bell is rung.

In file bellmult.cpp

```
//Repeated bell ringing.

#include   <iostream.h>
const char   BELL = '\a';

void ring(int k)
{
   int   i;

   for (i = 0; i < k; ++i)
      cout << BELL;
}

int main()
{
   int   n;

   cout << "\nInput a small positive integer:   ";
   cin >> n;
   ring(n);
}
```

3.3 The return Statement

The `return` statement is used for two purposes. When a `return` statement is executed, program control is immediately passed back to the calling environment. In addition, if an expression follows the keyword `return`, then the value of the expression is returned to the calling environment as well. This value must be assignment-convertible to the return type of the function definition header.

A `return` statement has one of the following two forms:

```
return;
return expression;
```

Some examples are:

```
return;
return 3;
return (a + b);
```

Parenthesizing the `return` expression is optional, and is a stylistic device that some programmers use to enhance readability. In Fortran, the returned value is assigned to the name of the function. In Fortran 90, the RESULT clause specifies the variable to be returned.

As an example, let us write a program that computes the sum of the squares of two integers.

In file sum_sq.cpp

```
//Find the sum of squares of two integers.
#include  <iostream.h>

int sum_of_squares(int x, int y)
{
    return x * x + y * y;
}
```

```
int main()
{
   int  j, k, m;

   cout << "Input two integers:   ";
   cin >> j >> k;
   m = sum_of_squares(j, k);
   cout << '\n' << m << " is the sum of squares of " << j
        << " and " << k << endl;
}
```

The equivalent Fortran program is

In file sum_sq.f

```
         INTEGER FUNCTION SUMSQ(X, Y)

         INTEGER X, Y

         SUMSQ = X * X + Y * Y
         END

         PROGRAM GETSUMSQ

         INTEGER  J, K, M

         PRINT *, 'Input 2 integers: '
         READ *, J, K
         M = SUMSQ(J, K)
         PRINT *, M, ' is the sum of squares of ', J, ' and ', K
         END
```

We have designed sum_of_squares() to work with integer values; but suppose we want to work with values of type double. We will rewrite sum_of_squares() to use double.

In file sum_sq_dbl.cpp

```cpp
//Find the sum of squares of two doubles.
#include <iostream.h>

double sum_of_squares(double x, double y)
{
   return x * x + y * y;
}
```

3.4 Function Prototypes

The syntax of functions in C++ is type safe where the types of parameters are listed inside the header parentheses. Explicitly listing the type and number of arguments makes strong type-checking and assignment-compatible conversions possible.

A function can be declared before it is defined. It can be defined later in the file, or can come from a library or a user-specified file. Such a declaration is called a *function prototype*. It has the following general form:

type name(argument-declaration-list) ;

The *argument-declaration-list* is typically a comma-separated list of types. If a function has no parameters, then the keyword `void` may be used. In C++, the preferred style for an empty parameter list is *function_name()*. This list can include the argument identifiers. This information allows the compiler to enforce type compatibility by converting the arguments to the types in the *argument-declaration-list* as if they were following rules of assignment.

To recode `main()`, taken from the program *bellmult* in Section 3.2, "Function Definition," on page 67, to introduce the function prototype for `ring()`:

```cpp
void   ring(int);       //definition in file ring.c

int main()
{
   int n;

   cout << "\nInput a small positive integer:   ";
   cin >> n;
   ring(n);
}
```

The declaration of the function prototype informs the compiler that ring() must be used with a single integer argument, and that it does not return a value when called.

In Section 3.3, "The return Statement," on page 68, we used the function sum_of_squares() in the *sum_sq.cpp* program. Its prototype in main() would be

```
int sum_of_squares(int, int);
```

Both the function return type and the argument-list types are explicitly mentioned. The definition of sum_of_squares() that occurs in the file must match this declaration. The function prototype can also include the identifier names of the arguments. In the case of sum_of_squares() this would be

```
int sum_of_squares(int x, int y);
```

C++ uses the ellipsis symbol (...) to represent an argument list that is unspecified. The *stdio.h* function printf() is declared as the prototype:

```
int printf(const char* cntrl_str, ...);
```

Such a function can be invoked on an arbitrary list of actual parameters. This practice should be avoided because of loss of type safety.

Here is another program that illustrates the use of function prototypes:

In file avg3.cpp

```
//Add three ints - illustrating function prototypes.

#include   <iostream.h>

int   add3(int, int, int);
double   average(int);
```

```
int main()
{
    int   score_1, score_2, score_3, sum;

    cout << "\nEnter 3 scores: ";
    cin >> score_1 >> score_2 >> score_3;
    sum = add3(score_1, score_2, score_3);
    cout << "\nTheir sum is " << sum;
    cout << "\nTheir average is " << average(sum);
    sum = add3(1.5 * score_1, score_2, score_3);
    cout << "\nThe weighted sum is " << sum << ".";
    cout << "\nTheir weighted average is "
         << average(sum) << "." << endl;
}

int add3(int a, int b, int c)
{
    return (a + b + c);
}

double average(int s)
{
    return (s / 3.0);
}
```

In Fortran the function average() would be written as follows:

In file avg3.f

```
      REAL FUNCTION AVE (S)
      INTEGER   S
      AVE = S / 3.0;
      END
```

Dissection of the *avg3* Program

- `int   add3(int, int, int);`
  `double   average(int);`

These declarations are function prototypes. They inform the compiler of the type and number of arguments to expect for each externally specified function. Since the list of arguments can optionally include variable names

```
int add3(int a, int b, int c);
double average(int s);
```

is also possible.

- `sum = add3(1.5 * score_1, score_2, score_3);`

In C++ this expression is converted to an integer value per the function prototype specification.

- ```
  int add3(int a, int b, int c)
  {
     return (a + b + c);
  }
  ```

This is the actual function definition. It could just as well have been imported from another file. It is compatible with the function prototype declaration in the source file containing `main()`.

C++ does not have keywords distinguishing between functions and subroutines. A function whose return type is `void` is the equivalent of a Fortran subroutine. C++ provides inline functions that are similar to Fortran statement functions, but where Fortran statement functions are restricted to functions expressible as a single assignment, C++ inlining can be applied to multiple statement functions as well.

3.4.1 Recursion

C++ functions can be recursive but they cannot nest; Fortran 90 functions work the same way. A recursive function calls itself as part of its definition. A simple recursive function has two main parts: the base case part, where it computes a value and terminates, and the recursive part, where it calls itself. It corresponds to mathematical induction in describing how functions such as factorial are proved correct.

```
//Recursive factorial function
long factorial(int n)
{
   if (n <= 1)
      return 1;
   else
      return n * factorial(n - 1);
}
```
```

Notice how the recursive call is with the expression n - 1. This guarantees that the function `factorial()` will terminate. Each recursion will reduce the called expression by one until the termination condition n <= 1 is true. In running this computation, be aware that for relatively small values of n (such as 13) the computation will fail because of integer overflow.

A pseudocode prescription for writing a simple recursion is:

```
//base case part
if (base-case condition)
    return base-case computed value;
//general case as a recursion
else
    return recursively computed expression;
```

3.5 Default Arguments

A formal parameter can be given a default argument. This is usually a constant that occurs frequently when the function is called. Use of a default argument saves writing this default value at each invocation. The following recursive function illustrates the point.

In file def_args.cpp

```
int sqr_or_power(int n, int k = 2)   //k=2 is default
{
    assert(k > 1);
    if (k == 2)
        return (n * n);
    else
        return (sqr_or_power(n, k - 1) * n);
}
```

We assume that most of time the function is used to return the value of n squared.

```
sqr_or_power(i + 5)         //computes (i + 5) * (i + 5)
sqr_or_power(i + 5, 3)      //computes (i + 5) cubed
```

Only trailing parameters of a function can have default values. Some examples are:

```
void foo(int i, int j = 7);                    //legal
void goo(int i = 3, int j);                    //illegal
void hoo(int i, int j = 3, int k = 7);         //legal
void moo(int i = 1, int j = 2, int k = 3);     //legal
void noo(int i, int j = 2, int k);             //illegal
```

3.6 Functions as Arguments

Functions in C++ can be thought of as the address of the compiled code residing in memory. They are therefore a form of pointer (see Section 3.11, "Pointer Types," on page 85), and can be passed as a pointer-value argument into another function. Using this idea, we write code that will print n values of a function starting at some initial value using a specific increment. This form of plotting function can be useful to generate a map of a function that will later be used to find properties of the function, such as its root.

In file root.cpp

```cpp
#include <iostream.h>

double f(double x)
{
   return (x*x + 1.0/x);
}

void plot(double fcn(double), double x0, double incr, int n)
{
   for (int i = 0; i < n; ++i){
      cout << " x :" << x0
           << "    f(x) : " << fcn(x0) << endl;
      x0 += incr;
   }
}

int main()
{
   cout << "mapping function x*x + 1.0/x " << endl;
   plot(f, 0.01, 0.01, 100);
}
```

Notice that the first argument to `plot()` is a function of a specific type. Functions as arguments are strongly typed. In this case `plot()` will take only a function returning `double` of one argument that is `double`.

3.7 Overloading Functions

The usual reason for picking a function name is to indicate the function's chief purpose. Readable programs generally have a diverse and literate choice of identifiers. Sometimes different functions are used for the same purpose. For example, consider a function that averages the values in an array of `double` versus one that averages the values in an array of `int` (see Section 3.14, "Arrays and Pointers," on page 95). Both are conveniently named `avg_arr()`, as in the following example.

Overloading refers to using the same name for multiple meanings of an operator or a function. The meaning selected depends on the types of the arguments used by the operator or function. Here we restrict our discussion to function overloading and leave operator overloading to later chapters (see Chapter 6, "Operator Overloading and Conversions"), as the latter is chiefly used in the context of classes. In the following code we overload `avg_arr()`:

In file avg_arr.cpp

```
//Average the values in an array.
double avg_arr(const int a[], int size)
{
   int  sum = 0;

   for (int i = 0; i < size; ++i)
      sum += a[i];         //performs int arithmetic
   return (double(sum) / size);
}

double avg_arr(const double a[], int size)
{
   double  sum = 0.0;

   for (int i = 0; i < size; ++i)
      sum += a[i];         //performs double arithmetic
   return (sum / size);
}
```

The following code shows how `avg_arr()` is invoked:

```
int main()
{
   int      w[5] = { 1, 2, 3, 4, 5 }; //initialization
   double   x[5] = { 1.1, 2.2, 3.3, 4.4, 5.5 };

   cout << avg_arr(w, 5) << " int average" << endl;
   cout << avg_arr(x, 5) << " double average" << endl;
}
```

The compiler chooses the function with matching types and arguments. The *signature-matching algorithm* gives the rules for performing this (see Section 6.2, "Overloading and Function Selection," on page 201). By *signature* we mean the list of types that are used in the function declaration.

3.8 Inlining

C++ provides the keyword `inline` to preface a function declaration when the programmer intends the code replacing the function call to be inline.

In file inline.cpp

```
inline double cube(double x)
{
   return (x * x * x);
}
```

The compiler parses this function, providing semantics that are equivalent to a non-inline version. The compiler limits prevent complicated functions, such as recursive functions, from being inlined. The Fortran statement function contains a single assignment expression and is analogous to the C++ inline function.

Macro expansion is a scheme for placing code inline that would normally use a function call. The `#define` preprocessor directive supports general macro substitution, as in the following:

```
#define  SQR(X)   ((X) * (X))
#define  CUBE(X)  (SQR(X)*(X))
#define  ABS(X)   (((X) < 0)? -(X) : X)
  .....
   y = SQR(t + 8) - CUBE(t - 8);
   cout << sqrt(ABS(y));
```

The preprocessor expands the macros and passes on the resulting text to the compiler. So the above is equivalent to:

```
   y = ((t+8) * (t+8)) - ((((t-8)) * (t-8)) * (t-8));
   cout << sqrt((((y) < 0)? -(y) : y));
```

One reason for all the parentheses is to avoid precedence mistakes, as would occur in the following:

```
#define  SQR(X)   X * X
  .....
   y = SQR(t + 8);        //expands to t + 8 * t + 8
```

Even so, such macro expansion provides no type safety such as is given by the C++ parameter-passing mechanism.

3.9 Scope and Storage Class

The kernel language has two principal forms of scope: *file scope* and *local scope*. Local scope is scoped to a block. Compound statements that include declarations are blocks. Function bodies are examples of blocks. They contain a set of declarations that include their parameters. File scope has names that are external (global). We will discuss class scope rules later.

The basic rule of scoping is that identifiers are accessible only within the block in which they are declared. They are unknown outside the boundaries of that block. A simple example is:

In file scope_t.cpp

```
{
   int   a = 2;                  //outer block a
   cout << a << endl;            //prints 2
   {                             //enter inner block
      int   a = 7;               //inner block a
      cout << a << endl;         //prints 7
   }                             //exit inner block
   cout << ++a << endl;          //3 is printed
}
```

Each block introduces its own nomenclature. An outer block name is valid unless an inner block redefines it. If redefined, the outer block name is hidden, or masked, from the inner block. Inner blocks may be nested to arbitrary depths that are determined by system limitations.

In C++, declarations can be internal to a block. In C, all block-scope declarations occur at the head of the block. An example that shows this is:

```
//C++ but not C

int max(int c[], int size)
{
   cout << "array size is " << size << endl;

   int   comp = c[0];                        //declare comp
   for (int i = 1; i < size; ++i)            //declare i
      if (c[i] > comp)
         comp = c[i];
   return comp;
}
```

In C++, the scope of an identifier begins at the end of its declaration and continues to the end of its innermost enclosing block.

Even though C++ does not require that declarations be placed at the head of blocks, it is frequently good practice to do so. Since blocks are often small, this provides a good documentation style where their associated use is commented on.

Placing declarations within blocks allows a computed or input value to initialize a variable; especially for large blocks, it is best to place declarations as close as possible to where they are used.

3.9.1 The Storage Class `auto`

Every variable and function in C++ kernel language has two attributes: *type* and *storage class*. The four storage classes are automatic, external, register, and static, with corresponding keywords

      `auto`   `extern`   `register`   `static`

Variables declared within function bodies are by default automatic. Thus automatic is the most common of the four storage classes. If a compound statement contains variable declarations, then these variables can be acted on within the scope of the enclosing compound statement. A compound statement with declarations is a *block*.

Declarations of variables within blocks are implicitly of storage class automatic. The keyword `auto` can be used to explicitly specify the storage class. An example is:

```
auto int    a, b, c;
auto float  f = 7.78;
```

Because the storage class is automatic by default, the keyword `auto` is seldom used.

When a block is entered, the system allocates memory for the automatic variables. The variables with initializers are initialized. Most systems use some form of stack allocation for these variables. Within that block those variables are defined, and they are considered *local* to the block. When the block is exited, the system no longer reserves the memory that was set aside for the automatic variables. Thus the values of these variables are lost. This is easy to implement with a stack, where space for these variables would be deallocated by resetting the stack top. If the block is reentered, the system once again allocates memory, but previous values are unknown. If a function definition contains a block, then each invocation of that function sets up a new environment.

3.9.2 The Storage Class `register`

The storage class `register` tells the compiler that the associated variables should be stored in high-speed memory registers, provided it is physically and semantically possible to do. Since resource limitations and semantic constraints sometimes make this impossible, the storage class `register` defaults to automatic whenever the compiler cannot allocate an appropriate physical register. Typically, the compiler has only a few such registers available. Many of these are required for system use and cannot be allocated for other purposes.

When speed is of concern, the programmer may choose a few variables that are most frequently accessed and declare them to be of storage class `register`. Common candidates for such treatment include loop variables and function parameters. Here is an example:

```
   {
      for (register i = 0; i < LIMIT; ++i) {
         .....
      }
   }
```

The declaration

    `register i;`   is equivalent to   `register int i;`

If a storage class is specified in a declaration and the type is absent, then the type is `int` by default.

The storage class `register` is of limited usefulness. It is taken only as *advice* to the compiler. Furthermore, contemporary optimizing compilers are often more astute than the programmer.

3.9.3 The Storage Class `extern`

One method of transmitting information across blocks and functions is to use external variables. When a variable is declared outside a function at the file level, storage is permanently assigned to it, and its storage class keyword is `extern`. A declaration for an external variable can look just like a declaration for a variable that occurs inside a function or block. Such a variable is considered to be global to all functions declared after it, and upon block exit or function exit, the external variable remains in existence. Such variables cannot have automatic or register storage class. The keyword `static` can be used. (See Section 3.9.4, "The Storage Class static," on page 82.)

The keyword `extern` is used to tell the compiler, "look for it elsewhere, either in this file or in some other file." Thus, two files can be compiled separately. The use of `extern` in the second file tells the compiler that the variable will be *defined* elsewhere, either in this file or in some other. The ability to compile files separately is important when writing large programs.

External variables never disappear. Since they exist throughout the execution life of the program, they can be used to transmit values across functions. They may, however, be hidden if the identifier is redefined. Another way to conceive of external variables is as being declared in a block that encompasses the whole file.

Information can be passed into a function two ways: by external variables and by the parameter mechanism. Although there are exceptions, the parameter mechanism is the preferred method. This tends to improve the modularity of the code and reduces the possibility of undesirable side effects.

Here is a simple example of using external declarations where the program sits in two separate files:

In file circle3.cpp

```cpp
const double  pi = 3.14159;
double circle(double radius)
{
   return (pi * radius * radius);
}
```

In file cir_main.cpp

```cpp
#include  <iostream.h>

double circle(double);      //functions are of extern scope

int main()
{
   double  x;

   .....
   cout << circle(x) << "is area of circle of radius "
        << x << endl;
}
```

With the GNU system this is compiled as *g++ circle.c main.c*.

The `const` modifier causes `pi` to have local file scope. It cannot be directly imported into another file. When such a definition is required elsewhere, it must be modified explicitly with the keyword `extern`.

3.9.4 The Storage Class `static`

Static declarations have two important and distinct uses. The more elementary use is to allow a local variable to retain its previous value when the block is reentered. This is in contrast to ordinary automatic variables, which lose their value upon block exit and must be reinitialized. The second and more subtle use is in connection with external declarations, and will be discussed in the next section.

As an example of the value-retention use of `static`, we will write a function that maintains a count of the number of times it is called:

In file stat_tst.cpp

```
int f()
{
   static int  called = 0;
   ++called;
   .....
   return called;
}
```

The first time the function is invoked, the variable `called` is initialized to zero. On function exit, the value of `called` is preserved in memory. When the function is invoked again, `called` is *not* reinitialized; instead, it retains its previous value from the last time the function was called.

The second and more subtle use of `static` is in connection with external declarations, with which it provides a privacy mechanism that is very important for program modularity. By privacy, we mean *visibility* or *scope* restrictions on otherwise accessible variables or functions.

This use restricts the scope of the function. Static functions are visible only within the file in which they are defined. Unlike ordinary functions, which can be accessed from other files, a static function is available throughout its own file, but in no other. Again, this facility is useful in developing private modules of function definitions. Note that in C++ systems with namespaces, this mechanism should be replaced by anonymous namespaces (see Section 3.10, "Namespaces," on page 84).

```
static int goo(int a)
{
   .....
}

int foo(int a)
{
   .....
   b = goo(a);
   //goo() is available here, but not in other files
   .....
}
```

In C++, both external variables and static variables that are not explicitly initialized by the programmer are initialized to zero by the system. This includes arrays, strings, pointers, structures, and unions. For arrays and strings this means that each element is initialized to zero; for structures and unions it means each member is initialized to zero. In contrast, automatic and register variables usually are not initialized by the system. This means they can start with "garbage" values.

3.9.5 Linkage Mysteries

Multifile programs require proper linkage. C++ requires some special rules to avoid hidden inconsistencies. As already indicated, a name declared at file scope that is explicitly `static` is local and hidden from other files. So are functions that are declared `inline` and variables declared `const`. A `const` variable that is at file scope but is not static can be given external linkage by declaring it `extern`. Finally, linkage to C code is possible using the form:

```
extern "C" { code or included file }
```

Linkage to languages other than C is system-dependent; for example, some systems might allow "FORTRAN". (See Section D.11.6, "Type-Safe Linkage for Functions," on page 443.)

3.10 Namespaces

C++ inherited C's single global namespace. Programs written by various parties inadvertently can have name clashes when combined. C++ encourages multivendor library use. This motivates the addition of a namespace scope to ANSI C++:

```
namespace LMPinc {
   class puzzles { ····· };
   class toys { ····· };
   ·····
}
```

The namespace identifier can be used as part of a scope-resolved identifier. This has the form:

namespace_id::*id*

There is also a `using` declaration that lets a client have access to all names from that namespace. For example:

```
using namespace LMPinc;
toys   top;                          //LMPinc::toys
```

Namespaces can nest:

In file namespac.cpp

```
namespace LMPout {
   int  n;
   namespace LMPin {
      int  sq(){ return n * n; }       //LMPout::n
      void  pr_my_logo();
   }
   void  LMPin::pr_my_logo()
      { cout << "LMPinc" << endl; }
}
```

As was mentioned in Section 3.9.4, "The Storage Class static," on page 83, namespaces can be used to provide a unique scope that replaces static global declarations. This is done by an anonymous namespace definition, as in:

```
namespace { int count = 0; }       //count is unique here
//count is available in the rest of the file
void  chg_cnt(int i) { count = i; }
```

ANSI C++-conforming library headers will no longer use the *.h* suffix. Files such as *iostream* and *complex* will be declared with the `namespace std`. Vendors no doubt will continue shipping old-style headers such as *iostream.h* or *complex.h* as well, so that old code can run without change.

3.11 Pointer Types

C++ *pointers* are used to reference variables and machine addresses. They are intimately tied to array and string processing. C++ arrays can be considered a special form of pointer associated with a contiguous piece of memory for storing a series of values that are indexible.

Pointers are used in programs to access memory and manipulate addresses. If v is a variable, then &v is the *address*, or location, in memory of its stored value. The address operator & is unary and has the same precedence and right-to-left associativity as the other unary operators. Pointer variables can be declared in programs then used to take addresses as values. Thus,

```
int*  p;
```

declares p to be of type "pointer to int." The legal range of values for any pointer always includes the special address zero, as well as a set of positive integers that are interpreted as machine addresses on a particular system.

Some examples of assignment to the pointer p are:

```
p = &i;                        //the address of object i
p = 0;                         //a special sentinel value
p = static_cast<int*>(1507);   //absolute address
```

In the first example, we think of p as "referring to i," "pointing to i," or "containing the address of i." The compiler decides what address to assign the variable i. This will vary from machine to machine, and may even be different for various executions on the same machine. The second example is the assignment of the special value zero to the pointer p. This value is typically used to indicate a special condition. For example, a pointer value of zero is returned by a call to the operator new when free storage is exhausted. It is also used to indicate the end of a dynamic data structure such as a tree or list. In the third example, the cast is necessary to avoid a type error, and an actual memory address is used.

3.11.1 Addressing and Dereferencing

The *dereferencing* or *indirection* operator * is unary, and has the same precedence and right-to-left associativity as the other unary operators. If p is a pointer, then *p is the value of the variable that p points to. The direct value of p is a memory location, whereas *p is the indirect value of p, namely, the value at the memory location stored in p. In a certain sense, * is the inverse operator to &. Here is code showing some of these relationships:

```
int    i = 5, j;
int*   p = &i;         //pointer init to address of i

cout << *p << " = i stored at " << p << endl;
j = p;                 //illegal pointer not convertible to integer
j = *p + 1;            //legal
p = &j;                //p points to j
```

3.11.2 Pointer-Based Call-by-Reference

When call-by-value is employed, variables are passed as arguments to a function, their values are copied to the corresponding function parameters, and the variables themselves are not changed in the calling environment. In this section, we describe how the *addresses* of variables can be used as arguments to functions so the stored values of the variables can be modified in the calling environment to simulate call-by-reference. Pointers must be used in the parameter list in the function definition. Then, when the function is called, addresses of variables must be passed as arguments. As an example of this, let us recode order():

In file call_ref.cpp

```cpp
//Pointer based call-by-reference.
#include <iostream.h>

void order(int*, int*);

int main()
{
   int i = 7, j = 3;

   cout << i << '\t' << j << endl;      //7   3 is printed
   order(&i, &j);
   cout << i << '\t' << j << endl;      //3   7 is printed
}

void order(int* p, int* q)
{
   int temp;

   if (*p > *q) {
      temp = *p;
      *p = *q;
      *q = temp;
   }
}
```

Most of the work of this program is carried out by the function call to order(). Notice that the addresses of i and j are passed as arguments. As we shall see, this allows the function call to change the values of i and j in the calling environment.

Dissection of the order() Function

- ```
  void order(int* p, int* q)
  {
      int   temp;
  ```

The parameters p and q are both of type pointer to int. The variable temp is local to this function and is of type int.

- ```
      if (*p > *q) {
          temp = *p;
          *p = *q;
          *q = temp;
      }
  }
  ```

If the value of what is pointed to by p is greater than the value of what is pointed to by q, then the following is done. First, temp is assigned the value of what is pointed to by p; second, what is pointed to by p is assigned the value of what is pointed to by q; and third, what is pointed to by q is assigned the value of temp. This interchanges in the calling environment the stored values of whatever p and q are pointing to.

Summarizing the rules for using pointer arguments to achieve call-by-reference:

Call-by-Reference Using Pointers

1. Declare a pointer parameter in the function header.

2. Use the dereferenced pointer in the function body.

3. Pass an address as an argument when the function is called.

3.12 Reference Declarations and Call-by-Reference

Reference declarations are a new feature of C++. They declare the identifier to be an alternative name or *alias* for an object specified in an initialization of the reference, and allow a simpler form of call-by-reference parameters. Some examples are:

```
int     n;
int&    nn = n          //nn is alternative name for n
double  a[10];
double& last = a[9];    //last is an alias for a[9]
```

Declarations of references that are definitions must be initialized, and are usually initialized to simple variables. The initializer is an lvalue expression, which gives the variable's location in memory. In these examples, the names n and nn are aliases for each other; that is, they refer to the same object. Modifying nn is equivalent to modifying n and vice versa. The name last is an alternative to the single array element a[9]. These names, once initialized, cannot be changed.

When a variable i is declared, it has an address and memory associated with it. When a pointer variable p is declared and initialized to &i, it has an identity separate from i. When a reference variable r is declared and initialized to i, it is identical to i. It does not have an identity separate from the other names for the same object.

The following definitions are used to demonstrate the use of pointers, dereferencing, and aliasing. They assume that memory at location 1004 is used for integer variable a, and memory at location 1008 is used for pointer variable p.

```
int    a = 5;           //declaration of a
int*   p = &a;          //p points to a
int&   ref_a = a;       //alias for a
*p = 7;                 //*p is lvalue of a, so a is assigned 7
a = *p + 1;             //rvalue 7 added to 1 and a assigned 8
```

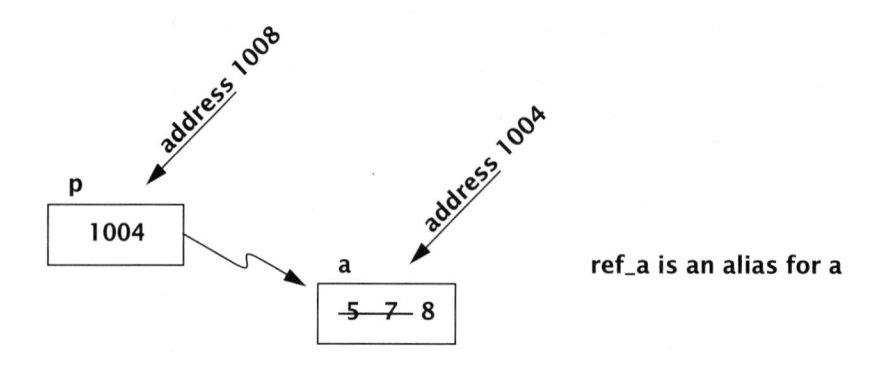

Pointer Declarations

Notice in the above figure that any change to the value of a is equivalent to changing ref_a. Such a change affects the dereferenced value of p. The pointer p can be assigned another address and lose its association with a. However, a and ref_a are aliases, and within scope must refer to the same object.

These declarations can be used for call-by-reference arguments, which allows C++ to have call-by-reference arguments directly. Since this is also the Fortran parameter mechanism, it allows the Fortran programmer an easy transition to coding C++ functions.

The function order() using this mechanism is recoded as:

In file order.cpp

```
void order(int& p, int& q)
{
   int  temp;

   if (p > q) {
      temp = p;
      p = q;
      q = temp;
   }
}
```

It is equivalent to

3.12 ▼ Reference Declarations and Call-by-Reference

In file order.f

```
SUBROUTINE  ORDER(P, Q);
INTEGER P, Q, TEMP

IF (P .GT. Q) THEN
    TEMP = P
    P = Q
    Q = TEMP
END IF
 END
```

Like a C++ function of return type `void`, a Fortran subroutine does not return a value back to its calling environment. It would be prototyped and invoked in `main()` as follows:

```
void  order(int&, int&);

int main()
{
   int  i, j;
   .....
   order(i, j);
   .....
}
```

Let us use this mechanism to write a function `greater` that exchanges two values if the first is greater than the second. In Fortran:

In file sim_call.f

```
      SUBROUTINE GREATR(A, B, ANS)

      INTEGER A, B, TEMP
      LOGICAL ANS

      IF (A .GT. B) THEN
         TEMP = A
         A = B
         B = TEMP
         ANS = .TRUE.
      ELSE
         ANS = .FALSE.
      END IF
       END
```

The same function coded in C++ is:

In file sim_call.cpp

```cpp
bool greater(int& a, int& b)
{
   if (a > b) {           //exchange
      int  temp = a;

      a = b;
      b = temp;
      return true;
   }
   else
      return false;
}
```

Now, if i and j are int variables, then

```
greater(i, j)
```

will use the reference to i and the reference to j to exchange, if necessary, their two values. In traditional C, this operation must be accomplished using pointers and dereferencing.

When function arguments are to remain unmodified, it can be efficient and correct to pass them `const` call-by-reference. This is the case for types that are structures:

```
struct large_size {
   int  mem[N];
   .....
};

void print(const large_size& s)
{
   //since s will not be modified
   //avoid call-by-value copying
   .....
}
```

3.13 The Uses of void

The keyword `void` is used as the return type of a function not returning a value. Its most important use is to declare the *generic* pointer type—pointer to `void`.

A `void` cast can inform the compiler that the expression's computed value is to be discarded. For example:

In file voidcast.cpp

```
//Simple use of a void cast.
#include  <iostream.h>

int  foo(int i)
{
   cout << "i is " << i;
   return i;
}

int main()
{
   int  k = 5;

   static_cast<void>(foo);        //remove return value
}
```

Most interesting, however, is the use of void* as a generic pointer type. A pointer declared as type pointer to void, as in void* gp, may be assigned a pointer value of any underlying base type, but may not be dereferenced. Dereferencing is the operation * acting on a pointer value to obtain what is pointed at. It would not make sense to dereference a pointer to a void value. Therefore:

```
void*   gp;                             //generic pointer
int*    ip;                             //int pointer
char*   cp;                             //char pointer

gp = ip;                                //legal conversion
ip = reinterpret_cast<int*> gp;         //legal conversion
cp = ip;                                //illegal conversion
*ip = 15;                               //legal dereference of pointer to int
*ip = *gp;                              //illegal generic pointer dereference
```

A key use for this type is as a formal parameter. For example, the library function memcpy() is declared in *cstring* (on older C++ systems or on C systems this is *string.h*) as

```
void* memcpy(void* s1, void* s2, size_t n);
```

This function copies n characters from the object based at s2 into the object based at s1. It works with any two pointer types as actual arguments. The type size_t is defined in *stddef.h*, and is often a synonym for unsigned int.

A further use of void given as the parameter list in a function declaration means the function takes no arguments.

```
int foo();      is equivalent in C++ to      int foo(void);
```

3.14 Arrays and Pointers

An array is a data type that is used to represent a large number of homogeneous values. The array is sequential storage. The elements of an array are randomly accessible through the use of subscripts. C++ arrays and records are derived types. In C++ terminology, a *record* is a *structure* or *class*, and its fields are called *members*. Arrays of all types are possible, including arrays of arrays. A typical array declaration allocates memory starting from a base address. An array name is, in effect, a pointer constant to this base address. In Fortran, arrays may be constructed of any type, and they may be multidimensional. They are accessed by subscripting, which in C++ is actually pointer arithmetic. In C++ only one-dimensional arrays are provided, with the first element always indexed as element zero.

To illustrate some of these ideas, let us write a small program that fills an array, prints out values, and sums the elements of the array:

In file sum_arr1.cpp

```
//Simple array processing.
#include   <iostream.h>
const int   SIZE = 5;

int main()
{
   int   a[SIZE];              //get space for a[0],·····,a[4]
   int   i, sum = 0;

   for (i = 0; i < SIZE; ++i) {
      a[i] = i * i;
      cout << "a[" << i << "] = " << a[i] << "   ";
      sum += a[i];
   }
   cout << "\nsum = " << sum << endl;
}
```

The output of this program is:

```
a[0] = 0   a[1] = 1   a[2] = 4   a[3] = 9   a[4] = 16
sum = 30
```

The above array requires enough memory to store five integer values. Thus, if `a[0]` is stored at location 1000, then on a system needing 4 bytes for an `int`, the remaining array elements are successively stored at locations 1004, 1008, 1012, and 1016. It is considered good programming practice to define the size of an array as a symbolic constant. Since much of the code may depend on this value, it is convenient to be able to change a single `#define` line to process different size arrays. Notice how the various parts of the `for` statement are neatly tailored to provide a terse notation for dealing with array computations.

The equivalent Fortran program is:

In file aprint.f

```
      PROGRAM APRINT

      INTEGER UB
      PARAMETER (UB = 4)

      INTEGER   I, SUM, A(0:UB)

      SUM = 0
      DO 10 I = 0, UB
         A(I) = I * I
         PRINT *, 'A[', I, '] = ', A(I)
         SUM = SUM + A(I)
   10 CONTINUE
      PRINT *, SUM = ', SUM
      END
```

3.14.1 Subscripting

Assume that a declaration of the form

```
    int   i, a[size];
```

has been made. Then we can write `a[i]` to access an element of the array. More generally, we may write `a[expr]`, where *expr* is an integral expression, to access an element of the array. We call *expr* a *subscript*, or *index*, of **a**. The value of a C++ subscript should lie in the range zero to *size* - 1. An array subscript value outside this range often causes a run-time error. When this happens, the condition is called "overrunning the bounds of the array" or "subscript out of bounds." It is a common programming error. The effect of the error in a C++ program is system-dependent, and can be quite confusing. One frequent result is that the value of some unrelated variable will be returned or modified. Thus, the programmer must ensure that all subscripts stay within bounds.

3.14.2 Initialization

Arrays can be initialized by a comma-separated list of expressions enclosed in braces:

```
int   array[4] = { 9, 8, 7 };     //a[0]=9, a[1]=8, a[2]=7
```

When the list of initializers is shorter than the size of the array, the remaining elements are initialized to zero. If uninitialized, external and static arrays are automatically initialized to zero. Not so for automatic arrays, which start with undefined values.

An array declared with an explicit initializer list and no size expression is given the size of the number of initializers.

```
char laura[] = { 'l', 'm', 'p' };
```

    is equivalent to

```
char laura[3] = { 'l', 'm', 'p' };
```

3.15 The Relationship Between Arrays and Pointers

An array name by itself is an address, or *pointer value*, and pointers and arrays are almost identical in terms of how they are used to access memory. However, there are differences, and these differences are subtle and important. A pointer is a variable that takes addresses as values. An array name is a particular fixed address that can be thought of as a constant pointer. When an array is declared, the compiler must allocate a base address and a sufficient amount of storage to contain all the elements of the array. The base address of the array is the initial location in memory where the array is stored; it is the address of the first element (index 0) of the array. Suppose we write the declaration

```
const int   N = 100;

int   a[N], *p;
```

and the system causes memory bytes 300, 304, 308, . . . , 696 to be the addresses of a[0], a[1], a[2], . . . , a[99], respectively, with location 300 being the base address of a. We are assuming that each byte is addressable, and that four bytes are used to store an int. The two statements p = a;   and   p = &a[0];

are equivalent and would assign 300 to p. Pointer arithmetic provides an alternative to array indexing. The two statements

p = a + 1;   and   p = &a[1];

are equivalent and would assign 304 to p. Assuming that the elements of a have been assigned values, we can use the following code to sum the array.

In file sum_arr2.cpp

```
sum = 0;
for (p = a; p < &a[N]; ++p)
    sum += *p;
```

is equivalent to

```
sum = 0;
for (i = 0; i < N; ++i)
    sum += a[i];
```

In this loop, the pointer variable p is initialized to the base address of the array a. Then the successive values of p are equivalent to &a[0], &a[1], ..., &a[N-1]. In general, if i is a variable of type int, then p + i is the ith offset from the address p. In a similar manner, a + i is the ith offset from the base address of the array a. Here is another way to sum the array:

```
sum = 0;
for (i = 0; i < N; ++i)
    sum += *(a + i);
```

Just as the expression *(a + i) is equivalent to a[i], the expression *(p + i) is equivalent to p[i].

In many ways, arrays and pointers can be treated alike, but there is one essential difference. Because the array a is a constant pointer and not a variable, and we cannot change the address of a, expressions such as the following are illegal.

a = p   ++a   a += 2

3.16 Passing Arrays to Functions

In a function definition, a formal parameter that is declared as an array is actually a pointer. When an array is being passed, its base address is passed call-by-value. The array elements themselves are not copied. As a notational convenience, the compiler allows array bracket notation to be used in declaring pointers as parameters. This notation reminds the programmer and other readers of the code that the function should be called with an array. To illustrate this, we write a function that sums the elements of an array of type `int`:

In file sum_arr3.cpp

```
int sum(int a[], int n)         //n is the size of a[]
{
   int  i, s = 0;

   for (i = 0; i < n; ++i)
      s += a[i];
   return s;
}
```

As part of the header of a function definition the declaration

    int a[];   is equivalent to   int *a;

In other contexts the two are not equivalent.

Suppose that v has been declared to be an array with 100 elements of type `int`. After the elements have been assigned values, we can use the function `sum()` to add various elements of v. The following table illustrates some of the possibilities.

Summing Elements of an Array	
Invocation	What Gets Computed and Returned
sum(v, 100)	v[0] + v[1] + . . . + v[99]
sum(v, 88)	v[0] + v[1] + . . . + v[87]
sum(v + 7, k)	v[7] + v[8] + . . . + v[k+6]

The last function call illustrates again the use of pointer arithmetic. The base address of v is offset by 7, and `sum()` initializes the local pointer variable a to this address. This causes all address calculations inside the function call to be similarly offset.

In C++, a function with a formal array parameter can be called with an actual array argument of any size, provided the array has the right base type. In Fortran, an array passed as an argument is generally followed by another argument giving the size of the array, or the size of the subset of the array, to be manipulated.

3.17 Strings: A Kernel-Language ADT

The C and C++ communities have agreed to treat the type char* as a form of string type. The understanding is that these strings will be terminated by the char value zero, and that the *cstring* (*string.h* on older systems) package of functions will be called on this abstraction. In ANSI C++, the library *string* provides as a template class a standardized string type that is preferred to this use of char*. The language partly supports this abstraction by defining string literals as being null-terminated. A char* or char[] can be initialized with a literal string. Note that the terminating zero is part of the initializer list.

```
char*   s = "C++";       //s[0] = 'c', s[1] = '+',
                         //s[2] = '+', s[3] = '0';
```

The *cstring* package contains more than 20 functions, including those listed below.

Some Functions in the c*string* Library

- `size_t strlen(const char* s);`
  Computes the string length. The number of characters before 0 is returned.

- `char* strcpy(char* s1, const char* s2);`
  Copies the string s2 into s1. The value of s1 is returned.

- `int strcmp(const char* s1, const char* s2);`
  Returns an integer that reflects the lexicographic comparison of s1 and s2. When the strings are the same, zero is returned. When s1 is less than s2, a negative integer is returned. When s2 is less than s1, a positive integer is returned.

By adhering to the above conventions the programmer benefits by being able to reuse lots of string code. The library routines insure that portable, readily understood code is available.

In file str_func.cpp

```
//string function implementations

size_t strlen(const char* s)
{
   for (int i = 0; s[i]; ++i)
      ;
   return i;
}

int strcmp(const char* s1, const char* s2)
{
   for (int i=0; s1[i] || s2[i] || (s1[i] != s2[i]); ++i)
      ;
   return (s1[i] - s2[i]);
}

char* strcpy(char* s1, const char* s2)
{
   for (int i = 0; s1[i] = s2[i]; ++i)
      ;
   return s1;
}
```

Notice how these functions use the convention that a string is null-terminated to end their major loops. The function strcpy() terminates when s2[i] == 0.

It is also good practice to place the const keyword in front of those strings whose contents will not be modified.

3.18 Multidimensional Arrays

Fortran allows arrays of up to seven dimensions. C++ allows arrays of any type, including arrays of arrays. With two bracket pairs we obtain a two-dimensional array. This idea can be iterated to obtain arrays of higher dimension. With each bracket pair we add another array dimension.

Declarations of Arrays	
`int a[100];`	a one-dimensional array
`int b[3][5];`	a two-dimensional array
`int c[7][9][2];`	a three-dimensional array

A *k*-dimensional array has a size for each of its *k* dimensions. If we let s_i represent the size of its *i*th dimension, then the declaration of the array will allocate space for $s_1 \times s_2 \times \ldots \times s_k$ elements. In the above table, b has 3×5 elements, and c has $7 \times 9 \times 2$ elements. Starting at the base address of the array, all the array elements are stored contiguously in memory row by row.

Initialization of multidimensional arrays can be a brace-enclosed list of initializers, where each row is initialized from a brace-enclosed list:

```
int    a[2][3] = { {1, 2, 3,}, {4, 5, 6} } ;
                        //same as {1, 2, 3, 4, 5, 6}
char   name[3][9] = { "laura", "michelle", "pohl"};
                        //pad with '\0'
```

This last example has `name[][]` representing three strings, each of which stores nine `char` values. So `name[0][0]` is `'l'`, `name[0][1]` is `'a'`, `name[0][2]` is `'u'`, `name[0][3]` is `'r'`, `name[0][4]` is `'a'`, `name[0][5]` is `'\0'`, `name[0][6]` is `'\0'`, `name[0][7]` is `'\0'`, and `name[0][8]` is `'\0'`.

3.19 Assertions and Program Correctness

An *assertion* is a program check for correctness that if violated forces an error exit. Our point of view is that an assertion is a contractual guarantee between the provider of a piece of code, the code's manufacturer, and the code's client or user. In this model, the client needs to guarantee that the conditions for applying the code exist, and the manufacturer needs to guarantee that the code will work correctly under these provisions. In this methodology, assertions provide various guarantees.

Program correctness can be viewed in part as a proof that the computation terminated with correct output dependent on correct input. The user of the computation has the responsibility of providing correct input. This is a *precondition*. The computation, if successful, satisfies a *postcondition*. Such assertions can be monitored at run time to provide very useful diagnostics. Indeed, the discipline of thinking out appropriate assertions frequently allows the programmer to avoid bugs and pitfalls.

In the C++ community there is an increasing emphasis on the use of assertions. The standard library *assert.h* provides a macro `assert`, and is invoked as though its function signature were

void assert(*expression*);

If the *expression* evaluates as false, then execution is aborted with diagnostic output. The assertions are discarded if the macro `NDEBUG` is defined.

In the following program we provide assertions to demonstrate this technique. The program examines a slice of an array for its minimum element, and places that minimum element in the first examined array position.

In file order.cpp

```
//Finding a minimum element in an array slice.
#include <iostream.h>
#include <assert.h>

void order(int& p, int& q)
{
   int temp = p;

   if (p > q) {
      p = q;
      q = temp;
   }
}

int place_min(int a[], int size, int lb = 0)
{
   int i, min;
   assert(size >= 0);                    //precondition

   for (i = lb; i < lb + size; ++i)
      order(a[lb], a[i + 1]);
   return a[lb];
}
```

```
int main()
{
   int   a[9] = { 6, -9, 99, 3, -14, 9, -33, 8, 11};

   cout << "Minimum = " << place_min(a, 3, 2) << endl;
   assert(a[2]<=a[3] && a[2]<=a[4]);          //postcondition
}
```

The precondition assertion in `place_min()` guarantees that a nonnegative number of elements will be searched. The postcondition in `main()` checks that the minimum element was found and placed in the correct position.

3.20 Free-Store Operators new and delete

The unary operators `new` and `delete` are available to manipulate *free store*. Dynamic allocation is not possible in FORTRAN 77, but Fortran 90 added the ALLOCATE and DEALLOCATE statements. Free store is a system-provided memory pool for objects whose lifetime is directly managed by the programmer. The programmer creates an object using `new`, and destroys the object using `delete`. This is important for dynamic data structures such as lists and trees.

In C++, the operator `new` is used in the following forms:

new *type-name*
new *type-name initializer*
new *type-name[expression]*

In each case there are at least two effects. First, an appropriate amount of store is allocated from free store to contain the named type. Second, the base address of the object is returned as the value of the `new` expression. The operator `new` returns the value zero when memory is unavailable. This value should be tested to see if `new` failed. The operator `new` either returns the value zero or throws an appropriate exception when memory is unavailable. (See Section 10.9, "Standard Exceptions and Their Uses," on page 362.)

The following example uses `new`:

```
int*   p, *q;
p = new int(5);          //allocation and initialization
q = new int[10];         //gets q[0] to q[9] with q = &q[0]
```

In this code, the pointer to `int` variable `p` is assigned the address of the store obtained in allocating an object of type `int`. The location pointed at by `p` is initialized to the value 5. This use is not usual for a simple type such as `int`, in that it is far more convenient and natural to automatically allocate an integer variable on the stack or globally. Usually, an array of elements is allocated to the pointer q.

The operator `delete` destroys an object created by `new`, in effect returning its allocated storage to free store for reuse. The operator `delete` is used in the following forms:

delete *expression*
delete [ ] *expression*

The first form is used when the corresponding `new` expression has not allocated an array. The second form has empty brackets indicating that the original allocation was an array of objects. The operator `delete` does not return a value. Equivalently, one can say its return type is `void`.

The following example uses these constructs to dynamically allocate an array:

In file dynarray.cpp

```
//Use of new to dynamically allocate an array.
#include   <iostream.h>
#include   <assert.h>

int main()
{
   int*   data;
   int    size;

   cout << "\nEnter array size: ";
   cin >> size;
   assert(size > 0);

   data = new int[size];         //allocate an array of ints
   assert(data != 0);            //data != 0 allocation succeeds
   for (int j = 0; j < size; ++j)
      cout << (data[j] = j) << '\t';
   cout << "\n\n";
   delete[] data;                //deallocate an array
}
```

Dissection of the *dynarray* Program

- ```
  int*   data;
  int    size;

  cout << "\nEnter array size: ";
  cin >> size;
  assert(size > 0);

  data = new int[size];          //allocate an array of ints
  assert(data != 0);             //data != 0 allocation succeeds
  ```

The pointer variable `data` is used as the base address of a dynamically allocated array whose number of elements is the value of `size`. The user is prompted for the integer valued `size`. The `new` operator is used to allocate storage from free store capable of storing an object of type `int[size]`. On a system where integers take two bytes, this would allocate 2 × `size` bytes. At this point, `data` is assigned the base address of this store. The second `assert` guarantees that allocation succeeded. In newer C++ systems, if the `new` operator fails it can throw an exception, automatically aborting the program.

- ```
  for (int j = 0; j < size; ++j)
     cout << (data[j] = j) << '\t';
  ```

This statement initializes the values of the `data` array and prints them.

- ```
  delete[] data;                 //deallocate an array
  ```

The operator `delete` returns the storage associated with the pointer variable `data` to free store. This can be done only with objects allocated by `new`. The bracket form is used because the corresponding allocation was of an array.

This introductory discussion of the free-store operators treats the basic cases. The free-store operators are addressed in greater detail in Chapter 5, "Constructors and Destructors."
  ```

Summary

1. The C++ code that describes what a function does is called the function definition. Its form is

    function header
    {
        statements
    }

    Whenever variables are passed as arguments to a function, their values are copied to the corresponding function parameters, and the variables themselves are not changed in the calling environment. This is call-by-value. For a function to effect call-by-reference, pointers must be used in the parameter list in the function definition. Then, when the function is called, addresses of variables must be passed as arguments. In C++, reference declarations are available for call-by-reference arguments.

2. In C++, a function cannot be used before it is declared. It can be defined later in the file, or can come from a library or a user-specified file. A function prototype provides the type and number of arguments explicitly. It has the following general form:

    type name(argument-declaration-list) ;

    The *argument-declaration-list* is typically a comma-separated list of types. This list can include the argument identifiers. The information allows the compiler to enforce type compatibility.

3. A `return` statement is used to exit a function. If the form `return` *expression* is used, it must have an expression that is assignment-convertible to the function's return type.

4. An array is a data type that is used to represent a large number of homogeneous values. Array allocation starts with element zero. The elements of an array are accessed by the use of subscripts. Therefore, an array of *size* number of elements is indexed or subscripted from zero to *size* – 1. Arrays of all types are possible, including arrays of arrays. C strings or `char*` strings are just arrays of characters. Conventionally, these strings are terminated with the character value `'\0'`. A typical array declaration allocates memory starting from a base

address. An array name is in effect a pointer constant to this base address. ANSI C++ introduces a string type in its standard library *string*.

5. Every variable and function in C++ kernel language has a storage class. The four storage classes are automatic, external, register, and static, and their corresponding keywords are

    auto   extern   register   static

    Variables declared within function bodies are by default automatic.

6. C++ pointers are used to reference variables and machine addresses. C++ arrays can be thought of as a special form of pointer associated with a contiguous piece of memory for storing a sequence of values that are indexible. Pointers are used in programs to access memory and manipulate addresses. For example, if v is a variable, then &v is the address, or location, in memory of its stored value. The declaration

    ```
    int*  p;
    ```

    declares p to be of type pointer to int. The legal range of values for any pointer always includes the special address zero.

7. Reference declarations allow an object to be given an alias or alternate name. These declarations can be used for call-by-reference arguments. For example, the function order() using this mechanism is declared as:

    ```
    void order(int &p, int &q);
    ```

8. The declaration void* is a generic pointer type. A pointer declared as type pointer to void, as in void* gp, can be assigned a pointer value of any underlying base type, but it may not be dereferenced.

9. In a function definition, a formal parameter declared as an array is actually a pointer. When an array is being passed, its base address is passed call-by-value. The array elements themselves are not copied. As a notational convenience, the compiler allows array bracket notation to be used in declaring pointers as parameters. This notation reminds the programmer and other readers of the code that the function should be called with an array.

10. The unary operators new and delete are available to manipulate free store. Free store is a system-provided memory pool for objects whose lifetime is directly managed by the programmer. The programmer creates an object by using new

and destroys the object by using `delete`. This is important for dynamic data structures such as lists and trees.

Exercises

1. Pointer to `char` strings are by convention terminated with the value zero. The following function implements a string-equality test. Note its use of pointer arithmetic. The construct `*s1++` means "dereference the pointer `s1`, and after using this value in the expression, add one to its pointer value":

    ```
    bool streq(const char* s1, const char* s2)
    {
       while ( *s1 != 0 && *s2 != 0)
          if ( *s1++ != *s2++)
             return false;
       return (*s1 == *s2);
    }
    ```

    Write and test a function

    ```
    bool strneq(const char* s1, const char* s2, int n);
    ```

    that returns `true` if the first `n` characters of the two strings are the same and otherwise returns `false`.

2. Reimplement the above functions using array notation.

    ```
    bool streq(char s1[], char s2[]);
    ```

3. The standard header file *cstring* contains the prototypes for a number of useful string functions found in the standard library. Among them is:

    ```
    size_t strlen(const char* s);
    ```

This returns the length of a string. The text in Section 3.17, "Strings: A Kernel-Language ADT," on page 101, gave a terse definition of this function; here is another way to code it:

```
//iterative string length
size_t strlen(const char *s)
{
    size_t  len = 0;

    while (*s != '\0') {        //string terminator
        ++len;                  //increment length
        ++s;                    //advance pointer
    }
    return len;
}
```

This algorithm marches the pointer s down the string looking for the termination character. External to the function, the pointer value has not been changed because it is call-by-value. Write a recursive version of this function.

4. The greatest common divisor of two integers is recursively defined in pseudocode as follows:

GCD(m,n) is:
   if m mod n equals 0 then n;
   else GCD(n, m mod n);

Recall that the modulo operator in C++ is %. Code this routine in C++.

5. We wish to count the number of recursive function calls by gcd(). It is generally bad practice to use globals inside functions. In C++, we can use a local static variable instead of a global.

```
int gcd(int m, int n)
{
    static int  fcn_calls = 1;      //happens once
    int         r;                  //remainder

    fcn_calls++;
    .....
}
```

Complete and test this C++ version.

6. The following C program uses traditional C function syntax:

   ```
   /* Compute a table of cubes. */

   #include <stdio.h>

   #define  N    15
   #define  MAX  3.5

   int main()
   {
       int     i;
       double  x, cube();

       printf("\n\nINTEGERS\n");
       for (i = 1; i <= N; ++i)
          printf("cube(%d) = %d\n", i, cube(i));
       printf("\n\nREALS\n");
       for (x = 1; x <= MAX; x += 0.3)
          printf("cube(%f) = %f\n", x, cube(x));
   }

   double cube(x)
   double  x;
   {
       return (x * x * x);
   }
   ```

   It gives the wrong answers for the integer arguments, because integer arguments are passed as if their bit representation were double. It is unacceptable as C++ code. Recode, as a proper function prototype, and run using a C++ compiler. C++ compilers enforce type compatibility on function argument values. Therefore, the integer values are properly promoted to double values.

7. Use sum_of_squares() to find all positive integer pairs with integer values less than 100, such that k = sqrt(sum_of_squares(i, j)) and k is an integer. The function double sqrt(double) is found in *math.h*. Write this for comparison purposes in Fortran and see which is faster on your system. Use inline if appropriate for C++ implementation.

8. Predict what the following program prints:

```
#include <iostream.h>

int foo(int n)
{
   static int  count = 0;

   ++count;
   if ( n <= 1) {
      cout << " count = " << count << endl;
      return n;
   }
   else
      foo(n / 3);
}

int main()
{
   foo(21);
   foo(27);
   foo(243);
}
```

9. The static storage class is useful in multifile compilation. Predict what the following program prints:

```
//  file A.c

static int  foo(int i)
{
   return (i * 3);
}
```

```
int goo(int i)
{
   return (i * foo(i));
}

// file B.c
#include <iostream.h>

int foo(int i)
{
   return (i * 5);
}

int goo(int i);        //imported from file A.c

int main()
{
   cout << "foo(5) = " << foo(5) << endl;
   cout << "goo(5) = " << goo(5) << endl;
}
```

The program is compiled as follows: *g++ A.c B.c*. File-scope functions are by default `extern`. The `foo()` in file *A.c* is private to that file, but `goo()` is not. Thus, redefining `foo()` in file *B.c* does not cause an error. Try this again, this time dropping `static`, to see what error message your compiler gives. Then try a third time, making `goo()` `inline` in *A.c*, to see what error message your compiler gives.

10. C++ provides a method to pass command-line arguments into the function `main()`. The following code prints its command-line arguments:

```
//Print command line arguments rightmost first.
#include <iostream.h>

int main(int argc, char **argv)
{
   for (--argc; argc >= 0; --argc)
      cout << argv[argc] << endl;
}
```

Compile this into an executable called *echo*. Run it with the following command-line arguments:

echo a man a plan a canal panama

The argument `argc` is passed the number of command-line arguments. Each argument is a string placed in the two-dimensional array `argv`.

11. Modify the previous program to print the command-line arguments from left to right, and to number each of them.

12. One advantage of C++ over traditional languages is type extensibility. Using `#include <complex.h>`, you can import a complex number type that can be mixed and matched with the native arithmetic types. Overload and test

    ```
    complex avg_arr(const complex a[], int size)
    ```

13. The problem with using `void*` is that it cannot be dereferenced. Thus, to perform useful work on a generic pointer, one must cast it to a standard working type such as a `char*`. Write and test:

    ```
    void* memcpy(void* s1, const void* s2, unsigned n)
    {
       char*  from = s2, *to = s1;     //uses char type
       .....
    }
    ```

14. Write a program that performs string reversal. Assume that `s1` ends up with the reverse of the string `s2`, and that `s1` points at enough store that is adequate for reversal.

    ```
    char* strrev(char* s1, const char* s2);
    ```

15. Write a program that performs string reversal using storage allocated with new. Assume that `s1` ends up with the reverse of the string `s2`, and use new to allocate `s1` of length `strlen(s2) + 1`, which is adequate store for `s1`.

    ```
    char* strrev(char*& s1, const char* s2);
    ```

16. Write a program that allocates a one-dimensional array from free store using user-provided lower and upper bounds. The program should check that the upper bound exceeds the lower bound. If not, perform an error exit using the *assert.h* package as follows:

```
#include <assert.h>
   ...                       ..//input lower bound and upper bound
assert(ub - lb > 0);
   .....
```

The size of this array will be (*upper bound* − *lower bound* + *1*) elements. Given a standard C++ array of this many elements, write a function that uses the standard array to initialize the dynamic array. Test this by writing out both arrays before and after initialization in a nicely formatted style.

17. Write a function

    ```
    double findmin(double fcn(double), double x0,
            double x1, double incr, double& xmin)
    ```

    that returns the value at `fcn(xmin)`, where `xmin` is the minimum value of `fcn(x)` in the interval `(x0, x1)`, evaluated at increments of `incr`.

18. Write a function `findzero()` that finds `xzero`, the value closest to zero in a specified interval. It should have the same arguments as `findmin()`.

19. Write a function to compute body mass index (BMI) as follows:

    BMI = (*weight in kilograms*) / (*height in meters*)^2

    If the BMI is over 25 you are considered overweight; if it is over 40 you are considered obese. Test the program on data taken from at least five individuals, printing out for each name a weight, height, BMI, and BMI category of normal, overweight, or obese.

Chapter 4

Classes

This chapter introduces the reader to structures and classes. The original name given by Stroustrup to his language was "C with classes." A *class* is an extension of the idea of `struct` found in C. A class packages a data type with its associated functions and operators. User-defined data types, such as stack, complex numbers, and card decks are examples. In C++, structures may have member functions, and also may have parts of their description hidden. Both of these extensions will be described here.

FORTRAN 77 does not have pointer or structure declarations, but Fortran 90 has introduced them as well as data hiding with the keywords `PRIVATE` and `PUBLIC`.

C++ classes bundle data declarations with function declarations. This couples data with its behavior. The class description also has access modifiers that allow data hiding. Public access is access available to any part of the code. Private access is restricted access, principally restricted to use by the class code itself.

Allowing private and public *visibility* for members gives the programmer control over what parts of the data structure are modifiable. The private parts are hidden from client code, and the public parts are available. It is possible to change the hidden representation, but not to change the public access or functionality. If this is done properly, client code need not change when the hidden representation is modified. A large part of the OOP design process involves thinking up the appropriate ADTs for a problem. Good ADTs not only model key features of the problem, but also are frequently reusable in other code.

4.1 The Aggregate Type `struct` and `class`

The structure type allows the programmer to aggregate components into a single named variable. A structure has components, called *members*, that are individually named. Since the members of a structure can be of various types, the programmer can create aggregates that are suitable for describing complicated data.

As a simple example, let us define a structure that will describe a point. We can declare the structure type:

```
struct point {
    double x, y;
}
```

In C++, the structure name, or *tag name*, is a type. In the above declaration, `struct` is a keyword, `point` is the structure tag name, and the variables `x` and `y` are members of the structure. The declaration `point` can be thought of as a blueprint; it creates the type `point`, but no actual instances are allocated. The declaration

```
point   pt;
```

allocates storage for the variable `pt`. To access the members of `pt`, we use the structure member operator, represented by a period, or dot. It is a construct of the form

structure_variable.member_name

and is used as a variable in the same way a simple variable or an element of an array is used. Suppose we want to assign to `pt` the value (-1, +0.5). To do this we can write:

```
pt.x = -1;
pt.y = 0.5;
```

The member name must be unique within the specified structure. Since the member must always be prefaced or accessed through a unique structure variable identifier, there is no confusion between two members that have the same name in different structures. An example is:

```
struct fruit {
    char   name[15];
    int    calories;
};
```

```
struct vegetable {
   char   name[15];
   int    calories;
};

fruit       a;         //struct fruit      a; in C
vegetable   b;         //struct vegetable  b; in C
```

Having made these declarations, we can access `a.calories` and `b.calories` without ambiguity.

In general, a structure is declared with the keyword `struct` followed by an identifier (tag name), followed by a brace-enclosed list of member declarations. The tag name is optional but should be expressive of the ADT concept being modeled. When the tag name is not present, the structure declaration is anonymous and can be used only to declare variables of that type immediately, as in:

```
struct {
   int a, b, c;
} triples [2] = { {3, 3, 6}, {4, 5, 5} };
```

4.2 Structure Pointer Operator

We have already seen the use of the member operator in accessing members. In this section we introduce the structure pointer operator ->.

C++ provides the structure pointer operator -> to access the members of a structure via a pointer. This operator is typed on the keyboard as a minus sign followed by a greater-than sign. If a pointer variable is assigned the address of a structure, then a member of the structure can be accessed by a construct of the form:

pointer_to_structure -> *member_name*

An equivalent construct is given by:

(**pointer_to_structure*) . *member_name*

The operators -> and ., along with () and [], have the highest precedence, and they associate left to right. In complicated situations the two accessing modes can be combined. The following table illustrates their use.

Declarations and Assignments
`point w, *p = &w;`
`point v[5];`
`w.x = 1;`
`w.y = 4;`
`v[0] = w;`

Expression	Equivalent Expression	Value
`w.x`	`p -> x`	1
`w.y`	`p -> y`	4
`v[0].x`	`v -> x`	1
`(*p).y`	`p -> y`	4

4.2.1 typedef Declarations

typedef declarations are used to provide synonyms for type declarations.

```
typedef int    miles;       //miles a synonym for int
typedef char*  cstring;     //pointer to char
typedef void*  gen_ptr;     //generic pointer type
typedef point* pPoint;      //pointer to point
```

Besides providing a form of documentation, `typedef` declarations reduce complicated declarations to simple identifiers.

4.3 Member Functions

The concept of `struct` or `class` is augmented in C++ to allow functions to be members. The function declaration is included in the structure declaration, and is invoked by using access methods for structure members. The idea is that the functionality required by the structure or class should be directly included in the `struct` declaration. This construct improves the encapsulation of the ADT `point` operations by packaging it directly with its data representation. Let us add a printing operation and an initializing operation to the ADT `point`.

In file point1.cpp

```cpp
struct point {
   double x, y;
   void print() { cout << "(" << x << "," << y << ")"; }
   void init(double u, double v) { x = u; y = v; }
};
```

The member functions are written much the way other functions are. One difference is that they can use the data member names without changing them. Thus the member functions in `point` use `x` and `y` in an unqualified manner. When invoked on a particular object of type `point` they act on the specified member in that object.

Let us use these member functions in an example:

```cpp
int main()
{
   point w1, w2;

   w1.init(0, 0.5);
   w2.init(-0.5, 1.5);
   cout << "\npoint w1 = ";
   w1.print();
   cout << "\npoint w2 = ";
   w2.print();
}
```

Which prints

```
point w1 = (0,0.5)
point w2 = (-0.5,1.5)
```

Member functions that are defined within the `struct` are implicitly inline. As a rule, only short, heavily used member functions should be defined within the `struct`, as in the example just given. To define a member function outside the `struct`, the scope resolution operator is used (see Section 4.6, "Class Scope," on page 125). Let us illustrate this by adding a member function `point::plus()`. We write it out fully using the scope resolution operator. In this case the function is not implicitly inline.

```
struct point {
    .....
    void  plus(point c);         //function prototype
    .....
};

void point::plus(point c)       //definition not inline
{
//offset the existing point by point c
    x += c.x;
    y += c.y;
}
```

Member functions within the same `struct` can be overloaded. Consider adding a print operation to the data type `point` that has a string parameter that is printed as the name of the point. It could be added as the following function prototype within the `struct`:

```
struct point {
    .....
    void print(string name);
    .....
};

void point::print(string name)
{
    cout << name << " (" << x << "," << y << ")";
}
```

The definition that is invoked depends on the actual arguments to `print()`:

```
w.print();                  //invokes standard print
w.print("point w = ");      //invokes print with name
```

A member function is conceptually part of the type. The `inline` specification can be used explicitly, with member functions defined at file scope. This avoids having to clutter the class definition with function bodies. The grouping of operations with data emphasizes their "objectness." Objects have a description and behavior. Think of an object as a noun and its behavior as the verbs that are most often associated with that noun. The OO approach is a data-centered design approach.

4.4 Access: Private and Public

In C++, structures have public and private members. Inside a `struct` or `class`, the use of the keyword `private` followed by a colon restricts the access to the members that follow this construct. The private members can be used by only a few categories of functions, whose privileges include access to these members. These functions include the member functions of the structure. Other categories of functions that have access will be discussed later.

We modify our example of `point` to hide its data representation:

In file point2.cpp

```
struct point {
public:
   void print(){ cout << "(" << x << "," << y << ")";}
   void init(double u, double v) { x = u; y = v; }
   void plus(point c);
private:
   double x, y;
};
```

An attempt by a nonmember function to access the now private members will result in a syntax error. So,

```
void foo(point w)
{
   .....
   cout << " x coordinate = " << w.x ;    //syntax error
   .....
}
```

Hiding data is an important component of OOP. It allows for more easily debugged and maintained code because errors and modifications are localized. Client programs need only be aware of the type's interface specification.

4.5 Classes

Classes in C++ are introduced by the keyword `class`. They are a form of `struct` whose default privacy specification is `private`. Thus, `struct` and `class` can be used interchangeably with the appropriate access specifications.

We modify our example of `point` to use `class`:

In file point3.cpp

```
class point {
   double x, y;            //implicitly private
public:
   void print() { cout << "(" << x << "," << y << ")"; }
   void init(double u, double v) { x = u; y = v; }
   void plus(point c);
};
```

Contemporary C++ style is to use access specifiers explicitly rather than to rely on defaults. The use of implicit features is labor-saving but error prone. Therefore it is better style to declare `point` as follows:

In file point4.cpp

```
class point {
public:                    //place public members first
   void print() { cout << "(" << x << "," << y << ")"; }
   void init(double u, double v) { x = u; y = v; }
   void plus(point c);
private:
   double x, y;
};
```

When access keywords are used, `struct` and `class` are interchangeable. Stylistically, professional C++ programmers use `class` in preference to `struct` unless the `struct` has only public data members.

As a second example, let us write an ADT for complex numbers, which many scientific computations require. Let us recode complex numbers:

In file complex2.cpp

```
class complex {
public:                     //need to know style - our preference
   void  assign(double r, double i) { real = r;   imag = i; }
   void  print() { cout << real << " + " << imag << "i "; }
private:
   double   real, imag;
};
```

It will be our style to use access keywords explicitly and to place public members first and private members last. We call this the "need-to-know" style, because everyone needs to know the public interface, but only the class provider needs to know the private implementation details.

The presence of member functions within the class shows the clear relationship of the data type `complex` and its associated operations `assign()` and `print()`. There is also less likelihood of a misuse of the representation since the implementation details `real` and `imag` are private. An attempt to directly alter these members would result in the syntactic error access violation, so a client of this version of complex must use member functions that properly act on complex variables.

4.6 Class Scope

Class adds a new set of scope rules to those of the kernel language. (See Section 3.9, "Scope and Storage Class," on page 78.) One point of classes is to provide an encapsulation technique. Conceptually it makes sense that all names declared within a class be treated within their own namespace as distinct from external names, function names, and other class names. This creates a need for the scope resolution operator.

4.6.1 Scope Resolution Operator ::

The scope resolution operator is the highest precedence operator in the language. It comes in two forms:

```
::i            //unary operator  - refers to external scope
foo_bar::i     //binary operator - refers to class scope
```

Its unary form is used to uncover or access a name that has external scope and has been hidden by local or class scope:

In file how_many.cpp

```
int  count = 0;                      //global count

void how_many(double w[], double x, int& count)
{
   for (int i = 0; i < N; ++i)
      count += (w[i] == x);          //parameter block
   ++ ::count;                       //global count tracks calls
}
```

Binary scope resolution is used to clarify names that are reused within classes:

```
class widgets { public: void f(); };
class gizmos  { public: void f(); };

void f() { ····· }                   //ordinary external f
void widgets::f() { ····· }          //f scoped to widgets
void gizmos::f() { ····· }           //f scoped to gizmos
```

One way to think about the scope resolution operator is to view it as providing a path to the identifier. No scope modifier means that normal scope rules apply.

Continuing with the previous example:

```
widgets   w;
gizmos    g;

g.f();
w.f();
g.gizmos::f();       //legal but redundant
g.widgets::f();      //illegal; widgets::f() cannot act on a gizmo
```

4.6.2 Nested Classes

Like blocks and namespaces, classes are scopes and can nest. Nesting allows local hiding of names and local allocation of resources. This is often desirable when a class is needed as part of the implementation of a larger construct (see Section 5.8, "Example: A Singly Linked List," on page 171, which nests `listelem` in `list`). The following nested classes illustrate current C++ rules.

In file nested.cpp

```
char  c;              //external scope   ::c

class X {             //outer class declaration  X::
public:
   char  c;           //X::c
   class Y {          //inner class declaration  X::Y::
   public:
      void foo(char e) { X t; ::c = t.X::c = c = e; }
   private:
      char  c;        //X::Y::c
   };
};
```

In class Y, the member function `foo()`, when using `::c`, references the global variable c; when using `X::c`, it references the outer class variable; when using c, it references the inner class variable `X::Y::c`. All three variables named c are accessible using the scope resolution operator.

Furthermore, purely locally scoped classes can be created within blocks. Their definitions are unavailable outside their local block context.

```
void foo()
{
   class local { ..... } x;
   .....
}

local y;           //illegal:local is scoped within foo()
```

Notice that C++ allows you to nest function definitions by using class nesting, which is a restricted form of function nesting. The member functions must be defined inside the local class, and cannot be referred to outside this scope. As in C, ordinary nested functions are not possible.

4.7 An Example: Flushing

We want to estimate the probability of being dealt a flush in poker. A flush occurs when at least five cards are of the same suit. We simulate shuffling cards by using a random-number generator to shuffle the deck. This is a form of *Monte Carlo* calculation. The program is written using classes to represent the necessary data types and functionality.

In file poker.cpp

```
//A poker calculation on flushing
#include  <iostream.h>
#include  <stdlib.h>     //for random-number generation
#include  <time.h>       //for random-number seed

enum suit { clubs, diamonds, hearts, spades };

class pips {
public:
   void  assign(int n) { p = n % 13 + 1; }
   int   getpip() { return p; }
   void  print() { cout << p };
private:
   int   p;
};

class card {
public:
   suit   s;
   pips   p;
   void   assign(int n)
      { cd = n; s = static_cast<suit>(n/13); p.assign(n); }
   void   pr_card();
private:
   int   cd;       //a cd is from 0 to 51
};
```

```
class deck {
public:
   void   init_deck();
   void   shuffle();
   void   deal(int, int, card*);
   void   pr_deck();
private:
   card   d[52];
};
```

Here, the clustering of member functions and the data members they act on improves modularity. Behavior and description are logically grouped together. Each level of declaration hides the complexity of the previous level.

```
void deck::init_deck()
{
   for (int i = 0; i < 52; ++i)
      d[i].assign(i);
}

void   deck::shuffle()
{
   for (int i = 0; i < 52; ++i) {
      int    k = i + ((rand() % (52 - i)));
      card   t = d[i];                    //swap cards
      d[i] = d[k];
      d[k] = t;
   }
}

void deck::deal(int n, int pos, card* hand)
{
   for (int i = pos; i < pos + n; ++i)
      hand[i - pos] = d[i];
}
```

The init_deck() function calls card::assign() to map the integers into card values. The shuffle() function uses the library-supplied pseudorandom-number generator rand() to exchange two cards for every deck position. The deal() function takes cards in sequence from deck and arranges them into hands.

```
int main()
{
   card one_hand[9];        //max hand is nine cards
   deck dk;
   int  i, j, k, fcnt = 0, sval[4];
   int  ndeal, nc, nhand;
   .....
   dk.init_deck();
   dk.print();
   .....
      dk.shuffle();
         .....
      for (j = 0; j < nc; ++j)          //deal nc cards
         sval[one_hand[j].s]++;         //many in each suit
   .....
}
```

4.8 static Member

Data members can be declared with the storage class modifier static. A data member that is declared static is shared by all variables of that class and is stored in only one place. Nonstatic data members are created for each instance of the class. Without static data members, data that was required by all instances of a class would have to be global. This would decouple the relationship between the data and the class. Static data allows class data that is not specific to any instance to be scoped to the class but still require only one object for its storage.

Since a static member is independent of a particular instance, it can be accessed in the form

class-name :: *identifier*

This is a use of the scope resolution operator. A static member of a global class must be explicitly declared and defined in file scope. An example is:

4.8 ▼ static Member

```
class str {
public:
   static int  how_many;       //declaration
   void  print();
   void  assign(const char*);
   .....
private:  //implement as fixed length char array
   char  s[100];
};

int str::how_many = 0;         //definition and init
```

In our example, how_many could track how much memory is being used to store str variables. So,

```
str   s1, s2, s3, *p;

str::how_many = 3;             //preferred style use ::
   .....
str  t;
t.how_many++;                  //dot operator to access
   .....
p = new str;
p -> how_many++;               //pointer operator to access
   .....
delete p;
str::how_many--;
```

The preferred style for accessing static members is to use scope resolution. Pointer and dot operator access are misleading and give no indication that the member is static.

Newly allowed is `static const` initialization within the class declaration:

```
class ch_stack {
.....
private:
   static const int max_len = 10000;   //initializer
.....
};

const stack::int max_len;                    //declaration required
```

4.9 The this Pointer

The keyword this denotes an implicitly declared self-referential pointer. It can be used only in a nonstatic member function. In a static member function the implicit arguments are not available. A simple illustration of its use follows.

In file point5.cpp

```
//The this pointer
class point {
public:      //place public members first
   void   print() { cout << "(" << x << "," << y << ")"; }
   void   init(double u, double v) { x = u; y = v; }
   void   plus(point c);
   point  inverse() { x = -x; y = -y; return (*this); }
   point* where_am_I() { return this; }
private:
   double x, y;
};

int main()
{
   point  a, b;

   a.init(1.5, -2.5);
   a.print();
   cout << "\na is at " << a.where_am_I() << endl;
   b = a.inverse();
   b.print();
   cout << "\nb is at " << b.where_am_I() << endl;
}
```

The output on our system is:

```
(1.5,-2.5)
a is at 0x0064fdd4
(-1.5,2.5)
b is at 0x0064fdc4
```

Note that machine addresses are displayed in hexadecimal, and are system dependent. In this case the two addresses differ by 0x10 or 16 bytes. This is the size of the two doubles required to represent a point.

The member function `inverse()` uses the implicitly provided pointer `this` to return the newly inverted value of a. The member function `where_am_I` returns the address of the given object. The `this` keyword provides for a built-in self-referential pointer, as if `point` implicitly declared the private member `point* const this`.

4.10 `static` and `const` Members

C++ allows static and constant members. The `const` modifier used in declaring a data member means that the data member is nonmodifiable after initialization. To use `const` properly, we need to understand constructors (see Chapter 5, "Constructors and Destructors"). The `static` modifier used in declaring a data member means that the data member is independent of any given class variable. It is part of the class, but separate from any single class object. For example, we might want a counter to keep track of how many points are declared at any time. We can add to class `point`:

```
class point {
public:
   static int how_many;          //declaration
   .....
};

int point::how_many = 0;         //initialization
   .....
++point::how_many;               //use independent of any instance
```

The static member `point::how_many` needs a definition separate from an ordinary `point` variable, since it exists independent from these variables. It can be used with scope resolution since it exists independent of `point` objects. Syntactically, a `static` member function has the modifier `static` precede the return type inside the class declaration. A definition outside the class must not have this modifier:

```
class foo {
.....
   static int  foo_fcn();        //static goes first
.....
};
```

```
int foo::foo_fcn()              //no static keyword here
{ /* definition */ }
```

Syntactically, a `const` member function has the modifier `const` follow the argument list inside the class declaration. A definition outside the class must also have this modifier:

```
class foo {
.....
   int  foo_fcn() const;
.....
};

int foo::foo_fcn() const        //const keyword needed
{ /* definition */ }
```

The `const` and `static` member function implementation can be understood in terms of `this` pointer access. An ordinary member function invoked as

```
x.mem(i, j, k);
```

has an explicit argument list i, j, k and an implicit argument list that includes the members of x. The implicit arguments can be thought of as a list of arguments accessible through the `this` pointer. In contrast, a `static` member function does not get the implicit arguments. A `const` member function cannot modify its implicit arguments. Writing out `const` member functions and parameter declarations is called *const-correctness*. Const-correctness is an important aid in writing code. In effect it is an assertion that the compiler should check that an object will not have its values modified. It can also allow the compiler to apply some special optimizations, such as placing a `const` object in read-only memory.

The following example illustrates these differences.

In file salary.cpp

```cpp
//Calculate salary using static members.
class salary {
public:
   void init(int b) { b_sal = b; your_bonus = 0; }
   void  calc_bonus(double perc) { your_bonus = b_sal * perc; }
   static void  reset_all(int p) { all_bonus = p; }
   int  comp_tot() const
      { return (b_sal + your_bonus + all_bonus); }
private:
   int        b_sal;
   int        your_bonus;
   static int  all_bonus;     //declaration
};

//declaration and definition
int salary::all_bonus = 100;

int main()
{
   salary  w1, w2;

   w1.init(1000);
   w2.init(2000);
   w1.calc_bonus(0.2);
   w2.calc_bonus(0.15);
   salary::reset_all(400);
   cout << " w1 " << w1.comp_tot() << "   w2 "
        << w2.comp_tot() << endl;
}
```

Dissection of the *salary* Program

- ```
  class salary {
       .....
     private:
        int          b_sal;
        int          your_bonus;
        static int   all_bonus;       //declaration
  };
  ```

  There are three private data members. The `static` member `all_bonus` requires a file-scope declaration. It can exist independent of any specific variables of type `salary` being declared.

- `void init(int b) { b_sal = b; your_bonus = 0; }`

  This assigns the value of b to the member `b_sal`. This member function initializes the base salary. The variable `your_bonus` is also initialized. While our small example did not require this, it is a good habit to initialize all member variables. In the next chapter, special functions called constructors are used when initialization and object creation are needed.

- `static void  reset_all(int p) { all_bonus = p; }`

  The modifier `static` must come before the function return type.

- ```
  int  comp_tot() const
     { return (b_sal + your_bonus + all_bonus); }
  ```

  The `const` modifier comes between the end of the argument list and the beginning of the code body. It indicates that no data member will have its value changed. Thus, it makes the code more robust. In effect, it means that the self-referential pointer is passed as `const salary* const this`.

- `salary::reset_all(400);`

  A `static` member function can be invoked using the scope resolution operator. It could also have been invoked as `w1.reset_all(400);` but this is misleading, since there is nothing special about the class variable w1.

Note: The `static` keyword is used only in the class definition, and must be omitted when the data or function member is defined outside the class.

4.10.1 Mutable

The keyword `mutable` allows data members of class variables that have been declared `const` to remain modifiable. This reduces the need to cast away constness using `const_cast<>`. This is a relatively new feature and is not implemented on all C++ compilers. It is used as follows.

In file mutable.cpp

```
//class with mutable members
class person {
public:
   person(const char*; int; unsigned long);
   void bday() { ++age; }
   .....
private:
   const char*     name;
   mutable int     age;          //always modifiable
   unsigned long   soc_sec;
};
.....
const person ira("ira pohl", 38, 1110111);
.....
ira.bday();                      //okay, ira.age is mutable
```

4.11 Unions

A *union* is a derived type whose syntax is the same as for structures, except that the keyword `union` replaces `struct`. The member declarations share storage, and their values will be overlaid. Therefore, a union allows its value to be interpreted as a set of types that correspond to the member declarations. This is similar to the Fortran EQUIVALENCE statement.

A union initializer is a brace-enclosed value for its first member. Consider the following declaration.

In file union.cpp

```
union int_dbl {
    int     i;
    double  x;
} n = { 0 };                    //i member is init to zero
```

The variable n can be used as either an integer type or a double type:

```
n.i  = 7;                       //int value 7 is stored in n
cout << n.i << " is integer. ";
cout << n.x << " is double - machine dependent.";
n.x  = 7.0;                     //double value 7.0 is stored in n
```

This example also illustrates why unions can be dangerous, and are often system-dependent. On some systems, it is possible that not all bit patterns are legal values for the overlaid types. In that case, a legal value with one type might, when accessed as the other type, lead to an exception.

A union can be anonymous, as in the following code.

In file weekend.cpp

```
enum week { sun, mon, tues, weds, thurs, fri, sat };

union {
   int   i;
   week  w;
};

i = 5;

if (w == sat || w == sun)
   cout << " It's the weekend! ";
```

This allows the individual member identifiers to be used as variables. The member names must be unique within scope, and no variables of the anonymous type can be declared. Note that an anonymous union declared in file scope must be static.

4.12 Bit Fields

A member that is an integral type can consist of a specified number of bits. Such a member is called a *bit field*, and the number of associated bits is called its *width*. The width is specified by a nonnegative constant integral expression following a colon. For example,

```
struct pcard {              //packed representation of card
   unsigned  s : 2;
   unsigned  p : 4;
};
```

The compiler will attempt to pack the bit fields sequentially within memory. It is at liberty to skip to a next byte or word for purposes of alignment. Arrays of bit fields are not allowed. Also, the address operator & cannot be applied to bit fields.

Bit fields are used to address information conveniently in packed form. On many machines, words are 32 bits, and bit operation can be performed in parallel. In this case, bit manipulation is an implementation technique for sets that contain up to 32 elements, as shown below.

In file set.cpp

```
struct word {
unsigned w0:1,w1:1,w2:1, w3:1, w4:1, w5:1, w6:1, w7:1,
   w8:1, w9:1,w10:1,w11:1, w12:1, w13:1, w14:1, w15:1,
   w16:1,w17:1,w18:1,w19:1, w20:1, w21:1, w22:1, w23:1,
   w24:1,w25:1,w26:1,w27:1, w28:1, w29:1, w30:1, w31:1;
};
```

We can overlay `word` and `unsigned` within a `union` to create a data structure for manipulating bits:

```
union set {
   word      m;
   unsigned  u;
};
```

```
int main()
{
   set   x, y;

   x.u = 0x0f100f10;
   y.u = 0x01a1a0a1;
   x.u = x.u | y.u;    //set union
   cout << "element 9 ="
        << ((x.m.w9)? "true" : "false") << endl;
}
```

The set operation union is performed as a word-parallel operation on most systems.

4.13 A Container Class Example: ch_stack

We develop code that is used to store character values in a *stack*, which is a *last-in-first-out* (LIFO) container. A *container* is a data structure whose main purpose is to store and retrieve a large number of values. In the kernel language an array acts as such a structure.

We develop code for a ch_stack that will store characters:

In file ch_stac3.h

```
class ch_stack {
public:
   void   reset() { top = EMPTY; }
   void   push(char c) { top++; s[top] = c; }
   char   pop() { return s[top--]; }
   char   top_of() { return s[top]; }
   bool   empty() { return (top == EMPTY);}
   bool   full() { return (top == FULL); }
private:
   enum { max_len = 100, EMPTY = -1, FULL = max_len-1 };
   char   s[max_len];
   int    top;
};
```

The basic operations on a stack are push and pop. The push operation places a value on the top of the stack, and the pop operation removes the value at the top of the stack. We use a fixed-length char array to implement the stack. Later we will talk about other implementations that are more flexible.

4.13 ▼ A Container Class Example: ch_stack

We now write main() to test the same operations:

In file ch_stac3.cpp

```
//Reverse a string with a ch_stack.
int main()
{
   ch_stack   s;
   char       str[40] = { "My name is Don Knuth!" };
   int        i = 0;

   cout << str << endl;
   s.reset();                      //s.top = EMPTY; would be illegal
   while (str[i] && !s.full())
      s.push(str[i++]);
   while (!s.empty())              //print the reverse
      cout << s.pop();
   cout << endl;
}
```

The output from this version of the test program is

```
My name is Don Knuth!
!htunK noD si eman yM
```

As the comment in main() states, access to the hidden variable top is controlled. It can be changed by the member function reset(), but cannot be accessed directly. Also, notice how the variable s is passed to each member function using the structure member operator form.

The ch_stack class has a private part that contains its data description, and a public part that contains member functions to implement ch_stack operations. It is useful to think of the private part as restricted to the implementor's use and the public part an interface specification that clients may use. The implementor could change the private part without affecting the correctness of a client's use of the ch_stack type.

4.14 Fortran 90 Equivalence

Ordinary `structs` in C are largely equivalent to Fortran 90 derived types. In C++, this is equivalent to `structs` having only public data members. Where `structs` or classes include member functions and private data members, there is an equivalence in Fortran 90 to the use of MODULE and PUBLIC and PRIVATE access. The following Fortran 90 code implements a stack ADT similar to our C++ `ch_stack` ADT. This type will be implemented in a Fortran 90 MODULE.

```
MODULE ch_stackT
    IMPLICIT NONE
    INTEGER, PARAMETER::  maxlen = 1000;

!Derived type with PRIVATE access implementation
TYPE ch_stack
   PRIVATE
      INTEGER :: top
      CHARACTER, DIMENSION(maxlen) :: s
END TYPE ch_stack

!reset the stacks top.
SUBROUTINE reset(stk)
TYPE(ch_stack), INTENT(IN)::stk
INTEGER::stk%top
   stk%top := 0              !the % is used like . in C++
END SUBROUTINE reset
```

```
SUBROUTINE pr_stk(stk)
TYPE(ch_stack), INTENT(IN)::stk
INTEGER :: stk%top
CHARACTER, DIMENSION(stk%top)::s(stk%top)
!local variables
   INTEGER i

   PRINT *, 'ch_stack contents:'
   DO i = 1, stk%top
      PRINT *, s[i], ', '
   END DO
END SUBROUTINE pr_stk

SUBROUTINE push(stk, c )
TYPE(ch_stack), INTENT(IN)::stk
INTEGER :: stk%top
CHARACTER, DIMENSION(maxlen)::s(maxlen)

   stk%top = stk%top + 1;
   stk%s[stk%top] = c
END SUBROUTINE push

!implement additional subprograms

.....
END MODULE ch_stackT
```

This Fortran 90 code implements a new type `ch_stack` within a MODULE. It can be used in a program with a USE statement, which acts like a C++ `include` in a header file that contains the class declaration of `ch_stack`. The following code tests the type `ch_stack` by importing it with the USE statement.

```
PROGRAM test_ch_stack
USE ch_stackT              !in C++ include a header file
IMPLICIT NONE

TYPE(ch_stack):: s1, s2

!test implementation of ch_stack
   PRINT "enter ch_stack program"
   CALL push(s1, 'M')
   CALL push('o')
   CALL push('M')
   CALL pr_stk(s1)          ! M o M is printed
   CALL push(s2, 'B')
   CALL pr_stk(s2)          ! B is printed
   CALL reset(s2)
   CALL pr_stk(s2)          ! s2 is empty
   PRINT "exit ch_stack program"
END PROGRAM test_ch_stack
```

4.15 Pragmatics

The access order for classes has traditionally been private first, as in:

```
class ch_stack {
private:
   int   top;
   enum { max_len = 100, EMPTY = -1, FULL = max_len-1 };
   char  s[max_len];
public:
   void  reset() { top = EMPTY; }
   void  push(char c) { top++; s[top] = c; }
   char  pop() { return s[top--]; }
   char  top_of() const { return s[top]; }
   bool  empty() const { return (top == EMPTY); }
   bool  full() const { return (top == FULL); }
};
```

This is because, in the original form of C++, the access keywords private and protected did not exist. By default, member access for class was private; therefore, the private members had to come first.

Our style of public first is becoming the norm. It follows the rule that the widest audience needs to see the public members. More specialized information is placed later in the class declaration.

Data members should in general be private. This is an important coding heuristic. Generally, data is part of an implementation choice. It should be accessed through public member functions. Such member functions are called *accessor functions* when they do not change, or mutate, the data. This is not necessarily inefficient, because simple accessor member functions can be inline. In the class `stack` the member functions `top_of()`, `empty()`, and `full()` are all inline accessor functions. Accessor functions should be declared `const`. The member function `reset()` is a *mutator*. It allows a constrained action on the hidden variable `top`. Notice how much safer such a design is. If `top` were directly accessible, it would be easy for it to be inappropriately changed.

In OO design the public members are usually functions, and are thought of as the type's *interface*. These are the actions or behaviors publicly expected of an object. If we think of the object type as a noun, the behaviors are verbs. In the implementation, data members are generally placed in private access. This is a key data-hiding principle, namely that implementation is kept inside a black box that cannot be directly exploited by the object's user.

Summary

1. The original name given by Stroustrup to his language was "C with classes." A class is an extension of the idea of structure in traditional C. It is a way of implementing a data type and associated functions and operators. It is the mechanism in C++ for implementing ADTs, such as complex numbers and stacks.

2. The structure type allows the programmer to aggregate components into a single named variable. A structure has components, called members, that are individually named. Critical to processing structures is the accessing of their members. This is done with either the member operator . or the structure pointer operator -> . These operators, along with () and [], have the second highest precedence. Highest precedence belongs to scope resolution, ::.

3. The concept of structure or class is augmented in C++ to allow functions to be members. The function declaration is included in the structure declaration, and is invoked by using access methods for structure members. The idea is that the functionality required by the `struct` data type should be directly included in the `struct` declaration.

4. Member functions that are defined within the structure or class are implicitly inline. As a rule, only short, heavily used member functions should be defined within the structure. To define a member function outside the structure, the scope resolution operator is used.

5. The scope resolution operator allows member functions of various structure types to have the same names. In this case, which member function is invoked depends on the type of object it acts upon. Member functions within the same `struct` can be overloaded.

6. Structures have public and private members. This provides data hiding. Inside a structure or class, the keyword `private` followed by a colon restricts the access of the members that follow it. The private members are used by only a few categories of functions, whose privileges include access to these members. These functions include the member functions of the class.

7. Classes in C++ are a form of struct whose default access specification is private. Thus, struct and class can be used interchangeably with the appropriate access specification.

8. Data members can be declared with the storage class modifier `static`. A data member that is declared `static` is shared by all variables of that class and is stored in one place only. Because of this it can be accessed in the form:

   class-name :: *identifier*

9. Classes can be nested. The inner class is inside the scope of the outer class. This is not in accordance with C semantics.

Exercises

1. Design a C++ structure to store a dairy-product name, portion weight, calories, protein, fat, and carbohydrates. Twenty-five grams of American cheese has 375 calories, 5 grams of protein, 8 grams of fat, and zero carbohydrates. Show how to assign these values to the member variables of your structure. Write a function that, given a variable of type `struct dairy` and a weight in grams (portion size), returns the number of calories for that weight.

2. Write a struct `point` that has three coordinates x, y, and z. How can you access the individual members?

3. Use the struct card defined in Section 4.7, "An Example: Flushing," on page 128, to write a hand-sorting routine. In card games, most players keep their cards sorted by pip value. The routine will place aces first, kings next, and so forth, down to twos. A hand will be five cards.

4. The following declarations do not compile correctly. Explain what is wrong.

   ```
   struct brother {
       char            name[20];
       int             age;
       struct sister   sib;
   } a;

   struct sister {
       char            name[20];
       int             age;
       struct brother  sib;
   } a;
   ```

5. In this exercise, use the class ch_stack, defined in Section 4.13, "A Container Class Example: ch_stack," on page 140. Write the function:

   ```
   void reverse(char s1[], char s2[]);
   ```

   The strings s1 and s2 must be the same size. String s2 should become a reversed copy of string s1. Internal to reverse, use a ch_stack to perform the reversal.

6. Rewrite the functions push() and pop() discussed in Section 4.13, "A Container Class Example: ch_stack," on page 140, to test that push() is not acting on a full ch_stack and pop() is not acting on an empty ch_stack. If either condition is detected, print an error message using cerr, and use exit(1) (in *stdlib.h*) to abort the program. Contrast this to an approach using asserts.

7. Write reverse() as a member function for type ch_stack, discussed in Section 4.13, "A Container Class Example: ch_stack," on page 141. Test it by printing normally and reversed the string:

   Gottfried Leibniz wrote Toward a Universal Characteristic

8. For the ch_stack type in Section 4.4, "Access: Private and Public," on page 123, write as member functions

   ```
   //push n chars from s1 onto the ch_stack
   void   pushm(int n, const char s1[]);

   //pop n chars from ch_stack into char string
   void   popm(int n, char s1[]);
   ```

   Hint: Be sure to put a terminator character into the string before outputting it.

9. Explain the difference in meaning between the structure

   ```
   struct a {
      int i, j, k;
   };
   ```

   and the class

   ```
   class a {
      int i, j, k;
   };
   ```

   Explain why the class declaration is not useful. How can you use the keyword `public` to change the class declaration into a declaration equivalent to `struct a`?

10. Recode as a class the data type `deque`, which is a double-ended queue that allows push and pop at both ends.

    ```
    class deque {
    public:
       void reset() { top = bottom = max_len / 2; top--; }
       . . . . .
    private:
       char   s[max_len];
       int    bottom, top;
    };
    ```

    Declare and implement push_t, pop_t, push_b, pop_b, out_stack, top_of, bottom_of, empty, and full. The function push_t() stands for push on top, and pop_t() for pop on top; push_b() stands for push on bottom, and pop_b() for pop on bottom. The out_stack() function should output the stack from bottom to top. An empty stack is denoted by having the top fall below the bottom. Test each function.

11. Extend the data type deque by adding a member function relocate(). If the deque is full, then relocate() is called, and the contents of the deque are moved to balance empty storage around the center max_len/2 of array s. Its function declaration header is

    ```
    //returns true if it succeeds, false if it fails
    bool deque::relocate()
    ```

12. Write a function that swaps the contents of two strings. If you pushed a string of characters onto a ch_stack and popped them into a second string, they would come out reversed. In a swap of two strings, we want the original ordering. Use a deque to do the swap. The strings will be stored in character arrays of the same length, but the strings themselves may be of differing lengths. The function prototype is

    ```
    void swap(char s1[], char s2[]);
    ```

13. Write the following member functions:

    ```
    void   pips::print();
    void   card::pr_card();
    void   deck::pr_deck();
    ```

    and add them to the *poker* program found in Section 4.7, "An Example: Flushing," on page 128. Let pr_deck() use pr_card() and pr_card() use print(). Print the deck after it is initialized.

14. Write a function pr_hand() that prints out card hands. Add it to the *poker* program, and use it to print out each flush.

15. In Section 4.7, "An Example: Flushing," on page 128, main() detects flushes. Write a function

    ```
    bool   isflush(const card hand[], int nc);
    ```

    that returns true if a hand is a flush.

16. Write a function

    ```
    bool   isstraight(const card hand[], nc);
    ```

that returns `true` if a `hand` is a straight. A straight is five cards that have sequential pip values. The lowest straight is ace, two, three, four, five, and the highest straight is ten, jack, queen, king, ace. Run experiments to estimate the probability that dealt cards will be a straight, and compare the results of five-card hands with results of seven-card hands. *Hint:* You may want to set up an array of 15 integers to correspond to counters for each pip value. Be sure that a pip value of 1 (corresponding to ace) is also counted as the high card corresponding to a pip value of 14.

17. Use the previous exercises to determine the probability that a poker hand will be a straight flush. This is the rarest poker hand and has the highest value. Note that, in a hand of more than five cards, it is not sufficient to merely check for the presence of both a straight and a flush to determine that the hand is a straight flush.

18. Change the `suit` declaration from an enumerated type to a class as follows:

    ```
    enum  suit_val { clubs, diamonds, hearts, spades };

    class suit {
    public:
       void  assign(int n) { s = n / 13; }
       int   getsuit() { return s; }
       void  print();
    private:
       suit_val   s;
    };
    ```

    We add the member function `getsuit()` to access the hidden integer value of a `suit` variable. Now recode all references to `suit` throughout the program.

19. Change class `ch_stack` to `int_stack` by substituting type `int` for type `char` in the class definition as appropriate. Later we will see how to use templates to automate this process.

Chapter 5

Constructors and Destructors

An *object* requires memory and some initial value. C++ provides this through declarations that are definitions. In most cases, when we discuss declarations, we mean declarations that are definitions. For example, in

```
void foo()
{
   int     n = 5;
   double  z[10] = { 0.0 };
   struct  gizmo { int i, j; } w = { 3, 4 };
   .....
}
```

all the objects are created at block entry when `foo()` is invoked. A typical implementation uses a run-time system stack. Thus, the `int` object `n` on a system with four-byte integers gets this allocated off the stack and initialized to the value 5. The `gizmo object` `w` requires eight bytes to represent its two integer members. The array of `double` object `z` requires 10 times `sizeof(double)` to store its elements. In each case, the system provides for the construction and initialization of these objects. Upon exit from `foo()`, deallocation occurs automatically.

In creating complicated aggregates, the user will expect similar management of a class-defined object. The class needs a mechanism to specify object creation and destruction, so that a client can use objects like native types.

A *constructor* is a member function whose name is the same as the class name; it constructs values of the class type. This process involves initializing data members and, frequently, allocating free store using `new`. A *destructor* is a member function whose name is the class name preceded by the tilde character ~. Its usual purpose is to finalize objects of the class type, typically by using `delete` to deallocate store assigned the object.

5 ▼ Constructors and Destructors

Constructors are the more complicated of these two specially named member functions. They can be overloaded and can take arguments, while destructors can do neither. A constructor is invoked when its associated type is used in a definition; when call-by-value is used to pass a value to a function, or when the return value of a function must create a value of associated type. Destructors are invoked implicitly when an object goes out of scope. Constructors and destructors do not have return types, and cannot use `return` *expression* statements.

5.1 Classes with Constructors

The simplest use of a constructor is for initialization. In this and later sections, we will develop some examples that use constructors to initialize the values of the data members of the class.

Our first example is an implementation of a data type `mod_int` to store numbers that are computed with a modulus.

In file modulo.cpp

```
//Modulo numbers and constructor initialization
class mod_int {
public:
   mod_int(int i);                   //constructor declaration
   void  assign(int i) { v = i % modulus; }
   void  print() const { cout << v << '\t'; }
   const static int modulus = 60;
private:
   int  v;
};

//constructor definition
mod_int::mod_int(int i) { v = i % modulus; }
const int  mod_int::modulus;
```

The integer v is restricted in value to 0, 1, 2, ..., modulus - 1. It is the programmer's responsibility to enforce this restriction by having all member functions guarantee this behavior.

The member function `mod_int::mod_int(int)` is a constructor. It does not have a return type. It is invoked when objects of type `mod_int` are declared. It is a function of one argument. When invoked, it requires an expression that is assignment-compatible with its `int` parameter. It then creates and initializes the declared variable.

Some examples of declarations using this type are:

```
mod_int   a(0);       //a.v = 0;
mod_int   b(61);      //b.v = 1;
```

but not:

```
mod_int   a;          //illegal:no parameter list
```

Since this class has only the one constructor of argument list `int`, a `mod_int` declaration must have an integral expression passed as an initializing value. Note that by not allowing a `mod_int` variable to be declared without an initializing expression, we prevent run-time errors due to uninitialized variables.

5.1.1 The Default Constructor

A constructor requiring no arguments is called the *default* constructor. This can be a constructor with an empty argument list or one whose arguments all have default values. It has the special purpose of initializing arrays of objects of its class.

It is often convenient to overload the constructor with several function declarations. In our example, it could be desirable to have the default value of v be zero. If we add the default constructor

```
mod_int() { v = 0; }
```

as a member function of `mod_int`, it is possible to have the following declarations:

```
mod_int   s1, s2;     //both init private member v to 0
mod_int   d[5];       //arrays are properly initialized
```

In both of these declarations, the empty parameter-list constructor is invoked.

If a class does not have a constructor, the system provides a default constructor. If a class has constructors but not a default constructor, array allocation causes a syntactic error.

Notice that in our `mod_int` example one constructor could serve as both a general initializer and a default constructor:

```
inline   mod_int::mod_int(int i = 0)
       { v = i % modulus; }
```

5.1.2 Constructor Initializer

There is a special syntax for initializing subelements of objects with constructors. *Constructor initializers* for structure and class members can be specified in a comma-separated list that follows the constructor parameter list and precedes the code body. Let us recode the previous example:

```
//Default constructor for mod_int
mod_int::mod_int(int i = 0) : v(i % modulus){}
```

Notice that initialization replaces assignment. The individual members must be initializable as:

member-name (expression list)

It is not always possible to assign values to members in the body of the constructor. An initializer list is required when a nonstatic member is either a `const` or a reference type.

5.1.3 Constructors as Conversions

Constructors of a single parameter are automatically conversion functions unless declared with the keyword `explicit`. For example, T1::T1(T2) provides code that can be used to convert a T2 object to a T1 object. Consider the following class, whose purpose is to print invisible characters with their ASCII designation; for example, the code 07 (octal) is `alarm` or `bel`.

In file printabl.cpp

```
//ASCII printable characters

class pr_char {
public:
   pr_char(int i = 0) : c(i % 128) { }
   void  print() const { cout << rep[c]; }
private:
   int  c;
   static const char*  rep[128];
};

const char*  pr_char::rep[128] = { "nul", "soh", "stx",
   . . . . .
      "w", "x", "y", "z","{", "|", "}", "~", "del" };
```

```
int main()
{
   pr_char   c;

   for (int i = 0; i < 128; ++i) {
      c = i;                  //or: c = static_cast<pr_char>(i);
      c.print();
      cout << endl;
   }
}
```

The constructor creates an automatic conversion from integers to pr_char. Notice that the statement in the loop

```
c = i;
```

implies this conversion. It is also possible to explicitly use a cast. Conversions are covered in detail in Chapter 6, "Operator Overloading and Conversions." One reason OOP has implicit conversions for ADTs is that it is desirable for them to have the look and feel of the native types.

5.1.4 Improving the point Class

The class point from Section 4.5, "Classes," on page 124 is readily improved by adding constructors. Notice that it contains the member function point::init(), which is similar to a constructor.

```
class point {
public:
   void print() { cout << "(" << x << "," << y << ")"; }
   void init(double u, double v) { x = u; y = v; }
   void plus(point c);
private:
   double x, y;
};
```

Adding constructors gives us:

```
class point {
public:
   point() { x = 0; y = 0; }                              //default
   point(double u) { x = u; y = 0;)                       //double to point
   point(const point& p) { x = p.x; y = p.y; } //copy
   point(double u, double v) { x = u; y = v; }
   .....
private:
   double x, y;
};
```

In this version of point, we have a full complement of constructors explicitly written out. The copy constructor code is essentially the same as the code that the compiler would have produced by default, namely member-by-member copy.

Many scientific problems require producing a table of points or a graph by using a function. For example, a parabola can be coded as:

```
double parabola(double x, double p) { return(x * x) / p; }
```

Let us use this function to produce a table of points that graphs the parabola from zero to two in increments of 0.1.

```
void graph(double a, double b, double incr,
   double f(double, double), double p, point gr[])
{
      double x = a;
      for (int i = 0; x <= b; ++i, x += incr)
         gr[i].init(x, f(x, p));
}
```

```
int main()
{
   point g[1000];              //uses the default constructor

   graph(0, 2, 0.1, parabola, 5, g );
}
```

5.2 Constructing a Dynamically Sized Stack

A constructor can also be used to allocate space from free store. We shall modify the ch_stack type from Section 4.13, "A Container Class Example: ch_stack," on page 140, so that its maximum length is initialized by a constructor.

The design of the object ch_stack includes hidden implementation detail. Data members are placed in the private access region of class ch_stack. The public interface provides clients with the expected stack abstraction. These are all public member functions, such as push() and pop(). Some of these functions are *accessor functions* that do not change the stack object, such as top_of() and empty(). It is usual to make these const member functions. Some of these functions are *mutator functions* that do change the ch_stack object, such as push() and pop(). The constructor member functions have the job of creating and initializing ch_stack objects.

In file ch_stac4.cpp

```
class ch_stack {
public:
//the public interface for the ADT ch_stack
   explicit ch_stack(int size): max_len( size), top(EMPTY)
      { assert(size > 0); s = new char[size]; assert(s ! = 0); }
   void  reset() { top = EMPTY; }
   void  push(char c) { s[++top]= c; }
   char  pop() { return s[top--]; }
   char  top_of() const { return s[top]; }
   bool  empty() const { return (top == EMPTY); }
   bool  full() const { return (top == max_len - 1); }
private:
   enum  { EMPTY = -1 };
   char*  s;                     //changed from s[max_len]
   int    max_len;
   int    top;
};
```

Now a client using `ch_stack` can decide on the size requirement. An example of a `ch_stack` declaration invoking this constructor is:

```
ch_stack  data(1000);          //allocate 1000 elements
ch_stack  more_data(2 * n);    //allocate 2 * n elements
```

Two alternate constructors would be an empty parameter constructor that would allocate a specific-length `ch_stack`, and a two-parameter constructor whose second parameter would be a `char*` used to initialize the `ch_stack`. They could be written as follows:

```
//default constructor for ch_stack
ch_stack::ch_stack():max_len(100),top(EMPTY)
{
   s = new char[100];
   assert(s != 0);
}

//domain transfer
ch_stack::ch_stack(int size, const char str[]):
   max_len(size)
{
   int i;
   assert(size > 0);
   s = new char[size];
   assert(s != 0);
   for (i = 0; i < max_len && str[i] != 0; ++i)
      s[i] = str[i];
   top = --i;
}
```

The corresponding function prototypes would be included as members of the class `ch_stack`. Let us use these constructors in the following:

```
ch_stack  data;              //creates s[100]
ch_stack  d[N];              //creates N 100 element ch_stacks
ch_stack  w(4, "ABCD");      //w.s[0]='A'...w.s[3]='D'
```

5.2.1 The Copy Constructor

We wish to examine our stack and count the number of occurrences of a given character. We can repeatedly pop the stack, testing each element in turn, until the stack is empty. But what if we want to preserve the contents of the stack? Call-by-value parameters accomplish this:

In file ch_stac4.cpp

```
int cnt_char(char c, ch_stack s)
{
   int  count = 0;

   while (!s.empty())
      count += (c == s.pop());
   return count;
}
```

The semantics of call-by-value require that a local copy of the argument type be created and initialized from the value of the expression passed as the actual argument. This requires a *copy constructor*. The compiler provides a copy constructor whose signature is:

```
ch_stack::ch_stack(const ch_stack&);
```

The compiler copies by *memberwise initialization*. This may not work in all circumstances, such as for complicated aggregates with members that are themselves pointers. In many cases, the pointer is the address of an object that is deleted when it goes out of scope. However, the act of duplicating the pointer value but not the object pointed at can lead to anomalous code. This deletion affects other instances that still expect the object to exist. It is appropriate for the class to explicitly define its own copy constructor:

In file ch_stac4.h

```
//Copy constructor for ch_stack of characters
ch_stack::ch_stack(const ch_stack& str):
   max_len(str.max_len),top(str.top)
{
   s = new char[str.max_len];
   assert(s != 0);
   memcpy(s, str.s, max_len);
}
```

The *stdlib.h* routine memcpy() copies max_len characters from the base address str.s into memory starting at base address s. This is called a *deep copy*. The character arrays are distinct because they refer to different memory locations. If, instead, the body of this routine were

```
s = str.s;
```

then this would be a *shallow copy*, with the ch_stack variables sharing the same representation. Any change to one variable would change the other.

5.3 Classes with Destructors

Destructors are member functions whose name is the class name preceded by a tilde. They are almost always called implicitly, usually at the exit of the block in which the object was declared. They are also invoked when a delete operator is called on a pointer to an object having a destructor, or where they are needed to destroy a subobject of an object being deleted.

Let us augment our ch_stack example with a destructor.

In file ch_stac4.h

```
//ch_stack implementation with constructors and destructor
class ch_stack {
public:
   ch_stack();                                  //default constructor
   explicit ch_stack(int size) : max_len(size), top(EMPTY)
      { assert(size > 0); s = new char[size]; assert(s != 0); }
   ch_stack(const stack& str)                   //copy constructor
   ch_stack(int size, const char str[]);
   ~ch_stack() { delete []s; }                  //destructor
   .....
private:
   enum   { EMPTY = -1 };
   char*  s;
   int    max_len;
   int    top;
};
```

The addition of the destructor allows the class to return unneeded heap-allocated memory during program execution. All of the public member functions perform in exactly the same manner as before. The difference is that the destructor will be implicitly invoked upon block and function exit to clean up storage that is no longer accessible. This is good programming practice, and allows programs to execute using less memory.

5.4 An Example: Dynamically Allocated Strings

A native string type is lacking in C++. The standard library provides a string template class, which is increasingly the normally used string type. An older style of string representation is as pointer to `char`. In this representation, the end-of-string is denoted by the null character \0. This convention has an important drawback, in that many basic string manipulations are proportional to string length. This use is reflected by the library *string.h* (or *cstring* in modern C++). In that library, the standard function `int strlen(const char*)` is used to compute the length of the character array delimited by the null character. In modern C++, the standard library *string* provides a string type that stores string length as part of its hidden implementation.

In this section, we shall develop some of the ways in which such a type can be implemented, and also a useful string ADT that stores its length privately. We want our type to be dynamically allocated and able to represent arbitrary-length strings. A variety of constructors will be coded to initialize and allocate strings, and a set of operations on strings will be coded as member functions. The implementation will use the *string.h* library functions to manipulate the underlying pointer representation of strings.

In file string5.cpp

```cpp
//An implementation of dynamically allocated strings.
class my_string {
public:
   my_string() : len(0)
      { s = new char[1];assert(s != 0); s[0] = 0; }
   my_string(const my_string& str);         //copy constructor
   my_string(const char* p);                //conversion constructor
   ~my_string() { delete []s; }
   void assign(const my_string& str);
   void print() const { cout << s << endl; }
   void concat(const my_string& a,const my_string& b);
private:
   char*  s;
   int    len;
};
```

```cpp
my_string::my_string(const char* p)
{
   len = strlen(p);
   s = new char[len + 1];
   assert(s != 0);
   strcpy(s, p);
}

my_string::my_string(const my_string& str) : len(str.len)
{
   s = new char[len + 1];
   assert(s != 0);
   strcpy(s, str.s);
}

void my_string::assign(const my_string& str)
{
   if (this == &str)         //a = a; do nothing
      return;
   delete []s;
   len = str.len;
   s = new char[len + 1];
   assert(s != 0);
   strcpy(s, str.s);
}

void my_string::concat(const my_string& a, const my_string& b)
{
   char*  temp = new char[a.len + b.len + 1];

   len = a.len + b.len;
   strcpy(temp, a.s);
   strcat(temp, b.s);
   delete []s;
   s = new char[len + 1];
   assert(s != 0);
   strcpy(s, temp);
}
```

This type allows you to declare my_strings, assign by copying one my_string to another, print a my_string, and concatenate two my_strings. The hidden representation is pointer to char, and it has a variable len in which to store the current my_string length.

Dissection of the `my_string` Class

- ```
  my_string() : len(0)
      { s = new char[1]; assert(s != 0); s[0] = 0; }
  my_string(const my_string& str);      //copy constructor
  my_string(const char* p);             //conversion constructor
  ```

There are three overloaded constructors. The first is the default constructor, needed when declaring an array of `my_strings`. The second is the copy constructor. The third has a pointer to char argument that can be used to convert the `char*` representation of strings to our `my_string` type. It uses two library functions: `strlen` and `strcpy`. We allocate one additional character to store the end-of-string character \0, although this character is not counted by `strlen`. The copy constructor will be explained below.

- `~my_string() { delete []s; }`

The destructor automatically returns memory allocated to `my_strings` back to free store for reuse. The empty bracket-pair form of `delete` is used because array allocation was used. The operator `delete[]` knows the amount of memory associated with the pointer s.

- ```
  my_string::my_string(const my_string& str) : len(str.len)
  {
      s = new char[len + 1];
      assert(s != 0);
      strcpy(s, str.s);
  }
  ```

This is a copy constructor. This form is used to copy one `my_string` into another.

Copy Constructor Use

1. A `my_string` is initialized by another `my_string`.

2. A `my_string` is passed as an argument in a function.

3. A `my_string` is returned as the value of a function.

In C++, if this constructor is not present explicitly, the compiler creates one that uses member-by-member initialization.

- ```
  void my_string::assign(const my_string& str)
  {
     if (this == &str)        //a = a; do nothing
        return;
     delete []s;    len = str.len;
     s = new char[len + 1];
     assert(s != 0);
     strcpy(s, str.s);
  }
  ```

The assignment semantics are based on deep-copy semantics. Recall that in deep copy, the entire aggregate must be replicated and the data values copied into its representation. The copying requires a check against copying over the same my_string. This is the case with a = a. If we had not tested for this case and had performed deletion on the left-hand argument, the value of a would have disappeared. Each time the value of a my_string is copied, the value is physically recopied using strcpy(). This is in distinction to a later implementation that will show how to use shallow-copy semantics. Recall that shallow copying sets a pointer to an existing value without replicating the aggregate. As we shall see, this can be very efficient.

- ```
  void my_string::concat(const my_string& a, const my_string& b)
  {
     char  temp[a.len + b.len + 1];

     len = a.len + b.len;
     strcpy(temp, a.s);
     strcat(temp, b.s);
     delete []s;
     s = new char[len + 1];
     assert(s != 0);
     strcpy(s, temp);
  }
  ```

This is a form of concatenation. Neither my_string argument is modified. The implicit argument, whose hidden member variables are s and len, is modified to represent the my_string a followed by the my_string b. Note that in this member function the use of len, a.len, and b.len is possible. Member functions have access not only to the private members of the implicit argument, but also to the private representation of any of the arguments of type my_string.

5.4 ▼ An Example: Dynamically Allocated Strings

The following code tests class `my_string` by concatenating several `my_strings`:

In file string5.cpp

```
int main()
{
   char* str = "The wheel that squeaks the loudest\n";
   my_string  a(str), b, author("Josh Billings\n"), both, quote;

   b.assign("Is the one that gets the grease\n");
   both.concat(a, b);
   quote.concat(both, author);
   quote.print();
}
```

The printout from this program is:

```
The wheel that squeaks the loudest
Is the one that gets the grease
Josh Billings
```

We deliberately used a variety of declarations to show how different constructors would be called. The `my_string` variables b, both, and quote all use the default constructor. The declaration for author uses the constructor whose argument type is char*. The concatenation takes place in two steps. First, `my_strings` a and b are concatenated into both. Next, `my_strings` both and author are concatenated into quote. Finally, the quotation is printed out.

The constructor `my_string::my_string(const char*)` is invoked to create and initialize objects a and author. This constructor is also called implicitly as a conversion operation when invoking `my_string::assign()` on the literal "Is the one that gets the grease\n".

5.5 The Class functor

In Fortran, we use subroutines and functions to provide many scientific calculations on functions of one variable. We have seen that C++ has the same facilities. But C++ can also encapsulate a function as a class object and then apply a series of member functions to produce various computations such as plotting of a function. This is done by creating a class whose private pointer variable stores the functions address (see Section 3.6, "Functions as Arguments," on page 75).

In file functor.cpp

```
//Create a class that represents a function.
#include <iostream.h>
#include <assert.h>

class functor {
public:
   functor(double f(double)) : fcn(f) { }
   void plot(double x0, double x1, double incr);
private:
   double (*fcn)(double) ;
};

void functor::plot(double x0, double x1, double incr)
{
   assert(x0 < x1 && incr > 0);
   for (; x0 <= x1 ; x0 += incr)
      cout << "f(" << x0 << ") =" << fcn(x0) << endl;
}
```

An object of type functor acts in much the same way as a function. We can provide a series of member functions, such as plot(), to provide various computations over these functions. This is a convenient way to encapsulate a library of useful related routines. In the following code, we construct two such functors and plot them.

```
double f(double x)
   { return (x * x + 1.0/x); }

double g(double x)
   { return (3 * x * x - 2 * x + 4); }
```

```
int main()
{
   functor fctr(f), gctr(g);

   cout << "mapping functions x * x + 1.0/x " << endl;
   fctr.plot(0.01, 2.01, 0.01);
   cout << "mapping functions 3*x*x -2*x + 4" << endl;
   gctr.plot(0.00, 2.01, 0.01);
}
```

5.6 The Class dbl_vect

The one-dimensional array in C++ is a very useful and efficient aggregate type. In many ways it is the prototypical container: easy to use and highly efficient. However, it is error prone. A common mistake is to access elements that are out of bounds. C++ allows us to control this problem by defining an analogous container type in which bounds can be tested. We will also be able to use this type as a mathematical vector type:

In file dbl_vect1.h

```
//Implementation of a safe array type dbl_vect
class dbl_vect {
public:
   explicit dbl_vect(int n = 10);
   ~dbl_vect() { delete []p; }
   double& element(int i);                   //access p[i]
   int  ub() const { return (size - 1); }    //upper bound
   void print() const;
private:
   double*   p;
   double    size;
};

dbl_vect::dbl_vect(int n) : size(n)
{
   assert(n > 0);
   p = new double[size];
   assert(p != 0);
}
```

```
double& dbl_vect::element(int i)
{
   assert (i >= 0 && i < size);
   return p[i];
}
```

The constructor dbl_vect::dbl_vect(int n) allows the user to build dynamically allocated arrays. Such arrays are much more flexible than those in languages such as Fortran, Pascal, and C, where array sizes must be constant expressions. The constructor also initializes the variable size, whose value is the number of elements in the array. Note that we declare this one-argument constructor explicit because it is not intended as an implicit conversion from int to dbl_vect.

The print() function outputs tab-separated elements of the vector.

```
void dbl_vect::print()const
{
   cout << " vector of size " << size << endl;
   for (int i = 0; i <size; ++i)
      cout << p[i] << "\t";
}
```

Access to individual elements is through the safe-indexing member function

```
double& dbl_vect::element(int i)
```

An index that is outside the expected array range zero through ub will cause an assertion failure. This safe-indexing member function returns a reference to int that is the address of p[i] and that can be used as the left operand of an assignment or lvalue. The technique is often used in C++, and is an efficient mechanism for operating on complicated types.

As an example, the declarations

```
dbl_vect a(10), b(5);
```

construct arrays of ten and five integers, respectively. Individual elements can be accessed by the member function element, which checks whether the index is out of range. The statements

```
a.element(1) = 5;
b.element(1) = a.element(1) + 7;
cout << a.element(1) - 2;
```

are all legal. In effect we have a safe dynamic array type.

Classes with default constructors use them to initialize a derived array type. For example,

```
dbl_vect a[5];
```

is a declaration that uses the default constructor to create an array a of five objects, each of which is a size 10 dbl_vect. The ith element's address in the jth array would be given by a[j].element(i).

In Chapter 10, "Exceptions," we discuss how exceptions can be used to check on error conditions. With this more powerful methodology,

```
assert(n > 0);
```

is replaced by

```
if (n < 1)
   throw(vect_allocation_error(n));
```

5.6.1 dbl_vect as a Linear Vector Type

The basic type in linear algebra is the vector. It allows a description of many scientific and engineering problems. To use dbl_vect effectively as a linear vector, we need to add mathematical operations, such as vector addition, vector subtraction, and vector scalar product. We can do this as a set of functions that use dbl_vect::element(), but this does not allow efficient access to the underlying representation. By including these operations as part of the class dbl_vect we support an efficient implementation and appropriate encapsulation. We display the dot_prod() function, leaving the others as exercises.

In file dbl_vect1.h

```
double dbl_vect::dot_prod(const dbl_vect& v) const
{
   assert(size == v.size);
   double sum = 0.0;

   for (int i = 0; i < size; ++i)
      sum += p[i] * v.p[i];
   return sum;
}
```

In file dbl_vect1.cpp

```cpp
int main()
{
    dbl_vect c(6);
    for (int i = 0; i <= c.ub(); ++i)
        c.element(i) = i + 0.1;
    c.print();
    cout << " dot product = " << c.dot_prod(c) << endl;
}
```

5.7 Members that Are Class Types

In this section we shall use the type `dbl_vect` as a member of the class `pair_vect`. In OO methodology this is known as the *HASA relationship*. Complicated objects can be designed from simpler ones by incorporating them with the HASA relationship.

In file pairvect.cpp

```cpp
#include "dbl_vect1.h"

class pair_vect {
public:
    pair_vect(int i) : a(i), b(i), size(i) { }
    double& first_element(int i);
    double& second_element(int i);
    int ub()const { return size -1; }
private:
    dbl_vect a, b;
    int size;
};

double& pair_vect::first_element(int i)
{   return a.element(i); }

double& pair_vect::second_element(int i)
{   return b.element(i);}
```

Notice that the `pair_vect` constructor is a series of initializers. The initializers of the `dbl_vect` members a and b invoke `dbl_vect::dbl_vect(int)`. Let us use this data type to build a table of age and weight relationships:

```cpp
int main()
{
   int      i;
   pair_vect age_weight(5);      //age and weight

   cout << "table of age, weight\n";
   for (i = 0; i <= age_weight.ub(); ++i) {
      age_weight.first_element(i) = 21 + i;
      age_weight.second_element(i) = 135 + i;
      cout << age_weight.first_element(i) << ","
           << age_weight.second_element(i) << endl;
   }
}
```

5.8 Example: A Singly Linked List

In this section, we develop a singly linked list data type. This is the prototype of many useful dynamic ADTs called *self-referential structures*. These data types have pointer members that refer to objects of their own type. They are the basis of many useful container classes.

The following declaration implements such a type.

In file slist.cpp

```cpp
class slist {                    //a singly linked list
public:
   slist() : h(0) { }            //0 denotes empty slist
   ~slist() { release(); }
   void  prepend(char c);        //adds to front of slist
   void  del();
   slistelem* first() const { return h; }
   void  print() const;
   void  release();
private:
   slistelem*  h;                //head of slist
};

struct slistelem {
   char       data;
   slistelem* next;
};
```

List Operations

1. `prepend`: adds to front of list
2. `first`: returns first element
3. `print`: prints list contents
4. `del`: deletes first element
5. `release`: destroys list

The link member `next` points to the next `slistelem` in the list. In this example, `data` is a simple variable, but it could be replaced by a complicated type capable of storing a range of information. The constructor initializes the head of `slist` pointer `h` to the value zero, which is called the *null-pointer constant* and can be assigned to any pointer type. In linked lists it typically denotes the empty list or end-of-list value. The member function `prepend()` builds the list structure:

```
void slist::prepend(char c)
{
   slistelem*  temp = new slistelem;    //create element
   assert(temp != 0);
   temp -> next = h;                    //link to slist
   temp -> data = c;
   h = temp;                            //update head of slist
}
```

A list element is allocated from free store, and its data member is initialized from the single argument c. Its link member `next` is set to the old list head. The head pointer h is updated to point at this element as the new first element of the list.

The member function `del()` has the inverse role:

```
void slist::del()
{
   slistelem*  temp = h;

   h = h -> next;              //presumes an nonempty slist
   delete temp;
}
```

It returns the first element of the list to free store. It does this by using the `delete` operator on the head of `slist` pointer h. The new head-of-list is the value of the `next` member. This function can be modified to work on the empty list without aborting (see exercise 19, on page 195).

Much of list processing is repetitively chaining down the list until the null-pointer value is found. The following two functions use this technique.

In file slist.cpp

```cpp
void slist::print() const              //object is unchanged
{
   slistelem*  temp = h;

   while (temp != 0) {                 //detect end of slist
      cout << temp -> data << " -> ";
      temp = temp -> next;
   }
   cout << "\n###" << endl;
}

//elements returned to free store
void slist::release()
{
   while (h != 0)
      del();
}
```

Dissection of the `print()` and `release()` Functions

- ```cpp
  void slist::print() const              //object is unchanged
  {
     slistelem*  temp = h;
  ```

An auxiliary pointer `temp` will be used to chain down the list. It is initialized to the address of the `slist` head h. The pointer h cannot be used because its value would be lost, in effect destroying access to the list.
  ```

- ```
  while (temp != 0) {                    //detect end of list
      cout << temp -> data << " -> ";
      temp = temp -> next;
  }
  ```

The value zero is guaranteed to represent the end-of-list value because the constructor `slist::slist()` initialized it as such, and the `slist::prepend()` function maintains it as the end-of-list pointer value. Notice that the internals of this loop could be changed to process the entire list in some other manner.

- `void slist::release()`

The `release` function is used to return all list elements to free store, and it marches down the list doing so.

- ```
  while (h != 0)
      del();
  ```

Each element of the list must be returned to free store in sequence. This is done for a single element by `slist::del()`, which manipulates the hidden pointer h. Since we are destroying the list, it is unnecessary to preserve the original value of pointer h. This function's chief use is as the body of the destructor `slist::~slist()`. We could not use a destructor written

```
slist::~slist()
{
    delete h;
}
```

because it deletes only the first element in the list.

We demonstrate the use of this type in the following code, in which we have modified the destructor to print a message.

In file slist.cpp

```
slist:: ~slist()
{
    cout << "destructor invoked" << endl;
    release();
}
```

```
int main()
{
   slist*  p;
   {
      slist   w;

      w.prepend('A');
      w.prepend('B');
      w.print();
      w.del();
      w.print();
      p = &w;
      p -> print();
      cout << "exiting inner block" << endl;
   }
   //p -> print();  gives system-dependent behavior
   cout << "exiting outer block" << endl;
}
```

Notice that there is an inner block in `main()`. That block is included to test that the destructor is invoked upon block exit, returning storage associated with w to free store. The output of this program is:

```
B -> A ->
###
A ->
###
A ->
###
exiting inner block
destructor invoked
exiting outer block
```

The first `print()` call prints the two-element `slist` that stores B and A. After a `del` operation is performed, the list contains one element that stores A. The outer block pointer to `slist` p is assigned the address of the `slist` variable w. When the list is accessed through p in the inner block, it prints A. This output shows that the destructor works at block exit on the variable w.

The commented-out invocation of `slist::print()` is system-dependent. It is a run-time error to dereference p here, because the address it refers to may have been overwritten at block exit by the deletion routine.

5.9 Two-Dimensional Arrays

Standard C does not have authentic higher-dimensional arrays. Instead, the programmer must be careful to map such an abstract data structure into a pointer to pointer to base type. In C++ the programmer can implement flexible, safe, dynamic higher-dimensional arrays. We shall demonstrate this by implementing a two-dimensional array type `matrix`. Notice its similarity to the class `dbl_vect`.

In file matrix1.cpp

```
//A two-dimensional safe array type matrix
class matrix {
public:
   matrix(int d1, int d2);
   ~matrix();
   int   ub1() const { return(s1 - 1); }
   int   ub2() const { return(s2 - 1); }
   double&  element(int i, int j);
private:
   double**  p;
   int    s1, s2;
};
```

The type `matrix` has a size for each dimension and a corresponding public upper bound. The hidden representation uses the pointer to pointer to `double` type. This will store the base address of an array of pointers to `double`, which in turn store a base address for each row of the `matrix` type.

```
matrix::matrix(int d1, int d2) : s1(d1), s2(d2)
{
   assert(d1 > 0 && d2 > 0);
   p = new double*[s1];
   assert(p != 0);
   for (int i = 0; i < s1; ++i){
      p[i] = new double[s2];
      assert(p[i] != 0);
   }
}
```

```
matrix::~matrix()
{
   for (int i = 0; i <= ub1(); ++i)
      delete p[i];
   delete []p;
}
```

The constructor allocates an array of pointer to `double`. The number of elements in this array is the value of `s1`. Next, the constructor iteratively allocates an array of `double` pointed at by each element `p[i]`. Therefore, there is space for `s1` x `s2` doubles allocated from free store, and additionally the space for `s1` pointers is allocated from free store. The destructor deallocates store in reverse order. This scheme generalizes to higher dimensions.

Obtaining the lvalue of an element in this two-dimensional array requires two index arguments:

```
double& matrix::element(int i, int j)
{
   assert(i >= 0 && i <= ub1() && j >= 0 && j <= ub2());
   return p[i][j];
}
```

Both are tested to see that they are in range. This is a generalization of the one-index case.

5.10 Polynomials as a Linked List

A polynomial is *sparse* when it has relatively few nonzero coefficients in comparison to its degree. The degree of the polynomial is simply the highest exponent of a nonzero term. For example, the degree-1,000 polynomial $P(x) = x^{1000} + x^1 + 1$ has only three nonzero terms. When manipulating large sparse polynomials, it is often efficient to base the representation on a linked list. In such a representation each list element contains a nonzero term of the polynomial.

We will write a routine that manipulates such polynomials and does polynomial addition, allowing only one term per exponent. The list is sorted with terms in descending order of their exponents.

In file poly1.cpp

```cpp
//A polynomial represented as a singly linked list
struct term {
   int        exponent;
   double     coefficient;
   term*      next;
   term(int e, double c, term* n = 0)
      : exponent(e), coefficient(c), next(n) { }
   void print()
      { cout << coefficient << "x^" << exponent << " "; }
};

class polynomial {
public:
   polynomial(): h(0), degree(0) { }
   polynomial(const polynomial& p);
   polynomial(int size, double coef[], int expon[]);
   ~polynomial() { release(); }
   void print() const;
   void plus(polynomial a, polynomial b);
private:
   term*   h;
   int     degree;
   void    prepend(term* t);              //add term to front
   void    add_term(term*& a, term*& b);
   void    release();                     //garbage collect
   void    rest_of(term* rest);           //add remaining terms
   void    reverse();                     //reverse terms
};
```

In this representation a polynomial is coded as a list of terms. Each term is a coefficient-exponent pair. A polynomial's terms will be listed in decreasing order by exponent. This canonical form makes addition and other operations simpler. A polynomial will either be empty, initialized using the copy constructor, or constructed from a pair of arrays that contains a properly ordered sequence of coefficient-exponent pairs.

We have several important auxiliary member functions that manipulate the underlying list representation. The `prepend()` function links a term to the head of the list. The `reverse()` function reverses a list in place. The `add_term()` function is used by `plus()` to add a next term and properly advance pointers within the two polynomials being added.

```
inline void polynomial::prepend(term*  t)
   { t -> next = h; h = t; }

void polynomial::reverse()         //in place
{
   term*  pred, *succ, *elem;

   if (h && (succ = h -> next)) {
      pred = 0;
      elem = h;
      while (succ) {
         elem -> next = pred;
         pred = elem;
         elem = succ;
         succ = succ -> next;
      }
      h = elem;
      h -> next = pred;
   }
}
```

The following figure shows a graphic representation of both the prepend and reverse operations.

180   5 ▼ Constructors and Destructors

prepend()

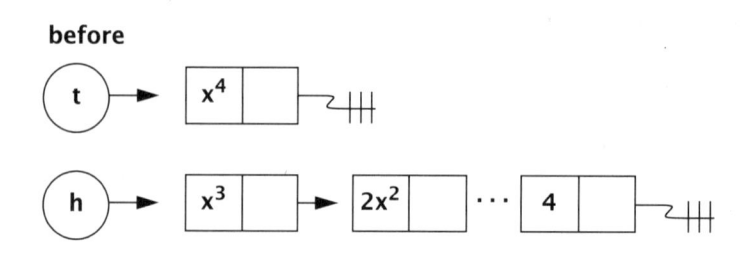

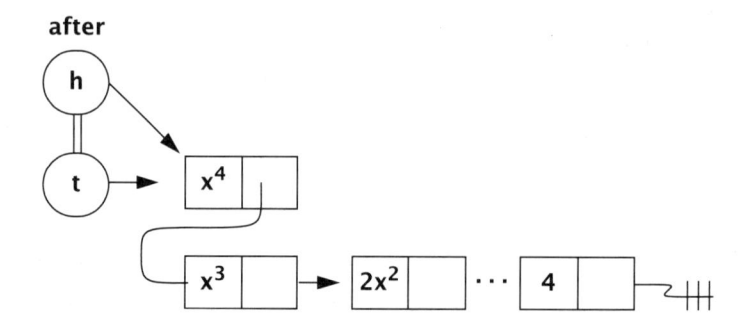

before

t → [x^4 |]⇝∦

h → [x^3 |] → [$2x^2$ |] ⋯ [4 |]⇝∦

after

h
‖
t → [x^4 |]
      ↓
   [x^3 |] → [$2x^2$ |] ⋯ [4 |]⇝∦

---

reverse()

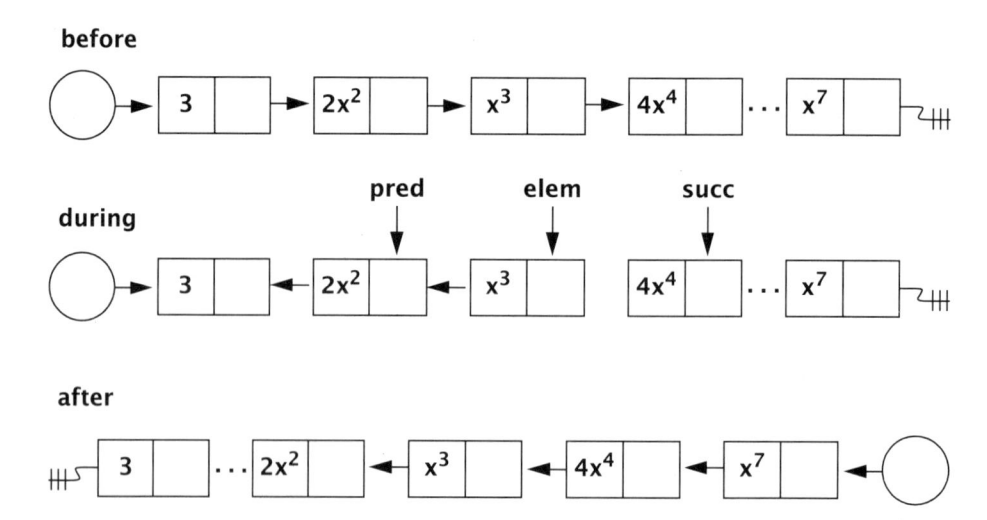

before

○ → [3 |] → [$2x^2$ |] → [x^3 |] → [$4x^4$ |] ⋯ [x^7 |]⇝∦

during

                  pred   elem   succ
                   ↓   ↓   ↓

○ → [3 |] ← [$2x^2$ |] ← [x^3 |]   [$4x^4$ |] ⋯ [x^7 |]⇝∦

after

∦⇜[3 |] ⋯ [$2x^2$ |] ← [x^3 |] ← [$4x^4$ |] ← [x^7 |] ← ○

5.10 ▼ Polynomials as a Linked List

The constructors build an explicit list for each polynomial. It would be incorrect to rely on the compiler-generated default copy constructor.

```
//assumes ordering is correct expon[i] < expon[i+1]
polynomial::polynomial(int size, double coef[], int expon[])
{
    term* temp = new term(expon[0], coef[0]);
    assert(temp != 0);

    h = 0;
    prepend(temp);                          //create initial term
    for (int i = 1; i < size; ++i) {
        assert(expon[i - 1] < expon[i]);
        temp = new term(expon[i], coef[i]);
        assert(temp != 0);
        prepend(temp);                      //add term
    }
    degree = h -> exponent;
}

polynomial::polynomial(const polynomial& p) : degree(p.degree)
{
    term* elem = p.h, *temp;

    h = 0;
    while (elem) {                          //term-by-term copying
        temp = new term(elem -> exponent, elem -> coefficient);
        assert(temp != 0);
        prepend(temp);
        elem = elem -> next;
    }
    reverse();
}
```

The next set of functions implements a merge-sort polynomial addition.

```
void polynomial::add_term(term*& a, term*& b)
{
   term*  c;

   if (a -> exponent > b -> exponent) {                    //add a
      c = new term(a -> exponent, a -> coefficient) ;
      assert(c != 0);
      a = a -> next;
      prepend(c);
   }
   else if (a -> exponent < b -> exponent){                //add b
      c = new term(b -> exponent, b -> coefficient);
      assert(c != 0);
      b = b -> next;
      prepend(c);
   }
    else {                                      //check on cancellation
       if (a -> coefficient + b -> coefficient != 0) {
          c = new term( a -> exponent,
                        a -> coefficient + b -> coefficient);
          assert(c != 0);
          prepend(c);
       }
       a = a -> next;
       b = b -> next;
   }
}
```

This merges the terms at the head of the two lists. The exponents can be of the same or different values. If the exponents are of different values, the larger term is the result, and only its list pointer is advanced. If the exponents are the same, both list pointers are advanced. Cancellation occurs when both exponents are the same and their coefficients sum to zero; no term is produced. Otherwise zero terms might proliferate and it would defeat our attempt at an efficient representation of a sparse polynomial.

When one list of terms is exhausted by the merge, the terms from the remaining list are added to the front of the list by `rest_of()`.

```
void polynomial::rest_of(term* rest)
{
   term* temp;

   while (rest) {
      temp = new term(rest -> exponent, rest -> coefficient);
      assert(temp != 0);
      prepend(temp);
      rest = rest -> next;
   }
}

//c.plus(a,b) means c = a + b;
void polynomial::plus(polynomial a, polynomial b)
{
   term*    aterm = a.h, *bterm = b.h;

   release();              //garbage collect c, assumes not a or b
   h = 0;
   while (aterm && bterm)    //merge step
      add_term(aterm, bterm);
   if (aterm)
      rest_of(aterm);
   else if (bterm)
      rest_of(bterm);
   reverse();
   degree = ((h) ? h -> exponent: 0);
}
```

The function `polynomial::plus()` uses `add_term()` and `rest_of()` to put the terms in the reverse order to the expected representation, and uses `reverse()` to correct this. The `print()` and `release()` functions for `polynomial` are needed to test this code (see exercise 23, on page 196).

5.11 Strings Using Reference Semantics

Allocation at run time of large aggregates can readily exhaust memory resources. Our list example in Section 5.8, "Example: A Singly Linked List," on page 172, showed one scheme for handling this in which the system reclaimed memory by traversing each list and disposing of each element. This model of reclamation is a form of *garbage collection*. In languages such as LISP and Smalltalk, the system itself is responsible for this reclamation. Such systems periodically invoke a garbage collector whose business it is to identify all cells that are currently accessible and reclaim those that are inaccessible. Most such schemes require traversal and marking of cells accessible from pointers with a computationally expensive procedure.

A disposal scheme that avoids this is *reference counting*. Here, each dynamically allocated object tracks its active references. When an object is created, its reference count is set to one. Every time the object is newly referenced, the reference count is incremented; every time it loses a reference, the count is decremented. When the reference count becomes zero, the object's memory is disposed of.

In the following example we create a my_string class that has reference semantics for copying. This class has shallow-copy semantics because pointer assignment replaces copying. The techniques illustrated are common for this type of aggregate. We use the class str_obj to create actual object values. The type str_obj is a required implementation detail for my_string. The detail could not be directly placed in my_string without destroying the potential many-one relationship between objects of type my_string and referenced values of type str_obj. The values of my_string are in the class str_obj, which is an auxiliary class for my_string's use only. The publicly used class my_string handles the str_obj instances, and is sometimes called a *handler* class.

In file string6.cpp

```
//Reference counted my_strings
#include   <string.h>
#include   <iostream.h>
#include   <assert.h>
```

5.11 ▼ Strings Using Reference Semantics

```
class str_obj {
public:
   int    len, ref_cnt;
   char*  s;
   str_obj() : len(0), ref_cnt(1)
      { s = new char[1]; assert(s != 0); s[0] = 0; }
   str_obj(const char* p) : ref_cnt(1)
      { len = strlen(p); s = new char[len + 1];
        assert(s != 0); strcpy(s, p); }
   ~str_obj() { delete []s; }
};
```

The `str_obj` declares objects that are used by `my_string`. We will explain later how these can be made private and accessed using the `friend` mechanism (see Section 6.3, "Friend Functions," on page 204). Notice how the `str_obj` class is basically used for construction and destruction of objects using free store. Upon construction of a `str_obj`, the `ref_cnt` variable is initialized to one.

```
class my_string {
public:
   my_string() { st = new str_obj; assert(st != 0);}
   my_string(const char* p)
      { st = new str_obj(p); assert(st != 0);}
   my_string(const my_string& str)
       { st = str.st; st -> ref_cnt++; }
   ~my_string();
   void  assign(const my_string& str);
   void  print() const { cout << st -> s; }
private:
   str_obj*  st;
};
```

The client will use objects of type `my_string`. These objects are implemented as pointers `st` to values of type `str_obj`. Notice the copy constructor for this class and how it uses reference semantics to produce a copy.

The semantics of `assign()` show some of the subtleties of using reference counting:

```
void my_string::assign(const my_string& str)
{
    if (str.st != st) {
        if (--st -> ref_cnt == 0)
            delete st;
        st = str.st;
        st -> ref_cnt++;
    }
}
```

The assignment occurs if the `my_string` is not being assigned its same value. The assignment causes the assigned variable to lose its previous value. This is equivalent to decrementing the reference count of the pointed-at `str_obj` value. Whenever an object's reference count is decremented, it gets tested for deletion.

The advantage of this over normal copying is clear. A very large aggregate is copied by reference using a few operations. There is a small amount of additional storage for the reference counter. Also, each possible change to a pointer adds a reference count operation. The destructor must also test the reference count before actual deletion.

```
my_string:: ~my_string()
{
    if (--st -> ref_cnt == 0)
        delete st;
}
```

5.12 No Constructor, Copy Constructor, and Other Mysteries

Object creation for native types is usually the task of the compiler. The writer of a class wishes to achieve the same ease of use for the defined ADT. Let us reexamine some issues in simple terms.

Does every class need an explicitly defined constructor? Of course not. Where no constructor is written by the programmer, the compiler provides a default constructor, if needed:

5.12 ▼ No Constructor, Copy Constructor, and Other Mysteries   187

In file tracking.cpp

```
//personal data tracking

struct pers_data {
   int    age;              //in years
   int    weight;           //in kilograms
   int    height;           //in centimeters
   char   name[20];         //last name
};

void print(pers_data d)
{
   cout << d.name << " is " << d.age
        << " years old\n";
   cout << "weight : " << d.weight << "kg,  height : "
        << d.height << "cm." << endl;
}

int main()
{
   pers_data   laura = { 3, 14, 88, "POHL" };
                        //construction off the stack

   print(laura);         //calls copy constructor
}
```

What if we use constructors and allow the copy constructor to be provided by the compiler? Recall that this means the copy constructor does member-by-member copy, which can result in the wrong semantics—namely, shallow-copy semantics. In shallow-copy semantics no new value is created; instead, a pointer variable is assigned the address of the existing value. Take the case of reference semantics, where a copy implies that the reference counter is incremented. This would not happen with the compiler-provided copy constructor. Thus, objects copied in this manner would be under-counted and prematurely returned to free store. As a rule of thumb, the class provider should explicitly write out the copy constructor unless it is self-evident that memberwise copy is safe. Always be cautious if the aggregate has any members that are pointer-based.

Are there special rules for unions? Yes. This should not be surprising, since unions are a technique for having different objects share space. Unions cannot have members that have constructors or destructors, nor can they have `static` data members. Anonymous unions can have only public data members, and a global anonymous union must be declared `static`.

5.12.1 Destructor Details

A destructor is implicitly invoked when an object goes out of scope. Common cases include block exit and function exit.

```
my_string sub_str(char c, my_string b)
{
   my_string  temp;
   .....
   return temp;
}
```

In `sub_str()` we have b, a call-by-value argument of type `my_string`. Therefore, the copy constructor is invoked to create a local copy when the function is invoked. Correspondingly, a destructor is called on function exit. There is a local `my_string` variable, `temp`, that is constructed upon block entry to this function, and therefore must have its destructor invoked upon block exit. Finally, the `return` argument must be constructed and passed back into the calling environment. The corresponding destructor will be invoked depending on the scope of the object to which it is assigned.

It is possible to explicitly call a destructor:

```
p = new my_string("I dont need you long");
    //invokes my_string::my_string(const char*);
.....
p -> ~my_string();       //or p -> my_string::~my_string()
.....                    //but delete p is strongly preferred
```

5.13 Pragmatics

In constructors, initialization is to be preferred to assignment. For example,

```
ch_stack::ch_stack(int size)
   { s = new char[size]; assert(s != 0);
     max_len = size; top = EMPTY;}
```

is better written as

```
ch_stack::ch_stack(int size) : max_len(size), top(EMPTY)
   { s = new char[size]; assert(s != 0); }
```

As mentioned, data members that are reference declarations or `const` declarations must be initialized. Also, the compiler is often more efficient about initialization.

In classes that use `new` to construct objects, a copy constructor should be explicitly provided. The default compiler-provided copy constructor usually has the wrong semantics for such an object. In general, it is usual to provide a default and copy constructor with any class that uses pointers in its implementation. In Section 6.7, "Overloading Assignment and Subscripting Operators," on page 213, we shall see that such classes should have their own explicit definition of `operator=()`, as well. This insures that copying and assignment will be done safely.

In cases where constructors of one argument are not intended as conversions, C++ has the recently added keyword `explicit` to disable its conversion semantics.

```
class ch_stack {
public:
   explicit stack(int n);      //not used for conversion
.....
};
```

Summary

1. A constructor is a member function whose name is the class name. It constructs objects of its class type. This process may involve initializing data members and allocating free store using the operator `new`. A constructor is invoked when its associated type is used in a definition:

   ```
   TYPE_foo y(3);              //invoke TYPE_foo::TYPE_foo(int)
   extern TYPE_foo x;          //declaration but not definition
   ```

   Again, not all declarations are definitions. In those cases, no constructor is invoked.

2. A destructor is a member function whose name is the class name preceded by the tilde character ~. Its usual purpose is to destroy values of the class type, typically by using `delete`.

3. A constructor requiring no arguments is called the default constructor. This can be a constructor with an empty argument list or one whose arguments all have default values. It has the special purpose of initializing arrays of objects of its class.

4. A copy constructor of the form

   type::*type*(const *type*& x)

   is used to perform copying of one type value into another when:
   - A type variable is initialized by a type value.
   - A type value is passed as an argument in a function.
   - A type value is returned from a function.

   If the copy constructor is not present, the compiler provides one that does member-by-member initialization of value.

5. A class having members whose type requires a constructor uses initializers—a comma-separated list of constructor calls following a colon. The constructor is invoked by using the member name followed by an argument list in parentheses. The initialization is in the order of the declaration of the members.

6. An efficient disposal scheme for large aggregates is reference counting. Here, each dynamically allocated object tracks its active references. When an object is created, its reference count is set to one. Every time the object is newly referenced, its reference count is incremented. Every time the object loses a reference, its count is decremented. When the reference count becomes zero, the object's memory is disposed of.

7. Constructors of a single parameter are automatically conversion functions. They convert from the parameter type to the class type. For example, my_type::my_type(int); is a conversion from int to my_type. This property can be disallowed by declaring the constructor explicit.

Exercises

1. Discuss why constructors are almost always public member functions. What goes wrong if they are private?

2. Write a member function for the class mod_int:

   ```
   void add(int i);    //add i to v modulo 60
   ```

It should add the number i to the current value of v while retaining the modulo 60 feature of v.

3. Run the following program and explain its behavior. Placing debugging information inside constructors and destructors is a very useful step in developing efficient and correct classes.

```
//Constructors and destructors invoked
#include   <iostream.h>

class A {
public:
   A(int n) : xx(n)
      { cout << "A(int " << n << ") called" << endl;}
   A(double y) : xx(y + 0.5)
      { cout << "A(fl " << y << ") called" << endl; }
   ~A()
      { cout << "~A() with A::xx = " << xx << endl; }
private:
   int   xx;
};

int main()
{
   cout << "enter main\n";
   int     x = 14;
   float   y = 17.3;
   A       z(11), zz(11.5), zzz(0);

   cout << "\nOBJECT ALLOCATION LAYOUT\n";
   cout << "\nx is at " << &x;
   cout << "\ny is at " << &y;
   cout << "\nz is at " << &z;
   cout << "\nzz is at " << &zz;
   cout << "\nzzz is at " << &zzz;
   cout << "\n_____\n";
   zzz = A(x);     zzz = A(y);
   cout << "exit main" << endl;
}
```

Add a default constructor for class A:

```
A::A() : xx(0) { cout << "A() called" << endl; }
```

Now modify the program by declaring an array of type A:

```
A  d[5];    //declares array of 5 elements of type A
```

Assign the values 0, 1, 2, 3, and 4 to the data member xx of each d[i]. Run the program and explain its behavior.

4. Using the ch_stack type discussed in Section 5.2, "Constructing a Dynamically Sized Stack," on page 157, add a default constructor to allocate a ch_stack of 100 elements. Write a program that swaps the contents of two ch_stacks, using an array of ch_stacks to accomplish the job. The ch_stacks will be the first two stacks in the array. One method would be to use four ch_stacks: st[0], st[1], st[2], and st[3]. Push the contents of st[1] into st[2], of st[0] into st[3], of st[3] into st[1], and of st[2] into st[0]. Verify that the contents of the ch_stacks are in the same order by implementing a print() function that outputs all elements in the ch_stack. Can this be done with only three ch_stacks?

5. Write a Fortran version of a ch_stack and its related routines. Discuss and compare the Fortran code with the C++ code. Which is more efficient on your machine? Which supports data hiding better?

6. Add a constructor to the type ch_stack with the following prototype:

```
ch_stack::ch_stack(const char* c);
//initialize from char array
```

When does this provide a conversion? Is this desirable? How can the conversion be avoided?

7. Using the my_string type discussed in Section 5.4, "An Example: Dynamically Allocated Strings," on page 161, code the following member functions:

```
//strcmp is negative if s < s1,
//         is 0 if s == s1,
//         and is positive if s > s1
//         where s is the implicit argument
int my_string::strcmp(const my_string& s1);
```

```
//strrev  reverses the my_string
void my_string::strrev();

//print overloaded to print the first n characters
void my_string::print(int n);
```

8. Write a function that swaps two `my_strings`. Use it and `my_string::strcmp` from the previous exercise to write a program that will sort an array of `my_strings`.

9. Write a member function for class `functor` from Section 5.5, "The Class functor," on page 166:

    ```
    double functor::minv(double x0, double x1, double incr)
    ```

    that returns the x value for which the `functor` has smallest value in the given range (x0, x1) using increments of `incr`.

10. Write a member function for class `functor` from Section 5.5, "The Class functor," on page 166:

    ```
    double functor::zerov(double x0, double x1, double incr)
    ```

    that returns the x value for which the `functor` has a nearest-to-zero value in the given range (x0, x1) using increments of `incr`.

11. Using the `dbl_vect` type in Section 5.6, "The Class dbl_vect," on page 167, code the following member functions:

    ```
    //adds all the element values and returns their sum
    double dbl_vect::sumelem();

    //prints all the elements
    void dbl_vect::print();

    //adds two vectors into a third  v(implicit) = v1+v2
    void dbl_vect::add(const dbl_vect& v1, const dbl_vect& v2);

    //adds two vectors and returns  v(implicit) + v1
    dbl_vect dbl_vect::add(const dbl_vect& v1);
    ```

12. Write a further constructor for dbl_vect that accepts an int array and its size and constructs a dbl_vect with these initial values:

    ```
    dbl_vect::dbl_vect(const dbl_vect* d, int sz);
    ```

13. Try to benchmark the speed differences between safe arrays, as represented by class dbl_vect, and ordinary integer arrays. Repeatedly run an element summation routine using int a[10000] and one using the dbl_vect a(10000). Time your trials. Useful timing functions can be found in *time.h*.

14. Using the class dbl_vect in Section 5.6, "The Class dbl_vect," on page 167, define the class multi_v as follows:

    ```
    class multi_v {
    public:
       multi_v(int i) : a(i), b(i), c(i), size(i) {}
       void  assign(int ind, int i, int j, int k);
       void  retrieve(int ind, int& i,
                      int& j, int& k) const;
       void  print(int ind) const;
       int   ub() const { return (size - 1); }
    private:
       dbl_vect   a, b, c;
       int    size;
    };
    ```

    Write and test code for the member functions assign(), retrieve(), and print(). The function assign() should assign i, j, and k to a[ind], b[ind], and c[ind], respectively. The function retrieve() does the inverse of assign(). The function print() should print the three values a[ind], b[ind], and c[ind].

15. Use the slist type discussed in Section 5.8, "Example: A Singly Linked List," on page 171, to code the following member functions:

    ```
    //slist constructor whose initializer is char array
    slist::slist(const char* c);

    //length returns the length of the slist
    int slist::length();

    //return number of elements whose data value is c
    int slist::count_c(char c);
    ```

16. Write a member function append() that will add a list to the end of the implicit list argument, then clear the appended slist by zeroing the head:

    void slist::append(slist& e);

17. Write a member function copy() that will copy a list:

    //the implicit argument ends up a copy of e
    void slist::copy(const slist& e);

    Be sure to destroy the implicit list before you do the copy. You want a special test to avoid the list's copying to itself.

18. Use the slist type and add the equivalent member functions that give you stack functions:

    reset   push   pop   top_of   empty

    Using one data structure as the implementation for another data structure is known as *adapting* the data structure. This idea is used extensively by the standard template library.

19. As written, slist::del() expects a nonempty list. What goes wrong if it is passed an empty list? See the effect on your system. Modify this routine to test for this condition and continue. Note that this can be tested as an assertion, but will then abort on the empty list.

20. Add a constructor to slistelem and use it to simplify the coding of the member function slist::prepend(char c).

21. Modify the matrix class to have a constructor that performs a transpose (see Section 5.9, "Two-Dimensional Arrays," on page 176). Its second argument will be an enumerated type that indicates what transformation should be made on the array.

    enum transform { transpose, negative, upper };

    matrix::matrix(const matrix& a, transform t)
    {
    //transpose   base[i][j] = a.base[j][i]
    //negative   base[i][j] = -a.base[i][j]
    //upper   base[i][j] = a.base[i][j] i <= j else 0
    }

22. Write a member function that will return the eigen values of a `matrix`.

23. Complete the polynomial package by writing the code for the routines `void polynomial::release()` and `void polynomial::print()`, which are not found in the text. (See Section 5.10, "Polynomials as a Linked List," on page 178.)

24. Write code for the polynomial addition routine `void polynomial::plus()`.

25. Rewrite `void polynomial::plus()` so that `c.plus(c, c)` works correctly. (See Section 5.10, "Polynomials as a Linked List," on page 183.)

26. Make the constructor for `polynomial` more robust. Assume that the coefficient-exponent pairs are not necessarily in sorted order and take this into account when writing the constructor. (See Section 5.10, "Polynomials as a Linked List," on page 181.

27. Improve the reference-counted form of class `my_string` by asserting in appropriate member functions that `ref_cnt` is not negative. Why would you want to do this? (See Section 5.11, "Strings Using Reference Semantics," on page 184.)

28. We wish to define a C++ class that will resemble sets in Pascal. The underlying representation will be a 32-bit machine word:

```
//Implementation of an ADT for type set.
const unsigned long int  masks[32] = {
   0x80000000, 0x40000000, 0x20000000, 0x10000000,
   0x8000000, 0x4000000, 0x2000000, 0x1000000,
   0x800000, 0x400000, 0x200000, 0x100000,
   0x80000, 0x40000, 0x20000, 0x10000,
   0x8000, 0x4000, 0x2000, 0x1000,
   0x800, 0x400, 0x200, 0x100,
   0x80, 0x40, 0x20, 0x10, 0x8, 0x4, 0x2, 0x1};
```

```
class set {
public:
   set(unsigned long int i) { t = i; }
   set() { t = 0x0; }
   void  u_add(int i) { t |= masks[i]; }
   void  u_sub(int i) { t &= ~masks[i]; }
   bool  in(int i) const
      { return bool( (t & masks[i]) != 0); }
   void  pr_mems() const;
   set   set_union(const set& v) const
      { return (set(t | v.t)); }
private:
   unsigned long int  t;
};
```

Write the code for pr_mems to print out all the elements of the set. Write the code for the member function intersection to return the resulting set intersection.

Chapter 6

Operator Overloading and Conversions

Polymorphism is a means of giving different meanings to the same message. The meanings are dependent on the type of data being processed. Object orientation takes advantage of polymorphism by linking behavior to the object's type. Operators such as + and << have distinct meanings overloaded by operand type.

Conversion is the explicit or implicit change of value between types. Conversions provide a form of polymorphism. Overloading of functions gives the same function name different meanings. The name has several interpretations that depend on function selection. This is called *ad hoc polymorphism*. This chapter discusses overloading, especially operator overloading, and conversions of data types.

Operators are overloaded and selected based on the signature-matching algorithm. Overloading operators gives them new meanings. For example, the expression a + b has different meanings depending on the types of the variables a and b. Overloading the operator + for user-defined types allows them to be used in addition expressions in much the same way native types would be used. The expression a + b could mean string concatenation, complex-number addition, or integer addition, depending on whether the variables were the ADT my_string, the ADT complex, or the native type int. Mixed type expressions are also made possible by defining conversion functions. This chapter also discusses friend functions and their importance to operator overloading.

One principle of OOP is that user-defined types must enjoy the same privileges as native types. The client expects the convenience of using these types without regard to a native/nonnative distinction. The ability of the manufacturer to achieve this result is the test of the adequacy of the language for OOP use. Native types in the kernel language can be mixed in expressions because it is convenient and would otherwise be burdensome to designate conventionally expected conversions.

6.1 ADT Conversions

Explicit type conversion of an expression is necessary when either the implicit conversions are not desired or the expression will not otherwise be legal. One aim of OOP using C++ is the integration of user-defined ADTs and built-in types. To achieve this, there is a mechanism for having a member function provide an explicit conversion.

In the last chapter we discussed a constructor of one argument's being a de facto type conversion from the argument's type to the constructor's class type.

```
point::point(double u);
```

This is automatically a type conversion from `double` to `point`, unless it is disabled by declaring such a conversion constructor with the modifier `explicit`. It is available both explicitly and implicitly. Explicitly, it is used as a conversion operation in either cast or functional form. Thus,

```
point s;
double  d = 3.5;

s = static_cast<point>(d);
```

and

```
s = d;            //implicit invocation of conversion
```

both work.

These are conversions from an already defined type to a user-defined type. However, it is not possible for the user to add a constructor to a built-in type such as `int` or `double`. A conversion function for a user-defined type can be created by defining a special conversion function inside the class. The general form of such a member function is:

```
operator type() { ····· }
```

Such a member function must be nonstatic. It cannot have parameters and does not have a declared return type. It must return an expression of the designated type.

In the `point` example, one may want a conversion from `point` to `double`. This can be done for the `point` class as follows.

In file point2.cpp

```
point::operator double()        //use distance from origin
{
    return sqrt(x * x + y * y);
}
```

Notice that we used a commonly accepted conversion that is by no means unique. Another possibility would have been to return the x value only. Unless there is universal agreement on a conversion, it is best to omit such functions, as they can readily lead to unintended results.

6.2 Overloading and Function Selection

Overloaded functions are an important addition in C++. The overloaded meaning is selected by matching the argument list of the function call to the argument list of the function declaration. When an overloaded function is invoked, the compiler must have a selection algorithm with which to pick the appropriate function. The algorithm that accomplishes this depends on what type conversions are available. A best match must be unique. It must be best on at least one argument and as good as any other match on all other arguments.

The matching algorithm for each argument is as shown in the following list.

Overloaded Function Selection Algorithm

1. Use an exact match if found.

2. Try standard type promotions.

3. Try standard type conversions.

4. Try user-defined conversions.

5. Use a match to ellipsis if found.

Standard promotions—conversions from `float` to `double`, and from `bool`, `char`, `short`, or `enum` to `int`—are better than other standard conversions. Standard conversions also include pointer conversions.

An exact match is clearly best. Casts can be used to force such a match. The compiler will complain about ambiguous situations. Thus, it is poor practice to rely on subtle type distinctions and implicit conversions that obscure the overloaded function. When in doubt, use explicit conversions to provide an exact match.

Let us write an overloaded function `greater()` and follow our algorithm for various invocations. In this example, the user type `rational` is available:

In file rational.cpp

```
//Overloading functions
class rational {
public:
   rational(int n = 0) : a(n),q(1){}
   rational(int i, int j) : a(i), q(j){}
   rational(double r) : q(BIG), a(r * BIG){}
   void  print() const { cout << a << " / " << q ; }
   operator double() { return static_cast<double>(a)/q; }
private:
   long  a, q;
   enum { BIG = 100 };
};

inline int     greater(int i, int j)
      { return ( i > j ? i : j); }
inline double  greater(double x, double y)
      { return ( x > y ? x : y); }
inline rational greater(rational w, rational z)
      { return ( w > z ? w : z); }

int main()
{
   int     i = 10, j = 5;
   float   x = 7.0;
   double  y = 14.5;
   rational w(10), z(3.5), zmax;

   cout << "\ngreater(" << i << ", " << j << ") = "
        << greater(i, j);
   cout << "\ngreater(" << x << ", " << y << ") = "
        << greater(x, y);
   cout << "\ngreater(" << i << ", " ;
   z.print();
   cout << ") = " << greater(static_cast<rational>(i), z);
   zmax = greater(w, z);
```

```
        cout << "\ngreater(";
        w.print();
        cout << ", ";
        z.print();
        cout << ") = ";
        zmax.print();
}
```

The output from this program is:

```
greater(10, 5) = 10
greater(7, 14.5) = 14.5
greater(10, 350 / 100) = 10
greater(10 / 1, 350 / 100) = 10 / 1
```

A variety of conversion rules, both implicit and explicit, are being applied. We explain these in the following dissection.

Dissection of the *rational* Program

- `rational(double r) : q(BIG), a(r * BIG){}`

This constructor converts from `double` to `rational`.

- `operator double() { return static_cast<double>(a)/q; }`

This member function converts from `rational` to `double`.

- ```
  inline int      greater(int i, int j)
                  { return ( i > j ? i : j); }
  inline double   greater(double x, double y)
                  { return ( x > y ? x : y); }
  inline rational greater(rational w, rational z)
                  { return ( w > z ? w : z); }
  ```

Three distinct functions are overloaded. The most interesting has `rational` type for its argument list variables and its return type. The conversion member function `operator double()` is required to evaluate `w > z`. Later, we shall show how to overload `operator>()` to take `rational` types directly.
  ```

- ```
  cout << "\ngreater(" << i << ", " << j << ") = "
       << greater(i, j);
  cout << "\ngreater(" << x << ", " << y << ") = "
       << greater(x, y);
  ```

The first statement selects the first definition of `greater()` because of the exact-match rule. The second statement selects the second definition of `greater()` because of the use of a standard widening conversion `float` to `double`. The value of variable `x` is widened to `double`.

- ```
  << greater(static_cast<rational>(i), z);
  ```

The second definition of `greater()` is selected because of the exact-match rule. The explicit conversion of `i` to a `rational` is necessary to avoid ambiguity.

- ```
  zmax = greater(w, z);
  ```

This is an exact match for the third definition.

See exercise 3, on page 234, for more on the *rational* program.

6.3 Friend Functions

The keyword `friend` is a function specifier. It gives a nonmember function access to the hidden members of the class, and provides a method of escaping the data hiding restrictions of C++. However, we must have a good reason for escaping these restrictions, as they are important to reliable programming.

One reason for using friend functions is that some functions need privileged access to more than one class. A second reason is that friend functions pass all of their arguments through the argument list, and each argument value is subject to assignment-compatible conversions. Conversions would apply to a class variable passed explicitly, and would be especially useful in cases of operator overloading, as seen in the next section.

A friend function must be declared inside the class declaration to which it is a friend. The function is prefaced by the keyword `friend`, and can appear in any part of the class without affecting its meaning. Our preferred style is to place the `friend` declaration in the public part of the class. Since access has no effect on `friend` declarations, they are conceptually public. Member functions of one class can be friend functions of another class. In this case, they are written in the `friend`'s class using
  ```

the scope resolution operator to qualify its function name. If all member functions of one class are friend functions of a second class, this can be specified by writing friend class *class-name*.

The following declarations illustrate the syntax.

```
class tweedledee {
   .....
   friend void  alice();        //friend function
   int  cheshire();             //member function
   .....
};

class tweedledum {
   .....
   friend int  tweedledee::cheshire();
   .....
};

class tweedledumber {
   .....
   friend class tweedledee;     //all member functions of
   .....                        //tweedledee have access
};
```

Consider the classes matrix (see Section 5.9, "Two-Dimensional Arrays," on page 176,) and dbl_vect (see Section 5.6, "The Class dbl_vect," on page 167). A function multiplying a vector by a matrix as represented by these two classes could be written efficiently if it had access to the private members of both classes. It would be a friend function of both classes. In our discussion, safe access was provided to the elements of dbl_vect and matrix with the member function element(). One could write a multiply function using element() without requiring friend status. However, the price in function-call overhead and array-bounds checking would make such a matrix multiply unnecessarily inefficient.

In file matrix2.cpp

```
class matrix;          //forward reference

class dbl_vect {
public:
   friend dbl_vect mpy(const dbl_vect& v, const matrix& m);
   .....
private:
   double*  p;
   int     size;
};

class matrix {
public:
   friend dbl_vect  mpy(const dbl_vect& v, const matrix& m);
   .....
private:
   double**   p;
   int       s1, s2;
};

   //use privileged access to p in both classes
dbl_vect mpy(const dbl_vect& v, const matrix& m)
{
   assert(v.size == m.s1);              //check sizes

   dbl_vect   ans(m.s2);
   int    i, j;

   for (i = 0; i <= m.ub2(); ++i) {
      ans.p[i] = 0;
      for (j = 0; j <= m.ub1(); ++j)
         ans.p[i] += v.p[j] * m.p[j][i];
   }
   return ans;
}
```

A minor point is that a forward declaration of the class matrix is necessary. This is because the function mpy() must appear in both classes, and it uses each class as an argument type.

The OOP paradigm is that objects (in C++, class variables) should be accessed through their public members. Only member functions should have access to the hidden implementation of the ADT. This is a neat, orderly design principle. The friend function, however, straddles this boundary. It has access to private members, but is not itself a member function. It can be used to provide quick fixes to code that needs access to the implementation details of a class. But the mechanism is easily abused.

6.4 Overloading Operators

The keyword `operator` is used to define a type-conversion member function. It is also used to overload the built-in C++ operators. Just as a function name, such as `print()`, can be given a variety of meanings that depend on its arguments, so can an operator, such as +, be given additional meanings. *Overloading operators* allows infix expressions of both ADTs and built-in types to be written. It is an important notational convenience, and in many instances leads to shorter and more readable programs.

Unary and binary operators can be overloaded as nonstatic member functions. Implicitly they are acting on a class value. Most unary operators can be overloaded as ordinary functions, taking a single argument of class or reference to class type. Most binary operators can be overloaded as ordinary functions, taking one or both arguments of class or reference to class type. The operators =, (), [], and -> must be overloaded with a nonstatic member function.

```
class foo {
public:
   foo   operator-();            //overload unary minus
   foo   operator-(int);         //binary minus foo-int
   foo   operator-(foo);         //binary minus foo-foo
};

foo operator-(int, foo);         //binary minus int-foo
foo operator-(int, foo*);        //illegal:need foo or foo&
```

The previous section's `mpy()` function could have been written as:

```
dbl_vect operator*(const dbl_vect& v, const matrix& m)
   .....
```

If this had been done, and if r and s were `dbl_vect` and t was a `matrix`, then the natural-looking infix expression

```
r = s * t;
```

would invoke the multiply function. This replaces the functional notation

    r = mpy(s, t);

Although meanings can be added to operators, their associativity and precedence remain the same. For example, the multiplication operator will remain of higher precedence than the addition operator. The operator precedence table for C++ is included in Appendix B, "Operator Precedence and Associativity." Almost all operators can be overloaded. The exceptions are the member operator ., the member object selector operator .*, the ternary conditional expression operator ? :, the `sizeof` operator, and the scope resolution operator ::. (See Section D.12.5, "Operator Overloading," on page 447.)

Available operators include all the arithmetic, logical, comparison, equality, assignment, and bit operators. Furthermore, the autoincrement and autodecrement operators, ++ and --, can have distinct prefix and postfix meanings. (See exercise 25, on page 240.) The subscript or index operator [] and the function call () can also be overloaded. The structure pointer operator -> and the member pointer selector operator ->* can be overloaded. (See exercise 26, on page 241.) It is also possible to overload `new` and `delete`. The assignment, function call, subscripting, and class pointer operators can be overloaded only by nonstatic member functions.

6.5 Unary Operator Overloading

We continue our discussion of operator overloading by demonstrating how to overload unary operators, such as !, ++, ~, and []. For this purpose, we develop the class `clock`, which can be used to store time as days, hours, minutes, and seconds. We shall develop familiar operations on `clock`.

In file clock.cpp

```
class clock {
public:
   clock(unsigned long i);        //construct & conversion
   void  print() const;           //formatted printout
   void  tick();                  //add one second
   clock  operator++() { tick(); return *this; }
private:
   unsigned long  tot_secs, secs, mins, hours, days;
};
```

This class overloads the prefix autoincrement operator; it is a member function, and can be invoked on its implicit single argument. The member function `tick` adds one second to the implicit argument of the overloaded ++ operator.

```
inline clock::clock(unsigned long i)
{
   tot_secs = i;
   secs = tot_secs % 60;
   mins = (tot_secs / 60) % 60;
   hours = (tot_secs / 3600) % 24;
   days = tot_secs / 86400;
}

void clock::tick()
{
   clock  temp = clock(++tot_secs);

   secs = temp.secs;
   mins = temp.mins;
   hours = temp.hours;
   days = temp.days;
}
```

The constructor performs the usual conversions from `tot_secs` to days, hours, minutes, and seconds. For example, there are 86,400 seconds in a day; therefore, integer division by this constant gives the whole number of days. The member function `tick()` constructs `clock temp`, which adds one second to the total time. The constructor acts as a conversion function that properly updates the time.

The overloaded `operator++()` also updates the implicit `clock` variable and returns the updated value as well. It could have been coded in the same way as `tick()`, except that the statement

```
return temp;
```

would be added.

Adding the following code, we can test our functions:

```
void clock::print() const
{
   cout << days << " d :" << hours << " h :"
        << mins << " m :" << secs << " s" << endl;
}
```

```
//Clock and overloaded operators
int main()
{
   clock  t1(59), t2(172799); //172799 = 2 days-1 sec

   cout << "initial times are" << endl;
   t1.print();
   t2.print();
   ++t1;   ++t2;
   cout << "after one second times are" << endl;
   t1.print();
   t2.print();
}
```

The output is:

```
initial times are
0 d :0 h :0 m :59 s
1 d :23 h :59 m :59 s
after one second times are
0 d :0 h :1 m :0 s
2 d :0 h :0 m :0 s
```

It is also possible to overload prefix ++ using an ordinary function:

```
clock operator++(clock& cl)
{
   cl.tick();
   return cl;
}
```

Notice that the clock variable must advance by one second; we use call-by-reference.

The decision to choose between a member function representation and a nonmember function typically depends on whether or not implicit conversion operations are available and desirable. Explicit argument passing allows the argument to be automatically coerced if necessary and possible. When overloaded as a member function,

++c   is equivalent to   c.operator++()

When overloaded as a nonmember function,

++c   is equivalent to   operator++(c)

6.6 Binary Operator Overloading

We continue with our `clock` example and show how to overload binary operators. Basically the same principles hold. When a binary operator is overloaded using a member function, it has as its first argument the implicitly passed class variable, and as its second argument the lone argument-list parameter. Friend functions and ordinary functions have both arguments specified in the parameter list. Of course, ordinary functions cannot access private members.

Let us create an operation for type `clock` that will add two values together.

In file clock.cpp

```
class clock {
    .....
    friend clock  operator+(clock c1, clock c2);
};

clock operator+(clock c1, clock c2)
{
    return (c1.tot_secs + c2.tot_secs);
}
```

The integer expression is implicitly converted to a `clock` by the conversion constructor `clock::clock(unsigned long)`. Both `clock` values are passed as function arguments, and both are candidates for assignment conversions. Because `operator+()` is a symmetric binary operator, the arguments should be treated identically. Thus, it is normal for symmetric binary operators to be overloaded by friend functions.

In contrast, let us overload binary minus with a member function:

```
class clock {
    .....
    clock  operator-(clock c);
};

clock clock::operator-(clock c)
{
    return (tot_secs - c.tot_secs);
}
```

Remember that there is an implicit first argument. This takes some getting used to. It would have been better to use a friend function for binary minus, because of the symmetric treatment of the arguments.

We shall define a multiplication operation as a binary operation with one argument an `unsigned int` and the second a `clock` variable. The operation will require the use of a friend function. It cannot be done with a member function because, as already stated, member functions have as their implicit first argument the `this` pointer.

```
clock operator*(unsigned long m, clock c)
{
   return (m * c.tot_secs);
}
```

This requirement forces the multiplication to have a fixed ordering that is type-dependent. In order to avoid this, it is common practice to write a second overloaded function:

```
clock operator*(clock c, unsigned long m)
{
   return (m * c.tot_secs);
}
```

An alternate defines the second function in terms of the first as follows:

```
clock operator*(clock c, unsigned long m)
{
   return (m * c);
}
```

Defining the second implementation in terms of the first implementation reduces code redundancy and maintains consistency.

6.7 Overloading Assignment and Subscripting Operators

The assignment operator for a class type is by default generated by the compiler to have member-by-member assignment. This is fine when shallow copying is suitable, for example with `rational` or `point`. For types, such as `my_string` and `dbl_vect`, that need deep copying, this is incorrect. As a rule of thumb, anytime a class needs an explicit copy constructor defined, it also needs an assignment operator defined.

The subscripting operator is usually overloaded where a class type represents an aggregate for which indexing is appropriate. The index operation is expected to return a reference to an element contained within the aggregate. Overloading assignment and subscripting share several characteristics. Both must be done as nonstatic member functions, and both usually involve a reference return type.

We shall reimplement the class `dbl_vect`, extending its functionality by applying operator overloading. (See Section 5.6, "The Class dbl_vect," on page 167.) The reimplemented class will have several improvements to make it both safer and more useful. A constructor that converts an ordinary integer array to a safe array will be added. This will allow us to develop code using safe arrays and later run the same code efficiently on ordinary arrays. The public data member `ub` has been changed to a member function. This prevents a user from inadvertently introducing a program error by modifying the member. Finally, the subscript operator is overloaded, and replaces the member function `element`.

In file dbl_vect2.h

```
//A safe array type dbl_vect with [] overloaded
class dbl_vect {
public:
   //constructors and destructor
   explicit dbl_vect(int n = 10);
   dbl_vect(const dbl_vect& v);
   dbl_vect(const double a[], int n);   //initialize by array
   ~dbl_vect() { delete []p; }
   //other member functions
   int  ub()const { return (size-1); }  //upper bound
   int& operator[](int i) ;              //range checked
private:
   double* p;                            //base pointer
   int    size;                          //number of elements
};
```

```
dbl_vect::dbl_vect(int n) : size(n)
{
   assert(n > 0);
   p = new double[size];
   assert(p != 0);
}

dbl_vect::dbl_vect(const double a[], int n) : size(n)
{
   assert(n > 0);
   p = new double[size];
   assert(p != 0);
   for (int i = 0; i < size; ++i)
      p[i] = a[i];
}

dbl_vect::dbl_vect(const dbl_vect& v) : size(v.size)
{
   p = new double[size];
   assert(p != 0);
   for (int i = 0; i < size; ++i)
      p[i] = v.p[i];
}

double& dbl_vect::operator[](int i)
{
   assert(i >= 0 && i < size);
   return p[i];
}
```

An overloaded subscript operator can have any return type and any argument list type. However, it is good style to maintain the consistency between a user-defined meaning and standard usage. Thus, the most common function prototype is:

class-name& operator[](*integral type*);

Such functions can be used on either side of an assignment.

It is also convenient to be able to assign one array to another. The user can specify the behavior of assignment by overloading it. It is good style to be consistent with standard usage. The following member function overloads assignment for class dbl_vect:

```
dbl_vect& dbl_vect::operator=(const dbl_vect& v)
{
   if (this != &v) {            //do nothing if assigned to self
      assert(v.size == size);
      for (int i = 0; i < size; ++i)
         p[i] = v.p[i];
   }
   return *this;
}
```

Dissection of dbl_vect::operator=(const dbl_vect& v) Function

- dbl_vect& dbl_vect::operator=(const dbl_vect& v)

The operator=() function returns reference to dbl_vect and has one explicit argument of type reference to dbl_vect. The first argument of the assignment operator is the implicit argument. The function could have been written to return void, but then it would not have allowed multiple assignment.

- if (this != &v) {

Don't do anything if assignment is to the current variable.

- assert(v.size == size);

A guarantee that the sizes are compatible.

- for (int i = 0; i < size; ++i)
     p[i] = v.p[i];
  return (*this);

The explicit argument v.p[] will be the right side of the assignment; the implicit argument p[] will be the left side. The self-referential pointer is dereferenced and passed back as the value of the expression. This allows multiple assignment with right-to-left associativity to be defined.

Expressions of type dbl_vect can be evaluated by overloading in appropriate ways the various arithmetic operators. As an example, let us overload binary + to mean element-by-element addition of two dbl_vect variables.

```
dbl_vect dbl_vect::operator+(const dbl_vect& v)
{
   assert(size == v.size);
   dbl_vect sum(size);
   for (int i = 0; i < size; ++i)
      sum.p[i] = p[i] + v.p[i];
   return sum;
}
```

Now with the class `dbl_vect`, the following expressions are meaningful:

```
a = b;                      //a, b are type dbl_vect
a = b = c;                  //a, b, c are type dbl_vect
a = dbl_vect(data, DSIZE);  //convert array data[DSIZE]
a = b + a;                  //assignment and addition
a = b + (c = a) + d;        //complicated expression
```

The class `dbl_vect` is a full-fledged ADT. It behaves and appears in client code much as any built-in type behaves and appears.

Notice that overloading both the assignment and plus operators does not imply that `operator+=` is overloaded. Indeed, it is the class designer's responsibility to make sure the various operators have consistent semantics. It is customary to overload related sets of operators consistently.

6.8 Polynomial: Type and Language Expectations

A type's behavior is largely dictated by expectations found in the community that uses it. So how a polynomial behaves is determined by the mathematical community's definitions. When we come to write a polynomial type, we expect that the basic mathematical operations, such as +, -, *, and /, are available and work appropriately. Furthermore, we expect that assignment operators, equality operators, and increment and decrement operators provided are consistent with the C++ community's expectations. A class provides a public interface that is easy to use insofar as it meets both expectations. Where there is no normal expectation for operators, they should not be overloaded.

A more realistic polynomial class based on the representation in Section 5.10, "Polynomials as a Linked List," on page 178, could have the following declaration.

6.8 ▼ Polynomial: Type and Language Expectations 217

In file poly2.cpp

```
//Polynomials with overloaded arithmetic operators
class polynomial {
public:
   polynomial();
   polynomial(const polynomial& p);
   polynomial(int size, double coef[], int expon[]);
   ~polynomial() { release(); }
   void print() const;
   double operator()(double x) const;   //evaluate P(x)
   polynomial& operator=(const polynomial& a);
   friend polynomial& operator+(const polynomial& a,
                                const polynomial& b);
   friend polynomial& operator-(const polynomial& a,
                                const polynomial& b);
   friend polynomial& operator*(const polynomial& a,
                                const polynomial& b);
   friend polynomial& operator/(const polynomial& a,
                                const polynomial& b);
   friend polynomial& operator-(const polynomial& a);
   friend polynomial& operator+=(polynomial& a,
                                 const polynomial& b);
   friend bool operator==(const polynomial& a,
                          const polynomial& b);
   friend bool operator!=(const polynomial& a,
                          const polynomial& b);
private:
   term*   h;
   int     degree;
   void    prepend(term* t);
   void    add_term(term*& a, term*& b);
   void    release();
   void    rest_of(term* rest);
   void    reverse();
};
```

We expect both the basic mathematical operations to work and the basic relationships among C++ operators to hold. It would be very undesirable to have operator=(), operator+(), and operator+=() all defined and not have a = a + b give the same result as a += b.

The code for overloading operator= is as follows.

In file poly2.cpp

```
polynomial& polynomial::operator=(const polynomial& a)
{
   if (h != a.h) {                    //avoid a = a case
      release();                      //garbage collect old value
      polynomial* temp = new polynomial(a);
      h = temp -> h;
      degree = temp -> degree;
   }
   return *this;
}
```

The implementation of the other operators is left as an exercise (see exercise 29, on page 242).

6.9 Overloading I/O Operators << and >>

In keeping with the spirit of OOP, it is important to overload << to output user-defined types as well as native types. The operator << has two arguments—an `ostream&` and the ADT—and it must produce an `ostream&`. You want to use a reference to a stream and return a reference to a stream, whenever overloading << or >>, because you do not want to copy a stream object. Let us write these functions for the type `rational`:

In file rational.cpp

```
class rational {
public:
   friend ostream&
      operator<<(ostream& out, rational x);
   friend istream&
      operator>>(istream& in, rational& x)
   .....
private:
   long  a, q;
};
```

```
ostream& operator<<(ostream& out, rational x)
{
    return (out << x.a << " / " << x.q << '\t');
}
```

When overloading the operator >> to produce input to a user-defined type, the typical form is:

```
istream& operator>>(istream& p, user-defined type& x)
```

If the function needs access to private members of x, it must be made a friend of its class. A key point is to make x a reference parameter so that its value can be modified. To do this for `rational` would require placing a `friend` declaration for this operator in the class `rational` and providing its function definition.

```
istream& operator>>(istream& in, rational& x)
{
    return (in >> x.a >> x.q);
}
```

6.10 Overloading Operator () for Indexing

A matrix type that provides dynamically allocated two-dimensional arrays can be designed with the function call operator overloaded to provide element selection. This is a good example of a container class that is useful with both scientific and nonscientific computation.

The function call operator () is overloadable as a nonstatic member function. It can be overloaded with respect to different signatures. It is frequently used to provide an iterator operation (see exercise 12, on page 236 through exercise 14, on page 237) or an operation requiring multiple indices.

In file matrix3.cpp

```cpp
//dynamic matrix type
class matrix {
public:
   matrix(int c, int r);
   ~matrix();
   double& operator()(int i, int j);
   matrix& operator=(const matrix& m);
   matrix& operator+=(matrix& m);
private:
   int c_size, r_size;
   double  **p;
};

matrix:: matrix(int c, int r):c_size(c), r_size(r)
{
   p = new double*[c];
   assert(p != 0);
   for (int i = 0; i < c; ++i){
      p[i] = new double[r];
      assert(p[i] != 0);
   }
}

matrix:: ~matrix()
{
   for (int i = 0; i < c_size; ++i)
      delete [] p[i];
   delete [] p;
}

inline double& matrix::operator()(int i, int j)
{
   assert( i >= 0 && i < c_size &&
           j >= 0 && j < r_size);
   return p[i][j];
}
```

6.10 ▼ Overloading Operator () for Indexing

```
matrix& matrix::operator=(const matrix& m)
{
   assert(m.c_size == c_size && m.r_size == r_size);
   int i, j;

   for (i = 0; i < c_size; ++i)
      for (j = 0; j < r_size; ++j)
         p[i][j] = m.p[i][j];
   return (*this);
}

matrix& matrix::operator+=(matrix& m)
{
   assert(m.c_size == c_size && m.r_size == r_size);
   int i, j;

   for (i = 0; i < c_size; ++i)
      for (j = 0; j < r_size; ++j)
         p[i][j] += m.p[i][j];
   return *this;
}
```

Dissection of the class matrix

- ```
  inline double& matrix::operator()(int i, int j)
  {
     assert( i >= 0 && i < c_size &&
             j >= 0 && j < r_size);
     return p[i][j];
  }
  ```

This member function gives a convenient multiple-argument notation for element access. This results in client code using expressions of the form m(i, j) to access explicit matrix elements. Notice how matrix indices are bounds-tested through an assertion.

- ```
  matrix& matrix::operator+=(matrix& m)
  {
     assert(m.c_size == c_size && m.r_size == r_size);
  ```

The assertion macro is used with a testable precondition for arguments needed by this member function. The matrix being assigned to must be the same size as the matrix expression being computed. The code replaces an `if-else` statement that would perform an error exit. Compare this to the code written for class `dbl_vect` (see Section 5.6, "The Class dbl_vect," on page 167).

- ```
  for (i = 0; i < c_size; ++i)
      for (j = 0; j < r_size; ++j)
          p[i][j] += m.p[i][j];
  ```

This inner loop is efficient and transparent. Elementwise addition is being accomplished without overhead.

- ```
  return (*this);
  ```

The return type is a *reference* to `matrix`. Dereferencing the `this` pointer causes the lvalue of the `matrix` object to be returned. This is the usual trick that allows multiple assignment to occur.

This code is expanded in exercise 31, on page 242.

6.11 Pointer Operators

The structure pointer operator `->` is overloaded as a nonstatic class member function. The overloaded structure pointer operator is a unary operator on its left operand. The argument must be either a class object or a reference of this type. It can return either a pointer to a class object, an object of a class for which `operator ->` is defined, or a reference to a class for which `operator ->` is defined.

In the following example we overload the structure pointer operator inside the class `t_ptr`. Objects of type `t_ptr` act as controlled-access pointers to objects of type `triple`.

In file triple.cpp

```cpp
// Overloading the structure pointer operator.
#include <iostream.h>

class triple {
public:
   triple(int a, int b, int c) { i = a; j = b; k = c; }
   void print() { cout << "\ni = " << i << ", j = "
                       << j << ", k = " << k; }
private:
   int     i, j, k;
};

triple   unauthor(0, 0, 0);

class t_ptr {
public:
   t_ptr(bool f, triple* p) { access = f; ptr = p; }
   triple*  operator ->() ;
private:
   bool   access;
   triple*  ptr;
};

triple* t_ptr::operator->()
{
   if (access)
      return (ptr);
   else {
      cout << "\nunauthorized access";
      return &unauthor;
   }
}
```

The variable `t_ptr::access` is tested by the overloaded `operator ->`, and, if `true`, access is granted. The following code illustrates this.

```
int main()
{
    triple  a(1, 2, 3), b(4, 5, 6);
    t_ptr ta(false, &a), tb(true, &b);

    ta -> print();              //access denied
    tb -> print();              //access granted
}
```

6.11.1 Pointer to Class Member

A pointer to class member is distinct from a pointer to class. A pointer to class member's type is *T::**, where *T* is the class name. C++ has two operators that act to dereference a pointer to class member. The pointer-to-member operators are:

```
.*
->*
```

Think of *obj.*ptr_mem* and *pointer->*ptr_mem* as first accessing the object and then accessing and dereferencing the member that is specified.

The following code shows how to use these operators.

In file showhide.cpp

```
//Pointer to class member.

#include <iostream.h>

class X {
public:
   int  visible;
   void print()
        { cout << "\nhide = " << hide
               << " visible = " << visible; }
   void reset() { visible = hide; }
   void set(int i) { hide = i; }
private:
   int  hide;
};
```

```
typedef void (X::*pfcn)();

int main()
{
   X   a, b, *pb = &b;
   int X::*pXint = &X::visible;
   pfcn pF = &X::print;

   a.set(8); a.reset();
   b.set(4); b.reset();
   a.print();
   a.*pXint += 1;
   a.print();
   cout << "\nb.visible = " << pb ->*pXint;
   (b.*pF)();
   pF = &X::reset;
   (a.*pF)();
   a.print();
   cout << endl;
}
```

The output is as follows:

```
hide = 8 visible = 8
hide = 8 visible = 9
b.visible = 4
hide = 4 visible = 4
hide = 8 visible = 8
```

Dissection of the *showhide* Program

- `typedef void (X::*pfcn)();`

This says that `pfcn` is a pointer to class X member whose base type is a function with no arguments that returns `void`. Member functions `X::print` and `X::reset` match this type.

- `int X::*pXint = &X::visible;`
  `pfcn pF = &X::print;`

This declares pXint to be a pointer to class X member whose base type is int. It is initialized to point at the member X::visible. The pointer pF is initialized to point at the member function X::print.

- `a.*pXint += 1;`

This is equivalent to ++a.visible.

- `cout << "\nb.visible = " << pb ->*pXint;`
  `(b.*pF)();`

The pointer expression is equivalent to pb -> visible. The function call is equivalent to b.print().

- `pF = &X::reset;`
  `(a.*pF)();`

The pointer pf is assigned the address of X::reset. The function call is equivalent to a.reset().

Consider the memory layout for representing an object. The object has a base address, and the various nonstatic members are offset relative to this base address. In effect, a pointer to class member is used as an offset and is not a true pointer; a true pointer has general memory addresses as values. A static member is not offset and, as such, a pointer to a static member is a true address.

6.12 Overloading new and delete

Most classes involve free-store memory allocation and deallocation. Sometimes more sophisticated use of memory than is provided by simple calls to operators new and delete is needed for efficiency or robustness.

Operator new has the general form

$::_{opt}$ new $placement_{opt}$ $type$ $initializer_{opt}$

Some examples are

```
::new char[10];      //insist on global new
new(buff) X(a);      //call with buff using X::X(a)
```

Up to now we have been using the global operator new() to allocate free store. The system provides a sizeof(*type*) argument to this function implicitly. Its function prototype is

```
void* operator new(size_t size);
```

The operators new and delete can be overloaded. This feature provides a simple mechanism for user-defined manipulation of free store. For example, traditional C programming uses malloc() to access free store and return a void* pointer to the allocated memory. In this scheme memory is deallocated by the *stdlib.h* function free(). We use operator overloading of new and delete to allow an X object to utilize C's traditional free-store management.

```
#include <stdlib.h>    //malloc() and free() defined

class X {
public:
   void* operator new(size_t size) { return (malloc(size)); }
   void  operator delete(void* ptr) { free(ptr); }
   X(unsigned size) { new(size); }
   ~X() { delete(this); }
   .....
};
```

In this example, the class X has provided overloaded forms of new() and delete(). When a class overloads operator new(), the global operator is still accessible using the scope resolution operator ::.

One reason to overload these operators is to give them additional semantics, such as providing diagnostic information or being more fault tolerant. Also, the class can have a more efficient memory-allocation scheme than that provided by the system.

The *placement* syntax provides a comma-separated argument list used to select an overloaded operator new() with a matching signature. These additional arguments are often used to place the constructed object at a particular address. This form of operator new uses the *new.h* header file.

In file over_new.cpp

```cpp
//Placement syntax and new overloaded.
#include <iostream.h>
#include <new.h>

char*  buf1 = new char[1000];      //in place of free store
char*  buf2 = new char[1000];

class object {
public:
   .....
private:
   .....
};

int main()
{
   object *p = new(buf1) object;   //allocate at buf1
   object *q = new(buf2) object;   //allocate at buf2
   .....
}
```

Placement syntax allows the user to have an arbitrary signature for the overloaded new operator. This signature is distinct from the initializer arguments used by calls to new that select an appropriate constructor.

The delete operator comes in two flavors. It can have as signatures

```cpp
void operator delete(void* p);
void operator delete(void* p, size_t);
```

The first signature makes no provision for the number of bytes to be returned by delete. In this case the programmer provides code that supplies this value. The second signature includes a size_t argument passed to the delete invocation. This is provided by the compiler as the size of the object pointed at by p. Only one form of delete can be provided as a static member function in each class.

The *new.h* file has the function pointer _new_handler, which calls the error handler for operator new(). If memory is exhausted, the function pointer _new_handler is used to call a default system routine. The user can specify an explicit *out-of-free-store* routine, which can replace the default function by using set_new_handler().

In file new_hdlr.cpp

```
//Simple fault tolerance using _new_handler.
#include <new.h>
#include <stdlib.h>      //for exit

void heap_exhausted()   //user-defined error handling
{
   cerr << "HEAP EXHAUSTED" << endl;
   exit(1);
}

int main()
{
   set_new_handler(heap_exhausted);
   ·····  //memory exhaustion is like heap_exhausted()

}
```

These class `new()` and `delete()` member functions are always implicitly `static`. The `new()` is invoked before the object exists and therefore cannot have a `this` yet. The `delete()` is called by the destructor, so the object is already destroyed.

6.13 Pragmatics

Explicitly casting arguments can be both an aid to documentation and a useful way to avoid poorly understood conversion sequences. It is not an admission of ignorance to cast or parenthesize arguments or expressions that otherwise could be converted or evaluated properly.

Operator overloading is easily misused. Do not overload operators when it can lead to misinterpretation. The domain of use should have a widely used notation that conforms to your overloading. Also, overload related operators in a manner consistent with C++ community expectations. For example, the relational operators <, >, <=, and >= should all be meaningful and provide expected inverse behaviors.

Generally speaking, overload symmetric binary operators, such as +, *, ==, !=, and &&, with friend functions. Both arguments are then passed as ordinary parameters. This subjects both arguments to the same rules of parameter passing. Recall that using a member function to provide overloading for symmetric binary operators causes the first argument to be passed via the `this` pointer.

Any time a class uses `new` to construct objects, it should provide an explicitly overloaded `operator=()`. This advice is analogous to our rule that such a class provide an explicit copy constructor. (See Section 5.2.1, "The Copy Constructor," on page 159.) The compiler-provided default assignment operator semantics would in most cases result in spurious behavior. This leads to a suggested normal form for classes with heap-managed memory.

```
//Normal form for heap-managed classes illustrated.
class dbl_vect {
public:
   dbl_vect();                              //default constructor
   dbl_vect(const dbl_vect&);               //copy constructor
   .....
   dbl_vect& operator=(const dbl_vect&);    //returns lvalue
   .....
};
```

This normal form rule also applies to reference-counted classes, such as the `my_string` type. (See Section 5.4, "An Example: Dynamically Allocated Strings," on page 161.) The `operator=()` returns a reference to allow assignment to work efficiently. This requires lvalue semantics.

6.13.1 Signature Matching

Signature matching rules are given in simplified form in Section 6.2, "Overloading and Function Selection," on page 201. A further clarification of these rules with examples is given in this section.

For a given argument, a best match is always an exact match. An exact match also includes *trivial conversions*. For type T these are shown in the following table.

Trivial Conversions	
From	To
T*	const T*
T*	volatile T*

The use of `volatile` is specialized. It means that a variable can be modified external to the program code. So, a variable representation of an address that gets data from an external device, such as a real-time clock, would be `volatile`. It is also used to suppress compiler optimizations that involve such variables.

These additional modifiers can be used in overloading resolution. Thus,

```
void   print(int i);
void   print(const int& i);
```

can be unambiguously overloaded.

It is important to remember that user-defined conversions include constructors of a single argument. These constructors can be implicitly called to perform conversions from the argument type to their class type. This can happen for assignment conversions, as in the argument-matching algorithm. An example is modified from Section 6.5, "Unary Operator Overloading," on page 208:

In file clock.cpp

```
//modify clock program
class clock {
public:
   clock(unsigned long i);      //construct & conversion
   void   print() const;        //formatted printout
   void   tick();               //add one second
   clock  operator++()  { this -> tick(); return(*this); }
   void   reset(const clock& c);
private:
   unsigned long  tot_secs, secs, mins, hours, days;
};


void clock::reset(const clock& c)
{
   tot_secs = c.tot_secs;
   secs = c.secs;
   mins = c.mins;
   hours = c.hours;
   days = c.days;
}

int main()
{
   clock  c1(900), c2(400);
   .....
   c1.reset(c2);
   c2.reset(100);
   .....
}
```

The call to `reset(100)` involves an argument match between `int` and `clock` that is a user-defined conversion invoking the constructor `clock(unsigned)`. Where these conversions are unintended a new keyword `explicit` can be used in declaring the constructor to disable its use as an implicit conversion.

Summary

1. Overloading operators gives them new meanings. For example, the expression `a + b` will have different meanings depending on the types of the variables `a` and `b`. The expression could mean string concatenation, complex number addition, or integer addition, depending on whether the variables were the ADT `my_string`, the ADT `complex`, or the built-in type `int`, respectively.

2. There are four cast types in C++:

   ```
   static_cast<type>(expression)
   reinterpret_cast<type>(expression)
   const_cast<type>(expression)
   dynamic_cast<type>(expression)
   ```

   These replace the two obsolete notations not used in this text:

   ```
   x = float(i);      //C++ functional notation
   x = (float) i;     //C style cast
   ```

3. A nonexplicit constructor of one argument is de facto a type conversion from the argument's type to the constructor's class type. A conversion from a user-specified type to a built-in type can be made by defining a special conversion function. The general form of such a member function is:

   ```
   operator type() { ..... }
   ```

   These conversions occur implicitly in assignment expressions, arguments to functions, and values returned from functions.

4. The overloaded meaning is selected by matching the argument list of the function call to the argument list of the function declaration. A best match must be unique. It must be best on at least one argument and as good as any other match on all other arguments. The matching algorithm for each argument is as shown in the following list.

Overloaded Function Selection Algorithm

1. Use an exact match if found.
2. Try standard type promotions.
3. Try standard type conversions.
4. Try user-defined conversions.
5. Use a match to ellipsis if found.

5. The keyword `friend` is a function specifier that allows a nonmember function access to the nonpublic members of the class of which it is a friend.

6. The keyword `operator` is also used to overload the built-in C++ operators. Just as a function name, such as `print()`, can be given a variety of meanings that depend on its arguments, so can an operator, such as +, be given additional meanings. Overloading operators allows infix expressions of both user and built-in types to be written. Operator precedence and associativity remain fixed.

7. Operator overloading typically uses either member functions or friend functions, because both have privileged access. When a unary operator is overloaded using a member function, it has an empty argument list because the single operator argument is the implicit argument. When a binary operator is overloaded using a member function, it has as its first argument the implicitly passed class variable and as its second argument the lone argument-list parameter.

8. An overloaded subscript operator can have any return type and any argument-list type. However, it is good style to maintain the consistency between a user-defined meaning and standard usage. Thus, a common function prototype is:

    class-name& `operator[]`(*integral type*);

    This is an lvalue that can be used on either side of an assignment.

Exercises

1. The following table contains a variety of mixed type expressions. Fill in both the type the expression is converted to and its value when well defined.

Declarations and Initializations		

`int    i = 3, *p = &i;`
 `char c = 'b';`
 `float x = 2.14, *q = &x;`		

Expression	Type	Value
`i + c`		
`x + i`		
`p + i`		
`p == & i`		
`* p - * q`		
`static_cast<int>(x + i)`		

2. For the type `rational` in Section 6.2, "Overloading and Function Selection," on page 202, explain why the conversions of integer 7 and double 7.0 lead to different internal representations.

3. The following line of code is from the *rational* program in Section 6.2, "Overloading and Function Selection," on page 202.

   ```
   cout << ") = " << greater(static_cast<rational>(i), z);
   ```

   If it is replaced by

   ```
   cout << ") = " << greater(i, z);
   ```

   what goes wrong?

4. Write a `rational` constructor that, given two integers as dividend and quotient, uses a greatest common divisor algorithm to reduce the internal representation to its smallest a and q value. (See Section 6.2, "Overloading and Function Selection," on page 202.)

5. Overload the equality and comparison operators for `rational`. Notice that two `rationals` are equal in the form given by the previous exercise if and only if their dividends and quotients are equal (see Section 6.2, "Overloading and Function Selection," on page 202).

6. Write a function that adds a `dbl_vect` v to a `matrix` m. The prototype to be added to class `matrix` and class `dbl_vect` is:

   ```
   friend dbl_vect  add(const dbl_vect& v, matrix& m);
   ```

   The `dbl_vect` v will be added element-by-element to each row of m. (See Section 6.3, "Friend Functions," on page 206.)

7. Define class `complex` as:

   ```
   class complex {
   public:
      complex(double r) { real = r; imag = 0; }
      void   assign(double r, double i)
         { real = r; imag = i; }
      void   print()
         { cout << real << " + " << imag << "i "; }
      operator double()
         { return (sqrt(real * real + imag * imag));}
   private:
      double real, imag;
   };
   ```

   We wish to augment the class by overloading a variety of operators. For example, the member function `print()` could be replaced by creating the friend function `operator<<()`:

   ```
   ostream& operator<<(ostream& out, complex x)
   {
      out << x.real << " + " << x.imag << "i ";
      return out;
   }
   ```

   Also, code and test a unary minus operator. It should return a `complex` whose value in each part is negated.

8. For the type `complex`, write the binary operator functions add, multiply, and subtract. Each should return `complex`. Write each as a friend function. Why not write them as member functions?

9. Write two friend functions:

   ```
   friend complex  operator+(complex, double);
   friend complex  operator+(double, complex);
   ```

   In the absence of a conversion from type `double` to type `complex`, both types are needed to allow completely mixed expressions of `complex` and `double`. Explain why writing one with an `int` parameter is unnecessary when these friend functions are available.

10. Overload assignment for `complex`:

    ```
    complex complex::operator=(complex c) { return c; }
    ```

    Would this be equivalent to the default assignment that the compiler generates, if this definition were omitted? In the presence of the conversion operator for converting `complex` to `double`, what is the effect of assigning a `complex` to a `double`? Try to overload assignment with a friend function in class `complex`.

    ```
    friend double  operator=(double d, complex c);
    //assign d = real_part(c)
    ```

    Why won't this work?

11. Program a class `vec_complex` that is a safe array type whose element values are `complex`. Overload operators + and * to mean, respectively, element-by-element `complex` addition and dot-product of two `complex` vectors. For added efficiency, you can make the class `vec_complex` a friend of class `complex`.

12. The following member function is a form of iterator:

    ```
    double& dbl_vect::iterate()
    {
       static int  i = 0;
       i = i % size;
       return p[i++];
    }
    ```

    It is called an *iterator* because it returns each element value of a `dbl_vect` in sequence. Use it to write a print function that is not a member function, and that writes out all element values of a given `dbl_vect`. Modify class `dbl_vect` given in Section 6.7, "Overloading Assignment and Subscripting Operators," on page 213.

13. The previous exercise has a serious limitation. By providing an iterator that is contained in the class, it does not allow the element sequencing to depend on the individual dbl_vect variable. Thus, if a and b are both dbl_vect variables, the first call of a.iterate() will get the first element of a, and a subsequent call of b.iterate() will get the second element of b. So, instead, we shall define a new class dbl_vect_iterator, as follows:

    ```
    class dbl_vect_iterator {
    public:
       dbl_vect_iterator(dbl_vect& v) : p(&v), position(0) { }
       double& iterate() const;
    private:
       dbl_vect  *p;
       int       position;
    };
    ```

    This class must be a friend of dbl_vect. Write the code for iterate. Then, for each declaration of a dbl_vect, there will be a corresponding declaration of its iterator. For example:

    ```
    dbl_vect            a(5), b(10);
    dbl_vect_iterator   it_a(a), it_b(b);
    ```

    Use this to write a function that finds the maximum element value in a dbl_vect.

14. Define a new class matrix_iterator as an iterator class that sequences through all elements of a matrix. (See Section 6.10, "Overloading Operator () for Indexing," on page 220.) Use it to find the maximum element in a matrix.

15. Redo the my_string ADT by using operator overloading. (See Section 5.4, "An Example: Dynamically Allocated Strings," on page 161.) The member function assign should be changed to become operator=. The member function concat should be changed to become operator+. Also, overload operator[] to return the ith character in the my_string. If there is no such character, the value -1 is to be returned.

16. Explain why friendship to str_obj was required when overloading << to act on objects of type my_string. (See Section 5.11, "Strings Using Reference Semantics," on page 185.) Rewrite my_string by adding a conversion member function operator char*(). This now allows << to output objects of type my_string. Discuss this solution.

17. What goes wrong with the following client code when the overloaded definition of operator=() is omitted from my_string? (See Section 5.11, "Strings Using Reference Semantics," on page 184.)

```
//Swapping my_strings that are reference counted.
#include <iostream.h>

class my_string {
   .....
};

void swap(my_string x, my_string y)
{
   my_string temp;

   temp = x;
   x = y;
   y = temp;
}

int main()
{
   my_string   b("dont try me "), c(" try me");

   cout << b << c << endl;
   swap(b, c);
   cout << b << c << endl;
}
```

18. We can develop our my_string class with a substring operation by overloading function call. The notation is my_string(from, to), where from is the beginning of the substring and to is the end.

```
my_string my_string::operator()(int from, int to)
{
   my_string temp(to - from + 1);

   for (int i = from; i < to + 1; ++i)
      temp.st -> s[i - from] = st -> s[i];
   temp.st[to - from + 1] = 0;
   return temp;
}
```

Use this substring operation to search a string for a given character sequence and return `true` if the subsequence is found.

19. Rewrite the substring function using a `char*` constructor. Is this better or worse? If you have a profiler, run this example with both forms of substring creation on the following client code:

    ```
    int main()
    {
       my_string large("A verbose phrase to search");

       for (i = 0; i < MANY; ++i)
          count += (large(i, i + 3) == "ver");}
    ```

    For this exercise, code `operator==()` to work on `my_strings`.

20. Write the function

    ```
    void reverse(double data[], int size);
    //data[size] will be reversed
    //internally declare a stack of generic pointers
    //push values onto stack, pop them back into data[]
    ```

21. Use a stack to write out subsequences in increasing order by value. In the sequence (7, 9, 3, 2, 6, 8, 9, 2), the subsequences are (7, 9), (3), (2, 6, 8, 9), (2). Use a stack to store increasing values. Pop the stack when a next sequence value is no longer increasing. Keep in mind that the stack pops values in reverse order. Redo this exercise using a queue, thus avoiding this reversal problem.

22. For the stack of generic pointers, add the constructor

    ```
    stack::stack(int size, generic_ptr[]);
    ```

23. Redo the list ADT by using operator overloading. (See Section 5.8, "Example: A Singly Linked List," on page 171.) The member function `prepend()` should change to `operator+()`, and `del()` should change to `operator--()`. Also, overload `operator[]()` to return the `i`th element in the list.

24. Modify the class `set` in Chapter 5, "Constructors and Destructors," in exercise 28, on page 196, to have overloaded operators +, –, and *.

```
class set {
    .....
        set   operator+(set& v);    //define union
        set   operator*(set& v);    //define intersection
        set   operator-(set& v);    //define difference
};
```

Test your complete set ADT with the following:

```
//The set ADT
{
    set   s(0x5555), t(0x10303021), w, x;
    s.pr_mems(); t.pr_mems();
    w.pr_mems(); x.pr_mems();
    w = s + t;                      //set union
    x = s * t;                      //set intersection
    t = t - s;                      //set difference
    s.pr_mems(); t.pr_mems();
    w.pr_mems(); x.pr_mems();
}
```

Notice that we now have added a set type that is similar to the built-in Pascal set type.

25. The postfix operators ++ and -- can be overloaded distinct from their prefix meanings. Postfix can be distinguished by defining the postfix overloaded function as having a single unused integer argument, as in

```
class T {
public:
    //postfix invoked as t.operator++(0);
    void   operator++(int);
    void   operator--(int);
};
```

There will be no implied semantic relationship between the postfix and prefix forms. Add postfix decrement and increment to class `clock` in Section 6.5, "Unary Operator Overloading," on page 208. Have them subtract a second and add a second, respectively. Write these operators to use an integer argument n that will be subtracted or added as an additional argument:

```
clock c(60);

    c++;                    //adds a second
    c--;                    //subtracts a second
    c.operator++(5);        //adds 1 + 5 seconds
    c.operator--(5);        //subtracts 6 seconds
```

26. The operator -> is overloadable provided it is a nonstatic member function returning either a pointer to a class object or an object of a class for which operator-> is defined. Such an overloaded structure pointer operator is called a *smart pointer operator*. It usually returns an ordinary pointer after doing some initial computation. One use could be as an iterator function:

    ```
    dbl_vect* dbl_vect::operator->();
    //maintain an internal i
    //increment and return &p[++i]
    ```

    Modify class dbl_vect in Section 6.7, "Overloading Assignment and Subscripting Operators," on page 213, to code and test this idea.

27. (*Difficult*) It is a better idea to make a smart pointer class:

    ```
    class dbl_vect {
    public:
        friend class smart_ptr_dbl_vect; //add to dbl_vect
        .....
    };

    class smart_ptr_dbl_vect {
    public:
        smart_ptr_dbl_vect(const dbl_vect& v);
        smart_ptr_dbl_vect&  operator->();
    private:
        int*  ptr;
        int   position;
    };
    ```

```
smart_ptr_dbl_vect::
   smart_ptr_dbl_vect(const dbl_vect& v) :
            position(0), ptr(v.p) { }
smart_ptr_dbl_vect& smart_ptr_dbl_vect::operator->()
{
   //write this code to access and test that
   //p[position] is not out of range
}
```

Modify class `dbl_vect` in Section 6.7, "Overloading Assignment and Subscripting Operators," on page 213, to test this idea.

28. Take the `polynomial::plus()` member function found in Section 5.10, "Polynomials as a Linked List," on page 183, and convert it to code for overloading `operator+`:

    ```
    polynomial operator+(const polynomial&, const polynomial&)
    ```

    This should be a friend of the class `polynomial`.

29. *(Project)* Write code to implement a polynomial multiplication operator. The code can repeatedly call the polynomial addition routine. Did you make sure that intermediate results would be properly garbage-collected? Write a full-blown polynomial package that is consistent with community expectations. You could include differentiation and integration of polynomials as well.

30. Use a conditional compilation flag `NDEBUG` to signal the compiler whether or not to include assertions. This gives a simple mechanism that allows both safe and unsafe classes to be compiled from the same source code. Run an application such as a large matrix addition with both forms of code, and measure the runtime overhead required by the assertion statements.

31. Write a `matrix_iterator` class with the same interface as `dbl_vect_iterator` from exercise 13, on page 237. It should contain `successor()`, `predecessor()`, `reset()`, and `item()`. If you want you can extend this with member functions `int row()` and `int column()`. (See Section 6.3, "Friend Functions," on page 206, for class `matrix`.)

32. Rewrite the `matrix` class to have row and column indices that go from one instead of zero.

33. *(Project)* Write code that fleshes out the `rational` type of Section 6.9, "Overloading I/O Operators << and >>," on page 218. Have it work appropriately for

all major operators. Allow it to properly mix with other number types, including integers, floats, and complex numbers. There are several ways to improve the `rational` implementation. You can try to improve the precision of going from `double` to `rational`. Also, many algorithms are more convenient when the `rational` is in some canonical form where the quotient and divisor are relatively prime. This can be accomplished by adding a greatest common division algorithm to reduce the representation to the canonical form.

Chapter 7

Visitation: Iterators and Containers

Container classes are data types used to hold a large number of individual items. The types `ch_stack` and `dbl_vect` are two such container classes. Many of the operations on container classes involve the ability to visit individual elements conveniently. Classes also are the means to attaining abstraction in C++. Abstraction is a question of ignoring detail, and a class hides detail; it publicly provides a convenient way to handle a computational task. In this chapter we explore a variety of techniques to perform visitation and the extraction of elements from a class. One technique is to create an iterator whose function is to visit the elements of an object in a container class. The iterator navigates over the elements of the class. Using visitation as the theme, we will write code that anticipates using the container classes, iterator objects, and algorithms found in the standard template library.

7.1 Visitation

In conventional programming the `for` statement in C++ or the `DO` statement in Fortran is the preferred means of structuring iteration, especially when processing arrays.

```
//visit each a[i] and do something
for (i = 0; i < size; ++i)
   sum += a[i];
```

The homogeneous aggregate `a[]` is processed element by element. The `for` statement specifies a specific order of visitation and is controlled by an index `i`, which is visibly modified. The order of visitation and the index used are generally details of implementation that do not affect the computation. Here is an alternate coding that performs the same computation:

```
for (j = size - 1; j != 0; --j)
    sum += a[j];
```

Abstractly the computation is:

until no new elements
    sum += *next element*

We could capture a *next element* with a pointer type that is suitable for selecting objects in the container. Let us modify the class dbl_vect from Section 6.4, "Overloading Operators," on page 207, to add iterator objects. We call the new class vector, anticipating similarities with the standard template library container of the same name.

In file vector.h

```
class vector {
public:
    typedef double* iterator;      //pointer type vector::double*
    explicit vector(int n = 1);
    vector(const vector& v);
    vector(const double a[], int n);
    ~vector() { delete []bp; }
    iterator begin()const { return bp; }
    iterator end()const { return bp + size; }
    int ub()const { return size - 1; }     //upper bound
    double& operator[](int i);             //range checked
    vector& operator=(const vector& v);
private:
    iterator bp;                           //base pointer
    int size;                              //number of elements
};
```

The functions begin() and end() return the boundaries of a given vector.

The code for summing such an aggregate using an iterator would be:

```
vector v(n);
vector::iterator p;
double   sum = 0;
.....
for (p = v.begin(); p != v.end(); ++p)
   sum += *p;
```

The visitation idiom here uses a pointer type and two boundary locations to perform a standard loop over all the elements of the container.

7.2 Iterators

The pointer object and iterator visitation idiom make it very easy to write many standard algorithms over container classes, such as class vector. We will write several such elementary algorithms.

In file vector.h

```
ostream& operator<<(ostream& out, const vector& v)
{
   vector::iterator p;

   for (p = v.begin(); p != v.end(); ++p)
      out << *p << '\t';
   out << endl;
   return out;
}

istream& operator>>(istream& in, vector& v)
{
   vector::iterator p;

   for (p = v.begin(); p != v.end(); ++p)
      in >> *p;
   return in;
}
```

Here we overloaded the two standard I/O operators for extraction and insertion. In each case the visitation is very straightforward. By staying with an efficient, idiomatic scheme, the programmer avoids common pitfalls such as out-of-range errors.

In file vectacum.cpp

```
//Summing over an iterator range.
double accumulate              //sum the container values
(   vector::iterator first,    //starting location
    vector::iterator last,     //end-of-range
    double initial_val         //initial sum
)
{
   vector::iterator   p;
   double sum = initial_val;

   for (p = first; p != last; ++p)
      sum += *p;
   return sum;
}
```

Notice how the location `last` is an end-of-range designator; `last` itself is not dereferenced. This is why the member function `vector::end()` returns `p + size`.

7.3 An Example: `quicksort()`

The *quicksort* sorting procedure, invented by Anthony Hoare, is a highly efficient internal sort. It is tricky to code because of the different indices that are tracked in a traditional implementation. (See Kelley and Pohl, *A Book on C: 3rd Edition*, New York: Benjamin/Cummings, 1995.) We will replace indexing with iterators.

The `quicksort` algorithm works by recursively decomposing unordered values into two subsets separated by a mid-value. The mid-value is larger than all elements in the first set and smaller than or equal to all elements in the second set. This segregation leads to increasingly smaller subsets that are in turn separated until they are trivially sorted. The use of `quicksort()` is an illustration of the effectiveness of the divide-and-conquer method of programming.

In file vectsort.cpp

```cpp
//QUICKSORT using an iterator
void quicksort(vector::iterator from, vector::iterator to)
{
   vector::iterator mid;

   if (from < to -1) {
      mid = partition(from, to);
      quicksort(from, mid);
      quicksort(mid + 1, to);
   }
}

vector::iterator partition(vector::iterator from,
                           vector::iterator to)
{
   vector::iterator front = from + 1, back = to - 1;
   double compare = *from;

   while (front < back) {
      //search forward for out of order element
      while ((front < back) &&(compare > *front))
         ++front;
      //search backward for out of order element
      while ((front < back) &&(compare <= *back))
         --back;
      swap(*front, *back);
   }
   //insert  mid position comparison element
   if (compare > *front) {
      swap(*from, *front);
      return front;
   }
   else {
      swap(*from, *(front - 1));
      return front - 1;
   }
}
```

The real work occurs in the partition() function. It arbitrarily uses the first element as the basis for separating all the elements into less-than and greater-than-or-equal-to piles. When it finds an out-of-order element that is on the less-than side, it switches to looking for an out-of-order element that is on the greater-than side. It swaps these elements pairwise until it completes the partitioning, as shown in the following figure.

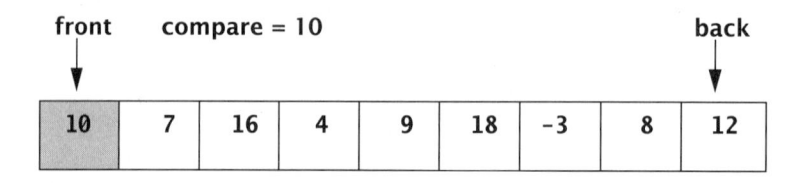

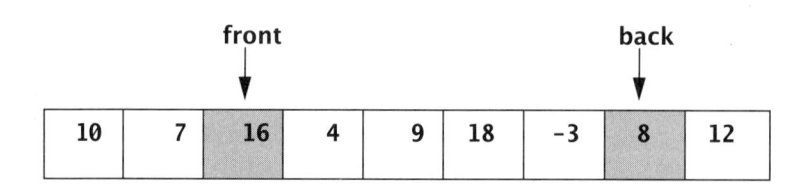

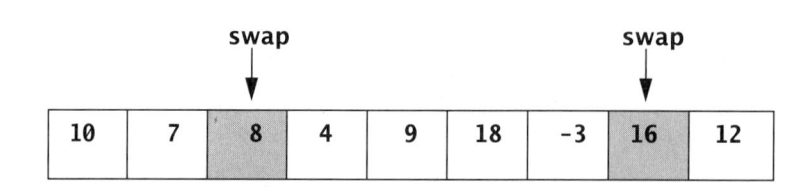

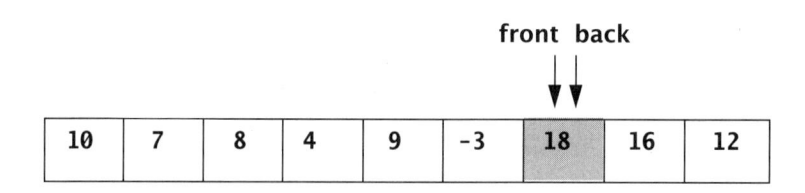

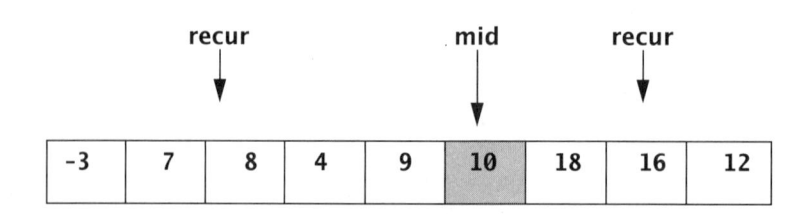

```
front    compare = 10                              back
  ↓                                                  ↓
┌────┬────┬────┬────┬────┬────┬────┬────┬────┐
│ 10 │  7 │ 16 │  4 │  9 │ 18 │ -3 │  8 │ 12 │
└────┴────┴────┴────┴────┴────┴────┴────┴────┘

              front                      back
                ↓                          ↓
┌────┬────┬────┬────┬────┬────┬────┬────┬────┐
│ 10 │  7 │ 16 │  4 │  9 │ 18 │ -3 │  8 │ 12 │
└────┴────┴────┴────┴────┴────┴────┴────┴────┘

              swap                       swap
                ↓                          ↓
┌────┬────┬────┬────┬────┬────┬────┬────┬────┐
│ 10 │  7 │  8 │  4 │  9 │ 18 │ -3 │ 16 │ 12 │
└────┴────┴────┴────┴────┴────┴────┴────┴────┘

                                  front back
                                    ↓    ↓
┌────┬────┬────┬────┬────┬────┬────┬────┬────┐
│ 10 │  7 │  8 │  4 │  9 │ -3 │ 18 │ 16 │ 12 │
└────┴────┴────┴────┴────┴────┴────┴────┴────┘

              recur            mid        recur
                ↓               ↓           ↓
┌────┬────┬────┬────┬────┬────┬────┬────┬────┐
│ -3 │  7 │  8 │  4 │  9 │ 10 │ 18 │ 16 │ 12 │
└────┴────┴────┴────┴────┴────┴────┴────┴────┘
```

The `swap()` function interchanges out-of-order elements. By making `swap()` inline, we make the inner loop code of `partition()` efficient at no additional effort to the programmer.

```
inline void swap(double& i, double& j)
{
   double temp = i;

   i = j;
   j = temp;
}
```

In Section 8.5, "Parameterizing quicksort()," on page 282, we show how to transform this to a generic algorithm as is found in STL.

7.4 Friendly Classes and Iterators

A class can define objects that are needed as internal detail for other classes. To preserve its anonymous role, such a class needs to be private. A class that handles these private objects must be on friendly terms with them.

Recall the `my_string` type defined with reference-counting semantics in Section 5.11, "Strings Using Reference Semantics," on page 184. Individual `my_string` values were ultimately referencing objects of type `str_obj`. This decoupling allowed one instance of `str_obj`, which might require many bytes of store, to be used by many instances of `my_string`. We can convert that example using friendship to preserve the privacy of the class `str_obj`.

In file string8.h

```
class str_obj {
private:
   friend class my_string;
   friend class string_iterator;
   friend ostream&
      operator<<(ostream& out, const my_string& str);
   int  len, ref_cnt;
   char* s;
   str_obj():len(0), ref_cnt(1) { s = new char[1]; }
   str_obj(int n):len(n), ref_cnt(1) { s = new char[n + 1]; }
   str_obj(const char* p):ref_cnt(1)
      { len = strlen(p); s = new char[len + 1]; strcpy(s, p); }
   ~str_obj() { delete [] s; }
};
```

This two-class design has the advantage of increasing flexibility by further segregating implementation detail from client code.

Iterators also typically need friendly relations to the object they are visiting. Let us add an iterator class and modify our my_string to overload assignment and the put to operator, filling out this example.

In file string8.h

```
class my_string {
public:
   my_string() { st = new str_obj; }
   my_string(int n) { st = new str_obj(n); }
   my_string(const char* p) { st = new str_obj(p); }
   my_string(const my_string& str)
      { st = str.st; st -> ref_cnt++; }
   ~my_string();
   void assign(const my_string& str);
   my_string& operator=(my_string& str)
      { assign(str); return str; }
   friend class string_iterator;
   friend ostream&
      operator<<(ostream& out, const my_string& str);
private:
   str_obj* st;
};
```

```
//The typical method for overloading << "put to"
ostream& operator<<(ostream& out,const my_string& str)
{
   out << str.st -> s;
   return out;
}
```

As written, the `ostream& operator<<(ostream&, const my_string&)` function requires friendly relations to `str_obj`. It uses private implementation details of the class `my_string`. It cannot be written as a member function because its first argument must be an `ostream`. Since its return value is an `ostream&`, it can be used in a multiple put to expression. This stays within the conventions of *iostream.h*.

We use the `assign()` member function to code `operator=()`. We return a reference value to permit multiple assignment. It is worth pointing out that if assignment is not overloaded, the default assignment semantics would fail. It would not properly handle the reference count.

The related iterator class follows a common design. A constructor associates the iterator object with the object to be visited by initializing `my_string* ptr_s`. We keep a private position variable `cur_ind`. Since the friendship relation between `my_string` and `str_obj` is not transitive, our design requires `string_iterator` to be friendly with `str_obj` as well.

In file string8.h

```
class string_iterator {
public:
   string_iterator(my_string& s) :cur_ind(0),ptr_s(&s) { }
   bool successor();
   char& item() { return ((ptr_s -> st -> s)[cur_ind]); }
   void reset(int n = 0) { cur_ind = n; }
   int position() { return cur_ind; }
private:
   my_string* ptr_s;
   int cur_ind;
};
```

```
bool string_iterator::successor()
{
   if (cur_ind >= ptr_s -> st -> len - 1)
      return false;
   else {
      ++cur_ind;
      return true;
   }
}
```

Let us use the iterator to search the string for the next word.

In file string8.cpp

```
void word(string_iterator& it_s, char* w)
{
   while (isspace(it_s.item()) && it_s.successor())
       ;     //find non-whitespace character
   if (!isspace(it_s.item())) {
      *w = it_s.item();          //first character of word
      while (it_s.successor()&& !isspace(it_s.item()))
          *++w = it_s.item();    //successive characters
   }
   *++w = 0;                     //add '\0' terminator
}
```

This routine skips over characters for which `isspace()` is true. It then collects a word as a series of `nonisspace()` characters and terminates this with 0.

7.5 Generic Programming with `void*`

The pointer type `void*` serves as a generic, or universal, pointer type. Any other pointer type can be assigned to it. This allows us to use it polymorphically by developing code that indirectly manipulates objects of any type. We can see this in the definition of the standard memory-copying function `memcpy`.

7.5 ▼ Generic Programming with void*   255

In file memcopy.cpp

```cpp
#include <stddef.h>              //define size_t
#include <iostream.h>

void* memcpy(void* to, const void* from, size_t n_bytes)
{
   const char* f= reinterpret_cast<const char*>(from);
   char *t = reinterpret_cast<char*>(to);

   for (int i = 0; i < n_bytes; ++i)
      t[i] = f[i];
   return to;
}

int main()
{
   char v[4];
   int  w  = 0x00424344;

   memcpy(v, &w, 4);            //polymorphic interface
   cout << w << " == " << v;
}
```

The function memcpy allows pointer arguments of any type to copy characters byte-wise starting at the address specified by from. In the sample code we initialize a four-byte character array using an integer value stored in w. This technique can also work to allow a container class, such as stack, to store arbitrary values indirectly.

In file genstack.h

```cpp
//generic stack implementation:genstack.h
typedef void* generic_ptr;

class stack {
public:
   explicit stack(int size = 1000) : max_len(size), top(EMPTY)
      { s = new generic_ptr[size]; assert(s != 0);}
   ~stack() { delete [] s; }
   void reset() { top = EMPTY; }
   void push(generic_ptr c) { s[++top] = c; }
   generic_ptr pop() { return s[top--]; }
   generic_ptr top_of() { return s[top]; }
   bool empty()const { return top == EMPTY; }
   bool full()const { return top == max_len - 1; }
private:
   enum   { EMPTY = -1};
   generic_ptr* s;
   int    max_len;
   int    top;
};
```

Of course, to do useful work with such a class, values must be properly cast. For example, assume that you have an array of words stored as a two-dimensional array of characters, and you wish to use the standard `stack` algorithm for printing the words in reverse order.

In file month.cpp

```cpp
#include <iostream.h>
#include "genstack.h"

char* months[12] = { "january", "february", "march",
     "april", "may", "june", "july", "august",
     "september", "october", "november", "december"};
```

```
int main()
{
   stack a;
   int i;

   for (i = 0; i < 12; ++i)
      a.push(months[i]);
   for (i = 0; i < 12; ++i)
      cout << reinterpret_cast<char*>(a.pop()) << endl;
}
```

7.6 List and List Iterator

In this section we develop a doubly linked list whose interface is similar to the STL type list. A doubly linked list trades off space and efficiency. By adding a link that explicitly points to a previous list element, operations such as deletion are simplified at the expense of maintaining this additional pointer in all list elements. We will give a basic design of this class and its associated iterator definitions.

In file list2.h

```
class list {
public:
   struct listelem;                       //forward declarations
   class iterator;
   friend iterator;
   list():h(0), t(0) {}                   //construct the empty list
   ~list() { release(); }
   iterator begin()const { return h; }
   iterator end()const { return t; }
   void push_front(char c);
   void pop_front();
   char& front() { return h -> data; }
   char& back() { return t -> data; }
   bool empty()const { return h == 0; }
   void release();
```

```
private:
   listelem* h, *t;                    //head and tail
   struct listelem                     //list cell
   {
      char data;
      listelem* next, *prev;
      listelem(char c, listelem* n, listelem* p)
            :data(c), next(n), prev(p) {}
   };
};
```

Let us examine this class design piecemeal starting with underlying implementation. We have struct listelem, which has a data member and pointers to the next and previous list elements. The list itself is represented as head and tail pointers. List traversal is easily accomplished in either a forward direction starting from h using the next member, or a backward direction starting from t using the prev member. Traversal halts when a pointer value is zero.

In our design, we add an iterator class nested inside the list class. This class list::iterator will be used to point at a current position inside a list. It will be akin to a pointer or cursor. Therefore, we also need to be able to navigate the list with autoincrement and autodecrement operators defined in the iterator class. We can do this as follows.

In file list2.h

```
//scoped within class list
class iterator {
public:
   iterator(listelem* p = 0):ptr(p) { }
   iterator operator++();
   iterator operator--();
   iterator operator++(int);
   iterator operator--(int);
   listelem* operator->() { return ptr; };
   char& operator*() { return ptr -> data; }
   operator listelem*() { return ptr; }     //conversion
private:
   listelem* ptr;                            //current listelem or 0
};
```

Where, for example, operator++() could be defined as follows:

```
list::iterator iterator::operator++()
{
   assert(ptr != 0);
   ptr = ptr -> next;
   return *this;
}
```

Let us use these ideas to write an overloaded operator<<() for printing out a list.

```
ostream& operator<<(ostream& out, list& x)
{
   list::iterator p = x.begin();   //gets x.h

   out << "list = (";
   while (p != 0) {
      out << *p << ",";            //gets a char&
      ++p;                         //advance iterator using next
   }
   cout << ")\n";
   return out;
}
```

The apparent dereferencing of p is accomplished by accessing the data member of the appropriate listelem using list::iterator:: operator*().

The STL member functions for list are very extensive; we will only show the code for a representative set and will place several more in the exercises (see exercise 7, on page 266, through exercise 10, on page 267). A basic operation on a list is the push_front() operation, where an element is prepended to the list. Here we have to take care of the special case of the empty list as well as the general case.

In file list2.h

```cpp
void list::push_front(char c)
{
   listelem* temp = new listelem(c, h, 0);

   if (h != 0) {                    //was a nonempty list
      h -> prev = temp;
      h = temp;
   }
   else                             //was an empty list
      h = t = temp;
}
```

The constructor for `listelem` builds the list cell that is prepended. If the list was previously empty both the head and tail must be properly initialized. Notice that the pointer `next` is set to h by the `listelem` constructor.

STL provides numerous constructors and a destructor.

In file list2.h

```cpp
//constructors
   list():h(0), t(0) {}             //0 denotes an empty list
   list(size_t n_elements, char c);
   list(const list& x);
   list(iterator b, iterator e);
   ~list() { release(); }
```

The default constructor producing an empty list has already been discussed. The second constructor produces a list of n elements, all initialized with a `data` member passed in as c.

```cpp
list::list(size_t n_elements, char c)
{
   assert(n_elements > 0);
   h = t = 0;
   for (size_t i = 0; i < n_elements; ++i)
      push_front(c);
}
```

This constructor builds its list by repeatedly calling `push_front()`.

In the copy constructor definition we combine list iteration and list creation. We traverse the original list getting data values used in creating the copy.

```
list::list(const list& x)
{
   list::iterator r = x.begin();
   h = t = 0; //needed for empty list
   while (r != 0)
      push_front(*r++);
}
```

The destructor calls the garbage-collection function `release()`.

```
void list::release()
{
   while (h != 0)
      pop_front();
}
```

The iterator logic and definitions are designed to be consistent with ordinary C++ pointer logic and operations.

7.7 Using Vectors for Numerical Processing

Many scientific problems are best solved numerically. Usually this involves finding some property of an equation or system of equations. In many cases a function is computed numerically over some interval of the reals, with the results being stored in a vector. These values can then be used to plot the function or examine the function for a desired property. For example, you can find a root of an equation, that place on the interval where the function evaluates to zero.

To find a root, we can compute the values of a function for a given interval and store them in a vector. Then we can search for the value that is nearest to zero. The function `find_zero()` will conduct that search. This is admittedly a simplistic method, but it is easy to illustrate and understand.

In file vector2.cpp

```
inline double abs(double x)
   { return (x > 0 ? x : -x); }
```

```
vector::iterator find_zero(const vector& v)
{
   vector::iterator u = v.begin(), t = u;
   double eps = abs(*t);

   while (++t != v.end())
      if (abs(*t)< eps) {
         u = t;
         eps = abs(*t);
      }
   return u;
}
```

The vector v is searched for the smallest absolute value; in other words, the value nearest to zero. It returns the iterator location of that element. We will use this to compute the zero of a simple quadratic.

```
inline double f(double x) { return 3*x*x + 4*x + 1; }

int main()
{
   vector y(1000);
   double x = -2, incr = 2.0/y.ub();

   for (int i = 0; i <= y.ub(); ++i) {
      y[i] = f(x);
      x += incr;
   }
   cout << y << endl;
   cout << "residual of y = " << *find_zero(y) << endl;
   cout << "zero at = "
        << (-2.0 + incr *
        static_cast<int>(find_zero(y) - y.begin()));
}
```

The code uses the vector size to determine how many points will be generated. It computes the increment as the length of the interval divided by the vector's upper bound, in this case 1,000. Knowing the position of the numerical zero in the vector lets us find the root. In this case we have searched from -2 to zero at increments of 2/1,000.

This method is ineffective for two reasons. First, it is computationally expensive for the resulting accuracy. Each digit of accuracy requires 10 times more points. Second, it might fail to properly detect a true zero. The nearest residual value to zero might still not be in the neighborhood of a zero. We can avoid this pitfall by looking for a place where the function crosses the x-axis. The residual would have opposite signs at adjacent points. This works for functions that have continuity as a property. We leave this modification as an exercise (see exercise 13, on page 267).

Another approach, which beats the above method, is to use bisection. Starting with an interval whose function has a different sign on each end, we examine the value at its midpoint. We use the midpoint to shorten the interval at each iteration. We stop when the interval is sufficiently accurate for our needs. This method is guaranteed to converge. It provides one binary digit of accuracy per function evaluation, so it is reasonably efficient when compared to the above search.

In file vector2.cpp

```
double bisect(double f(double),    //function
   double a,                       //f(a) < 0
   double b,                       //f(b) > 0
   double eps                      //accuracy of result
)
{
   if ((b - a) < eps)
      return ( (b + a) / 2);
   else
      if ( f((b+a)/2) <= 0)
         bisect(f, ( b+a )/ 2, b, eps);
      else
         return bisect(f, a, ( b+a )/ 2,  eps);
}
```

The function `bisect()` is naturally recursive. We leave as an exercise writing a noniterative form of this function (see exercise 12, on page 267).

7.8 Pragmatics

Notice that the class `list::iterator` mimics definitions that are appropriate for post- and pre- autoincrement and autodecrement. This is done to be consistent with the behavior of these operators on native types. The post operators return the existing object's value to the expression being evaluated and only then perform incrementation. We will show how this is done for list iterators.

In file list2.h

```
list::iterator iterator::operator++()
{
   assert(ptr != 0);
   ptr = ptr -> next;
   return *this;
}
```

Notice that in the preincrement operator we test for the end-of-list pointer value with an assertion. Other schemes are possible, such as resetting the iterator to the front of the list (see exercise 7, on page 266).

In the postincrement operator the initial value of the iterator is saved and returned as `temp`.

```
list::iterator iterator::operator++(int)
{
   assert(ptr != 0);
   iterator temp = *this;
   ptr = ptr -> next;
   return temp;
}
```

Summary

1. Visitation of the elements of an aggregate is a fundamental operation. When the aggregate is a class, an elegant solution to providing visitation operations is to create a separate but related class, called an iterator class, whose function is to visit and retrieve elements from the aggregate.

2. Containers should designate a `begin()` and an `end()` member returning an iterator. The STL conventions are that `begin()` returns the first position in the container, and `end()` returns an out-of-range value used for terminating the iteration over the container.

3. The pointer type `void*` serves as a generic, or universal, pointer type. Any other pointer type can be assigned to it. This allows us to use it polymorphically by developing code that indirectly manipulates objects of any type.

4. We developed a doubly linked list whose interface is similar to the STL library type `list`. A doubly linked list trades off space and efficiency. By adding a link that points to a previous list element, operations such as deletion are simplified at the expense of maintaining this additional pointer in all list elements.

5. Iterators are either pointers or pointer-like objects. Their semantics should be consistent with pointers in the kernel language.

Exercises

1. Write the indexing member function

    ```
    double& vector::operator[];
    ```

    It should use assertions to test whether indexing is out-of-range. (See the class `vector` in Section 7.1, "Visitation," on page 246.)

2. Write the member function

    ```
    vector::iterator vector::find(double x);
    //return position of first item containing x
    ```

3. Write the member function

   ```
   int vector::count(double x);
   //return the number of items containing x
   ```

4. Write a bubble sort on vector in which visitation uses iterator conventions.

5. Write a function:

   ```
   //Fill the designated range with random numbers
   void fill_rand(vector::iterator first, vector::iterator last)
   {
      vector::iterator   p;
   .....
   }
   ```

   that fills the designated vector range with randomly generated integer values.

6. Write a Monte Carlo root finder. Generate *n* random points in the function range and keep track of the point that is nearest in absolute value to zero. Return this point as the functions root. Test this on the function x*x - 2*x + 1. As you increase the number of points generated, how much added accuracy do you find?

7. Rewrite the list iterator operator postincrement:

   ```
   list::iterator iterator::operator++();
   //resets to front
   ```

   If it hits the last element of its range, namely end(), it is reset to the first element of the range, namely begin() (see Section 7.6, "List and List Iterator," on page 258).

8. Write both list iterator decrement operators:

   ```
   list::iterator iterator::operator--();
   list::iterator iterator::operator--(int);
   ```

9. Write the list member functions (see Section 7.6, "List and List Iterator," on page 257):

   ```
   void list::push_back(char c);    //adds to back of list
   void pop_back();                 //pop back of list element
   ```

10. Write the code for the constructor:

    ```
    list::list(iterator b, iterator e);
    ```

11. *(Project)* Code your own text editor. The model will be a page of text. The text will be made up of strings as a primary unit. You are to design an iterator class that can usefully navigate across the text. It can go to a next word, a next string, a next line—whatever you decide is useful. Minimally you should be able to enter, delete, and print text with or without line numbers. The text replacement commands should allow you to substitute one word for another. Also, try to use file-oriented I/O (see Section E.5, "Files," on page 477). You want text to be persistent, which means when you are done with it, it should be written to an output file.

12. Write the nonrecursive form of `bisect()` (see Section 7.7, "Using Vectors for Numerical Processing," on page 263).

13. Write a function that examines a vector and computes the first position at which the values change sign, and use it to find the roots of the equation

    $$f(x) = 3x^2 + 4x + 1$$

    Remember they are both in the interval (-2, 0).

14. Bisection gets one bit of accuracy per iteration. This is known as linear convergence. It is much better than finding a root by generating a random set of points. Better still is the Newton-Raphson method, in which the next iteration is equal to the previous value minus the function at that value divided by its derivative. Computationally this is

    ```
    x[n+1] = x[n] - f(x[n])/f_deriv(x[n])
    ```

    This iteration is repeated until a desired accuracy is obtained. Program this method for the equation $x^2 - 2$. Start the iteration at the value x[0] = 1. The solution should be the square root of 2.

Chapter 8

Templates, Generic Programming, and STL

C++ uses the keyword `template` to provide *parametric polymorphism*, which allows the same code to be used with respect to different types, where the type is a parameter of the code body. This is a form of generic programming. Many of our classes have been used to contain data of a particular type, though the data is processed in the same way regardless of type. Template class definitions and template function definitions allow us to reuse code in a simple, type-safe manner that lets the compiler automate the process of type *instantiation*, which is when an actual type replaces a type parameter that appeared in the template code.

> Which form do you need, master?

Polymorphism: Capable of assuming various forms

8.1 Template Class `stack`

We shall modify the `ch_stack` type from Section 5.2.1, "The Copy Constructor," on page 159, to have a parameterized type.

In file stack_t1.cpp

```
//template stack implementation
template <class TYPE>
class stack {
public:
   explicit stack(int size = 100)
      : max_len(size), top(EMPTY),s(new TYPE[size])
        { assert(s != 0;); }
   ~stack() { delete []s; }
   void  reset() { top = EMPTY; }
   void  push(TYPE c) { s[++top] = c; }
   TYPE  pop() { return s[top--]; }
   TYPE  top_of()const { return s[top]; }
   bool  empty()const { return top == EMPTY;}
   bool  full()const { return top == max_len - 1;}
private:
   enum    { EMPTY = -1 };
   TYPE*   s;
   int     max_len;
   int     top;
};
```

The syntax of the class declaration is prefaced by:

```
template <class identifier>
```

This identifier is a template argument that essentially stands for an arbitrary type. Throughout the class definition, the template argument can be used as a type name. This argument is instantiated in the actual declarations. A template declaration usually has global or namespace scope. It can be a member of a class or it can be declared within another template class. An example of a `stack` declaration using this is:

```
stack<char>     stk_ch;            //100 char stack
stack<char*>    stk_str(200);      //200 char* stack
stack<complex>  stk_cmplx(500);    //500 complex stack
```

This mechanism saves us rewriting class declarations where the only variation would be the type declarations. It is an alternate scheme to using void* as a universal pointer type. When processing such a type, the code must always use the angle brackets as part of the declaration, as shown below.

In file stack_t1.cpp

```
//Reversing an array of char* represented strings
void reverse(char* str[], int n)
{
   stack<char*>  stk(n);

   for (int i = 0; i < n; ++i)
      stk.push(str[i]);
   for (i = 0; i < n; ++i)
      str[i] = stk.pop();
}

//Initializing stack of complex numbers from an array
void init(complex c[], stack<complex>& stk, int n)
{
   for (int i = 0; i < n; ++i)
      stk.push(c[i]);
}
```

Member functions, when declared and defined inside the class, are, as usual, inline. When defining them externally, you must use the full angle-bracket declaration. So, when defined outside the template class,

```
TYPE  top_of() const { return s[top]; }
```

would be written as

```
template<class TYPE> TYPE stack<TYPE>::top_of() const
   { return s[top]; }
```

Yes, this is ugly and takes some getting used to, but the compiler otherwise would not know that TYPE was a template argument. As another example, we write the file-scope definition of the destructor for template<class TYPE> stack.

```
template<class TYPE> stack<TYPE>::~stack()
   { delete []s; }
```

8.2 Function Templates

Many functions have the same code body, regardless of type; for example, initializing the contents of one array from another of the same type uses the same code body. The essential code is:

```
for (i = 0; i < n; ++i)
   a[i] = b[i];
```

Most C programmers automate this with a simple macro:

```
#define  COPY(A, B, N) \
   { int i; for(i = 0; i < (N); ++i) (A)[i] = (B)[i]; }
```

Programming that works regardless of type is a form of generic programming. Using define macros can often work, but is not type safe. Another problem with define macros is that they can lead to repeated evaluation of a single parameter (see exercise 3, on page 311). A user could readily mix types among which conversions were inappropriate. C++ programmers can make use of various forms of conversion and overloading to achieve similar affects. However, in the absence of appropriate conversions and signatures, no action would be taken. Templates provide a further generic programming mechanism for this.

In file copy1.cpp

```
template<class TYPE>
void copy(TYPE a[], TYPE b[], int n)
{
   for (int i = 0; i < n; ++i)
      a[i] = b[i];
}
```

The invocation of copy() with specific arguments causes the compiler to generate the actual function based on those arguments. If it cannot, a compile-time error results. What are the effects of the following calls?

In file copy1.cpp

```
double  f1[50], f2[50];
char    c1[25], c2[50];
int     i1[75], i2[75];
char*   ptr1, *ptr2;
copy(f1, f2, 50);
copy(c1, c2, 10);
copy(i1, i2, 40);
copy(ptr1, ptr2, 100);
copy(i1, f2, 50);
copy(ptr1, f2, 50);
```

The last two invocations of copy() fail to compile because their types cannot be unified, according to the syntax error issued by the *g++* compiler. The types of the actual arguments do not conform to the template. If we were to cast f2 as

```
copy(i1, (int* )f2, 50);
```

compilation would occur. However, this would result in an inappropriate form of copying. Instead, we need to have a generic copying procedure that accepts two distinct class type arguments.

In file copy2.cpp

```
template<class T1, class T2>
void copy(T1 a[], T2 b[], int n)
{
    for (int i = 0; i < n; ++i)
        a[i] = b[i];
}
```

In this form, there is an element-by-element conversion. This is usually the appropriate and safer conversion.

8.2.1 Signature Matching and Overloading

A generic routine often cannot work for special cases. The following form of swapping template works on basic types.

In file swap.cpp

```
//generic swap
template <class T>
void swap(T& x, T& y)
{
   T  temp;

   temp = x;
   x = y;
   y = temp;
}
```

A function template is used to construct an appropriate function for any invocation that matches its arguments unambiguously:

```
int       i, j;
char      str1[100], str2[100], ch;
complex   c1, c2;

swap(i, j);                  //i j int -  okay
swap(c1, c2);                //c1, c2 complex -okay
swap(str1[50], str2[33]);    //both char variables -okay
swap(i, ch);                 //i int ch char - illegal
swap(str1, str2);            //illegal
```

In the last case, `str1` and `str2` are array names. They are pointer values that cannot be modified.

To have `swap()` work for strings represented as character arrays, we write the following special case:

```
void swap(char* s1, char* s2)
{
   int  max_len;

   max_len = (strlen(s1) >= strlen(s2)) ?
             strlen(s1) : strlen(s2);
   char* temp = new char[max_len + 1];

   strcpy(temp, s1);
   strcpy(s1, s2);
   strcpy(s2, temp);
   delete []temp;
}
```

With this specialized case added, an exact match of this nontemplate version to the signature of a swap() invocation takes precedence over the exact match found by a template substitution.

Overloaded Function-Selection Algorithm

1. Exact match with some trivial conversions allowed on nontemplate functions.

2. Exact match using function templates.

3. Ordinary argument resolution on nontemplate functions.

8.3 Class Templates

In the stack<T> example given in Section 8.1, "Template Class stack," on page 270, we have an ordinary case of class parameterization. In this section, we wish to discuss various special features of parameterizing classes.

8.3.1 Friends

Template classes can contain friends. A friend function that does not use a template specification is universally a friend of all instantiations of the template class. A friend function that incorporates template arguments is specifically a friend of its instantiated class:

```
template <class T>
class matrix {
public:
   friend void  foo_bar();                    //universal
   friend vect<T>  product(vect<T> v);        //instantiated
   .....
};
```

8.3.2 Static Members

Static members are not universal, but are specific to each instantiation:

```
template <class T>
class foo {
public:
   static int  count;
   .....
};

   .....
foo<int>     a;
foo<double>  b;
```

The static variables foo<int>::count and foo<double>::count are distinct.

8.3.3 Class Template Arguments

Both classes and functions can have several class template arguments. Let us write a function that will convert one type of value to a second type, provided the first type is at least as wide as the second.

In file coerce.cpp

```
template <class T1, class T2>
bool coerce(T1& x, T2 y)
{
   if (sizeof(x) < sizeof(y))
      return false;
   x = static_cast<T1>(y);
   return true;
}
```

In this template function there are two possibly distinct types specified as template arguments.

Other template arguments include constant expressions, function names, and character strings.

In file array_tm.cpp

```
template <class T, int n>
class assign_array {
public:
    T  a[n];
};

. . . . .
assign_array<double,50>  x, y;
. . . . .
x = y;       //should work efficiently
```

The benefits of this parameterization include allocation of the stack, as opposed to allocation from free store. On many systems this is the more efficient regime. The type is bound to the particular integer constant, so that operations involving compatible-length arrays are type safe and are checked at compile time.

8.4 Parameterizing the Class vector

The class vector is a natural candidate for parameterization. We will parameterize it and discuss how it is used in conjunction with iterators and algorithms. It is a typical sequential container class that approximates a similar class available in the standard template library:

In file vect_it.h

```
//Template based vector type
template <class T>
class vector {
public:
   typedef T* iterator;
   explicit vector(int n=100);      //create a size n array
   vector(const vector<T>& v);      //copy vector
   vector(const T a[], int n);      //copy an array
   ~vector() { delete []p; }
   iterator begin(){ return p;}
   iterator end(){ return p + size;}
   T& operator[](int i);            //range checked element
   vector<T>& operator=(const vector<T>& v);
private:
   T* p;                            //base pointer
   int size;                        //number of elements
};
```

Basically, everywhere the previous vector class used int as the value to be stored in individual elements, the template definition uses T. So the declaration of the private base pointer p is now of type T.

The definition of member functions in file scope include the scope-resolved label *classname<T>*. The following constructors for vector<T> use T as the type specification to new:

```
template <class T>
vector<T>::vector(int n = 100): size(n)
{
   assert(n > 0);
   p = new T[size];
   assert(p != 0);
}
```

This is the default constructor, because of the default argument of 100. We use the keyword explicit to disallow its use as a conversion from int to vector. Assertions are used to guarantee that the constructor performs its contractual obligations when given appropriate input.

```
template <class T>
vector<T>::vector(const T a[], int n)
{
   assert(n > 0);
   size = n;
   p = new T[size];
   assert(p != 0);
   for (int i = 0; i < size; ++i)
      p[i] = a[i];
}
```

This constructor converts an ordinary array to a vector. The copy constructor defines a deep copy of the vector v.

```
template <class T>
vector<T>::vector(const vector<T>& v)
{
   size = v.size;
   p = new T[size];
   assert(p != 0);
   for (int i = 0; i < size; ++i)
      p[i] = v.p[i];
}
```

The following code defines vector indexing by overloading the bracket operator. The return type for the bracket operator is reference to T, as this is an alias for the item stored in the container. Using this return type allows the bracket operator to access the item in the container as an lvalue.

```
template <class T> T& vector<T>::operator[](int i)
{
   assert (i >= 0 && i < size );
   return (p[i]);
}
```

Notice that we can test to make sure the array bounds are not exceeded. With operator[] overloaded, we can access vectors as if they were native C++ arrays. We also need to provide an overloaded assignment operator (see exercise 7, on page 312).

```
template <class T>
vector<T>& vector<T>::operator=(const vector<T>& v)
{
   assert(v.size == size);
   for (int i = 0; i < size; ++i)
      p[i] = v.p[i];
   return *this;
}
```

Client code is almost as simple as with nonparameterized declarations. To use these declarations, you simply add within angle brackets the specific type that instantiates the template. These types can be native types, such as int in the example, or user-defined types. The following code uses these templates.

In file vect_it.cpp

```
int main()
{
   vector<double> v(5);
   vector<double>::iterator p ;
   int i = 0;

   for (p = v.begin() ; p != v.end(); ++p)
      *p = 1.5 + i++;

   do {
      --p;
      cout << *p << " , ";
   } while (p != v.begin());
   cout << endl;
}
```

The output from this program is:

```
5.5, 4.5, 3.5, 2.5, 1.5,
```

The values are in reverse order to how they are stored. This is a consequence of iterating back from the iterator value v.end().

8.5 Parameterizing `quicksort()`

We use the `vector<T>` and templates to build a parameterized `quicksort()` routine. Each piece of the traditional `quicksort` is parameterized.

In file quicksort.cpp

```
//QUICKSORT using a vector class

template<class T>
void swap(T& i, T& j) { T temp = i; i = j; j = temp; }
```

At the heart of any sorting routine is the reordering of elements. In this case, `swap()` is parameterized to accept an arbitrary type.

The `quicksort` routine itself is a simple recursion. It uses a partitioning routine to divide the parameterized array `vector<T>` into two parts. The elements in the range from to mid - 1 are smaller than the elements in the range (mid + 1, to).

```
template<class T>
void quicksort(T* from, T* to)
{
   T* mid;

   if (from < to - 1) {
      mid = partition(from, to);
      quicksort(from, mid);
      quicksort(mid + 1, to);
   }
}
```

The `partition()` routine is parameterized and uses iterators to track where it is when exchanging out-of-order elements. The iterators `front` and `back` maintain the current position in their respective parts of the array being partitioned.

```
template<class T>
T* partition(T* from, T* to)
{
   T* front = from;
   T* back = to - 1;
   T  compare;

   compare = *front;            //comparison element
   ++front;                     //advance to next element
   while (front < back) {
      //search forward for out of order element
      while ((front < back) &&(compare > *front))
            ++front;
      //search backward for out of order element
      while ((front < back) &&(compare <= *back))
            --back;
      swap(*front, *back);
   }
   //insert mid position comparison element
   if (compare >= *front) {
      swap(*from, *front);
      return (front);
   }
   else {
      swap(*from, *(front - 1));
      return (front - 1);
   }
}
```

Using this in client code is very easy. We instantiate the angle brackets with the desired type; for example:

```
vector<int> v(n);       //create a vector of n integers
```

Then we invoke the instantiated sorting algorithm as

```
quicksort(v.begin(), v.end());
```

Note that the parameterized type being sorted needs to have the comparison operators defined for it.

8.6 Parameterized Binary Search Tree

Parametric polymorphism is achievable using both void* generic pointers and templates. This technique has some advantages over using void* or templates alone. We want to show how it works in implementing a binary sorted tree.

In file gentree1.cpp

```
//A generic binary sorted tree.
template <class T>  class gen_tree;        //forward decl

template <class T>
class bnode {
private:
   friend class gen_tree<T>;
   bnode<T>*  left;
   bnode<T>*  right;
   T          data;
   int        count;
   bnode(T d, bnode<T>* l, bnode<T>* r) :
         data(d), left(l), right(r), count(1) { }
   void   print() const
      { cout << data << " : " << count << '\t'; }
};
```

The tree will store type T data. Notationally, the internal self-referential pointers left and right are of type bnode<T>*. The notation is ugly but necessary. The inline bnode<T>::print() function is expected to have operator<<() defined as an output operator. If this is not the case, the instantiation will fail at compile time.

```
template <class T>
class gen_tree {
public:
   gen_tree() { root = 0; }
   void  insert(T d);
   T  find(T d) const { return (find(root, d)); }
   void  print() const { print(root); }
private:
   bnode<T>*   root;
   T  find(bnode<T>* r, T d) const;
   void  print(bnode<T>* r) const;
};
```

The generic tree type gentree<T> will be instantiated to store T data using the insertion routine insert() to build the binary sorted tree.

The function comp() is a parameterized external function. It has two forms. In its general form, it uses existing or user-supplied meanings for == and <. When lexicographic compare on const char* is needed, a specialization of this function is required:

```
#include  <string.h>
template <class T>         //general case
int comp(T i, T j)
{
   if (i == j)             //assumes ==  < defined for T
      return 0;
   else
      return ( (i < j) ? -1 : 1 );
}

//specialization for const char*
int comp(const char* i, const char* j)
{
   return (strcmp(i, j));
}
```

The gen_tree<T>::insert() function needs to find and insert a node in sorted order. Notice that the new operator needs to create a bnode<T> object:

```
template <class T>
void gen_tree<T>::insert(T d)
{
   bnode<T>*  temp = root;
   bnode<T>*  old;

   if (root == 0) {
      root = new bnode<T>(d, 0, 0);
      return;
   }

   while (temp != 0) {
      old = temp;
      if (comp(temp -> data, d) == 0) {
         (temp -> count)++;
         return;
      }
      if (comp(temp -> data, d) > 0)
         temp = temp -> left;
      else
         temp = temp -> right;
   }
   if (comp(old -> data, d) > 0)
      old -> left = new bnode<T>(d, 0, 0);
   else
      old -> right = new bnode<T>(d, 0, 0);
}
```

Member functions require simple modifications to accommodate parameterization. Almost all changes to the concrete case occur in declarations:

```
template <class T>
T gen_tree<T>::find(bnode<T>* r, T d) const
{
   if (r == 0)
      return 0;
   else if (comp(r -> data, d) == 0)
      return (r -> data);
   else if (comp(r -> data, d) > 0)
      return (find( r -> left, d));
   else
      return (find( r -> right, d));
}
```

```
template <class T>
void gen_tree<T>::print(bnode<T> *r) const
{
   if (r != 0) {
      print( r -> left);
      r -> bnode<T>::print();
      print ( r -> right);
   }
}
```

Client code needs only instantiation of the particular type to be stored in the binary trees. Below we show two uses—one to sort `char*` strings and the second to sort integers.

In file gentree1.cpp

```
int main()
{
   char              dat[256];
   gen_tree<char*>   t;
   char*             p;

   while (cin>>dat){
      p = new char[strlen(dat) + 1];
      strcpy(p, dat);
      t.insert(p);
   }
   t.print();
   cout << "EOF" << endl << endl;

   gen_tree<int>  i_tree;

   for (int i = 15; i > -5; --i)
      i_tree.insert(i);
   i_tree.print();
}
```

In Section 9.3, "Code Reuse: A Binary Tree Class," on page 321, we reexamine this data structure and use inheritance to achieve some of the same results of code reuse and polymorphism that are found here using templates. These two approaches have different advantages and trade-offs with respect to ease of use, efficiency, and extensibility.

8.7 STL

The standard template library (STL) is the C++ library providing generic programming for many standard data structures and algorithms. The STL library provides three components—containers, iterators, and algorithms—that support a standard for generic programming.

The library is built using templates and is highly orthogonal in design. Components can be used with one another on native and user-provided types through proper instantiation of the various elements of the STL library.

We will use the list container, an iterator, and the generic algorithm `accumulate()` in our first example program using STL.

In file stl_cont.cpp

```cpp
//Using the list container.
#include <iostream>
#include <list>              //list container
#include <numeric>           //for accumulate
using namespace std;

void print(const list<double> &lst)
{                   //using an iterator to traverse lst
   list<double>::const_iterator p;

   for (p = lst.begin(); p !=lst.end(); ++p)
      cout << *p << '\t';
   cout << endl;
}

int main()
{
   double w[4] = { 0.9, 0.8, 88, -99.99 };
   list<double> z;
   for (int i = 0; i < 4; ++i)
      z.push_front(w[i]);
   print(z);
   z.sort();
   print(z);
   cout << "sum is "
        << accumulate(z.begin(), z.end(), 0.0) << endl;
}
```

In this example, a list container is instantiated to hold `doubles`. An array of doubles is pushed into the list. The `print()` function uses an iterator to print each element of the list in turn. Notice that iterators work like pointers. They have standard interfaces that include `begin()` and `end()` member functions for starting and ending locations of the container. Also, the list interface includes a stable sorting algorithm, the `sort()` member function. The `accumulate()` function is a generic function in the *numeric* package that uses 0.0 as an initial value and computes the sum of the list container elements by going from the starting location `z.begin()` to the ending location `z.end()`.

Notice that `print()` itself could be parameterized and made a generic algorithm. Try to do this in a most general way (see exercise 14, on page 313).

8.8 Containers

Containers come in two major families: sequence and associative. Sequence containers include vectors, lists, and deques. These containers are ordered by having a sequence of elements. Associative containers include sets, multisets, maps, and multimaps, and have keys for looking up elements. The map container is a basic associative array and requires that a comparison operation on the stored elements be defined. The two varieties of container share a similar interface.

STL Typical Container Interfaces

- Constructors, including default and copy constructors
- Element access
- Element insertion
- Element deletion
- Destructor
- Iterators

Containers are traversed using iterators. These are pointer-like objects that are available as templates and optimized for use with STL containers.

In file stl_deq.cpp

```
//A typical container algorithm
double sum(const deque<double> &dq)
{
   deque<double>::const_iterator p;
   double s = 0.0;

   for (p=dq.begin(); p != dq.end(); ++p)
      s += *p ;
   return s;
}
```

The deque (double-ended queue) container is traversed using a `const_iterator`. The iterator p is dereferenced to obtain each stored value in turn. This algorithm will work with sequence containers and with all types that have `operator+=()` defined.

Container classes will be designated as CAN in the following table, which describes their interface.

STL Container Definitions	
CAN::value_type	what is held in the CAN
CAN::reference	reference type to value
CAN::const_reference	const reference
CAN::pointer	pointer to reference type
CAN::iterator	iterator type
CAN::const_iterator	const iterator
CAN::reverse_iterator	reverse iterator
CAN::const_reverse_iterator	const reverse iterator
CAN::difference_type	the difference between two CAN::iterator values
CAN::size_type	size of a CAN

All container classes have these definitions available. For example, `vector<char>::value_type` means a character value is stored in the vector container. Such a container could be traversed with a `vector<char>::iterator`.

Containers allow equality and comparison operators. They also have an extensive list of standard member functions, as shown in the following table.

STL Container Members	
CAN::CAN()	default constructor
CAN::CAN(c)	copy constructor
c.begin()	beginning location of CAN c
c.end()	ending location of CAN c
c.rbegin()	beginning for a reverse iterator
c.rend()	ending for a reverse iterator
c.size()	number of elements in CAN
c.max_size()	largest possible size
c.empty()	true if the CAN is empty
c.swap(d)	swap two CANs

8.8.1 Sequence Containers

The sequence containers are vector, list, and deque. They have a sequence of accessible elements. The C++ array type in many cases can also be treated as a sequence container.

In file stl_vect.cpp

```
//Sequence Containers- insert a vector into a deque.
#include <iostream>
#include <deque>
#include <vector>
using namespace std;
```

```
int main()
{
   int data[5] = { 6, 8, 7, 6, 5 };
   vector<int> v(5, 6);               //5 element vector
   deque<int> d(data, data + 5);
   deque<int>::iterator p;
   cout << "\nDeque values" << endl;
   for (p = d.begin(); p != d.end(); ++p)
      cout << *p << '\t';             //print:6 8 7 6 5
   cout << endl;
   d.insert(d.begin(), v.begin(), v.end());
   for (p = d.begin(); p != d.end(); p++)
      cout << *p << '\t';             //print:6 6 6 6 6 8 7 6 5
}
```

The five-element `vector` v is initialized with the value 6. The `deque` d is initialized with values taken from the `data` array. The `insert()` member function places the v values in the specified range `v.begin()` to `v.end()`, at the location `d.begin()`.

Dissection of the *stl_vect* Program

- ```
  int data[5] = { 6, 8, 7, 6, 5 };
  vector<int> v(5, 6);               //5 element vector
  deque<int> d(data, data + 5);
  deque<int>::iterator p;
  ```

  The vector v initializes a five-element `int` container to value 6. The deque d uses the iterator values `data` and `data + 5` to initialize a five-element double-ended queue container. Ordinary array pointers can be used as iterators. The iterator p is declared but not initialized.

- ```
  for (p = d.begin(); p != d.end(); ++p)
     cout << *p << '\t';     //print:6 8 7 6 5
  ```

  This is a standard traversal idiom when using containers and iterators. Notice that `d.end()` is used to terminate the loop, because it is in effect the end-of-container iterator value. Also notice the ++ autoincrement has pointer semantics advancing the iterator to the next container position. Dereferencing also works analogously to pointer semantics.

- `d.insert(d.begin(), v.begin(), v.end());`

The `insert()` member function places the range of iterator values `v.begin()` up to but not including `v.end()` at the position `d.begin()`.

- ```
  for (p = d.begin(); p != d.end(); ++p)
      cout << *p << '\t';   //print:6 6 6 6 6 8 7 6 5
  ```

As a consequence of inserting five new elements of value 6 at the front of the deque d, the output of the traversal loop for d is now the 10 elements, as shown in the comment.

Sequence classes will be designated as SEQ in the following table. Keep in mind that these are in addition to the already described CAN interface.

STL Sequence Members	
SEQ::SEQ(n, v)	n elements of value v
SEQ::SEQ(b_it, e_it)	starts at b_it and goes to e_it - 1
c.insert(w_it, v)	inserts v before w_it
c.insert(w_it, v, n)	inserts n copies of v before w_it
c.insert(w_it, b_it, e_it)	inserts b_it to e_it before w_it
c.erase(w_it)	erases the element at w_it
c.erase(b_it, e_it)	erases b_it to e_it

Some examples of using these members are:

```
double w[6] = { 1.1, 1.2, 2.2, 2.3, 3.3, 4.4 };
vector<double> v(15, 1.5);   //15 elements of value 1.5
deque<double> d(w + 2, w + 6);     //use 2.2 to 4.4
d.erase(d.begin() + 2);            //erase 3rd element
v.insert(v.begin() +1, w[3]);      //insert w[3]
```
```

8.8.2 Associative Containers

The associative containers are set, map, multiset, and multimap. They have key-based accessible elements, and an ordering relation Compare, which is the comparison object for the associative container.

In file stl_age.cpp

```
//Associative Containers - looking up ages.
#include <map>
#include <string>
#include <iostream>
using namespace std;

int main()
{
   map<string, int, less<string> > name_age;

   name_age["Pohl,Laura"] = 7;
   name_age["Dolsberry,Betty"] = 39;
   name_age["Pohl,Tanya"] = 14;
   cout << "Laura is " << name_age["Pohl,Laura"]
        << " years old." << endl;
}
```

The map name_age is an associative array where the key is a string type. The Compare object is less<string>.

Associative classes will be designated as ASSOC in the following table describing their interface. Keep in mind that these are in addition to the already described CAN interface.

STL Associative Definitions	
ASSOC::key_type	the retrieval key type
ASSOC::key_compare	the comparison object type
ASSOC::value_compare	the type for comparing ASSOC::value_type

The associative containers have several standard constructors for initialization.

STL Associative Constructors	
ASSOC()	default constructor using Compare
ASSOC(cmp)	constructor using cmp as the comparison object
ASSOC(b_it, e_it)	uses element range b_it to e_it using Compare
ASSOC(b_it, e_it, cmp)	uses element range b_it to e_it and cmp as the comparison object

What distinguishes these constructors from sequence container constructors is the use of a comparison object.

STL Insert and Erase Member Functions	
c.insert(t)	inserts t, if no existing element has the same key as t; returns position of insertion
c.insert(w_it, t)	inserts t with w_it as a starting position for the search; fails on sets and maps if key value is already present; returns position of insertion
c.insert(b_it, e_it)	inserts the element range
c.erase(k)	erases elements whose key value is k, returning the number of erased elements
c.erase(w_it)	erases the pointed to element
c.erase(b_it, e_it)	erases the range of elements

The insertions work when no element of the same key is already present. Here are some examples of using these members:

```
int m[4] = { 1, 2, 3, 4 };
set<int, less<int> > s;        //set of ints ordered on less
set<int, less<int> > t(m, m +4);    //use 1, 2, 3, 4
s.insert(3);                   //place 3 in set s
t.insert(3);                   //no insertion as 3 is in set t
s.erase(2);                    //s had no such element
t.erase(4);                    //t now contains 1, 2, 3
```

More member functions may be found in Section F.1.2, "Associative Containers," on page 490.

8.8.3 Container Adaptors

Container adaptor classes are container classes that modify existing containers to produce various public behaviors based on an existing implementation. Three provided container adaptors are `stack`, `queue`, and `priority_queue`.

The `stack` can be adapted from `vector`, `list`, and `deque`. It needs an implementation that supports `back`, `push_back`, and `pop_back` operations.

STL Adapted Stack Functions	
`void push(const value_type& v)`	places v on the stack
`void pop()`	removes the top element of the stack
`value_type& top() const`	returns the top element of the stack
`bool empty() const`	returns `true` if the stack is empty
`size_type size() const`	returns the number of elements in the stack
`operator==` and `operator<`	equality and lexicographically less than

The `queue` can be adapted from `list` or `deque`. It needs an implementation that supports `empty`, `size`, `front`, `back`, `push_back`, and `pop_front` operations. This is a first-in-first-out data structure.

STL Adapted Queue Functions	
`void push(const value_type& v)`	places v on the end of the queue
`void pop()`	removes the front element of the queue
`value_type& front() const`	returns the front element of the queue
`value_type& back() const`	returns the back element of the queue
`bool empty() const`	returns `true` if the queue is empty
`size_type size() const`	returns the number of elements in the queue
`operator==` and `operator<`	equality and lexicographically less than

We adapt the `stack` from an underlying `vector` implementation. Notice the STL ADTs replace our individually designed implementations of these types.

In file stl_stak.cpp

```cpp
//Adapt a stack from a vector.
#include <iostream>
#include <stack>
#include <vector>
#include <string>
using namespace std;

int main()
{
   stack<string, vector<string> > str_stack;
   string quote[3] =
    { "The wheel that squeaks the loudest\n",
      "Is the one that gets the grease\n",
      "Josh Billings\n" };

   for (int i =0; i < 3; ++i)
      str_stack.push(quote[i]);
   while (!str_stack.empty()) {
      cout << str_stack.top();
      str_stack.pop();
   }
}
```

8.9 Iterators

Navigation over containers is by iterator. Iterators can be thought of as an enhanced pointer type. They are templates that are instantiated according to the container class type they iterate over. There are five iterator types: input, output, forward, bidirectional, and random-access. Not all iterator types may be available for a given container class. For example, random-access iterators are available for vectors but not for maps.

Input iterators support equality operations, dereferencing, and autoincrement. An iterator that satisfies these conditions can be used for one-pass algorithms that read values of a data structure in one direction. A special case of the input iterator is the `istream_iterator`.

Output iterators support dereferencing restricted to the left-hand side of assignment and autoincrement. An iterator that satisfies these conditions can be used for one-pass algorithms that write values to a data structure in one direction. A special case of the output iterator is the `ostream_iterator`.

Forward iterators support all input/output iterator operations as well as unrestricted use of assignment. This allows position within a data structure to be retained from pass to pass. Therefore, general one-directional multipass algorithms can be written with forward iterators.

Bidirectional iterators support all forward iterator operations as well as both autoincrement and autodecrement. Therefore, general bidirectional multipass algorithms can be written with bidirectional iterators.

Random access iterators support all bidirectional iterator operations as well as address arithmetic operations such as indexing. In addition, random-access iterators support comparison operations. Therefore, algorithms such as `quicksort` that require efficient random access in linear time can be written with these iterators.

Container classes and algorithms dictate the category of iterator available or needed, so `vector` containers allow random-access iterators, but `lists` do not. Sorting generally requires a random-access iterator, but finding requires only an input iterator.

8.9.1 The `istream_iterator` and `ostream_iterator`

An `istream_iterator` is derived from an input iterator to work specifically with reading from streams. An `ostream_iterator` is derived from an output iterator to work specifically with writing to streams. We will write a program that prompts for five numbers, reads them, and computes their sum, where IO uses these iterators. The template for `istream_iterator` is instantiated with a *<type, distance>*. This distance is usually specified by `ptrdiff_t`. As defined in *cstddef* or *stddef.h*, it is an integer type representing the difference between two pointer values.

In file stl_io.cpp

```
//Use of istream_iterator and ostream_iterator.

#include <iterator>
#include <iostream>
#include <vector>
using namespace std;
```

```cpp
int main()
{
   vector<int> d(5);
   int  i, sum ;
   istream_iterator<int, ptrdiff_t> in(cin);
   ostream_iterator<int> out(cout, "\t");

   cout << "enter 5 numbers" << endl;
   sum = d[0] = *in;              //input first value
   for (i = 1; i < 5; ++i) {
      d[i] = *++in;               //input consecutive values
      sum += d[i];
   }
   for (i = 0; i < 5; ++i)
      *out = d[i] ;               //output consecutive values
   cout << " sum = " << sum << endl;
}
```

The `istream_iterator` in is instantiated with type `int` and parameter `ptrdiff_t`. The `ptrdiff_t` is a distance type that the iterator uses to advance in getting a next element. In the above declaration `in` is constructed with the input stream `cin`. The autoincrement operator advances `in` and reads a next value of type `int` from the designated input stream. The `ostream_iterator` out is constructed with the output stream `cout` and the `char*` delimiter "\t". Thus the tab character will be issued to the stream `cout` after each `int` value is written. In this program the iterator `out`, when it is dereferenced, writes the assigned `int` value to `cout`.

8.9.2 Iterator Adaptors

Iterators can be adapted to provide backward traversal and traversal with insertion. Reverse iterators reverse the order of iteration; with insert iterators, insertion takes place instead of the normal overwriting mode. In the following example we use a reverse iterator to traverse a sequence.

In file stl_iadp.cpp

```cpp
//Use of the reverse iterator.
#include <iostream>
#include <vector>
using namespace std;
```

```
template <class ForwIter>
void print(ForwIter first, ForwIter last, const char* title)
{
   cout << title << endl;
   while ( first != last)
      cout << *first++ << '\t';
   cout << endl;
}

int main()
{
   int     data[3] = { 9, 10, 11};
   vector<int> d(data, data + 3);
   vector<int>::reverse_iterator p = d.rbegin();

   print(d.begin(), d.end(), "Original");
   print(p, d.rend(), "Reverse");
}
```

This program uses a reverse iterator to change the direction in which the `print()` function prints the elements of vector d.

Other algorithms in the *iterator* library are discussed in Section F.2.4, "Iterator Adaptors," on page 494.

8.10 Algorithms

The STL algorithms library contains the following four categories.

Categories of STL Algorithms Library
- Sorting algorithms
- Nonmutating sequence algorithms
- Mutating sequence algorithms
- Numerical algorithms

These algorithms generally use iterators to access containers instantiated on a given type. The resulting code can be competitive in efficiency with special-purpose codes.

8.10.1 Sorting Algorithms

Sorting algorithms include general sorting, merges, lexicographic comparison, permutation, binary search, and selected similar operations. These algorithms have versions that use either `operator<()` or a `Compare` object. They often require random-access iterators.

The following program uses the quicksort function `sort()` from STL.

In file stl_sort.cpp

```
//Using sort() from STL.
#include <iostream>
#include <algorithm>
using namespace std;

const int N = 5;

int main()
{
   int    d[N], i, *e = d + N;

   for (i = 0; i < N; ++i)
      d[i] = rand();
   sort(d, e);
   for (i = 0; i < N; ++i)
      cout << d[i] << '\t';
}
```

This is a straightforward use of the library `sort` algorithm operating on the built-in array `d[]`. Notice that ordinary pointer values can be used as iterators.

The library prototype for the `sort` algorithm is:

- ```
  template<class RandAcc>
  void sort(RandAcc b, RandAcc e);
  ```

    This is a quicksort algorithm over the elements b to e. The `RandAcc` iterator type must be a random-access iterator.

More algorithm prototypes may be found in Section F.3.1, "Sorting Algorithms," on page 496.
  ```

8.10.2 Nonmutating Sequence Algorithms

Nonmutating algorithms do not modify the contents of the containers they work on. A typical operation is searching a container for a particular element and returning its position.

In the following program the nonmutating library function `find()` is used to locate the element t.

In file stl_find.cpp

```
//Use of the find function.
#include <iostream>
#include <algorithm>
#include <string>
using namespace std;

int main()
{
   string words[5] = { "my", "hop", "mop", "hope", "cope"};
   string*   where;

   where = find(words, words + 5, "hop");
   cout << *++where << endl;                //mop
   sort(words, words + 5);
   where = find(words, words + 5, "hop");
   cout << *++where << endl;                //hope
}
```

This uses `find()` to look for the position of the word *hop*. We print the word following *hop* before and after sorting the array `words[]`.

The library prototypes for two find algorithms are:

- template<class InputIter, Class T>
  InputIter find(InputIter b, InputIter e, const T& t);

  This finds the position of t in the range b to e.

- template<class InputIter, Class Predicate>
  InputIter find(InputIter b, InputIter e, Predicate p);

  This finds the position of the first element that makes the predicate true in the range b to e; otherwise the position e is returned.

More mutating function algorithm prototypes are given in Section F.3.2, "Nonmutating Sequence Algorithms," on page 499.

8.10.3 Mutating Sequence Algorithms

Mutating algorithms can modify the contents of the containers they work on. A typical operation is reversing the contents of a container.

In the following program the mutating library functions `reverse()` and `copy()` are used.

In file stl_revr.cpp

```cpp
//Use of mutating copy and reverse.
#include <string>
#include <algorithm>
#include <vector>
using namespace std;

int main()
{
   string first_names[5] = {"laura", "ira",
       "buzz", "debra", "twinkle"};
   string last_names[5] = {"pohl", "pohl",
       "dolsberry", "dolsberry", "star"};
   vector<string> names(first_names, first_names + 5);
   vector<string> names2(10);
   vector<string>::iterator p;

   copy(last_names, last_names + 5, names2.begin());
   copy(names.begin(), names.end(), names2.begin()+5);
   reverse(names2.begin(), names2.end());
   for (p = names2.begin(); p != names2.end(); ++p)
      cout << *p <<'\t';
}
```

The first invocation of the mutating function `copy()` places `last_names` in the container `vector names2`. The second call to `copy()` copies in the `first_names` that had been used in the construction of the `vector names`. The function `reverse()` reverses all the elements, which are then printed out.

The library prototypes for two copy algorithms are:

- ```
  template<class InputIter, class OutputIter>
  OutputIter copy(InputIter b1,
        InputIter e1, OutputIter b2);
  ```

  This is a copying algorithm over the elements b1 to e1. The copy is placed starting at b2. The position returned is the end of the copy.

- ```
  template<class BidiIter1, class BidiIter2>
  BidiIter2 copy_backward(BidiIter1 b1,
        BidiIter1 e1, BidiIter2 b2);
  ```

  This is a copying algorithm over the elements b1 to e1. The copy is placed starting at b2. The copying runs backward from e1 into b2, which also go backward. The position returned is b2 - (e1 - b1).

More algorithms are given in Section F.3.3, "Mutating Sequence Algorithms," on page 500.

8.10.4 Numerical Algorithms

Numerical algorithms include sums, inner product, and adjacent difference.

In the following program the numerical function accumulate() performs a vector summation, and inner_product() performs a vector inner product.

In file stl_numr.cpp

```cpp
//Vector accumulation and innerproduct.
#include <iostream>
#include <numeric>
using namespace std;

int main()
{
   double v1[3] = { 1.0, 2.5, 4.6 },
          v2[3] = { 1.0, 2.0, -3.5 };
   double sum, inner_p;

   sum = accumulate(v1, v1 + 3, 0.0);
   inner_p = inner_product(v1, v1 + 3, v2, 0.0);
   cout << "sum = " << sum
        << ",product = " << inner_p << endl;
}
```

These functions behave as expected on numerical types where + and * are defined. The `accumulate` algorithm has the starting and ending position and as a third argument the initial value, normally 0.0 to start accumulating the sum with.

The library prototypes for two accumulate algorithms are:

- ```
  template<class InputIter, class T>
  T accumulate(InputIter b, InputIter e, T t);
  ```

  This is a standard accumulation algorithm whose sum is initially t. The successive elements from the range b to e are added to this sum.

- ```
  template<class InputIter, class T, class BinOp>
  T accumulate(InputIter b, InputIter e, T t, BinOp bop);
  ```

  This is an accumulation algorithm whose sum is initially t. The successive elements from the range b to e are summed with `sum = bop(sum, element)`.

- ```
  template<class InputIter, class T>
  T inner_product(InputIter b1, InputIter e1, InputIter b2, T t);
  ```

  This is an inner-product algorithm whose sum is initially t. The successive elements from the range b1 to e1 are multiplied by the elements beginning at b2.

See also Section F.3.4, "Numerical Algorithms," on page 503.

8.11 Functions

Function objects are useful to further leverage the STL library. For example, many of the previous numerical functions had a built-in meaning using + or *, but also had a form in which user-provided binary operators could be passed in as arguments. Defined function objects can be found in the library *function*, or they can be built. Function objects are classes that have `operator()` defined. These are inlined and are compiled to produce efficient object code.
  ```

In file stl_fucn.cpp

```
//Using a function object minus<int>.
#include <iostream>
#include <numeric>
using namespace std;

int main()
{
   double v1[3] = { 1.0, 2.5, 4.6 }, sum;

   sum = accumulate(v1, v1 + 3, 0.0, minus<int>());
   cout << "sum = " << sum << endl;      //sum = -7
}
```

Accumulation is done using integer minus for the binary operation over the array v1[]. Therefore the double values are truncated, with the result being -7.

There are three defined function object classes, as shown in the following list.

Defined Function Object Classes

- Arithmetic objects
- Comparison objects
- Logical objects

We will use a table to briefly list algorithms and their purpose as found in the library *function*.

STL Function Objects	
template <class T> struct plus<T>	Arithmetic function for type T; also minus, times, divides, modulus
template <class T> struct greater<T>	Comparison function for type T; also less, equal_to, greater_equal, less_equal
template <class T> struct logical_and<T>	Logical function on type T; also logical_or, logical_not

The arithmetic objects are often used in numerical algorithms, such as `accumulate()`. The comparison objects are frequently used with sorting algorithms, such as `merge()`. Expanded tables of these three types are given in Section F.4, "Functions," on page 504.

8.12 Function Adaptors

Function adaptors allow for the creation of function objects using adaption.

Function Adaptors

- Negators for negating predicate objects
- Binders for binding function arguments
- Adaptors for pointer to function

In the following example we use a binder function `bind2nd` to transform an initial sequence of values to these values doubled.

In file stl_adap.cpp

```
//Use of the function adaptor bind2nd.
#include <iostream>
#include <algorithm>
#include <functional>
#include <string>
using namespace std;

template <class ForwIter>
void print(ForwIter first, ForwIter last, const char* title)
{
   cout << title << endl;
   while (first != last)
      cout << *first++ << '\t';
   cout << endl;
}

int main()
{
   int data[3] = { 9, 10, 11};

   print(data, data + 3, "Original values");
   transform(data, data + 3, data,
             bind2nd(times<int>(), 2));
   print(data, data + 3, "New values");
}
```

Other algorithms in this library are discussed in Section F.4.1, "Function Adaptors," on page 506. Allocators are discussed in Section F.5, "Allocators," on page 507, and the *string* library is discussed in Section F.6, "String Library," on page 507.

8.13 Numerical Integration Made Easy

STL provides the basic computations for many more sophisticated algorithms. By using STL we can easily implement these algorithms. We will use numerical integration as an example. The idea is to generate a series of points using a *generator*. A generator is a class that defines the function by overloading operator(), the function call operator. The STL algorithm generate(iterator b, iterator e, generator g) is used to produce a vector of values in the range (0, 1) for the function.

In file stl_inte.cpp

```
//Simple integration routine for x*x over (0, 1)
//The function is represented in class gen

#include <iostream>
#include <algorithm>
#include <numeric>              //need for accumulate
#include <vector>
using namespace std;

class gen {            //generator for function to be integrated
public:
   gen(double x_zero, double increment) : x(x_zero),
   incr(increment) { }
   double operator()() { x += incr; return x*x; }
private:
   double x, incr;
};

double integrate( gen g, int n)    //integrate on (0,1)
{
   vector<double> fx(n);

   generate(fx.begin(),fx.end(), g );
   return(accumulate(fx.begin(), fx.end(), 0.0) / n );
}
```

```cpp
int main()
{
   const int n = 10000;

   gen g(0.0, 1.0/n);
   cout << "integration program x**2" << endl;
   cout << integrate(g, n) << endl;
}
```

We approximate the area under the curve by a sequence of rectangles whose height is the value of the function and whose width is the increment. An increment gives us two choices for a height. We could improve the numerical accuracy of integration by bounding the area between rectangles based on the smaller heights and one based on the larger heights.

```cpp
double integrate( gen g, int n, double& diff)
{
   vector<double> fx(n), sm(n), lg(n);
   double s, l;

   generate(fx.begin(),fx.end(), g );
   for (int i = 0; i < n - 1; ++i)
      if (fx[i] > fx[i + 1]) {
         sm[i] = fx[i + 1]; lg[i] = fx[i];
      }
      else {
         sm[i] = fx[i]; lg[i] = fx[i + 1];
      }
   s = accumulate(sm.begin(), sm.end(), 0.0)/n ;
   l = accumulate(lg.begin(), lg.end(), 0.0)/n ;
   diff = l - s;
   return ( s + l ) / 2;
}
```

The above produces a more reliable estimate with an error estimate calculated in diff. It can be further improved by being adaptive as discussed in the exercises (see exercise 18, on page 314).

8.14 Pragmatics

Many current C++ template implementations make a distinction between what can be a template parameter for functions versus what can be a template parameter for classes. Functions allow only class arguments. Furthermore, these class arguments must occur in the template function as part of the type description of at least one of the function parameters.

This is okay:

```
template <class TYPE>
void   maxelement(TYPE a[], TYPE& max, int size);

template <class TYPE>
int   find(TYPE* data);
```

This:

```
template <class TYPE>
TYPE   convert(int i) { TYPE temp(i); return temp; }
```

was previously illegal, but is now legal according to the proposed ANSI standard. In the ANSI standard it is invoked as follows:

```
convert<double>(i + j);         //newly allowed explicit
                                //function instantiation
```

Since it was previously illegal, it may not work on many current systems. The restriction exists because current compilers must use the arguments at function invocation to deduce which actual functions will be created. A work-around is possible by creating a class whose sole member is a parameterized static function:

```
template <class TYPE>            //other arguments are possible
class convert_it {
   static TYPE   convert(int i)
      { TYPE   temp(i); return temp; }
};
```

Summary

1. C++ uses templates to provide parametric polymorphism. The same code is used with different types where the type is a parameter of the code body.

2. Both classes and functions can have several class template arguments. In addition to class template arguments, class template definitions can include constant expressions, function names, and character strings as template arguments. A common case is to have an `int` argument that parameterizes a size characteristic.

3. A nontemplate, specialized version of a function may be needed when the generic routine will not work. When multiple functions are available, an algorithm determines which to use.

   Overloading Function-Selection Algorithm

   1. Exact match on a nontemplate function.
   2. Exact match using a function template.
   3. Ordinary argument resolution on a nontemplate function.

4. The standard template library (STL) is the C++ library that provides generic programming for many standard data structures and algorithms.

5. Containers come in two major families: sequence and associative. Sequence containers include vectors, lists, and deques. These are ordered by having a sequence of elements. Associative containers include sets, multisets, maps, and multimaps, and have keys for looking up elements.

6. Container adaptor classes are container classes that modify existing containers to produce different public behaviors based on an existing implementation. Three provided container adaptors are `stack`, `queue`, and `priority_queue`.

7. Iterators can be thought of as an enhanced pointer type. There are five iterator types: input, output, forward, bidirectional, and random-access. Not all iterator types may be available for a given container class. For example, random access iterators are available for vectors but not for maps.

8. The STL algorithms library contains the following four categories:

   - Sorting algorithms
   - Nonmutating sequence algorithms
   - Mutating sequence algorithms
   - Numerical algorithms

   These algorithms generally use iterators to access containers instantiated on a given type. The resulting code can be competitive in efficiency with special-purpose codes.

Exercises

1. Rewrite stack<T> in Section 8.1, "Template Class stack," on page 270 to accept an integer value for the default size of the stack. Now client code can use declarations such as:

   ```
   stack<int, 100>    s1, s2;
   stack<char, 5000>  sc1, sc2, sc3;
   ```

   Discuss the pros and cons of this additional parameterization.

2. Define a template for fixed-length stacks that allocates a compile-time-determined size array to store the stacked values.

3. The code

   ```
   #define CUBE(X) ((X)*(X)*(X))
   ```

   behaves differently from the code

   ```
   template<class T> T cube (T x){ return x * x * x;}
   ```

   Explain the difference when cube(sqrt(7)); is invoked. When would the two coding schemes give different results?

4. Write a generic `cycle()` function with the following definition and test it:

   ```
   template<class TYPE>
   void cycle(TYPE& a, TYPE& b, TYPE& c)
   {
   // replace a's value by b's and b's by c's
   // and c's by a's
   }
   ```

5. Write a generic function that, given an arbitrary array and its size, rotates its values with:

   ```
   a[1] = a[0] , a[2] = a[1], ·····,
   a[size - 1] = a[size - 2], a[0] = a[size - 1]
   ```

6. Write the member function template:

   ```
   <class T> void vector<T>::print()
   ```

   This function prints the entire vector range.

7. Rewrite the overloaded assignment operator to be more general:

   ```
   template <class T>
   vector<T>& vector<T>::operator=(const vector<T>& v)
   //allow different size vectors to be assigned
   //must delete and reallocate storage for left-hand
   //argument and avoid in a = a
   ```

8. Write a generic function that requires that two `vector<T>`s of different types be swapped. (See Section 8.4, "Parameterizing the Class vector," on page 278.) Assume that both array types have elements that are assignment-convertible.

9. Using `vector<T>` and its associated iterator class, code a generic vector internal sorting routine of your choice, but not quicksort (see Section 8.4, "Parameterizing the Class vector," on page 278). Compare its running time with the STL library sort routine for 100- 1,000- and 10,000-element vectors.

10. *(Project)* Create a parametric string type. The basic type is to act as a container class that contains a `class T` object. The prototype case is where the object is a `char`. The normal end-of-string sentinel will be 0. The standard behavior should model the functions found in *string.h*. The class definition could parameterize the sentinel as well. Such a type exists in the standard library *string*.

11. Sorting functions are natural candidates for parameterization. The following is a generic bubble sort:

    ```
    template <class T>
    void bubble(T d[], int how_many)
    {
       T  temp;

       for (int i= 0; i < how_many - 2;  ++i)
          for (int j= 0; j < how_many - 1 - i; ++j)
             if (d[j] < d[j+1]) {
                temp = d[j];
                d[j ]= d[j + 1];
                d[j+1] = temp;
             }
    }
    ```

    What happens if this is instantiated with a class in which operator<() is not defined?

12. Modify quicksort() by using a three-element sample to select the partitioning element. (See Section 8.5, "Parameterizing quicksort()," on page 281.) This is an attempt to obtain on average a better partition at the expense of a small number of additional comparisons per iteration. Can you demonstrate that in the worst case this algorithm still exhibits n^2 behavior?

13. Using a random-number generator, generate 10,000 integers between zero and 9,999. Place them in a list<int> container. (See Section 8.7, "STL," on page 287.) Compute and print the median value. What did you expect? Compute the frequencies of each value; in other words, how many zeros were generated, how many ones were generated, and so forth. Print the value with the greatest frequency. Use a vector<int> to store the frequencies.

14. Recode print(const list<double> &lst) to be a template function that is as general as possible. (See Section 8.7, "STL," on page 287.)

15. For list<T> write the member function:

    ```
    iterator list<T>::insert(iterator w_it, T v);
    ```

    It inserts v before w_it and returns an iterator pointing at the inserted element. (See Section 8.7, "STL," on page 287.)

16. For list<T> write the member function:

    void list<T>::erase(iterator w_it);

    It erases the element pointed at by w_it. (See Section 8.7, "STL," on page 287.)

17. Write an algorithm to find the second largest element stored in an arbitrary container class. Use STL containers vector<T>, list<T>, and set<T> to test that it works regardless of the container. Write the algorithm assuming a forward iterator is available and comparison is understood.

18. We wish to perform simple numerical integration using STL containers and algorithms. Write a function that, given:

    double f(double x);

    generates a vector of doubles from a to b with an interval of s. Then accumulate the values s times f(x) over this interval. (See Section 8.13, "Numerical Integration Made Easy," on page 307.)

Chapter 9

Inheritance

Inheritance is the mechanism of deriving a new class from an old one. That is, the existing class can be added to or altered to create the derived class. This is a powerful code-reuse mechanism. Through inheritance, a hierarchy of related types can be created that share code and interfaces.

Many useful types are variants of one another, and it is frequently tedious to produce the same code for each. A derived class inherits the description of the *base* class; it can then be altered by adding members, modifying existing member functions, and modifying access privileges. The usefulness of this concept can be seen by examining how taxonomic classification compactly summarizes large bodies of knowledge. For example, knowing the concept "mammal" and knowing that an elephant and mouse are both mammals allows our descriptions of them to be considerably more succinct than they would be otherwise. The root concept contains the information that mammals are warm-blooded, higher vertebrates, and that they nourish their young through mammary glands. This information is inherited by the concept of both "mouse" and "elephant," but it is expressed only once: in the root concept. In C++ terms, both elephant and mouse are derived from the base class mammal.

C++ supports *virtual member functions*. These are functions declared in the base class and redefined in a derived class. A class hierarchy that is defined by public inheritance creates a related set of user types, all of whose objects may be pointed at by a base class pointer. By accessing the virtual function through this pointer, C++ selects the appropriate function definition at run-time. The object being pointed at must carry around type information so that this distinction can be made dynamically, a feature typical of OOP code. Each object "knows" how it is to be acted on. This is a form of polymorphism called *pure polymorphism*.

Inheritance should be designed into software to maximize reuse and allow a natural modeling of the problem domain. With inheritance, the key elements of the OOP design methodology are as follows.

OOD Design Methodology

1. Decide on an appropriate set of types.

2. Design in their relatedness, and use inheritance to share code.

3. Use virtual functions to process related objects polymorphically.

9.1 A Derived Class

A class can be derived from an existing class using the form:

```
class class-name : (public|protected|private)opt base-name
{
    member declarations
};
```

As usual, the keyword `class` can be replaced by the keyword `struct`, with the implication that members are by default `public`. One aspect of the derived class is the visibility of its inherited members. The keywords `public`, `protected`, and `private` are used to specify how the base class members are to be accessible to the derived class.

The keyword `protected` is introduced to allow data hiding for members that must be available in derived classes, but that otherwise act like private members. It is an intermediate form of access between public and private.

Consider developing a class to represent students at a college or university:

In file student2.h

```
class student {
public:
   enum year { fresh, soph, junior, senior, grad };
   student(char* nm, int id, double g, year x);
   void  print() const;
protected:
   int      student_id;
   double   gpa;
   year     y;
   char     name[30];
};
```

We could write a program that lets the registrar track such students. While the information stored in `student` variables is adequate for undergraduates, it omits crucial information needed to track graduate students. Such additional information might include their means of support, their department affiliations, and their thesis topics. Inheritance lets us derive a suitable `grad_student` class from the base class `student` as follows:

In file student2.h

```
class grad_student : public student {
public:
   enum support { ta, ra, fellowship, other };
   grad_student(char* nm, int id, double g, year x,
         support t, char* d, char* th);
   void  print() const;
protected:
   support  s;
   char     dept[10];
   char     thesis[80];
};
```

In this example, `grad_student` is the derived class, and `student` is the base class. The use of the keyword `public` following the colon in the derived class header means that the protected and public members of `student` are to be inherited as protected and public members of `grad_student`. Private members are inaccessible. Public inheritance also means that the derived class `grad_student` *is a* subtype of `student`. Thus, a graduate student is a student, but a student does not have to be a graduate student. This subtyping relationship is called the *ISA* relationship. This is also called *interface inheritance.*

A derived class is a modification of the base class; it inherits the public and protected members of the base class. Only constructors, its destructor, and any member function `operator=()` cannot be inherited. Thus, in the example of `grad_student`, the `student` members `student_id`, `gpa`, `name`, `y`, and `print()` are inherited. Frequently, a derived class adds new members to the existing class members. This is the case with `grad_student`, which has three new data members and a redefined member function `print()`, which is *overridden*. The function definitions of `student::print()` and `grad_student::print()` appear in the next section. The derived class has a different implementation of the member function than the base class. This is different from overloading, where the same function name can have different meanings for each unique signature.

Benefits of Using a Derived Class

- Code is reused: `grad_student` uses existing, tested code from `student`.
- The hierarchy reflects a relationship found in the problem domain. When speaking of students, the special grouping "graduate student" is an outgrowth of the real world and its treatment of this group.
- Various polymorphic mechanisms will allow client code to treat `grad_student` as a subtype of `student`, simplifying client code while granting it the benefits of maintaining these distinctions among subtypes.

9.2 Typing Conversions and Visibility

A publicly derived class is a *subtype* of its base class. A variable of the derived class can in many ways be treated as if it were the base class type. A pointer whose type is pointer to base class can point to objects that have the derived class type.

We shall examine our example of `student` and `grad_student`. Let us first examine the base and derived class constructors.

In file student2.h

```
student::student(char* nm, int id, double g,
    year x):student_id(id), gpa(g), y(x)
{
    strcpy(name, nm);
}
```

The constructor for the base class does a series of simple initializations. It then calls `strcpy()` to copy over the student's name.

```
grad_student::grad_student (char* nm, int id,   double g, year
x, support t, char* d,
    char* th):student(nm, id, g, x), s(t)
{
    strcpy(dept, d);
    strcpy(thesis, th);
}
```

Notice that the constructor for `student` is invoked as part of the initializer list. This is usual, and, logically, the base class object needs to be constructed before the object can be completed.

The `grad_student` is a publicly derived type whose base class is `student`. In the class `student`, the members `student_id` and `gpa` are protected. This makes them visible to the derived class but otherwise treated as private.

A reference to the derived class may be implicitly converted to a reference to the public base class. For example:

```
grad_student gs("Morris Pohl", 200, 3.2564, grad, ta,
            "Pharmacy", "Retail Pharmacies");
student& rs = gs;
```

In this case, the variable `rs` is a reference to `student`. The base class of `grad_student` is `student`. Therefore, this reference conversion is appropriate.

The `print()` member functions are implemented as follows:

In file student2.h

```
void student::print() const
{
   cout << name << " , " << student_id
        << " , " << y << " , " << gpa << endl;
}

void grad_student::print() const
{
   student::print(); //base class info is printed
   cout << dept << " , " << s << '\n'
        << thesis << endl;
}
```

For `grad_student::print()` to invoke `student::print()`, the scope-resolved identifier `student::print()` must be used. Otherwise, there will be an infinite loop caused by a recursive call to `grad_student::print()`. To see which versions of these functions get called, and to demonstrate some of the conversion relationships between base and publicly derived classes, we write a simple test:

In file student2.cpp

```
//Test pointer conversion rules.

#include   "student2.h"      //include relevant declarations
```

```
int main()
{
   student  s("Mae Pohl", 100, 3.425, student::fresh), *ps = &s;
   grad_student  gs("Morris Pohl", 200, 3.2564,
       student::grad, grad_student::ta, "Pharmacy",
       "Retail Pharmacies"), *pgs;

   ps -> print();           //student::print
   ps = pgs = &gs;
   pgs -> print();          //grad_student::print
   ps ->print();            //student::print
}
```

This function declares both class variables and pointers to them. The conversion rule is that a pointer to a publicly derived class may be converted implicitly to a pointer to its base class. In our example, the pointer variable ps can point at objects of both classes, but the pointer variable pgs can point only at objects of type grad_student. We wish to study how various pointer assignments affect the invocation of a version of print().

The first instance of the statement

```
ps -> print();
```

invokes student::print(). It is pointing at the variable s of type student. The multiple assignment statement

```
ps = pgs = &gs;
```

has both pointers pointing at an object of type grad_student. The assignment to ps involves an implicit conversion. The statement

```
pgs -> print();       //grad_student::print
```

invokes the grad_student::print() function. The variable pgs is of type pointer to grad_student and, when invoked with an object of this type, selects a member function from this class. The second instance of the statement

```
ps -> print();
```

invokes student::print(). That this pointer is pointing at a grad_student variable gs is not relevant. In Section 9.4, "Virtual Functions," on page 327, we explain how to use virtual member functions to make function invocation a run-time property depending on what is being pointed at.

9.3 Code Reuse: A Binary Tree Class

Private inheritance does not have a subtype, or ISA, relationship. In private inheritance, we reuse a base class for its code. We will call private derivation a *LIKEA* relationship. This is also called *implementation inheritance*, as opposed to interface inheritance. It comes in handy when diagramming the class relationships in a complicated software system. Because private and protected inheritance do not create type hierarchies, they have more limited utility than public inheritance. In a first pass in understanding these concepts, nonpublic inheritance can be skipped.

Code reuse is often all you want from inheritance. We shall see how private inheritance is used by designing a generic container class that is a binary tree (see Section 8.6, "Parameterized Binary Search Tree," on page 283). This tree structure was also used as the basis for a `template` class. Templates and inheritance are reuse techniques with different advantages. Normally templates are a simpler design and generate faster but larger executables.

The class will store `void*` data members. The idea will be to inherit this class privately, so as to make the `void*` pointer nongeneric:

In file gentree2.h

```
//generic binary search trees
typedef void*  p_gen;                   //generic pointer type
int   comp(p_gen a, p_gen b);

class bnode {
private:
   friend  class gen_tree;
   bnode*  left;
   bnode*  right;
   p_gen   data;
   int     count;
   bnode(p_gen d, bnode* l, bnode* r) :
        data(d), left(l), right(r), count(1) { }
   friend void   print(bnode* n);
};
```

```
class gen_tree {
public:
   gen_tree() { root = 0; }
   void   insert(p_gen d);
   p_gen  find(p_gen d) const { return (find(root, d)); }
   void   print() const { print(root); }
protected:
   bnode*  root;
   p_gen   find(bnode* r, p_gen d) const;
   void    print(bnode* r) const;
};
```

The individual nodes in this binary tree store a generic pointer data and an int count that will count duplicate entries. The pointer data will match a pointer type in the derived class. The tree will be a binary search tree that will store nodes of smaller values to the left and larger values to the right. We need a method of comparing values that is appropriate to the specific derived type. We use a friend function comp() that is a friend of bnode and will be coded appropriately for the derived class.

The insert() function places nodes in a tree; it must find a position in the tree for the new nodes.

```
void gen_tree::insert(p_gen d)
{
   bnode*  temp = root;
   bnode*  old;
   //Body is found in Section 9.6:
   //template<class T> void gen_tree<T>::insert(T d)
}
```

The body of the insert() function is the same as that shown in Section 8.6, "Parameterized Binary Search Tree," on page 284, except that references to <T> in the new() operator statements disappear.

The function p_gen find(bnode* r, p_gen d) searches the subtree rooted at r for the information represented by d.

```
p_gen gen_tree::find(bnode* r, p_gen d) const
{
   . . . . .
}
```

The body of the find() function is also the same as that shown in Section 8.6, "Parameterized Binary Search Tree," on page 285.

9.3 ▼ Code Reuse: A Binary Tree Class 323

The print() function is yet another standard recursion. At each node, the external function ::print() is applied.

```
void gen_tree::print(bnode* r) const
{
   if (r != 0) {
      print (r -> left);
      ::print(r);
      print (r -> right);
   }
}
```

We next derive a class capable of storing a pointer to char as its data member:

In file gentree2.cpp

```
#include  "gentree2.h"
#include  <cstring> //older systems use string.h
using namespace std;

class s_tree : private gen_tree {
public:
   s_tree() { }
   void  insert(char* d) { gen_tree::insert(d); }
   char*  find(char* d) const
      { return static_cast<char*>(gen_tree::find(d)); }
   void  print() const { gen_tree::print(); }
};
```

The base class insertion function gen_tree::insert takes a generic pointer type as its argument. The derived class insertion function s_tree::insert takes a pointer to char as its argument. Therefore, in the derived class s_tree,

```
void  insert(char* d) { gen_tree::insert(d); }
```

uses the implicit conversion char* to void*.

We need a function to perform comparison:

```
int comp(p_gen i, p_gen j)
{
   return (strcmp(static_cast<char*>(i),
                  static_cast<char*>(j) ));
}
```

We also need an external `print()` that can properly print the values stored in a single node to be used recursively by `s_tree::print()` to output the entire tree.

```
void print(bnode* n)
{
   cout << static_cast<char*>(n -> data) << '\t' ;
   cout << n -> count << '\t';
}
```

Notice that the generic pointer type `p_gen` is used in this version of the program for `gen_tree`, where the corresponding template code used a template parameter.

The template methodology is simpler and more run-time efficient. It is simpler because instantiation requires only a single actual type placed in the template declaration. In inheritance we need to derive the whole interface, substituting appropriate types. It is more run-time efficient because it often avoids indirection. Inheritance allows special cases to be developed for each type if necessary; it does not lead to large object-code modules. Remember, each template instantiation is compiled to object code.

9.4 Virtual Functions

Overloaded member functions are invoked by a type-matching algorithm that includes having the implicit argument matched to an object of that class type. All this is known at compile time, and it allows the compiler to select the appropriate member directly. As will become apparent, it would be nice to dynamically select at run time the appropriate member function from among base and derived class functions. The keyword `virtual` is a function specifier that provides such a mechanism, but it may be used only to modify member function declarations. The combination of *virtual functions* and public inheritance will be our most general and flexible way to build a piece of software. This is a form of pure polymorphism.

An ordinary virtual function must be executable code. When invoked, its semantics are the same as those of other functions. In a derived class, it can be overridden, and the function prototype of the derived function must have a matching signature and return type. The selection of which function definition to invoke for a virtual function is dynamic. In the typical case, a base class has a virtual function, and derived classes have their versions of this function. A pointer to base class can point at either a base class object or a derived class object. The member function selected will depend on the class of the object being pointed at, not on the pointer type. In the absence of a derived type member, the base class virtual function is used by default.

Note the difference in selection of the appropriate overridden virtual function from an overloaded member function. The overloaded member function is selected at compile time based on its signature, and it can have distinct return types. A virtual function is selected at run time based on the object's type, which is passed to it as its `this` pointer argument. Also, once it is declared `virtual`, this property is carried along to all redefinitions in derived classes. It is unnecessary in the derived class to use the function modifier `virtual`.

Consider the following example.

In file virt_sel.cpp

```
//virtual function selection.
class B {
public:
   int  i;
   virtual void  print_i() const
      { cout << i << " inside B" << endl; }
};

class D : public B {
public:
   //virtual as well
   void  print_i() const
      { cout << i << " inside D" << endl; }
};

int main()
{
   B   b;
   B*  pb = &b;              //points at a B object
   D   f;

   f.i = 1 + (b.i = 1);
   pb -> print_i();          //call B::print_i()
   pb = &f;                  //points at a D object
   pb -> print_i();          //call D::print_i()
}
```

The output of this program is:

```
1 inside B
2 inside D
```

Compare this behavior to the program *student* shown in Section 9.2, "Typing Conversions and Visibility," on page 319. There, the selection of print() is based on the pointer type, known at compile time. Here, print_i() is selected based on what is being pointed at. In this case, a different version of print_i() is executed. In OOP terminology, the object is *sent the message* print_i(), and it selects its own version of the corresponding method. Thus, the pointer's base type is not the determining method (function) selection. Different class objects are processed by different functions, determined at run time. Facilities that allow the implementation of ADTs, inheritance, and the ability to process objects dynamically are the essentials of OOP.

Virtual functions and member function overloading cause confusion. Consider the following.

In file virt_err.cpp

```
class B {
public:
   virtual void foo(int);
   virtual void foo(double);
};

class D : public B {
public:
   void foo(int);
};

int main()
{
   D  d;
   B  b, *pb = &d;

   b.foo(9);                //selects B::foo(int);
   b.foo(9.5);              //selects B::foo(double);
   d.foo(9);                //selects D::foo(int);
   d.foo(9.5);              //selects D::foo(int);
   pb -> foo(9);            //selects D::foo(int);
   pb -> foo(9.5);          //selects B::foo(double);
}
```

The base class member function B::foo(int) is overridden, and the base class member function B::foo(double) is hidden in the derived class. In the statement d.foo(9.5), the double value 9.5 is converted to the integer value 9. We could have used d.B::foo(double) to call the hidden member function.

The declaration of an identifier in a scope hides all declarations of that identifier in outer scopes. A base class is an outer scope of any class derived from it. This rule is independent of whether the names are declared virtual. Access restrictions (private, protected) are orthogonal to function selection. If the selected function is inaccessible, that is a compile-time error.

Only nonstatic member functions can be virtual. The virtual characteristic is inherited. Thus the derived class function is automatically virtual, and the presence of the virtual keyword is usually a matter of taste. Constructors cannot be virtual, but destructors can. As a rule of thumb, any class having virtual functions should have a virtual destructor.

Virtual functions allow run-time decisions. Consider a computer-aided design application where the area of the shapes in a design has to be computed. The various shapes will be derived from the shape base class:

In file shape2.cpp

```
class shape {
public:
   virtual double  area() const { return 0; }
   //virtual double area is default behavior
protected:
   double  x, y;
};

class rectangle : public shape {
public:
   double  area() const { return (height * width); }
private:
   double  height, width;
};

class circle : public shape {
public:
   double  area() const
       { return (PI * radius * radius);}
private:
   double   radius;
};
```

In such a class hierarchy, the derived classes correspond to important, well understood types of shapes. The system is readily expanded by deriving further classes. The area calculation is a local responsibility of a derived class.

Client code that uses the polymorphic area calculation looks like this:

```
shape*   p[N];

 . . . . .
for (i = 0; i < N; ++i)
    tot_area += p[i] -> area();
```

A major advantage here is that the client code will not need to change if new shapes are added to the system. Change is managed locally and propagated automatically by the polymorphic character of the client code.

9.5 Abstract Base Classes

A type hierarchy usually has its root class contain a number of virtual functions. Virtual functions provide for dynamic typing. In the root class they are often dummy functions, and have an empty body. In the derived classes, however, they will be given specific meanings. In C++, the *pure virtual function* is introduced for this purpose. A pure virtual function is a virtual member function whose body is normally undefined. Notationally, it is declared inside the class as follows:

```
virtual function prototype = 0;
```

The pure virtual function is used to defer the implementation decision of the function. In OOP terminology it is called a *deferred method*.

A class that has at least one pure virtual function is an *abstract class*. It is useful for the root class in a type hierarchy to be an abstract class. It would have the basic common properties of its derived classes, but cannot itself be used to declare objects. Instead, it is used to declare pointers that can access subtype objects derived from the abstract class.

We will explain this concept while developing a primitive form of ecological simulation. OOP was originally developed as a simulation methodology using Simula 67. Hence, many of its ideas are easily understood as an attempt to model a particular reality.

The world in our example will have various forms of life interacting, which will inherit the interface of an abstract base class called `living`. We shall have foxes as an archetypal predator, with rabbits as prey. The rabbits will eat grass.

In file predator.cpp

```cpp
//Predator-Prey simulation using class living
const int  N = 40;                      //size of square board
enum state { EMPTY , GRASS , RABBIT , FOX, STATES };
const int DRAB = 3, DFOX = 6, CYCLES = 5;

class living;                           //forward declaration
typedef living* world[N][N];

class living {                          //what lives in world
public:
   virtual state  who() = 0;            //state identification
   virtual living*  next(world w) = 0;
protected:
   int  row, column;                    //location
   void sums(world w,int sm[]);
};

void living::sums(world w, int sm[])
{
   int  i, j;

   sm[EMPTY] = sm[GRASS] = sm[RABBIT] = sm[FOX] = 0;
   for (i = -1; i <= 1; ++i)
      for ( j = -1; j <= 1; ++j)
         sm[w[row + i][column +j] -> who()]++;
}
```

There are two pure virtual functions and there is one ordinary member function, sums(). Virtual functions incur a small added run-time cost over normal member functions. Therefore, we use them only when necessary to our implementations. Our simulation will have rules for deciding who goes on living in the next cycle based on the populations in the neighborhood of a given square. These populations are computed by sums(). This is akin to Conway's "Game of Life" simulation.

The inheritance hierarchy will be one level deep:

```cpp
//currently only predator class
class fox : public living {
public:
   fox(int r, int c, int a = 0) : age(a)
      { row = r; column = c; }
   state  who() { return FOX; }    //deferred method for foxes
   living*  next(world w);
protected:
   int  age;                        //used to decide on dying
};

//currently only prey class
class rabbit : public living {
public:
   rabbit(int r, int c, int a = 0) : age(a)
      { row = r; column = c; }
   state  who() { return RABBIT; }
   living*  next(world w);
protected:
   int  age;
};

//currently only plant life
class grass : public living {
public:
   grass(int r, int c) { row = r; column = c; }
   state who() { return GRASS; }
   living* next(world w);
};

//nothing lives here
class empty : public living {
public:
   empty(int r, int c) { row = r; column = c; }
   state  who() { return EMPTY; }
   living*  next(world w);
};
```

Notice that the design allows other forms of predator, prey, and plant life to be developed using a further level of inheritance. The characteristics of how each life form behaves are captured in its version of next().

Grass can be eaten by rabbits. If there is more grass than rabbits in the neighborhood, the grass remains; otherwise the grass is eaten up (feel free to substitute your own rules, as these are highly limited and artificial):

```
living* grass::next(world w)
{
   int  sum[STATES];

   sums(w, sum);
   if (sum[GRASS] > sum[RABBIT])              //eat grass
      return (new grass(row, column));
   else
      return (new empty(row, column));
}
```

Rabbits die of old age if they exceed some defined limit DRAB, or they are eaten if there are an appropriate number of foxes in the neighborhood:

```
living* rabbit::next(world w)
{
   int  sum[STATES];

   sums(w, sum);
   if (sum[FOX] >= sum[RABBIT] )              //eat rabbits
      return (new empty(row, column));
   else if (age > DRAB)                       //rabbit is too old
      return (new empty(row, column));
   else
      return (new rabbit(row, column, age + 1));
}
```

Foxes die of overcrowding or old age:

```
living* fox::next(world w)
{
   int  sum[STATES];

   sums(w, sum);
   if (sum[FOX] > 5)                       //too many foxes
      return (new empty(row, column));
   else if (age > DFOX)                    //fox is too old
      return (new empty(row, column));
   else
      return (new fox(row, column, age + 1));
}
```

Empty squares are competed for by the various life forms:

```
living* empty::next(world w)     //how to fill an empty square
{
   int  sum[STATES];
   sums(w, sum);
   if (sum[FOX] > 1)
      return (new fox(row, column));
   else if (sum[RABBIT] > 1)
      return (new rabbit(row, column));
   else if (sum[GRASS])
      return (new grass(row, column));
   else
      return (new empty(row, column));
}
```

The rules in the different versions of next() determine a possibly complex set of interactions. Of course, to make the simulation more interesting, other behaviors, such as sexual reproduction, where the animals have gender and can mate, could be simulated.

The array type world is a container for the life forms. The container will have the responsibility of creating its current pattern. It needs to have ownership of the living objects so as to allocate new ones and delete old ones:

```
//world is all empty
void init(world w)
{
   int   i, j;

   for (i = 0; i < N; ++i)
      for (j = 0; j < N; ++j)
         w[i][j] = new empty(i,j);
}

//new world w_new is computed from old world w_old
void update(world w_new, world w_old)
{
   int   i, j;

   for (i = 1; i < N - 1; ++i)          //borders are taboo
      for (j = 1; j < N - 1; ++j)
         w_new[i][j] = w_old[i][j] -> next(w_old);
}

//clean world up
void dele(world w)
{
   int   i, j;

   for (i = 1; i < N - 1; ++i)
      for (j = 1; j < N - 1; ++j)
         delete(w[i][j]);
}
```

The simulation will have odd and even worlds, which alternate as the basis for the next cycle's calculations:

```
int main()
{
   world   odd, even;
   int     i;

   init(odd);   init(even);
   eden(even);                     //generate initial world
   pr_state(even);                 //print Garden of Eden state
```

```
      for (i = 0; i < CYCLES; ++i) {      //simulation
         if (i % 2) {
            update(even, odd);
            pr_state(even);
            dele(odd);
         }
         else {
            update(odd, even);
            pr_state(odd);
            dele(even);
         }
      }
   }
```

We leave as exercises the writing of `pr_state()` and `eden()` (see exercise 16, on page 350).

9.6 Templates and Inheritance

Templates and inheritance are jointly an extremely powerful reuse technique. Parameterized types can be reused through inheritance. Such use parallels the use of inheritance in deriving ordinary classes. Templates and inheritance are both mechanisms for code reuse, and both can involve polymorphism. They are distinct features of C++, and as such combine in different forms. A template class can derive from an ordinary class, an ordinary class can derive from an instantiated template class, and a template class can derive from a template class. Each of these possibilities leads to different relationships.

In some situations, templates lead to unacceptable cost in the size of the object module. Each instantiated template class requires its own compiled object module. Consider the `gen_tree` class in Section 9.3, "Code Reuse: A Binary Tree Class," on page 322. It provided reuse by supplying code that was readily converted through inheritance and casting to specifically useful pointer types. Its drawback was that each pointer type required individual coding of its class definition. This can be remedied by using a template to inherit the base class:

9.6 ▼ Templates and Inheritance

```cpp
//Base class is used to keep code body small.

template <class T>
class pointer_tree : private gen_tree {
public:
   pointer_tree() { }
   void   insert(T* d) { gen_tree::insert(d); }
   T*  find(T* d)  const
      { return reinterpret_cast<T*>(gen_tree::find(d)); }
   void  print() { gen_tree::print(); }
};
```

The object code for `gen_tree` is relatively large, and is needed only once. The interface `pointer_tree<type>` requires only a small object module for each instantiation. This is a major saving over the template solution presented earlier. (See Section 8.6, "Parameterized Binary Search Tree," on page 284.)

The derivation of a class from an instantiated template class is basically no different than ordinary inheritance. In the following example we reuse `stack<char>` as a base class for a safe character stack.

In file stack_t2.cpp

```cpp
//safe character stack
#include   <assert.h>

class safe_char_stack : public stack<char> {
public:
   // test push and pop
   void   push(char c)
      { assert (!full()); stack<char>::push(c); }
   char   pop()
      { assert (!empty()); return (stack<char>::pop()); }
};
```

The instantiated class `stack<char>` is generated and reused by `safe_char_stack`.

This example can be usefully generalized to a template class:

In file stack_t3.cpp

```
//parameterized safe stack
template <class TYPE>
class safe_stack : public stack<TYPE> {
public:
   void  push(TYPE c)
      { assert (!full()); stack<TYPE>::push(c); }
   TYPE  pop()
      { assert (!empty()); return (stack<TYPE>::pop()); }
};
```

It is important to notice the linkage between the base class and the derived class. Both require the same instantiated type. Each pair of base and derived classes is independent of all other pairs.

9.7 Multiple Inheritance

The examples in the text thus far require only single inheritance; that is, they require that a class be derived from a single base class. This feature can lead to a chain of derivations wherein class B is derived from class A, class C is derived from class B, ..., and class N is derived from class M. In effect, N ends up being based on A, B, ..., M. This chain must not be circular, however; a class cannot have itself as an ancestor.

Multiple inheritance allows a derived class to be derived from more than one base class. The syntax of class headers is extended to allow a list of base classes and their privacy designations. For example:

```
class student {
   .....
};

class worker {
   .....
};

class student_worker: public student, public worker {
   .....
};
```

In this example, the derived class `plans` publicly inherits the members of both base classes. This parental relationship is described by the inheritance *directed acyclic graph* (DAG). The DAG is a graph structure whose nodes are classes and whose directed edges point from base to derived class. To be legal a DAG cannot be circular, so no class may, through its inheritance chain, inherit from itself.

When identically named members are derived from different classes, ambiguities may arise. These derivations are allowed, provided the user does not make an ambiguous reference to such a member. For example:

```
class worker {
public:
   const int   soc_sec;
   const char* name;
   .....
};

class student {
public:
   const char* name;
   .....
};

class student_worker: public student, public worker {
public:
   void print() { cout << "ssn: " << soc_sec << "\n" ;
      cout << name;  ..... }                            //error
   .....
};
```

In the body of `student_worker::print()`, the reference to `soc_sec` is fine, but the reference to `name` is inherently ambiguous. It can be resolved by properly qualifying `name` using the scope resolution operator.

With multiple inheritance, two base classes can be derived from a common ancestor. If both base classes are used in the ordinary way by their derived class, that class will have two subobjects of the common ancestor. If this duplication is not desirable, it can be eliminated using virtual inheritance. An example is:

```
class student: public virtual person {
   .....
};
```

```
class worker: public virtual student {
   .....
};

class student_worker: public student, public worker {
   .....
};
```

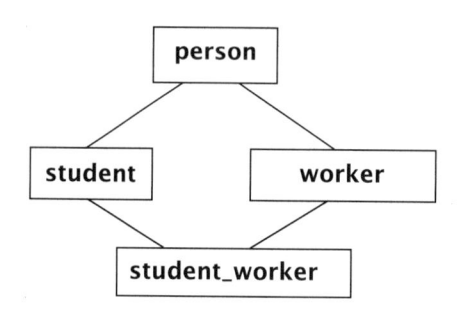

```
              person
             /      \
        student    worker
             \      /
          student_worker
```

Without the use of `virtual` in this example, `class student_worker` would have objects of `class::student::person` and `class::worker::person`. The order of execution for initializing constructors in base and member constructors is given in the following list.

Order of Constructor Execution

1. Base classes initialized in declaration order.

2. Members initialized in declaration order.

3. The body of the constructor.

Virtual base classes are constructed before any of their derived classes, and before any nonvirtual base classes. Their construction order depends on their DAG. It is a depth-first, left-to-right order. Destructors are invoked in the reverse order of constructors. These rules, although complicated, are intuitive.

On many systems, a concrete example of multiple inheritance can be found in *iostream.h*. This contains the class `iostream`, which can be derived from `istream` and `ostream`. However, it is an interesting comment on multiple inheritance that more recent implementations have gone back to single-inheritance designs.

9.8 Inheritance and Design

At one level, inheritance is a code-sharing technique. At another level it reflects an understanding of the problem and relationships between parts of the problem space. Much of public inheritance is the expression of an ISA relationship between the base and derived classes. The rectangle is a shape: This is the conceptual underpinning for making shape a superclass and allowing the behavior described by its public member functions to be interpretable on objects within its type hierarchy; in other words, subclasses derived from it share its interface.

There is no way to specify a completely optimal design. Design involves trade-offs between the various objectives one wishes to achieve. For example, generality is frequently at odds with efficiency. Using a class hierarchy that expresses ISA relationships increases our effort to understand how to compartmentalize coding relationships and potentially introduces coding inefficiencies by having various layers of access to the (hidden) state description of an object. However, a reasonable ISA decomposition can simplify the overall coding process. For example, a shape-drawing package need not anticipate shapes that might be added in the future. Through inheritance the class developer imports the base class "shape" interface and provides code that implements operations such as "draw." What is primitive or held in common remains unchanged. Also unchanged is the client's use of the package.

An undue amount of decomposition imposes its own complexity, and ends up being self-defeating. There is a granularity decision, where highly specialized classes do not provide enough benefit and are better folded into a larger concept.

Single inheritance (SI) conforms to a hierarchical decomposition of the key objects in the domain of discourse. Multiple inheritance (MI) is more troubling as a modeling or problem-solving concept. In MI we are saying that the new object is composed of several preexisting objects and is usefully thought of as a form of each. The term *mixin* is used to mean a class composed using MI, where each base class is orthogonal. Much of the time there is an alternate *HASA* formulation. For example, is a vampire bat a mammal that happens to fly, a flying machine that happens to be a mammal, or both a flying machine and a mammal. Depending on what code is available, developing a proper class for vampire bat might involve an MI derivation or an SI with appropriate HASA members.

MI presents problems for the type theorist. Student might be derived from person. Employee might be derived from person. But what about a student-employee? Generally, types are best understood as SI chains.

None of this diminishes the attraction of MI as a code-reuse technique. It is clearly a powerful generalization of SI. As such it probably fits in with the style of some programmers. Just as some programmers prefer iteration to recursion, some prefer SI and aggregation to MI and composition.

9.8.1 Subtyping Form

ADTs are successful insofar as they behave like native types. Native types such as the integer types in C act as a subtype hierarchy. This is a useful model for publicly derived type hierarchies, and promotes ease of use through polymorphism. Here is a recipe for building such a type hierarchy. The base class is made abstract and is used for interface inheritance. The derived classes will implement this interface concretely.

```
class Abstract_Base {
public:
   //interface - largely virtual
   Abstract_Base();                         //default constructor
   Abstract_Base(const Abstract_Base&);     //copy constructor
   virtual ~Abstract_Base() = 0;            //pure virtual
      .....
protected:
   //used in place of private because of inheritance
      .....
private:
   //often empty - else it constrains future designs
      .....
};

class Derived: virtual public Abstract_Base {
public:
   //Concrete instance
   Derived();                               //default constructor
   Derived(const Derived&);                 //copy constructor
   ~Derived();                              //destructor
   Derived& operator=(const Derived&);      //assignment
      .....
protected:
   //used in place of private if inheritance expected
      .....
private:
   //used for implementation details
      .....
};
```

It is usual to leave the root of the hierarchy abstract. This yields the most flexible design. Generally no concrete implementation is developed at this point. By using pure virtual functions, we are precluded from declaring objects of this type. Notice that the ~Abstract_Base() function is pure.

This level of the design focuses on public interface. These are the operations expected of any subtype in the hierarchy. In general, basic constructors are expected and they may not be virtual. Also, most useful aggregates require an explicit definition of assignment that differs from default assignment semantics. The destructor is virtual because response must be at run time and is dependent on the object's size, which can vary across the hierarchy. Finally, virtual public inheritance ensures that in MI schemes, we will not have multiple copies of the abstract base class.

9.9 Run-Time Type Identification

Run-time type identification (RTTI) provides a mechanism for safely determining the type pointed at by a base class pointer at run time. It involves dynamic_cast, an operator on a base class pointer; typeid, an operator for determining the type of an object; and type_info, a structure providing run-time information for the associated type.

The dynamic_cast operator has the form:

dynamic_cast< *type* >(*v*)

where *type* must be a pointer or reference to a class type and *v* must be a corresponding pointer value or reference value. This cast is used with classes having virtual functions. It is used as follows:

```
class Base { virtual void foo(); ····· };
class Derived : public Base { ····· };

void fcn(Base* ptr)
{
    Derived* dptr = dynamic_cast<Derived*>(ptr);
    ·····
}
```

In this example, the cast converts the pointer value ptr to a Derived*. If the conversion is inappropriate, a value of zero, the NULL pointer, is returned. This is called a *down-cast*. Dynamic casts also work with reference types.

The operator `typeid()` can be applied to a *type-name* or to an expression to determine the exact type of the argument. The operator returns a reference to the class `type_info`, which is supplied by the system and is defined in the header file *type_info.h* (some compilers use *typeinfo.h*). The class `type_info` provides a `name()` member function that returns a string that is the type name. It also provides overloaded equality operators. Remember to check the local implementation for the complete interface of this class.

In file typeid.cpp

```
Base* bptr;
. . . . .
//print the type name of what bptr currently points at
cout << typeid(bptr).name() << endl;
. . . . .
if (typeid(bptr) == typeid(Derived)) {
//do something appropriate for Derived
. . . . .
}
```

Bad dynamic casts and `typeid` operations can be made to throw the exceptions `bad_cast` and `bad_typeid`, so the user can choose between dealing with the NULL pointer or catching an exception. (See Section 10.9, "Standard Exceptions and Their Uses," on page 362.)

9.10 Pragmatics

A difficulty in learning C++ is the many distinctions and rules pertaining to the use of functions. We have now described most of the extensions, and shall mention some of the distinctions.

Function Use in C++

1. A virtual function and its derived instances that have the same signature must have the same return type with some minor exceptions. The virtual function redefinition is called *overriding*. Notice that nonvirtual member functions with the same signature can have different return types in derived classes. (See exercise 14, on page 348.)
2. All member functions except constructors and overloaded new and delete can be virtual.
3. Constructors, destructors, overloaded operator=, and friends are not inherited.
4. The operators =, (), [], and -> can be overloaded only with nonstatic member functions. Conversion functions that are operator *type*() must also be done only with nonstatic member functions. Overloading operators new and delete can be done only with static member functions. Other overloadable operators can be done with friend, member, or ordinary functions.
5. A union may have constructors and destructors, but not virtual functions. It cannot serve as a base class, nor can it have a base class. Members of a union cannot require constructors or destructors.
6. Access modification is possible, but using it with public inheritance destroys the subtype relationship. Access modification cannot broaden visibility. For example:

In file acc_mod.cpp

```
//Access modification
class B {
public:
   int  k;
protected:
   int  j, n;
private:
   int  i;
};
```

```
class D : public B {
public:
    int  m;
    B::n;        //illegal protected access can't be broadened
private:
    B::j;        //otherwise default is protected
};
```

Summary

1. Inheritance is the mechanism of deriving a new class from old ones. That is, the existing classes can be added to or altered to create the derived class. Through inheritance, a hierarchy of related, code-sharing ADTs can be created.

2. A class can be derived from an existing class using the form:

    class *class-name* : (public|protected|private)$_{opt}$*base-name*
    {
        member declarations
    };

    As usual, the keyword class can be replaced by the keyword struct, with the usual implication that members are by default public.

3. The keywords public, private, and protected are available as visibility modifiers for class members. A public member is visible throughout its scope. A private member is visible to other member functions within its own class and to friend functions. A protected member is visible to other member functions within its class, within friend functions, and within any class immediately derived from it. These visibility modifiers can be used within a class declaration in any order and with any frequency.

4. The derived class has its own constructors, which will invoke the base class constructor. There is a special syntax to pass arguments from the derived class constructor back to the base class constructor:

    function header : *base-classname* (*argument list*)

5. A publicly derived class is a subtype of its base class. A variable of the derived class can in many ways be treated as if it were the base class type. A pointer whose type is pointer to base class can point to objects of the publicly derived class type.

6. A reference to the derived class may be implicitly converted to a reference to the public base class. It is possible to declare a reference to a base class and initialize it to a reference to an object of the publicly derived class.

7. The keyword `virtual` is a function specifier that provides a mechanism to dynamically select at run time the appropriate member function from among base and derived class functions. It may be used only to modify member function declarations. This is called overriding. This ability to dynamically select a routine appropriate to an object's type is also a form of polymorphism.

8. Inheritance provides for code reuse. The derived class inherits the base class code, and typically modifies and extends the base class. Public inheritance also creates a type hierarchy. It allows further generality by providing additional implicit type conversions. Also, at a run-time cost, it allows for run-time selection of overridden virtual functions. Facilities that allow the implementation of ADTs, inheritance, and the ability to process objects dynamically are the essentials of OOP.

9. A pure virtual function is a virtual member function whose body is normally undefined. Notationally, it is declared inside the class as follows:

    `virtual` *function prototype* `= 0;`

    The pure virtual function is used to defer the implementation decision of the function. In OOP terminology it is called a *deferred method*. A class that has at least one pure virtual function is an *abstract class*. It is useful for the root class in a type hierarchy to be an abstract class. It would define the interface for its derived classes, but cannot itself be used to declare objects.

Exercises

1. For student and grad_student code, input member functions that read input for each data member in their classes. (See Section 9.1, "A Derived Class," on page 317.) Use student::read to implement grad_student::read.

2. Pointer conversions, scope resolution, and explicit casting create a wide selection of possibilities. Using main(), discussed in Section 9.2, "Typing Conversions and Visibility," on page 319, which of the following work, and what is printed?

   ```
   reinterpret_cast<grad_student *>(ps) -> print();
   dynamic_cast<student *>(pgs) -> print();
   pgs -> student::print();
   ps -> grad_student::print();
   ```

   Print out and explain the results.

3. Modify class D in Section 9.4, "Virtual Functions," on page 325, to be:

   ```
   class D2 : private B {
   public:
      B::i;                    //access modification
      void  print_i()
      {
         cout << i << " inside D2 and B::i is "
              << B::i << endl;
      }
   };
   ```

   What is changed in the output from that program?

4. The following uses class s_tree found in Section 9.3, "Code Reuse: A Binary Tree Class," on page 323.

   ```
   int main()
   {
      s_tree   t;
      char     dat[80], *p;

      cout << "\nEnter strings; exit "
           << "with an end-of-file" << endl;
      while ( cin >> dat ) {
         p = new char[strlen(dat) + 1];
         strcpy(p, dat);
         t.insert(p);
      }
      t.print();
      cout << "\n\n" << endl;
   }
   ```

   Use this with redirection to produce an ordered count of each string occurrence in a file. The function cin >> dat returns true if the operation succeeds.

5. Change the code in the above exercise so as to use an arbitrary input file. To accomplish this, read a file name from a command-line argument, and use that to open an ifstream. (See Section E.5, "Files," on page 477.)

6. Write a destructor for class gen_tree. Remember that it must traverse and individually delete nodes.

7. Write a destructor for class s_tree.

8. The printing routine for s_tree as written in Section 9.3, "Code Reuse: A Binary Tree Class," on page 323, is an *inorder* tree traversal.

   ```
   void gen_tree::print(bnode* r)
   {
      if (r != 0) {
         print (r -> left);
         ::print(r);              //inorder
         print (r -> right);
      }
   }
   ```

Run the program using both preorder and postorder traversal. For preorder, the statement ::print(r) goes first; for postorder it goes last.

9. Develop a class gen_vect that is a safe array of generic pointers. Derive a class s_vect that is a safe array of char*.

10. *(Difficult)* Using gen_tree, derive a class itree that stores a vector of type int pointed at by the data member of each node. You must write an appropriate comp function.

11. Rewrite the code for gen_tree::insert to be more efficient. Do this by assigning the value of comp(temp -> data, d) to a temporary variable. This avoids the recomputation of a potentially expensive function call.

12. Derive an integer vector class from the STL class vector<int> that has 1 as its first index value and n as its last index value.

    ```
    int_vector x(n);      //vector whose range is 1 to n
    ```

13. Generalize the previous exercise by deriving a template class that creates the index range 1 to n.

    ```
    vec_1<double> x(n);   //vector whose range is 1 to n
    ```

14. For the following program, explain when both overriding and overloading take place.

    ```
    class B {
    public:
       B(int j = 0) : i(j) {}
       virtual void  print() const
          { cout << " i = " << i << endl; }
       void  print(char *s) const
          { cout << s << i << endl; }
    private:
       int i;
    };
    ```

```
class D : public B {
public:
    D(int j = 0) : B(5), i(j) {}
    void  print() const
        { cout << " i = " << i << endl; }
    int  print(char *s) const
        { cout << s << i << endl; return i; }
private:
    int  i;
};

int main()
{
    B  b1, b2(10), *pb;
    D  d1, d2(10), *pd = &d2;

    b1.print(); b2.print(); d1.print(); d2.print();
    b1.print("b1.i = "); b2.print("b2.i = ");
    d1.print("d1.i = "); d2.print("d2.i = ");
    pb = pd;
    pb -> print(); pb -> print("d2.i = ");
    pd -> print(); pd -> print("d2.i = ");
}
```

15. Define a base class person that will contain universal information, including name, address, birth date, and gender. Derive from this class the following classes:

    ```
    class student : virtual public person {
    // ..... relevant additional state and behavior
    };

    class worker: virtual public person {
    // ..... relevant additional state and behavior
    };

    class student_worker:public student,public worker {
    // .....
    };
    ```

    Write a program that reads a file of information and creates a list of persons. Process the list to create, in sorted order by last name, a list of all people, a list of people who are students, a list of people who are employees, and a list of people who are student-employees. On your system, can you easily produce a list in sorted order of all students who are not employees?

16. *(Project)* Design and implement a graphical user interface (GUI) for the predator-prey simulation. It is beyond the scope of this book to describe various available GUI tool kits. The InterViews package works on top of X and is written in C++. The program should draw each iteration of the simulation on the screen. You should be able to directly input a "Garden of Eden" starting position. (See Section 9.5, "Abstract Base Classes," on page 329, for the game-of-life simulation.) You should also be able to provide other settings for the simulation, such as the size of the simulation. Can you allow the user to define other life forms and their rules for existing, eating, and reproducing? Make the graphical interface as elegant as possible. The user should be able to position it on the screen, resize it, and select icons for the various available life forms.

Chapter 10

Exceptions

This chapter describes exception handling in C++. *Exceptions* are generally unexpected error conditions. Normally these conditions terminate the user program with a system-provided error message. An example is floating-point divide-by-zero. Usually the system aborts the running program. C++ allows the programmer to attempt to recover from these conditions and continue program execution.

Assertions are a program check for correctness that forces an error exit when it is violated. One point of view is that an exception is based on a breakdown of a contractual guarantee between the provider of a code, the code's manufacturer, and the code's client. (See Section 11.3, "Clients and Manufacturers," on page 372.) In this model, the client needs to guarantee that the conditions for applying the code exist, and the manufacturer needs to guarantee that the code will work correctly under these conditions. In this methodology, assertions provide the various guarantees.

10.1 Using *assert.h*

Program correctness can be viewed in part as a proof that the computation terminated with correct output dependent on correct input. The user of the computation had the responsibility of providing correct input. This was a *precondition*. The computation, if successful, satisfied a *postcondition*. Providing a fully formal proof of correctness is an ideal, but is not usually done. Nevertheless, such assertions can be monitored at run time to provide very useful diagnostics. Indeed, the discipline of thinking out appropriate assertions frequently causes the programmer to avoid bugs and pitfalls.

In the C and C++ community there is an increasing emphasis on the use of assertions. The standard library *assert.h* provides a macro `assert`, and is invoked as though its function signature were:

```
void assert(bool expression);
```

If the *expression* evaluates as `false`, then execution is aborted with diagnostic output. The assertions are discarded if the macro `NDEBUG` is defined.

Consider allocation to our safe array type `dbl_vect` (see Section 5.6, "The Class dbl_vect," on page 167).

```
dbl_vect::dbl_vect(int n) : size(n)
{
   assert(n > 0);
   p = new int[size];
   assert(p != 0);
}
```

The use of assertions replaces the ad hoc use of conditional tests with a more uniform methodology. This is better practice. The downside is that the assertion methodology does not allow a retry or other repair strategy to continue program execution. Also, assertions do not allow a customized error message, though it would be easy to add this capability.

It is possible to make this scheme slightly more sophisticated by providing various testing levels as are found in the Borland C++ *checks.h* file. Under this package, the flag _DEBUG can be set to:

```
_DEBUG 0    no testing
_DEBUG 1    PRECONDITION tests only
_DEBUG 2    CHECK tests also
```

The idea is that once the library functions are thought to be correct, the level of checking is reduced to testing preconditions only. Once the client code is debugged, all testing can be suspended.

10.2 C++ Exceptions

C++ introduces an exception-handling mechanism that is sensitive to context. It is not intended to handle the asynchronous exceptions defined in *signal.h*, such as `SIGFPE`, which indicates a floating-point exception. The context for handling an exception is a try block. Handlers are declared at the end of a try block using the keyword `catch`.

C++ code can raise an exception in a try block by using the `throw` expression. The exception is handled by invoking an appropriate handler selected from a list found at the end of the handler's try block. An example of this follows.

In file dbl_vect4.h

```
dbl_vect::dbl_vect(int n): size(n)
{
   if (n < 1)  //1                //precondition assertion
      throw (n);
   p = new int[n];
   if (p == 0)                    //postcondition assertion
      throw ("FREE STORE EXHAUSTED");
}

void g()
{
   try {
      dbl_vect  a(n), b(n);
      .....

   }
   catch(int n) {.....}           //catches incorrect size
   catch(char* error) {.....}     //catches no free store
}
```

The first throw() has an integer argument and matches the catch(int n) signature. This handler is expected to perform an appropriate action where an incorrect array size has been passed as an argument to the constructor. For example, an error message and abort are normal. The second throw() has a pointer to character argument and matches the catch(char* error) signature.

10.3 Throwing Exceptions

Syntactically, *throw expressions* come in two forms:

>   throw *expression*
>   throw

The `throw` *expression* raises an exception. The innermost try block in which an exception is raised is used to select the `catch` statement that processes the exception. The `throw` with no argument can be used inside a `catch` to *rethrow* the current exception. It is typically used when you want a second handler called from the first handler to further process the exception.

The expression thrown is a static temporary object that persists until exception handling is exited. The expression is caught by a handler that may use this value:

In file throw1.cpp

```
#include <iostream.h>

void foo()
{
   int i;
   //will illustrate how an exception is thrown
   i = -15;
   throw i;
}

int main()
{
   try {
      foo();
   }
   catch(int n)
      { cerr << "exception caught\n " << n << endl; }
}
```

The integer value thrown by `throw i` persists until the handler with the integer signature `catch(int n)` exits. This value is available for use within the handler as its argument.

When a nested function throws an exception, the process stack is "unwound" until an exception handler is found. This means that block exit from each terminated local process causes automatic objects to be destroyed:

In file throw2.cpp

```
void foo()
{
   int  i, j;
   .....
   throw i;
   .....
}

void call_foo()
{
   int  k;
   .....
   foo();
   .....
}

int main()
{
   try {
      call_foo();         //foo exits with i and j destroyed
   }
   catch(int n) { ..... }
}
```

10.3.1 Rethrown Exceptions

Using `throw` without an expression rethrows a caught exception. The `catch` that rethrows the exception cannot complete the handling of the existing exception. It passes control to the nearest surrounding try block, where a handler capable of catching the still-existing exception is invoked. The exception expression exists until all handling is completed. Control resumes after the outermost try block that last handled the rethrown expression.

An example of rethrowing of an exception is:

```
catch(int n)
{
    .....
    throw;         //rethrown
}
```

Assuming the thrown expression was of integer type, the rethrown exception is the same persistent integer object that is handled by the nearest handler suitable for that type.

10.3.2 Exception Expressions

Conceptually, the thrown expression "passes" information to the handlers. Frequently the handlers will not need this information. For example, a handler that prints a message and aborts needs no information from its environment. However, the user might want additional information printed so that it can be used to select or help decide the handler's action. In this case, it is appropriate to package the information as an object:

```
class dbl_vect_error {
private:
    enum  error { bounds, heap, other } e_type;
    int   ub, index, size;
public:
    dbl_vect_error(error, int, int);    //out of bounds
    dbl_vect_error(error, int);         //out of memory
    .....
};
```

Now throwing an expression using an object of type dbl_vect_error can be more informative to a handler than just throwing expressions of simple types:

```
    .....
    throw dbl_vect_error(bounds, i, ub);
    .....
```

10.4 Try Blocks

Syntactically, a try block has the form:

```
try
compound statement
handler list
```

The try block is the context for deciding which handlers are invoked on a raised exception. The order in which handlers are defined determines the order in which a handler for a raised exception of matching type will be tried:

```
try {
   .....
   throw ("SOS");
   .....
   io_condition eof(argv[i]);
   throw (eof);
   .....
}

catch(const char*) {.....}
catch(io_condition& x) {.....}
```

Throw Expression Matches the Catch Handler Type if It Is

1. An exact match.

2. A derived type of the public base class handler type.

3. A thrown object type that is convertible to a pointer type that is the `catch` argument.

It is an error to list handlers in an order that prevents them from being called. An example would be:

```
catch(void*)              //any char* would match
catch(char*)
catch(BaseTypeError&)     //always on DerivedTypeError
catch(DerivedTypeError&)
```

A try block can be nested. If no matching handler is available in the immediate try block, a handler is selected from its immediately surrounding try block. If no handler can be found that matches, then a default behavior is used. This is by default `terminate()` (see Section 10.7, "terminate() and unexpected()," on page 359).

10.5 Handlers

Syntactically, a handler has the form

>   catch (*formal argument*)
>   *compound statement*

catch looks like a function declaration of one argument without a return type.

In file catch.cpp

```
catch(char* message)
{
   cerr << message << endl;
   exit(1);
}

catch( ... )         //default action to be taken
{
   cerr << "THAT'S ALL FOLKS." << endl;
   abort();
}
```

An ellipsis signature matching any argument type is allowed. Also, the formal argument can be an abstract declaration, meaning it can have type information without a variable name.

   The handler is invoked by an appropriate `throw` expression. At that point the try block is exited. The system calls clean-up functions that include destructors for any objects that were local to the try block. A partially constructed object will have destructors invoked on any parts of it that are constructed subobjects. The program resumes at the statement after the try block.

10.6 Exception Specification

Syntactically, an *exception specification* is part of a function declaration or function definition, and has the form

> *function header* `throw` (*type list*)

The *type list* is the list of types that a throw expression within the function can have. The function definition and the function declaration must write out the exception specification identically.

If the list is empty the compiler may assume that no throw will be executed by the function, either directly or indirectly.

```
void foo() throw(int, over_flow);
void noex(int i) throw();
```

If an exception specification is left off, the assumption is that an arbitrary exception can be thrown by such a function. Violations of these specifications are run-time errors. They are caught by the function `unexpected()`.

10.7 `terminate()` and `unexpected()`

The system-provided function `terminate()` is called when no handler has been provided to deal with an exception. The `abort()` function is called by default. It immediately terminates the program, returning control to the operating system. Another action can be specified by using `set_terminate()` to provide a handler. These declarations are found in *except* or *except.h*.

The system-provided handler `unexpected()` is called when a function throws an exception that was not in its exception-specification list. By default, the `terminate()` function is called; otherwise, a `set_unexpected()` can be used to provide a handler.

10.8 Example Exception Code

In this section, we discuss some examples of exception code and their effects. Let us return to catching a size error in our dbl_vect constructor from Section 6.7, "Overloading Assignment and Subscripting Operators," on page 213:

In file dbl_vect4.h

```
dbl_vect::dbl_vect(int n): size(n)
{
   if (n < 1)               //precondition assertion
      throw (n);
   p = new int[n];
   if (p == 0)              //postcondition assertion
      throw ("FREE STORE EXHAUSTED");
}
```

In file dbl_vect4.cpp

```
void g(int m)
{
   try {
      dbl_vect  a(m);
      .....
   }

   catch(int n)
   {
      cerr << "SIZE ERROR " << n << endl;   //retry g with
      g(10);                                //legal size
   }

   catch(const char* error)
   {
      cerr << error << endl;
      abort();
   }
}
```

The handler has replaced an illegal value with a default legal value. This may be reasonable in a system's debugging phase, when many routines are being integrated and tested. The system attempts to provide further diagnostics. It is analogous to a compiler attempting to continue to parse an incorrect program after a syntax error. Frequently, the compiler provides additional error messages that prove useful.

The above constructor checks that only one variable has a legal value. It looks artificial in that it replaces code that could directly replace the illegal value with a default by throwing an exception and allowing the handler to repair the value. However, in this form the separation of what is an error and how it is handled is clear. It is a clear methodology for developing fault-tolerant code.

More generally, one could have an object's constructor look like:

```
Object::Object(arguments)
{
   if (illegal argument1 )
      throw expression1;
   if (illegal argument2 )
      throw expression2;
   .....
   //attempt to construct
   .....
}
```

The `Object` constructor now provides a set of thrown expressions for an illegal state. The try block can now use the information to repair or abort incorrect code.

```
try {

   //..... fault tolerant code

}
catch(declaration1) { /* fixup this case */ }
catch(declaration2) { /* fixup this case */ }
   .....
   catch(declarationK) { /* fixup this case */ }
//correct or repaired - state values are now legal
```

When many distinct error conditions are useful for the state of a given object, a class hierarchy can be used to create a selection of related types to be used as throw expressions.

```
   Object_Error {
   public:
      Object_Error(arguments);        //capture useful info
      members that contain thrown expression state
      virtual void repair()
         { cerr << "Repair failed in Object " << endl;
           abort(): }
   };

   Object_Error_S1 : public Object_Error {
   public:
      Object_Error_S1(arguments);
      added members that contain thrown expression state
      void repair(); //override to provide repair
   };

   ..... //other derived error classes as needed
```

These hierarchies allow an appropriately ordered set of catches to handle exceptions in a logical sequence. Recall that a base class type should come after a derived class type in the list of catch declarations.

10.9 Standard Exceptions and Their Uses

Standard exceptions are provided by C++ compilers and library vendors. For example, the exception type xalloc is thrown by the Borland compiler if the new operator fails to return with storage from free store.

Here is a simple program that lets you test this behavior.

In file except.cpp

```
   #include <iostream.h>
   #include <except.h>         //for xalloc and xmsg
```

10.9 ▼ Standard Exceptions and Their Uses

```
int main()
{
   int *p, n;

   try {
      while (true) {
         cout << "enter allocation request:" << endl;
         cin >> n;
         p = new int[n];
      }
   }
   catch(xalloc x ) { cout << "xalloc caught" << endl; }
   catch(...) { cout << "default catch" << endl; }
}
```

This program loops until it is interrupted by an exception. On our system, a request for one billion integers will invoke the xalloc handler. In the ANSI standard, the exception class bad_alloc is provided for this purpose.

A frequent use of standard exceptions is in testing casts. The standard exception bad_cast is declared in file *exception*. Here is a simple program that uses RTTI as well as this exception:

In file bad_cast.cpp

```
#include <iostream.h>
#include <typeinfo.h>
#include <stdexception>
using namespace std;

class A {
public:
   virtual void foo() { cout << "in A" << endl; }
};

class B: public A {
public:
   void foo() { cout << "in B" << endl; }
};
```

```
int main()
{
   try {
      A a, *pa; B b, *pb;
      pa = &b;
      pb = dynamic_cast<B*>(pa);      //succeeds
      pb -> foo();
      pa = &a;
      pb = dynamic_cast<B*>(pa);      //fails
      pb -> foo();
   }
   catch(bad_cast) { cout << "bad cast" << endl; }
}
```

In systems that do not throw these exceptions, the pointer should be tested with an assertion to see that it is not converted to zero.

The standard library exceptions are derived from the base class `exception`. Two derived classes are `logic_error` and `runtime_error`. Logic-error types include `bad_cast`, `out_of_range`, and `bad_typeid`, which are intended to be thrown as indicated by their names. The run-time error types include `range_error`, `overflow_error`, and `bad_alloc`.

The base class defines a virtual function:

```
virtual const char* exception::what() const throw();
```

This member function should be defined in each derived class to give more helpful messages. The empty throw specification list indicates that the function should not itself throw an exception.

10.10 Pragmatics

Paradoxically, error recovery is chiefly concerned with writing correct programs. Exception handling is about error recovery. It is also a transfer-of-control mechanism. The client/manufacturer model gives the manufacturer the responsibility of making software that produces correct output given acceptable input. The question for the manufacturer is how much error detection, and, conceivably, correction, should be built in. The client is often better served by fault-detecting libraries, and can decide on whether to attempt to continue the computation.

Error recovery is based on the transfer of control. Undisciplined transfer of control leads to chaos. In error recovery, one assumes that an exceptional condition has corrupted the computation, making it dangerous to continue. It is analogous to driving a car after realizing the steering is damaged. Useful exception handling is the disciplined recovery when damage occurs.

In most cases, programming that raises exceptions should print a diagnostic message and gracefully terminate. Special forms of processing, such as real-time processing and fault-tolerant computing, require that the system not go down. In these cases, heroic attempts at repair are legitimate.

What can be agreed upon is that classes can usefully be provided with error conditions. In many of these conditions, the object has member values in illegal states—values it is not allowed to have. The system raises an exception for these cases, with the default action being program termination. This is analogous to the native types raising system-defined exceptions, such as `SIGFPE`.

But what kind of intervention is reasonable to keep the program running? And where should the flow of control be returned? C++ uses a termination model that forces the current try block to terminate. Under this regime, one will either retry the code or ignore or substitute a default result and continue. Retrying the code seems most likely to give a correct result.

Code is usually too thinly commented. It is hard to imagine the program that would be too rich in assertions. Assertions and simple throws and catches that terminate the computation are parallel techniques. A well thought out set of error conditions detectable by the user of an ADT is an important part of a good design. An overreliance on exception handling in normal programming, beyond error detection and termination, is a sign that a program was ill-conceived, with too many holes, in its original form.

Summary

1. Exceptions are generally unexpected error conditions. Normally these conditions terminate the user program with a system-provided error message. An example is floating-point divide-by-zero.

2. The standard library *assert.h* provides the macro

   `assert(`*expression*`);`

   If the *expression* evaluates as `false`, execution is aborted with diagnostic output. The assertions are discarded if the macro `NDEBUG` is defined.

3. The *signal.h* file provides a standard mechanism for handling system-defined exceptions in a straightforward manner. Some examples are:

   ```
   #define  SIGINT    2    /*interrupt signal */
   #define  SIGFPE    8    /*floating-point exception */
   #define  SIGABRT  22    /*abort signal */
   ```

   The system can raise these exceptions. For example, on many systems hitting control-C on the keyboard generates an interrupt. The normal action is to kill the current user process. These exceptions can be handled by use of the signal() function, which associates a handler function with a signal.

4. C++ code can raise an exception by using the throw expression. The exception is handled by invoking an appropriate handler selected from a list of handlers found at the end of the handler's try block.

5. Syntactically, throws come in two forms:

   throw
   throw *expression*

   The throw expression raises an exception in a try block. The throw with no argument may be used in a catch to rethrow the current exception.

6. Syntactically, a try block has the form:

   try
   compound statement
   handler list

   The try block is the context for deciding which handlers are invoked on a raised exception. The order in which handlers are defined determines the order in which a handler for a raised exception of matching type is tried.

7. Syntactically, a handler has the form:

   catch (*formal argument*)
   compound statement

   The catch looks like a function declaration of one argument without a return type.

8. Syntactically, an exception specification is part of a function declaration, and has the form:

   function header throw (*type list*)

   The *type list* is the list of types that a throw expression within the function can have. If the list is empty the compiler may assume that no throw will be executed by the function, either directly or indirectly.

9. The system-provided handler `terminate()` is called when no other handler has been provided to deal with an exception. The system-provided handler `unexpected()` is called when a function throws an exception that was not in its exception-specification list. By default `terminate()` calls the `abort()` function. The default `unexpected()` behavior is to call `terminate()`.

Exercises

1. The following bubble sort does not work correctly:

   ```
   //Incorrect bubble sort.
   #include  <iostream.h>

   void swap(int a, int b)
   {
      int  temp = a;

      a = b;
      b = temp;
   }

   void bubble(int a[], int size)
   {
      int  i, j;

      for (i = 0; i != size; ++i)
         for (j = i ; j != size; ++j)
            if (a[j] < a [j + 1])
               swap (a[j], a[j + 1]);
   }
   ```

```
int main()
{
   int  t[10] = { 9, 4, 6, 4, 5, 9, -3, 1, 0, 12};

   bubble(t, 10);
   for (int i = 0; i < 10; ++i)
      cout << t[i] << '\t';
   cout << "\nsorted? " << endl;
}
```

Place assertions in this code that will test that the code is working properly. Use this technique to write a correct program.

2. Use templates to write a generic version of the correct bubble sort, complete with assertions. Use a random-number generator to generate test data. On what types can this be made to work generically?

3. Code the member function dbl_vect::operator[](int) to throw an out-of-range exception if an incorrect index is used. (See Section 6.7, "Overloading Assignment and Subscripting Operators," on page 213.) Also, code a reasonable catch that prints out the incorrect value and terminates. Execute a try block in which the exception occurs to test the code. Write a catch that would allow user intervention at the keyboard to produce a correct index and continue or retry the computation. Can this be done in a reasonable manner?

4. Recode the ch_stack class to throw exceptions for as many conditions as you think are reasonable. (See Section 5.2, "Constructing a Dynamically Sized Stack," on page 157.) Use an enumerated type to list the conditions:

```
enum stack_error { overflow, underflow, ····· };
```

Write a catch that will use a switch statement to select an appropriate message and terminate the computation.

5. Write a stack_error class that replaces the enumerated type of the previous exercise. Make this a base class for a series of derived classes that encapsulates each specific exception condition. The catches should be able to use overridden virtual functions to process the various thrown exceptions.

Chapter 11

OOP Using C++

C++ is a hybrid language. The kernel language developed from C is classically used as a systems-implementation language. As such, C++ is suitable to writing very efficient code. The class-based additions to the language support the full range of OOP requirements. As such, C++ is suitable to writing reusable libraries, and it supports a polymorphic coding style.

Object-oriented programming (OOP) and C++ were embraced by the industry very quickly. C++ is a hybrid OOP language. As such, it allows a multiparadigmatic approach to coding. The traditional advantages of C as an efficient, powerful programmer's language are not lost. The key new ingredients are inheritance and polymorphism; that is, its capability to assume many forms.

11.1 OOP Language Requirements

OOP Language Characteristics

- Encapsulation with data hiding: The ability to distinguish an object's internal state and behavior from its external state and behavior.

- Type-extensibility: The ability to add user-defined types to augment the native types.

- Inheritance: The ability to create new types by importing or reusing the description of existing types.

- Polymorphism with dynamic binding: The ability of objects to be responsible for interpreting function invocation.

These features cannot substitute for programmer discipline and community-observed convention, but they can be used to promote such behavior.

Typical procedural languages like Fortran, Pascal, and C have limited forms of type-extensibility and encapsulation. These languages have pointer and record types that provide these features. C also has an ad hoc scheme of file-oriented privacy, in its `static` file-scope declarations. Languages like Modula-2 and Ada have more complete forms of encapsulation, namely module and package, respectively. These languages readily allow users to build ADTs, and they provide significant library support for many application areas. A language like pure LISP supports dynamic binding. The elements in OOP have been available in different languages for at least 25 years.

LISP, Simula, and Smalltalk have long been in widespread use in both the academic and research communities. These languages are in many ways more elegant than C and C++. However, not until OOP elements were added to C was there any significant movement to using OOP in industry. Indeed, the late 1980s saw a bandwagon effect in adopting C++ that cut across companies, product lines, and application areas; industry needed to couple OOP with the ability to program effectively at a low level.

Also crucial was the ease of migration from C to C++. Unlike PL/1, which is rooted in Fortran and COBOL; and Ada, which is rooted in Pascal; C++ had C as a nearly proper subset. As such, the installed base of C code need not be abandoned. These other languages required a nontrivial conversion process to modify existing code from their ancestor languages.

The conventional academic wisdom is that excessive concern with efficiency is detrimental to good coding practices. This concern misses the obvious, that product competition is based on performance. Consequently, industry values low-level technology. In this environment C++ is a very effective tool.

11.2 ADTs in Non-OOP Languages

Existing languages and methodology supported much of the OOP methodology by combining language features with programmer discipline. Programmer discipline and community conventions do work. It is possible in a non-OOP language to create and use ADTs. Three examples in C are the pseudotypes string, boolean, and file. They are pseudotypes in that they do not enjoy the same privileges as true types. What is gained by looking at these examples is a better understanding of the limits of extensibility in the non-OOP context.

A boolean type is implicit in C. Namely, logical expressions treat zero as false and nonzero as true. Since zero is a universal value, available for all native types, it is by convention used as a sentinel value. In pointer-based processing, using zero to represent an end-of-list condition is an idiom.

```
while (p) {              //p == 0  NULL pointer
   .....                 //process list
   p = p -> next;        //traverse
}
```

Enumerated types are often used explicitly to provide better documentation:

```
enum boolean { FALSE, TRUE };

boolean search(int table[], int x, int& where)
{
   where = -1;
   for (int i = 0; i < N; ++i)
      if (x == table[i]){
         where = i;
         break;
      }
   return boolean(where != -1);
}
```

The string type is a combination of programmer discipline and community convention in using the library *string.h*. This library is applicable to the type pointer to character. The end-of-string is again the zero value. Concatenation, copying, length, and other operations are given by functions in *string.h*. A measure of this success is the extent to which C is used for string-processing applications.

The file type is based on the use of *stdio.h*. A system-dependent structure type is defined with the name FILE. Functions such as file opening, closing, and seeking are given in *stdio.h*. These routines expect file pointers as parameters. Specific structure members are not directly manipulated when the programmer stays with these conventions. Again, C has been very successfully used in writing operating systems and in writing code that manipulates file systems.

These successes do not argue for the status quo. Instead, they argue for object-oriented programming as implemented in a language that insures the library conventions are not circumvented.

Notice that C++ has a real boolean type, namely bool, a standard string type defined in the standard library file *string*, and better file handling as defined by fstream.

11.3 Clients and Manufacturers

To fully appreciate the OOP paradigm, we must view the overall coding process as an exercise in shared and distributed responsibilities. We have used the terms *client* to mean a user of a class and *manufacturer* to mean the provider of the class.

A client of a class expects an approximation to an abstraction. A stack, to be useful, has to be of reasonable size. A complex number must be of reasonable precision. A deck of cards must be shufflable with random outcome in dealing hands. The internals of how these behaviors are computed is not a direct concern of the client. The client is concerned with cost, effectiveness, and ease of operation, but not with implementation. This is the *black box* principle.

Black Box for the Client

- Simple to use, easy to understand, and familiar
- In a component relationship within the system
- Cheap, efficient, and powerful

Black Box for the Manufacturer

- Easy to reuse and modify, and hard to misuse and reproduce
- Profitable to produce with a large client base
- Cheap, efficient, and powerful

The manufacturer competes for clients by implementing an ADT product that is reasonably priced and efficient. It is in the manufacturer's interest to hide details of an implementation. This simplifies what the manufacturer needs to explain to the client, and it frees the manufacturer to allow internal repairs or improvements that do not affect the client's use. It restrains the client from dangerous or inadvertent tampering with the product.

Structures and ordinary functions in C allow you to build useful ADTs, but do not support a client/manufacturer distinction. The client has ready access to internal details and may modify them in unsuitable ways. Consider a stack in C represented as an array with an integer variable **top**. A client of such a stack in C can extract an internal member of the array used to represent the stack. This violates the LIFO abstraction that the stack is implementing.

Encapsulation of objects prevents these violations. A data-hiding scheme that restricts access of implementation detail to manufacturers guarantees client conformance to the ADT abstraction. The private parts are hidden from client code, and the public parts are available. It is possible to change the hidden representation without changing the public access or functionality. If done properly, client code need not change when the hidden representation is modified.

The two keys to fulfilling these conditions are inheritance and polymorphism.

11.4 Reuse and Inheritance

Library creation and reuse are crucial indicators of successful language strategies. Inheritance, or deriving a new class from an old one, is used both for code sharing and reuse, and for developing type hierarchies. Through inheritance, a hierarchy of related ADTs can be created that share code and a common interface, a feature critical to the ability to reuse code.

Inheritance influences overall software design by providing a framework that captures conceptual elements that become the focus for system building and reuse. For example, InterViews is a C++ library that supports building graphical user interfaces. Major categories of objects include interactive, text, and graphics objects. These categories are readily composed to produce various applications, such as a CAD system, browser, or WYSIWYG editor.

The OOP Design Methodology

1. Decide on an appropriate set of ADTs.

2. Design in their relatedness, and use inheritance to share code and interface.

3. Use virtual functions to process related objects dynamically.

Inheritance also facilitates the black-box principle, and is an important mechanism for suppressing detail. It is hierarchical, and each level provides functionality to the next level that is built on it. In retrospect, structured programming methodology, with its process-centered view, relied on stepwise refinement to nest routines, but did not adequately appreciate the need for a corresponding view of data.

11.5 Polymorphism

Polymorphism is the genie in OOP, taking instruction from a client and properly interpreting its wishes. A polymorphic function has many forms. Following Cardelli and Wegner 1985, we make the distinctions:

Types of Polymorphism

1. Coercion (ad hoc polymorphism): A function or operator works on several different types by converting their values to the expected type. An example in ANSI C is assignment conversions of arithmetic types upon function call.

   ```
   a / b          //divide determined by native coercions
   ```

2. Overloading (ad hoc polymorphism): A function is called based on its signature, defined as the list of argument types in its parameter list. The C integer-divide operator and float-divide operator are distinguished based on their argument list.

   ```
   cout << a      //function overloading
   ```

3. Inclusion (pure polymorphism): A type is a subtype of another type. Functions available for the base type will work on the subtype. Such a function can have different implementations that are invoked by a run-time determination of subtype.

   ```
   p -> draw()    //virtual function call
   ```

4. Parametric polymorphism (pure polymorphism): The type is left unspecified and is later instantiated. Manipulation of generic pointers and templates provides this in C++.

   ```
   stack <window*> win[40]
   ```

Polymorphism localizes responsibility for behavior. The client code frequently requires no revision when additional functionality is added to the system through manufacturer-provided code additions.

Polymorphism directly contributes to the black box principle. The virtual functions specified for the base class are the interface used by the client throughout. The client knows that an overridden member function takes responsibility for a specific implementation of a given action relevant to the object. The client need not know different routines for each calculation or different forms of specification. These details are suppressed.

11.6 Language Complexity

For all of its advantages, C++ extracts a major price. Language complexity is substantial. This leads to additional training costs and to subtle misuse. Also, the rapid evolution of the language while it is in widespread use is nearly unprecedented. C is a small, elegant language. The syntax of C++ is similar to that of C, but its semantics are complex. To appreciate these difficulties, the following table compares some characteristics of Pascal, Modula-2, Modula-3, C++, and Ada.

Language Complexity				
Language	Keywords	Statements	Operators	Pages
Pascal	35	9	16	28
Modula-2	40	10	19	25
Modula-3	53	22	25	50
C	29	13	44	40
C++ v1.0	42	14	47	66
C++ v3.0 1990	48	14	52	155
Ada 1980	63	17	21	241
C++: ANSI 1995	62	15	54	650

These numbers only suggest the underlying language complexity. Modula-2 by these measures is slightly more complicated than its ancestor, Pascal; both are on a par with C. C++ is intentionally constructed as an extension of C, and follows the C style manual. C++ v3.0 adds 19 keywords to the 29 found in traditional C, a two-thirds increase. The C++ v3.0 reference manual has 155 pages, quadruple that of the C reference manual. These two measures suggest that C++ v3.0 is much more complicated than C. The draft ANSI standard for 1995 is roughly 650 pages long. Again, it is a quadrupling over the language as of 1990. While this document includes a large amount of additional material on an enhanced standard library, it still reflects great complexity. Furthermore, many C++ constructs are orthogonal, so their interactions greatly affect complexity.

An example of this occurs on page 306 of the *C++ Annotated Reference Manual* by Ellis and Stroustrup, where a 13-by-5 table is used to outline the distinct cases and features of different function types. The five function characteristics are: inherited, virtual, return type, member or friend, and default generation. For example, constructors, destructors, and conversion functions cannot have return type declarations, and `new()` and `delete()` must have `void*` and `void`, respectively. C has effectively one form of function semantics. This sixty-five-fold expansion is awe inspiring; and though regularities exist in this table and many characteristics can be derived from a conceptual understanding of the language design, the authors still felt it advisable to list these distinctions.

C++ overloads key concepts with several meanings, which causes a great deal of confusion. A candidate for the worst offender is the keyword `static`. There can be a local static variable, meaning a variable that retains value upon block exit. There can be a static file-scope identifier, meaning a name that has visibility restricted to that file. There can be a class variable that is static, meaning a variable whose existence is independent of the class. There can be static member functions, meaning member functions that do not receive the `this` pointer arguments. These meanings are related but distinct enough that is difficult to understand them as derived from a single concept.

11.7 C++ OOP Bandwagon

OOP using C++ has gained dazzling acceptance in industry, despite acknowledged flaws. The reason for this is that it brings OOP technology to industry in an acceptable way. That is, it is based on an existing, successful language in widespread use. It allows portable code to be written that is tight and efficient. Type safety is retained, and type extensibility is general. C++ coexists with standard languages, and does not require special resources from the system.

C was initially designed as a systems-implementation language, and as such allows coding that is readily translated to efficiently use machine resources. Software products gain competitive advantage from such efficiency. Hence, despite complaints that traditional C was not a safe or robust language to code in, C grew in its range of application. The C community, by ad hoc convention and discipline, used structured programming and ADT extensions. OOP made inroads into this professional community only when it was wed to C within a conceptual framework that maintained its traditional point of view and advantages. Key to the bandwagon change to C++ has been the understanding that inheritance and polymorphism gain additional important advantages over traditional coding practice.

Polymorphism in C++ allows a client to use an ADT as a black box. Success in OOP is characterized by the extent to which a user-defined type can be made indistinguishable from a native type. Polymorphism allows coercions to be specified that integrate the ADT with the native types. It permits objects from subtype hierarchies to respond dynamically to function invocation, the messaging principle in OOP. It also simplifies client protocols, and name proliferation is controlled by function and operator overloading. The availability of all four forms of polymorphism encourages the programmer to design with encapsulation and data hiding in mind.

OOP is many things to many people. Attempts to define it are like the blind men's attempts to describe an elephant. Recall our equation describing object-orientation as *OOP = type-extensibility + polymorphism.*

In many languages and systems, the cost of detail suppression was run-time inefficiency or undue rigidity in the interface. C++ has a range of choices that allow both efficiency and flexibility. As a consequence, industry will increasingly adopt it.

11.8 Platonism: Tabula Rasa Design

C++ gives the programmer a tool to implement an OOP design. But how do you develop such a design? Tabula rasa—given an empty slate—no simple methodology exists, because each design must be strongly tied to the problem domain and must reflect its abstractions. Discovering these abstractions is a design philosophy we call *Platonism*.

In the Platonic paradigm, there is an ideal object. For example, imagine the ideal chair and attempt to describe its characteristics. These would be characteristics shared by all chairs. Such a chair would be a subcategory of another ideal—furniture. Chair would have subcategories, such as swivel chair, beach chair, reclining chair, rocking chair, and so on. Useful descriptions would require expertise on chairs and agreement on the nature of "chairness" among producers and users of chairs. The Platonic chair should be easily modified to describe most commonly occurring chairs. The Platonic chair should be described in terms that are consistent with existing chair terminology.

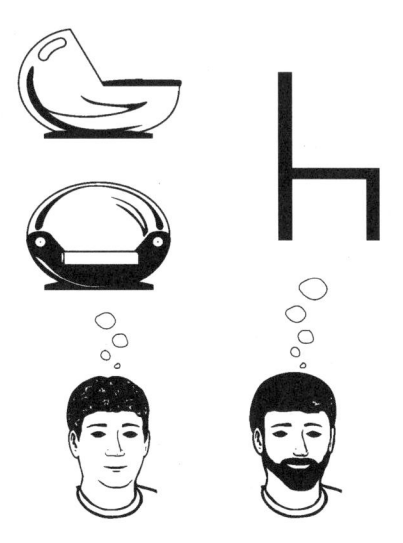

C++ was influenced by Simula 67, a language specifically invented for simulations. The Platonic paradigm is a modeling, or simulation, of the concrete world. It involves extra effort in determining a software OOP design. The OOP design typically provides a public interface that is convenient, general, and efficient. These considerations can be in conflict, and again, there are no simple rules for deciding which trade-offs to make.

The extra effort should be very beneficial to offset the increased initial design cost. First and foremost, it imposes an additional level of discipline to the programming process. Second, it encapsulates into classes meaningful, related pieces of code. Third, it enhances code reuse through inheritance and ADTs. Fourth, it improves prototyping by deferring implementation decisions and providing access to large, conveniently used general libraries. All of these things pay dividends.

The Platonic paradigm using OOP techniques is quietly revolutionizing the programming process. It does not displace older techniques, such as structured programming, but instead uses them when programming in the small to effectively manage the composition of large software projects.

11.9 Design Principles

Most programming should involve the use of existing designs. For example, the mathematical and scientific community have standard definitions of complex numbers, rationals, matrices, and polynomials. Each of these can be readily coded as an ADT. The expected public behavior of these types is widely agreed upon.

The programming community has widespread experience with standard container classes. Reasonable agreement exists as to the behavior of stack, associative array, binary tree, and queue. Also, the programming community has many examples of specialized programming language oriented around a particular domain. For example, SNOBOL and its successor language ICON have powerful string-processing features that can be captured as ADTs in C++.

Occam's razor is a useful design principle. It states that entities should not be multiplied beyond necessity—or beyond completeness, invertibility, orthogonality, consistency, simplicity, efficiency, or expressiveness. Such ideals can be in conflict, and frequently involve trade-offs in arriving at a design.

Invertibility means the program should have member functions that are inverses. In the mathematical types, addition and subtraction are inverses. In a text editor, add and delete are inverses. Some commands are their own inverses, such as negation. The importance of invertibility in a nonmathematical context can be seen by the brilliant success of the undo command in text editing and the recover commands in file maintenance.

Completeness is best seen in Boolean algebra, where the nand operation suffices to generate all possible Boolean expressions. But Boolean algebra is usually taught with negation, conjunction, and disjunction as the basic operations. Completeness by itself is not enough to judge a design by. A large set of operators is frequently more expressive.

Orthogonality is a principle that says each element of a design should integrate and work with all other elements without overlapping or being redundant. For example, on a system that manipulates shapes you should have a horizontal move, a vertical move, and a rotate operation. In effect, these would be adequate to position the shape at any point on the screen.

Hierarchy is captured through inheritance. Designs should be hierarchical. It is a reflection of two principles—decomposition and localization. Both principles are methods of suppressing detail, a key idea in coping with complexity. However, there is a scale problem in such a design. How much detail is enough to make a concept useful as its own class? It is important to avoid a proliferation of specialized concepts. Too much detail renders the class design hard to master.

11.10 Schema, Diagrams, and Tools

Designs can be aided by a diagramming process. Several OO-design (OOD) notations exist, and a number have been incorporated in CASE (computer-assisted software engineering) tools. We will describe two schemes that we have found useful. The first is the CRC notecard scheme (Budd 1991), and the second is the Wasserman-Pircher diagram (Wasserman et al. 1990; Booch 1991, for an alternative).

CRC stands for class, responsibility, and collaboration. A responsibility is an obligation the class must keep. For example, complex-number objects must provide an implementation of complex arithmetic. A collaborator is another object that cooperates with this object to provide some overall set of behaviors. For example, integers and reals collaborate with complex numbers to provide a comprehensive set of mathematical behaviors.

A CRC notecard is used to design a given class. The responsibilities of the class and the collaborators for that class are initially described. The front of the card corresponds to public behavior, and the back is used to describe implementation detail.

CRC Cards

card front

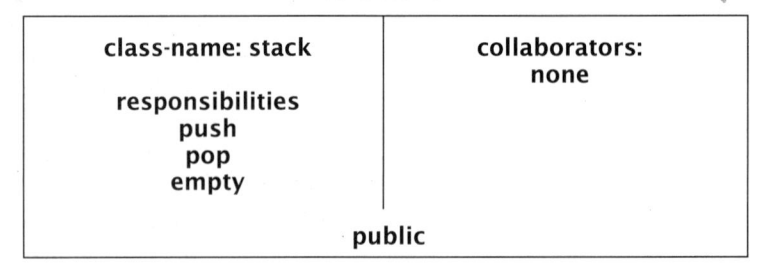

class-name: stack	collaborators: none
responsibilities push pop empty	
public	

card back

state/description

top

base_pointer

As the design process proceeds, the cards are rewritten and refined, becoming more detailed and closer to a set of member function headers. The back of the card can be used to show implementation details, including ISA, LIKEA, and HASA relationships.

The attractiveness of this scheme is its flexibility. In effect it represents a pseudocode refinement process that can reflect local tastes. The number of revisions and the level of detail and rigor are a matter of taste (Budd 1991).

Wasserman-Pircher diagrams are derived from entity-relation modeling and structured design.

11.10 ▼ Schema, Diagrams, and Tools

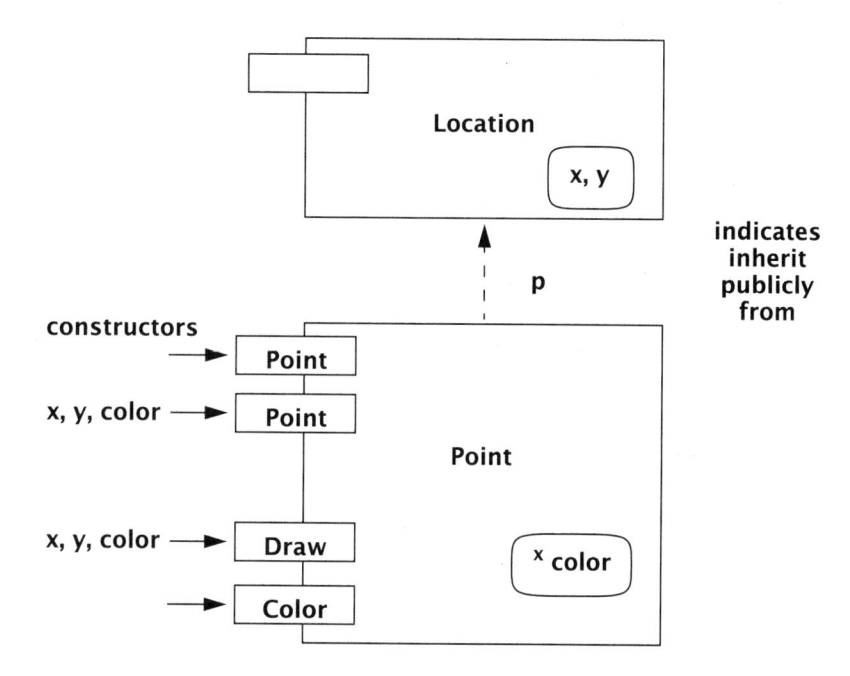

A sophisticated integrated software environment that uses these to develop OOP code is provided by Interactive Development Environments (IDE) of San Francisco. The software design is captured in the diagrams.

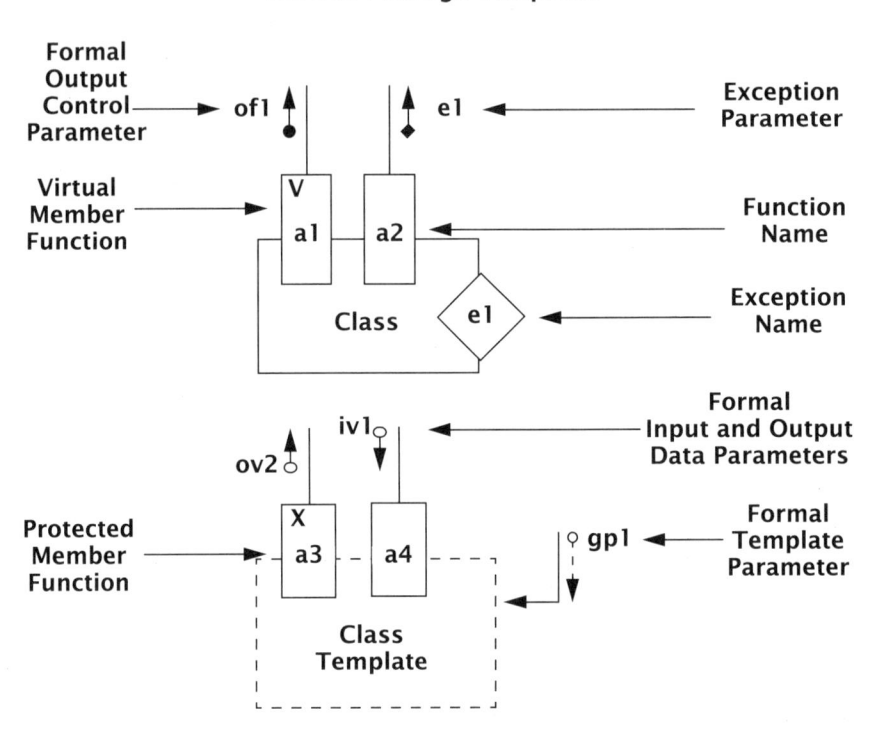

IDE's C++ Design Templates

```
Formal
Output
Control ─────► of1 ▲        ▲ e1 ◄───── Exception
Parameter                              Parameter
                 ┌───┬───┐
Virtual          │ V │   │
Member ─────►    │a1 │ a2│ ◄───────── Function
Function         │   │   │             Name
              ┌──┴───┴───┴──┐
              │             │ ◄e1►─── Exception
              │    Class    │         Name
              └─────────────┘

                      iv1       ◄───── Formal
                 ov2  ▼                Input and Output
                  ▲                    Data Parameters
                 ┌───┬───┐
Protected        │ X │   │             Formal
Member ─────►    │a3 │ a4│     gp1 ◄── Template
Function         │   │   │             Parameter
              ┌──┴───┴───┴──┐
              │    Class    │
              │   Template  │
              └─────────────┘
```

The level of detail is such that code stubs can be automatically produced from this design. Also, documentation and style rules can be semiautomatically tested for or generated.

11.11 Design Patterns

Reuse is a primary theme in modern programming. Reuse in early times was limited to simple libraries of functions, such as the math functions found in *math.h* or the string functions in *string.h*. In OOP, the class or template becomes a key construct for reuse. Classes and templates encapsulate code that conforms to certain designs. Thus the iterator classes of STL are a *design pattern*. Recently the concept of design pattern has proved very popular in defining medium-scale reuse (Gamma 1994). A design pattern has four elements:

Elements of a Design Pattern

1. The pattern terminology; for example, *iterator*.
2. The problem and conditions; for example, visitation over a container.
3. The solution; for example, pointer-like objects with a common interface.
4. The evaluation; for example, the trade-off between defining an iterator on a vector or using a native array.

A design pattern is an abstraction that suggests a useful solution to a particular programming problem. Often reuse is inexpensive. Such is the case with STL container and iterator design patterns that require only instantiation. Sometimes reuse is expensive, such as inventing from scratch a balanced tree class with an interface conforming to STL sequence containers.

Design Patterns in This Text

1. *Iterator.* For example, `vector::iterator`. Organizes container visitation.
2. *Composite.* For example, `class grad_student`. Composes complex objects out of simpler ones.
3. *Template method.* For example, the `quicksort()` template.

11.12 C++: A Critique

To an extent, C++ is the 90s version of PL/1 (1965) or Ada (1980). It is an attempt within the professional programming community to provide a nearly universal programming language. The defect of PL/1 was that it mixed too many styles—it combined COBOL, Fortran, and elements of ALGOL into the same language. Defects of Ada were its size, complexity, and inefficiency. C++ has problems with size and complexity, but what is very important is that it builds on existing resources and practice. It also emphasizes efficiency—sometimes to a fault.

Some of C++'s problems with complexity can be avoided by keeping to a conceptual view of its features. For example, a pure virtual function can be defined with executable code:

```
class ABC {
public:
    virtual void  f() = 0;
};
```

```
void ABC::f() { cout << "pure virtual foo " << endl; }

//must be called with qualified name,e.g.  x.ABC::f();
```

It is an eccentricity that this is possible. Conceptually, a pure virtual is used to defer a definition.

Other complexity issues are fundamental to the C++ language design, such as lack of garbage collection (GC). Several proposals exist (see Edelson 1991 and 1992, and Boehm 1988), and their implementation supports the contention that they can be done without degrading performance in most applications. Most other major OOP languages, such as Smalltalk, CLOS, and Eiffel, support GC. The argument for GC is that it makes the programmer's task distinctly easier. Memory leaks and pointer errors are common when each class provides for its own storage management. These are very hard errors to find and debug. GC is a well understood technology, so why not use it?

The argument against GC is that it extracts a hidden cost from all users when employed universally. Also, it manages memory but not other resources. Managing other resources would still require destructors for finalization, which is the return of resources and other behavior when an object's lifetime is over. For example, the object might be a file, and finalization might require closing the file. Finally, it is not in the tradition of the C community to have free store managed automatically.

OOP attempts to emphasize reuse, which is possible on several scales. The grandest scale is the development of libraries that are effective for an entire problem domain. The upside is that reuse contributes in the long run to more easily maintained code. The downside is that a particular application does not need costly library development.

OOP requires programmer sophistication. More sophisticated programmers are better programmers. The downside is high training cost and the potential misuse of sophisticated tools.

OOP makes client code simpler and more readily extensible. Polymorphism can be used to incorporate local changes into a large-scale system without global modification. The downside can be run-time overhead.

C++ provides programming encapsulations through classes, inheritance, and templates. Encapsulations hide and localize. As systems get bigger and more complex, there is an increasing need for such encapsulations. Simple block structure and functional encapsulation of languages such as Pascal are not enough. The 1970s taught us the need for the module as a programming unit. The 1980s taught us that modules need to have a logical coherence supported in the language, and that they must be derivable from one another. When supported by a programming language, encapsulations and relationships lead to increased programmer discipline. The art of programming is to blend rigor and discipline with creativity.

Summary

1. Object-oriented programming (OOP) and C++ were embraced by industry very quickly. C++ is a hybrid OOP language. As such, it allows a multiparadigmatic approach to coding. The traditional advantages of C as an efficient, powerful programmer's language are not lost. The key new ingredient is polymorphism, or the ability to assume many forms.

2. Existing languages and methodology supported much of the OOP methodology by combining language features with programmer discipline. It is possible to create and use ADTs in a non-OOP language. Three examples in the C community are string, boolean, and file, which are pseudotypes in that they do not enjoy the same privileges as true types. What is gained by looking at these examples is a better understanding of the limits of extensibility in non-OOP.

3. A black box for the client should be simple to use, easy to understand, and familiar; cheap, efficient, and powerful; and in a component relationship within the system. A black box for the manufacturer should be easy to reuse and modify, and hard to misuse and reproduce; cheap, efficient, and powerful; and profitable to produce for a large client base.

   The OOP Design Methodology
   - Decide on an appropriate set of ADTs.
   - Design in their relatedness, and use inheritance to share code and interface.
   - Use virtual functions to process related objects dynamically.

4. Polymorphism directly contributes to the black-box principle. The virtual functions specified for the base class are the interface used by the client throughout. The client knows that an overridden member function takes responsibility for a specific implementation of a given action relevant to the object.

5. As a hybrid OOP language, C++ can cause the programmer a dialectical tension headache. The penchant of C programmers to focus on efficiency and implementation conflicts with the penchant of objectivists to focus on elegance, abstraction, and generality. The two demands on the coding process are reconcilable, but require a measure of coordination and respect for the process.

6. OOP is many things to many people. My equation for it is *OOP = type-extensibility + polymorphism.* In many languages and systems, the cost of detail suppres-

sion was run-time inefficiency or undue rigidity in the interface. C++ has a range of choices that allow both efficiency and flexibility.

7. Tabula rasa—given an empty slate—no simple methodology exists for object-oriented design, because each design must be strongly tied to the problem domain and must reflect its abstractions. Discovering these abstractions is a design philosophy called Platonism. In the Platonic paradigm, there is an ideal object whose characteristics are shared by all objects of its type.

8. Occam's razor is a useful design principle. It states that entities should not be multiplied beyond necessity—or beyond completeness, invertibility, orthogonality, consistency, simplicity, efficiency, or expressiveness. These principles can be in conflict and frequently involve trade-offs in arriving at a design.

Exercises

1. Consider the following three ways to provide a Boolean type:

   ```
   //Traditional C using the preprocessor
   #define   TRUE   1
   #define   FALSE  0
   #define   Boolean int

   //ANSI C and C++ using enumerated types
   enum Boolean { false, true };

   //C++ as a class
   class Boolean {
      .....
   public:
      //various member functions
      //including overloading  !  &&  ||  ==  !=
   };
   ```

   Discuss the advantages and disadvantages of each style. Keep in mind scope, naming, and conversion problems. In what ways is it desirable for C++ to now have a native type bool?

2. C++ originally allowed the `this` pointer to be modifiable. One use was to have user-controlled storage management by assigning directly to the `this` pointer. The assignment of zero meant that the associated memory could be returned to free store. Discuss why this is a bad idea.

3. The rules for deciding which definition of an overloaded function to invoke have changed since the first version of C++. One reason for this is to reduce the number of ambiguities. A criticism is that the rules allow matching through conversions that may be unintended by the programmer. This can cause difficult to detect run-time bugs. One strategy is to have the compiler issue a diagnostic warning in such cases; another is to use casting defensively to inform the compiler of the intended choice. Discuss these alternatives after investigating how the rules have changed.

4. List three things that you would drop from the C++ language. Argue why each would not be missed. For example, it is possible to have protected inheritance, though it was never discussed in this text. Should it be in the language for completeness' sake?

5. Describe at least two separate concepts for the keyword `virtual` as used in C++. Does this cause conceptual confusion?

6. The package *string.h* is a pseudotype. It employs traditional C technology and programmer discipline to provide the ADT string. Why is it preferable to provide the standard library class `string`?

Appendix A

ASCII Character Codes

American Standard Code for Information Interchange										
	0	1	2	3	4	5	6	7	8	9
0	nul	soh	stx	etx	eot	enq	ack	bel	bs	ht
1	nl	vt	np	cr	so	si	dle	dc1	dc2	dc3
2	dc4	nak	syn	etb	can	em	sub	esc	fs	gs
3	rs	us	sp	!	"	#	$	%	&	'
4	(	)	*	+	,	-	.	/	0	1
5	2	3	4	5	6	7	8	9	:	;
6	<	=	>	?	@	A	B	C	D	E
7	F	G	H	I	J	K	L	M	N	O
8	P	Q	R	S	T	U	V	W	X	Y
9	Z	[	\	]	^	_	`	a	b	c
10	d	e	f	g	h	i	j	k	l	m
11	n	o	p	q	r	s	t	u	v	w
12	x	y	z	{	|	}	~	del		

Some Observations

- Character codes zero through 31 and 127 are nonprinting.
- Character code 32 prints a single space.
- Character codes for digits zero through nine are contiguous.
- Character codes for letters A through Z are contiguous.
- Character codes for letters a through z are contiguous.
- The difference between a capital letter and the corresponding lowercase letter is 32.

The Meaning of Some of the Abbreviations			
bel	audible bell	ht	horizontal tab
bs	backspace	nl	newline
cr	carriage return	nul	null
esc	escape	vt	vertical tab

Appendix B

Operator Precedence and Associativity

Operators	Associativity
:: (global scope) :: (class scope)	left to right
() [] -> . *(postfix)* ++ *(postfix)* --	left to right
++ *(prefix)* -- *(prefix)* ! ~ sizeof(*type*) & *(address)* + *(unary)* - *(unary)* * *(indirection)* delete new	right to left
.* ->*	left to right
* / %	left to right
+ -	left to right
<< >>	left to right
< <= > >=	left to right
== !=	left to right
&	left to right
^	left to right
|	left to right
&&	left to right
||	left to right
?:	right to left
= += -= *= /= %= >>= <<= &= ^= |=	right to left
, *(comma operator)*	left to right

In case of doubt, parenthesize.

Appendix C

Fortran 90 and C++

This appendix shows the similarities between Fortran 90 and C++. It presents, largely through examples, near-equivalent forms for the languages. Fortran 90 allows multifile programs. It has many extensions to standard Fortran.

C.1 Program Structure

A program in C++ is a collection of functions and declarations, which may be declared in different files. In C++, program execution always begins with the function `main()`. The language is block structured, and variables declared within blocks are automatically allocated upon block entry. Parameters, unless otherwise specified, are call-by-value. The general program structure of Fortran 90 and C++ is demonstrated in the following programs for computing the greatest common denominator of two integers.

In file gcd90.f

```fortran
! Greatest common divisor program.

PROGRAM GCD

   INTEGER  X, Y

   PRINT *, 'PROGRAM GCD FORTRAN 90'

   X = 1; Y = 2;            ! To force first time in
   DO WHILE (X /= Y)        ! /= or .NE.
      PRINT *, 'Enter two integers: '
      READ *, X, Y
      PRINT *, 'GCD[', X, ', ', Y, '] = ', GCD (X, Y)
   END DO
END

INTEGER FUNCTION GCD (M, N)

   INTEGER M, N, R          ! R is remainder

   DO WHILE (N /= 0)
      R = MOD(M, N)
      M = N
      N = R
   END DO
   GCD = M                  ! Returned result
   RETURN
END
```

In Fortran a program starts with the keyword PROGRAM, followed by an identifier naming the program. The program may contain a series of declarations and statements. Older Fortrans had a rigid structure that reserved columns 1 through 5 for comment symbols and line numbers, column 6 for continuation, and columns 7 through 72 for statements, and allowed only one statement per line. Fortran 90 is freeform.

The corresponding program in C++ is:

In file gcd.cpp

```cpp
//Greatest common divisor program.
#include   <iostream.h>
#include   <assert.h>

int gcd(int m, int n)       //function definition
{                           //block
   int   r;                 //declaration of remainder

   while (n != 0) {         //not equal
      r = m % n;            //modulos operator
      m = n;                //assignment
      n = r;
   }                        //end while loop
   return m;                //exit gcd with value m
}

int main()
{
   int   x, y, g;

   cout << "\nPROGRAM Gcd C++";
   do {
      cout << "\nEnter two integers: ";
      cin >> x >> y;
      assert(x * y != 0); //precondition on gcd
      cout << "\nGCD(" << x << ", " << y << ") = "
           << (g = gcd(x, y)) << endl;
      assert(x % g || y % g);//postcondition on g
   } while (x != y);

   return 0;
}
```

Some minor differences are easily seen in these two versions of the greatest common divisor program.

Some Differences Between C++ and Fortran

- The C++ comment symbols are either // or /* */. Fortran does not have a multiline comment form.
- C++ uses braces for blocks and compound statements.
- Fortran groups statements implicitly within its control constructs.
- C++ uses libraries such as *iostream.h* for input/output.
- The Fortran keyword FUNCTION is omitted in the C++ function declaration.
- C++ distinguishes subroutine from function by using void as a return type.
- Fortran offers extensive intrinsic functions for a reasonable set of types for scientific computation.
- C++ must add types like complex using libraries.
- Fortran requires a continuation character (the &) when text is broken across lines. C++ automatically continues across lines.

C.2 Identifiers

Fortran is not case sensitive; C++ is. Older Fortrans allowed up to six characters for an identifier and did not allow the underbar character; C++ and Fortran 90 do.

```
!Fortran Identifiers
INTEGER M, N, SIZE
I, J         !Integer by default (starts with I-N)
R, S         !Real by default
MULTI_WORD   !Allowed in Fortran 90, not FORTRAN 77
```

is equivalent to

```
int    M, N, Size;      //distinct from m, n, size
int    i, j;
float  R, S;
int    Multi_Word       //C++
```

Fortran 90 has qualified identifiers that are used with TYPE names. This corresponds to using the scope resolution operator in C++ to select a name.

```
TYPE FOOD
   CHARACTER (LEN = 20) :: NAME
   INTEGER :: CALORIES
END TYPE FOOD

TYPE (FOOD) :: CARROT

CARROT % CALORIES = 10
```

is equivalent to

```
struct food
   char* name;
   int   calories;

food carrot, apple;

carrot::calories = 10;      //C++ scope resolution
```

C.3 Simple Data Types

Fortran has five intrinsic data types: INTEGER, REAL, COMPLEX, CHARACTER, and LOGICAL. Additional data types can be derived from these types.

```
! Fortran 90 data types
INTEGER    i, j
REAL       x1, x2
CHARACTER (LEN=8) c1
CHARACTER (LEN=7) c2
PARAMETER (c1 = 'A string', c2 = "Another")
LOGICAL    flag
DOUBLE PRECISION Z
```

is equivalent to

```
int          i, j;
double       x1, x2;
char*        c1 = "A string", c2 = "Another";
bool         flag;     //may not be available
long double  z;
```

C.4 Statements

Statement	Fortran 90	C++
empty		`;`
assignment	`i = i + k`	`i = i + k;`
compound	`X ..... END X`	`{.....}`
goto	`GO TO 10`	`goto 110;`
simple if	`IF (x == y) PRINT *, x`	`if (x == y)` `    cout << x;`

if	`IF (X == Y) THEN`
	`    PRINT *, 'same'`
	`ELSE`
	`    PRINT *, 'unequal'`
	`END IF`
		`if (x == y)`
		`    cout << "same\n";`
		`else`
		`    cout << "unequal\n";`

for	`DO 10 i= 0, N - 1, 1`
	`    a[i] = b[i] + c[i];`
	`10 CONTINUE`
		`for (i = 0; i < n; ++i)`
		`    a[i] = b[i] + c[i];`

while	`DO WHILE (x /= y)`
	`.....`
	`END DO`
		`while (x != y) {`
		`.....`
		`}`

case	`SELECT CASE (s)`
	`CASE (1)`
	`    PRINT *, 'A '`
	`CASE (2)`
	`    PRINT *, 'B'`
	`.....`
	`END SELECT`
		`switch (s) {`
		`case 1:  cout << "A ";`
		`    break;`
		`case 2:  cout << "B ";`
		`    break;`
		`.....`
		`};`

return	`subname = x * x * x` `RETURN`	`return x * x * x;`

Table heading: Statements in Fortran 90 and C++

Expressions in Fortran 90 and C++		
Expression	**Fortran**	**C++**
arithmetic	a + b - c	a + b - c
	a * (b - c)	a * (b - c)
integer	i / j	i / j
	MOD(i, 10)	i % 10
real	x / y	x / y
and	flag1 .AND. flag2	flag1 && flag2
or	flag1 .OR. flag2	flag1 || flag2
not	.NOT. flag1	!flag1
relational	a == b	a == b
	a /= b	a != b
	(a < b) .AND.(b < c)	a < b && b < c
exponentiation	a ** b	pow(a, b)

Reference declarations allow C++ to have call-by-reference arguments.

\multicolumn{3}{c}{Subroutines and Functions in Fortran and C++}		
Declaration	Fortran	C++

function	`REAL FUNCTION CUBE(X)`
	`    REAL X`
	`    CUBE = X * X * X`
	`END`
		`double cube(double x)`
		`{`
		`    return x * x * x;`
		`}`

statement function	`REAL CUBE, X`
	`CUBE (X) = X * X * X`
		`double cube(double x)`
		`{`
		`    return x * x * x;`
		`}`

subroutine	`SUBROUTINE POW(X,SQ,CU)`
	`    REAL X, SQ, CU`
	`    SQ = X * X`
	`    CU = X * SQ`
	`END`
		`void pow(double x,`
		`    double& sq,`
		`    double& cu)`
		`{`
		`    sq = x * x;`
		`    cu = x * sq;`
		`}`

recursive function	`RECURSIVE FUNCTION`
	`F(N)  RESULT (ANS)`
	`INTEGER N, ANS`
	`IF (N <= 1) THEN`
	`    ANS = 1`
	`ELSE`
	`    ANS = N * F(N - 1)`
	`END IF`
	`END`
		`int f(int n)`
		`{`
		`    if (n <= 1)`
		`        return 1;`
		`    else`
		`        return n * f(n-1);`
		`}`

Both languages allow recursion. Ordinary functions cannot nest. C++ allows static local variables, akin to the Fortran SAVE. For example:

```
void foo()
{
   static int count = 0;

   cout <<  "count is " << count << endl;
   ++count;
}
```

Static variables retain their value and are not reinitialized. The first execution of foo() prints 0. The second execution of foo() prints 1.

Fortran 90 has arrays, derived data types, and strings. The analogs in C++ are arrays, structures, and character arrays, respectively.

Structured Types in Fortran and C++		
Declaration	**Fortran 90**	**C++**
array type	INTEGER A(0:N - 1)	int a[N]; //0 to N - 1
string type	CHARACTER (LEN = 20) c	char c[20];

record and pointer type	TYPE node
	   INTEGER data
	   TYPE (node), &
	      POINTER ::next
	END TYPE node
		struct node {
		   int data;
		   node* next;
		};

A C++ array is declared with a single integer expression that is its number of elements. These arrays are indexed from element zero. C++ strings must end with the sentinel character \0.

C++ does not have a native file type. Appendix E, "Input/Output," describes *fstream.h*, which defines library provided support for file I/O.

Appendix D

Language Guide

This appendix is a concise guide to C++. It summarizes many of the key language elements that are not found in older procedural languages, such as Pascal and C. It is intended as a convenient guide to the language.

D.1 Program Structure

C++ Program Organization

- C++ relies on an external standard library to provide input and output (I/O). The information the program needs to use this library resides in *iostream.h.*

- C++ uses a preprocessor to handle a set of directives, such as the `include` directive, to convert the program from its preprocessing form to pure C++ syntax. Directives start with the symbol #.

- A C++ program consists of declarations that may be in different files. Each function is on the external, or global, level and may not be declared in a nested manner. The files act as modules and may be separately compiled.

- The function `main()` is the starting point for program execution. It obeys the C++ rules for function declaration. It is normal practice for `main()` to implicitly return the integer value zero, indicating normal program completion. Other values need to be returned explicitly and would indicate an error condition.

- The `assert` macro tests a condition for correctness, and terminates the program if the test fails.

D.2 Lexical Elements

A C++ program is a sequence of characters that are collected into tokens, which comprise the basic vocabulary of the language. There are six categories of tokens: keywords, identifiers, constants, string constants, operators, and punctuators.

Characters that can be used to construct tokens are:

```
a b c d e f g h i j k l m n o p q r s t u v w x y z
A B C D E F G H I J K L M N O P Q R S T U V W X Y Z
0 1 2 3 4 5 6 7 8 9
+ - * / = ( ) { } [ ] <> ' " ! # ~ % ^ & _ : ; , . ? \ |
```
White space characters such as blank and tab

In producing tokens, the compiler selects the longest string of characters that constitutes a token.

D.2.1 Comments

C++ has a rest-of-line comment symbol, //. The C style comment pairs, /* */, are also available. Comments do not nest. Some examples are:

```
//OOP Using C++: Addison-Wesley Program GCD

const int N = 200;        //N is number of trials

/*    *   *   *   *   *
    Programmer:    Laura M. Pohl
    Compiler:      Borland 5.0
    Modifications: 5-2-96    Stack Overflow
*    *   *   *   *   *   */
```

Except for lengthy multiline comments, the rest-of-line comment should be used. This style is easier to use and is less error prone.

D.2.2 Identifiers

An identifier can be one character or more. The first character must be a letter or underscore. Subsequent characters can be letters, digits, or an underscore. Though in principle identifiers can be arbitrarily long, many systems distinguish only up to the first 31 characters. Identifiers that contain a double underscore or begin with an underscore followed by an uppercase letter are reserved for use by the system.

Identifier Examples			Comments
multiWord	vector	flag_x	normal style
q213	sb3	abx1w	opaque
speed	Speed	speedy	distinct but confusing
_Sys1	_Adriver	__C__	reserved for system use
9illegal	wrong-2	il$form	illegal
typeid	this	register	keywords can't be used

D.2.3 Keywords

Keywords are explicitly reserved identifiers that have a strict meaning in C++. They cannot be redefined or used in other contexts. There are other keywords that are specific to implementations, such as near and far in Borland C++. The following keywords are in use in most current C++ systems.

Keywords			
asm	else	operator	throw
auto	enum	private	true
bool	explicit	protected	try
break	extern	public	typedef
case	false	register	typeid
catch	float	reinterpret_cast	typename

Keywords			
char	for	return	union
class	friend	short	unsigned
const	goto	signed	using
const_cast	if	sizeof	virtual
continue	inline	static	void
default	int	static_cast	volatile
delete	long	struct	wchar_t
do	mutable	switch	while
double	namespace	template	
dynamic_cast	new	this	

D.3 Constants

C++ has constants for each basic type. These include integer, floating-point, and character constants. String constants are character sequences surrounded by double quotes. There is one universal pointer constant, namely zero. Some examples follow.

Constant Examples	Comments
156 0156 0x156	integer: dec, oct, hex
156l 156u	integer: long, unsigned
'A' 'a' '7' '\t'	character: A, a, 7, tab
3.14f 3.1415 3.14159L	floating-point constants
"A string."	string constant
true false	bool constants

The suffixes u or U, l or L, and f or F are used to indicate unsigned, long, and float, respectively. The unsigned constants are positive numbers. The long constants have greater precision than normal. The float constants are usually less precise than ordinary double constants.

The character constants are usually given in single quotes; for example, `'s'`. Some nonprinting and special characters require an escape sequence.

Character Constants	
`'\a'`	alert
`'\\'`	backslash
`'\b'`	backspace
`'\r'`	carriage return
`'\"'`	double quote
`'\f'`	formfeed
`'\t'`	tab
`'\n'`	newline
`'\0'`	null character
`'\''`	single quote
`'\v'`	vertical tab
`'\101'`	octal 101 in ASCII 'A'
`'\x041'`	hexadecimal ASCII 'A'
`L'oop'`	`wchar_t` constant

Floating-point constants can be specified with or without signed integer exponents.

Floating-Point Constant Examples			Comments
`3.14f`	`1.234F`		narrow `float` constants
`0.123456`	`.123456`		`double` constants
`0.12345678L`	`0.123456781`		`long double` constants
`3.`	`3.0`	`0.3E1`	all express `double` 3.0
`300e-2`	`.03e2`	`30e-1`	also 3.0

String constants are considered `static char[]` constants. A string constant is a contiguous array of characters. String constants that are separated only by white space are implicitly concatenated into a single string. A backslash character at the end of the line indicates string continuation. A backslash preceding a double quote makes the double quote part of the string. The compiler places a null character at the end of a complete string as a sentinel or termination character.

String Constant Examples	Comments
`""`	empty string is '\0'
`"OOP 4ME"`	'O' 'O' 'P' ' ' '4' 'M' 'E' '\0'
`"my \"quote \" is escaped"`	\" used for embedding "
`"a multiline string \` `is also possible"`	\ at end of line indicates string continuation

`"This is a single string, "`
`"since it is only separated "`
`"by whitespace."`
	implicitly concatenated

Enumerations define a collection of named constants called enumerators. The constants are a list of identifiers that are implicitly consecutive integer values starting with zero. They can be anonymous, or they can be distinct types.

Enumeration Constants	Comments
`enum { off, on };`	off == 0, on == 1
`enum color { red, blue, white, green };`	color is a type
`enum { BOTTOM = 50, TOP = 100, OVER };`	OVER == 101
`enum grades { F = 59, D = 60, C = 70,` `               B = 80, A = 90 };`	all initialized

Enumeration constants are promoted to type `int` in expressions.

The keyword `const` is used to declare that an object's value is constant throughout its scope.

Using the const Keyword	Comments
`const int   N = 100;`	N can't change
`double      w[N];`	[uses constant expressions]
`const int   bus_stops[5] =` `   { 23, 44, 57, 59, 83 };`	element values, `bus_stops[i]`, are constant

C++ uses a preprocessor to handle a set of directives, such as the `include` directive, to convert the program from its preprocessing form to pure C++ syntax. These directives are introduced by the symbol #.

The use of `const` differs from the use of `#define`, as in

```
#define N 100
```

In the case of the `const int N` declaration, N is a nonmodifiable lvalue of type `int`. In the case of the `define` macro, N is a constant. Also, the macro replacement of N occurs as a preprocessor substitution without regard to other scope rules.

D.4 Declarations and Scope Rules

Declarations associate meaning with a given identifier. The syntax of C++ declarations is highly complex because it incorporates many disparate elements that are context-dependent. A declaration provides an identifier with a type, a storage class, and a scope. (See Section 2.4.1, "Initialization," on page 36.) A simple declaration is often a definition as well. For a simple variable, this means the object is created and possibly initialized. For a function, it means the function body—that is, the brace-enclosed statements the function executes—are written out.

```
const int n = 17;     //n is declared and defined
int sqrt(double);     //sqrt is declared not defined
void foo()            //foo is declared and defined
{
   int  i = 5;        //i is defined and initialized
   .....              //i is automatic and local to foo
}
```

Complex declarations, such as class, function, and template declarations, are described in separate sections of this appendix.

The `typedef` mechanism can be used to create a synonym for the type it defines.

Typedefs	Comments
typedef int BOOLEAN	used prior to `bool` type
typedef char *c_string;	`c_string` pointer to `char`
typedef void (*ptr_f)();	pointer to `void fcn()`

C++ has file scope, function scope, block scope, class scope, function prototype scope, and namespace scope. File scope, also known as global scope, extends from the point of declaration in a file to the end of that file. Function prototype scope is the scope of identifiers in the function prototype argument list, and extends to the end of the declaration. Blocks nest in a conventional way, and functions cannot be declared inside other functions or blocks.

Declarations can occur almost anywhere in a block. A declaration can also be an initializer in a for statement. For a code example, see Section 2.8.5, "The for Statement," on page 52 (in file for_test.cpp).

Selection statements, such as the if or switch statement, cannot merely control a declaration. In general, jumps and selections cannot bypass an initialization. This is not true of C.

```
if (flag)
    int  j = 6;                      //illegal
else
    j = 19;

if (flag) {
    int  j = 6;                      //legal within block
    cout << j;
}
```

C++ has a scope resolution operator ::. When used in the form :: *variable*, it allows access to the externally named variable. Other uses of this notation are important for classes and namespaces. Class member identifiers are local to that class. The scope resolution operator can be used to resolve ambiguities. When used in the form *class-name* :: *variable*, it accesses the named variable from that class:

```
class A {
public:
    static void  foo();
};

class B {
public:
    void  foo() { A :: foo();  ····· }
};
```

A hidden external name can be accessed by using the scope resolution operator:

In file scope1.cpp

```
int  i;                    //external i
void foo(int i)            //parameter i
{
   i = ::i;                //parameter i is assigned external i
   .....
}
```

Classes can be nested. C++ rules scope the inner class within the outer class. This is a source of confusion, since the rules have changed and are different from C rules. For a code example, see Section 4.6.2, "Nested Classes," on page 127 (in file nested.cpp).

Enumerations declared inside a class give the enumerator's class scope, as in:

```
class foo {
public:
   enum  button { off, on } flag;
};

int main()
{
   foo  c;

   c.flag = foo::off;
   .....
}
```

D.5 Namespaces

C++ traditionally had a single, global namespace. Since programs written by different people can have inadvertent name clashes when combined, and C++ encourages multivendor library use, namespace scope was added:

```
//file gotten by including <iostream>
namespace std {                     //turn vendor library into ansi
   #include <iostream.h>
}
```

```
namespace LMPinc {                    //LMP toy company software
    class puzzles { ..... };
    class toys { ..... };
    .....
}
```

In effect, encapsulated declarations are given an outermost, or qualified, name. The *using* declaration allows these names to be used without the namespace identifier.

```
using namespace std;
using namespace LMPinc;
toys   top;                           //LMPinc::toys
```

The namespace declaration, like the class declaration, can be used as part of a scope resolved identifier.

Namespaces can nest. For a code example, see Section 3.10, "Namespaces," on page 85 (in file namespac.cpp).

Namespaces can be used to provide a unique scope similar in effect to the use of static global declarations. This is done with an unnamed namespace definition:

```
namespace { int count = 0; }          //count is unique here
//count is available in the rest of the file
void  chg_cnt(int i) { count = i; }
```

The new ANSI-conforming library headers will no longer use the *.h* suffix. Files, such as *iostream* or *complex*, will be declared with the `namespace std`. Vendors will no doubt continue shipping old-style headers such as *iostream.h* or *complex.h* as well, so that old code can run without change.

Most C++ programs will now begin with includes of standard library headers followed by a *using* declaration.

```
#include <iostream>       //std::cout is fully qualified name
#include <vector>          //STL vector templates
#include <cstddef>         //Old C libraries
using namespace std;
```

D.6 Linkage Rules

Modern systems are built around multifile inclusion, compilation, and linkage. For C++, it is necessary to understand how multifile programs are combined. Linking separate modules requires resolving external references. The key rule is that external nonstatic variables must be defined in only one place. Use of the keyword `extern`, together with an initializer, constitutes defining a variable. Using the keyword `extern` without an initializer constitutes a declaration but not a definition. If the keyword `extern` is omitted, the resulting declaration is a definition, with or without an initializer. The following example, where these files would all be linked, illustrates these rules:

In file prog1.cpp

```
char   c;                //definition of c
.....
```

In file prog2.cpp

```
extern char   c;         //declaration of c
.....
```

In file prog3.cpp

```
extern int   n = 5;      //definition of n
.....
```

In file prog4.cpp

```
char          c;         //illegal second definition
extern float  n;         //illegal type mismatch
extern int    k;         //illegal no definition
.....
```

Constant definitions and inline definitions at file scope are local to that file; in other words, they are implicitly static. Constant definitions can be explicitly declared `extern`. It is usual to place them in a header file to be included with any code that needs them.

A `typedef` declaration is local to its file. An enumeration constant declaration has linkage internal to its file. Enumerators and typedefs that are needed in a multifile program should be placed in a header file. Enumerators defined within a class are local to that class, and access to them requires the scope resolution operator.

Typically, declarations are placed in header files and used in code files:

```
//LMPstack.h
#ifndef LMP_stack           //avoid reinclusion
#define LMP_stack
namespace LMP {
class stack { ..... };
}
#endif

//LMPstack.cpp
#include <LMPstack.h>       //include above file as source
using namespace LMP;
.....
```

D.7 Types

The fundamental types in C++ are integral and floating-point types. The char type is the shortest integral type. The long double is the longest floating-point type.

The following table lists these types from shortest to longest. Reading across the table, the leftmost, topmost element is shortest, and the rightmost, bottommost element is longest.

Fundamental Data Types		
bool		
char	signed char	unsigned char
wchar_t		
short	int	long
unsigned short	unsigned	unsigned long
float	double	long double

Two of these data types, bool and wchar_t, were recently added by the ANSI committee, and should be available on more recent commercial compilers. (See adjunct program *newtyp.cpp*.)

The type `wchar_t` is intended for character sets, such as the Japanese Kana alphabet, that require characters not representable by `char`. Literals of this type are wide character constants. This type is an integral type, and in mixed expression follows the same rules for integral promotion.

The type `bool` is a break with C tradition. Over the years, many schemes have been used to achieve a Boolean type, and the new `bool` type removes these inconsistencies in practice. It is also an integral type. It becomes the type returned by relational, logical, and equality expressions. The `bool` constants `true` and `false` are promotable to one and zero, respectively. Nonzero values are assignment-convertible to `true`, and zero is assignment-convertible to `false`. It is anticipated that as compiler vendors add this type, they will provide switches or options that allow the old practice of not using `bool`.

Types can be derived from the basic types. A simple derived type is the enumeration type. The derived types allow pointer types, array types, and structure types. A generic pointer type `void*` is allowed. Both anonymous unions and anonymous enumerations are allowed, and there is also a reference type. An anonymous union can have only nonstatic public data members. A file-scope anonymous union has to be declared `static`. The `class` and `struct` types are structure types. Union, enumeration, and structure names are type names.

Types	Comments
`void*    gen_ptr;`	a generic pointer
`int      i, &ref_i = i;`	ref_i is an alias for i
`enum     button { off, on };`	enumeration
`button   flag;`	button is now a type name
`wchar_t  w = L'yz';`	new wide character type
`bool mine = false, yours = true;` `bool* p = &my_turn;`	new boolean type
`button   set[10];`	array

`class card {`
`public:`
`   suit  s;`
`   pips  p;`
`   void  pr_card();`
`private:`
`   int cd;`
`};`
	user-defined type
	
	public data member
	
	member function
	
	private data member

`suit card::* ptr_s = &card::s;`	pointer to member

There are five storage class keywords, as shown in the table below.

Storage Class	
auto	local to blocks and implicit
register	optimization advice and automatic
extern	global scope
static	within blocks, value retained
typedef	creates synonyms for types

The keyword `auto` can be used within blocks, but it is redundant and is normally omitted. Automatic variables are created at block entry and destroyed at block exit. The keyword `register` can be used within blocks and for function parameters. It advises the compiler that for optimization purposes the program wants a variable to reside in a high-speed register. The behavior of register variables is semantically equivalent to that of automatic variables.

The keyword `extern` can be used within blocks and at file scope. It indicates that a variable is linked in from elsewhere. The keyword `static` can be used within blocks and at file scope. Inside a block, it indicates that a variable's value is retained after block exit. At file scope, it indicates that declarations have internal linkage.

There are two special type-specifier keywords:

```
const                    //nonmodifiable
volatile                 //suppresses compiler optimization
```

The keyword `const` is used to indicate that a variable or function parameter has a nonmodifiable value. The keyword `volatile` implies that an agent undetectable to the compiler can change the variable's value; therefore the compiler cannot readily perform optimizations on code accessing this variable. Variables getting values from external agents would be `volatile`.

```
volatile const gmt;      //expect external time signal
```

D.8 Conversion Rules and Casts

C++ has both explicit conversions, called casts, and implicit conversions. The implicit conversions can occur in expressions, and in passing in arguments and returning expressions from functions. Many conversions are implicit, which makes C++ convenient but potentially dangerous for the novice. Implicit conversions can induce run-time bugs that are hard to detect.

The general rules are straightforward.

Automatic Expression Conversion *x op y*

1. Any `char`, `wchar_t`, `short`, `bool`, or `enum` is promoted to an `int`. Integral types unrepresentable as `int` are promoted to `unsigned`.

2. If, after the first step, the expression is of mixed type, then, according to the hierarchy of types,

   ```
   int < unsigned < long < unsigned long
       < float < double < long double
   ```

   the operand of lower type is promoted to that of the higher type, and the value of the expression has that type. Note that `unsigned` is promoted to `unsigned long`, if `long` cannot contain all the values of `unsigned`.

The new type `bool` is an integral type, with the `bool` constant `true` promoted to one, and the `bool` constant `false` promoted to zero.

Implicit pointer conversions also occur in C++. Any pointer type can be converted to the generic pointer of type `void*`. However, unlike in ANSI C, a generic pointer is not assignment-compatible with an arbitrary pointer type. This means C++ requires that generic pointers be cast to an explicit type for assignment to a nongeneric pointer variable:

```
char*   mem;
void*   gen_p;

gen_p = mem;                              //C and C++
mem   = (char*)gen_p;                     //C and (obsolete) C++
mem   = static_cast<char*>(gen_p);        //C++
mem   = gen_p;                            //legal C and illegal C++
```

The name of an array is a pointer to its base element. The null-pointer constant can be converted to any pointer type:

```
char*  p = 0;                    //p is a null pointer
int*   x = p;                    //illegal need static_cast
int*   y = 0;                    //legal
```

A pointer to a class can be converted to a pointer to a publicly derived base class. This also applies to references.

In addition to implicit conversions, which can occur across assignments and in mixed expressions, there are explicit conversions or casts. If i is an int, then

```
static_cast<double>(i)
```

will cast the value of i so that the expression has type double. The variable i itself remains unchanged. The static_cast is available for a conversion that is portable, well-defined, and invertible. Some more examples are:

```
static_cast<char>('A' + 1.0)
x = static_cast<double>(static_cast<int>(y) + 1)
```

Casts that are representation- or system-dependent use reinterpret_cast.

```
i = reinterpret_cast<int>(&x)          //system-dependent
```

These casts are undesirable and generally should be avoided.

Two other special casts exist in C++, const_cast and dynamic_cast. A useful discussion of dynamic_cast requires understanding inheritance (see Section D.13.5, "Run-Time Type Identification," on page 454). The const modifier means a variable's value is nonmodifiable. Very occasionally it is convenient to remove this restriction. This is known as casting away constness. This is done with the const_cast, as in:

```
foo(const_cast<int>(c_var));     //used to invoke foo
```

Older C++ systems allow the following unrestricted forms of cast:

   (type) expression   or   *type(expression)*

Some examples are:

```
y = i/double(7);                 //would do division in double
ptr = (char*)(i + 88);           //int to pointer value
```

These older forms are considered obsolete and are not used in this text, but many older compilers and older source code still use them. The older casts do not differentiate among relatively safe casts, such as `static_cast`, and system-dependent unsafe casts, such as `reinterpret_cast`. The newer casts are self-documenting as well; for example, a `const_cast` suggests its intent through its name.

In file stcast.cpp

```
enum  peer { king, prince, earl } a;
enum  animal { horse, frog, snake } b;
.....
a = static_cast<peer>(frog);
```

These new casts are safer and can replace all existing cast expressions. Still, casting should be avoided, as turning a `frog` into a `prince` is rarely a good idea.

Casts	Comments
`x = float(i);`	C++ functional notation
`x = (float) i;`	C cast notation
`x = static_cast<float>(i);`	ANSI C++
`static_cast<char>('A' + 1.0)`	ANSI C++
`i = reinterpret_cast<int>(&x)`	ANSI C++ system-dependent
`foo(const_cast<int>(c_var));`	used to invoke `foo()` while casting away constness

A constructor of one argument is a de facto type conversion from the argument's type to the constructor's class type unless preceded by the keyword `explicit`. (See Section 5.1.3, "Constructors as Conversions," on page 154.) Consider an example of a `my_string` constructor:

```
my_string::my_string(const char* p)
{
   len = strlen(p);
   s = new char[len + 1];
   assert (s != 0);
   strcpy(s, p);
}
```

This is automatically a type transfer from `char*` to `my_string`. These conversions are from an already defined type to a user-defined type. However, it is not possible for the user to add a constructor to a built-in type—for example, to `int` or `double`. In the `my_string` example, you may also want a conversion from `my_string` to char*. You can do this by defining a special conversion function inside the my_string class as follows.

```
operator char*() { return s; }          //char* s is a member
```

The general form of such a member function is:

```
operator type() { ····· }
```

These conversions occur implicitly in assignment expressions and in argument and return conversions from functions. Hidden temporaries can be created by the compiler to perform these operations, and can affect execution speeds.

In systems implementing the bool type, implicit conversion to bool is required for expressions controlling the if or while statement, and for the first operand of the ternary ?: operator. The obvious conversion of zero to false and nonzero to true occurs.

D.9 Expressions and Operators

C++ is an operator-rich, expression-oriented language. The operators have 17 precedence levels. Operators can also have side effects. The following table lists their precedence and associativity.

Operator Precedence and Associativity	
Operators	Associativity
:: (*global scope*) :: (*class scope*)	left to right
() [] -> . (*postfix*)++ (*postfix*)-- sizeof typedef	left to right
++ (*prefix*) -- (*prefix*) ! ~ & (*address*) + (*unary*) - (*unary*) *(*indirection*) delete new *casts*	right to left
.* ->*	left to right
* / %	left to right
+ -	left to right
<< >>	left to right
< <= > >=	left to right
== !=	left to right
&	left to right

Operator Precedence and Associativity	
Operators	Associativity
^	left to right
|	left to right
&&	left to right
||	left to right
?:	right to left
= += -= *= /= %= >>= <<= &= ^= |=	right to left
, (comma operator)	left to right

D.9.1 `sizeof` Expressions

The `sizeof` operator can be applied to an expression or a parenthesized type name. It gives the size in bytes of the type to which it is applied. Its results are system-dependent.

Declarations	
`int a, b[10];`	
Expression	Value on gnu C++ Running on a DEC Station
`sizeof(a)`	4
`sizeof(b)`	40 the array storage
`sizeof(b[1])`	4
`sizeof(5)`	4
`sizeof(5.5L)`	8

D.9.2 Autoincrement and Autodecrement Expressions

C++ provides autoincrement (++) and autodecrement (--) operators in both prefix and postfix form. The postfix form behaves differently than the prefix form by changing the affected lvalue after the rest of the expression is evaluated.

Autoincrement and Autodecrement	Equivalent Expression
j = ++i;	i = i + 1; j = i;
j = i++;	j = i; i = i + 1;
j = --i;	i = i - 1; j = i;
j = i--;	j = i; i = i - 1;

D.9.3 Arithmetic Expressions

Arithmetic expressions are consistent with expected practice. The following examples are grouped by precedence, highest first.

Arithmetic Expressions	Comments
-i +w	unary minus unary plus
a * b a / b i % 5	multiply divide modulus
a + b a - b	binary addition subtraction
a = 3 / 2.0;	a is assigned 1.5
a = 3 / 2;	a is assigned 1

The modulus operator % is the remainder from the division of the first argument by the second argument. It may be used only with integer types. Arithmetic expressions depend on the conversion rules given earlier. (See Section 5.1.3, "Constructors as Conversions," on page 154.) In the table above, see how the result of the division operator / depends on its argument types.

D.9.4 Relational, Equality, and Logical Expressions

This discussion is based on ANSI C++ adopting a `bool` type with constants `false` and `true`. Prior to the introduction of the `bool` type, the values zero and nonzero were thought of as false and true, and were used to effect the flow of control in various statement types. The following table contains the C++ operators that are most often used to affect flow of control.

Relational, Equality, and Logical Operators		
Relational operators	less than	<
	greater than	>
	less than or equal to	<=
	greater than or equal to	>=
Equality operators	equal	==
	not equal	!=
Logical operators	(unary) negation	!
	logical and	&&
	logical or	||

The negation operator ! is unary. All the other relational, equality, and logical operators are binary. They operate on expressions, and yield either `true` or `false`. Logical negation can be applied to an arbitrary expression, which is then converted to `bool`. When negation is applied to a `true` value it results in `false`; when it is applied to a `false` value it results in `true`.

In the evaluation of expressions that are the operands of && and ||, the evaluation process stops as soon as the outcome `true` or `false` is known. This is called short-circuit evaluation. For example, suppose that *expr1* and *expr2* are expressions. If *expr1* has `false` value, then in

    expr1 && *expr2*

expr2 will not be evaluated because the value of the logical expression is already determined to be `false`. Similarly, if *expr1* has `true` value, then in

    expr1 || *expr2*

expr2 will not be evaluated because the value of the logical expression is already determined to be `true`.

On systems that do not implement the `bool` type, these expressions will evaluate to one and zero instead of `true` and `false`.

Declarations and Initialization		
`int a = -5, int b = 3, c = 0;`		
Expression	**Equivalent**	**Value**
`a + 5 && b`	`((a + 5) && b)`	false or 0
`!(a < b) && c`	`((!(a < b)) && c)`	false or 0
`1 || (a != 7)`	`(1 || (a != 7))`	true or 1

Note that the last expression always short-circuits to value `true`.

D.9.5 Assignment Expressions

In C++, assignment occurs as part of an assignment expression. The effect is to evaluate the right side of the assignment and convert it to a value compatible with the left-side variable. Assignment conversions occur implicitly, and include narrowing conversions; simple variables are lvalues.

C++ allows multiple assignments in a single statement:

`a = b + (c = 3);`   is equivalent to   `c = 3; a = b + c;`

C++ provides assignment operators that combine an assignment and some other operator:

`a` *op*`= b;`   is equivalent to   `a = a` *op* `b`

Declarations and Initialization	
`int     a, i, *p = &i;` `double  w, *q = &w;`	
Assignment Expressions	**Comments**
`a = i + 1;`	assigns (i + 1) to a
`i = w;`	legal w value converted to `int`
`*q = i;`	legal integer value promoted to `double`
`*q = *p;`	legal
`q = p;`	illegal conversion between pointer types
`q = (double*)p;`	legal
`a *= a + b;`	equivalent to a = a * (a + b);
`a += b;`	equivalent to a = a + b;

D.9.6 Comma Expressions

The comma operator has the lowest precedence. It is a binary operator with expressions as operands. In a comma expression of the form

expr1, *expr2*

expr1 is evaluated first, then *expr2*. The comma expression as a whole has the value and type of its right operand. The comma operator is a control point. Therefore, each expression in the comma-separated list is evaluated completely before the next expression to its right. An example would be:

    sum = 0, i = 1

If `i` has been declared an `int`, then this comma expression has value 1 and type `int`. The comma operator associates from left to right.

D.9.7 Conditional Expressions

The conditional operator ?: is unusual in that it is a ternary operator. It takes as operands three expressions. In a construct such as

expr1 ? *expr2* : *expr3*

expr1 is evaluated first. If it is `true`, then *expr2* is evaluated and its value is the value of the conditional expression as a whole. If *expr1* is `false`, then *expr3* is evaluated and its value is the value of the conditional expression as a whole. The following example uses a conditional operator to assign the smaller of two values to the variable x:

```
x = (y < z) ? y : z;
```

The parentheses are not necessary because the conditional operator has precedence over the assignment operator. However, parentheses are good style because they clarify what is being tested for.

The type of the conditional expression

expr1 ? *expr2* : *expr3*

is determined by *expr2* and *expr3*. If they are different types, then the usual conversion rules apply. The conditional expression's type cannot depend on which of the two expressions is evaluated. The conditional operator ?: associates right to left.

D.9.8 Bit-Manipulation Expressions

C++ provides bit-manipulation operators. They operate on the machine-dependent bit representation of integral operands. It is customary that the shift operators be overloaded to perform I/O.

Bitwise Operators	Meaning
~	unary one's complement
<<	left shift
>>	right shift
&	and
^	exclusive or
|	or

D.9.9 Address and Indirection Expressions

The address operator & is a unary operator that yields the address, or location, where an object is stored. The indirection operator * is a unary operator that is applied to a value of type pointer. It retrieves the value from the location being pointed at. This is also known as *dereferencing*. (See adjunct program *lval.cpp*.)

Declarations and Initialization	
`int   a = 5;`	`//declaration of a`
`int*  p = &a;`	`//p points to a`
`int&  ref_a = a;`	`//alias for a`

Expression	Value
`*p = 7;`	lvalue in effect a is assigned 7
`a = *p + 1;`	rvalue 7 added to 1 and a assigned 8

D.9.10 new and delete Expressions

The unary operators new and delete are available to manipulate free store, which is a system-provided memory pool for objects whose lifetime is directly managed by the programmer, creating an object by using new and destroying it by using delete.

The new operator is used in the following simple forms:

new *type-name initializer*$_{opt}$
new *type-name*[*integer expression*]

The first form allocates an object of the specified type from free store. If an initializing expression is present it performs the initialization. The second form allocates an array of objects of the specified type from free store. A default initializer must be available for these objects.

The new Operator	Comments
`new int`	allocates an `int`
`new char[100]`	allocates an array of 100 `int`s
`new int(99)`	allocates an `int` initialized to 99
`new char('c')`	allocates a `char` initialized to c
`new int[n][4]`	allocates an array of pointers to `int`

In each case there are at least two effects. First, an appropriate amount of store is allocated from free storage to contain the named type. Second, the base address of the object is returned as the value of the new expression. If new fails, either the null-pointer value 0 is returned, or the exception `bad_alloc` or `xalloc` is thrown (see Section 10.9, "Standard Exceptions and Their Uses," on page 362). It is desirable to test for failure.

An initializer is a parenthesized list of arguments. For a simple type, such as an `int`, it would be a single expression. It cannot be used to initialize arrays, but it can be an argument list to an appropriate constructor. If the type being allocated has a constructor, the allocated object will be initialized.

The operator `delete` is used in the following forms:

delete *expression*
delete [ ] *expression*

In both forms the expression is typically a pointer variable used in a previous new expression. The second form is used when returning storage that was allocated as an array type. The brackets indicate that a destructor should be called for each element of the array. The operator `delete` returns a value of type `void`.

The delete Operator	Comments
delete ptr	deletes the pointer to an object
delete p[i]	deletes object p[i]
delete [] p	deletes each object of type p

The operator `delete` destroys an object created by new, in effect returning its allocated storage to free store for reuse. If the type being deleted has a destructor, it will be called. There are no guarantees on what values will appear in objects allocated from free store. The programmer is responsible for properly initializing such objects. For a code example, see Section 3.20, "Free-Store Operators new and delete," on page 105 (in file dynarray.cpp).

Placement Syntax and Overloading

The operator new has the general form:

$::_{opt}$ new *placement$_{opt}$* *type-name* *initializer$_{opt}$*

The global operator `new()` is typically used to allocate free store. The system provides a `sizeof(`*type*`)` argument to this function implicitly. Its function prototype is:

```
void* operator new(size_t size);
```

The operator new can be overloaded at the global level by adding parameters and calling it using placement syntax. It can be overloaded and used to override the global versions at the class level. But when allocating an array of objects, only the default global `void* operator new(size_t size)` will be called.

The delete operator can also be overloaded. The global version is:

```
void operator delete(void* ptr)
```

A class-specific version can be declared as

```
void operator delete(void* ptr)
```

or as

```
void operator delete(void* ptr, size_t size)
```

but only one of these forms can be used by any one class. When deallocating an array of objects, the global version will be called. This feature provides a simple mechanism for user-defined manipulation of free store. For example:

```
#include <stddef.h>     //size_t type defined
#include <stdlib.h>     //malloc() and free() defined

class X {
    .....
public:
    void* operator new(size_t size)
        { return (malloc(size)); }
    void  operator delete(void* ptr) { free(ptr); }
    X(unsigned size) { new(size); }
    ~X() { delete(this); }
    .....
};
```

In this example, the class X provides overloaded forms of new() and delete(). When a class overloads operator new(), the global operator is still accessible using the scope resolution operator ::.

The *placement* syntax provides for a comma-separated argument list that is used to select an overloaded operator new() with a matching signature. These additional arguments are often used to place the constructed object at a particular address. One form of this can be found in *new.h*.

Class `new()` and `delete()` member functions are always `static`. For a code example, see Section 6.12, "Overloading new and delete," on page 228 (in file *over_new.cpp*).

Error Conditions

In the absence of implemented exception handling, `new` returns a zero value, indicating an allocation failure.

The standard library *new.h* has the function `set_new_handler()`, which installs the function to be called when `new` fails. Calling this with value zero means a version of `new` that does not throw exceptions will be used. Otherwise a `bad_alloc` or an `xalloc` exception will be thrown. The implementation of *new.h* can be system-dependent.

D.9.11 Other Expressions

C++ considers *function call* () and *indexing* or *subscripting* [] to be operators. They have the same precedence as the member and structure pointer operators:

```
a[j + 6]            //means    *(a + j + 6)
sqrt(z + 15.5);     //returns a double
```

The global scope resolution operator is of highest precedence. The class scope resolution operator is used with a class-name to qualify a local-to-class identifier.

```
::i                 //access global i
A::foo()            //invoke member foo() defined in A
```

The pointer to member operators are `*` and `->*`, and their precedence is below the unary operators and above the multiplicative operator. Their use is described in Section D.13.4, "Pointer to Class Member," on page 454.

D.10 Statements

C++ has a large variety of statement types. It uses the semicolon as a statement terminator. Braces are used to enclose multiple statements and treat them as a single unit. Statements are control points. Before a new statement is executed, the actions of the previous statements must be completed. Inside statements, the compiler has some liberty to pick which parts of subexpressions are first evaluated. For example:

```
a = f(i);         //call f() and assign to a
a += g(j);        //call g() and add to a
a = f(i) + g(j);  //compiler decides calling order
```

C++ is a block-structured language in which declarations are often at the head of blocks. Unlike C, declarations are statements and can be intermixed with other statements. Structured programming principles should still be followed when writing C++ code. Namely, the goto should be avoided and care should be taken that the program's flow of control is easy to follow.

Because C++ has many side-effect possibilities in expressions, care should be exercised in avoiding system-dependent effects. For example, the side-effect operators autoincrement and autodecrement should be used sparingly in expressions where order-of-evaluation and possible compiler optimizations can lead to system dependencies.

In many cases, C++ statements are overly unrestrictive, and good programming discipline is required to avoid error-prone constructions. For example,

```
for (double x = 0.1; !(x == y); x += 0.1)
   .....
```

is problematic because machine accuracy and roundoff problems will in most cases cause a failure in the terminating condition.

The following table gives a summary of general C++ statements.

Statement	C++	Comments
empty	`;`	
expression	`i = i + k;`	assignment may use conversions
compound	`{ .....` `}`	used for function definitions and structuring; same as block
goto	`goto l1;`	avoid
if	`if (p == 0)` `    cerr << "new error";`	one-branch conditional

if-else	`if (x == y)`
	`    cout << "same\n";`
	`else`
	`    cout << "unequal\n";`
		two-branch conditional

for	`for (i = 0; i < n; ++i)` `    a[i] = b[i] + c[i];`	declarations allowed in the first component
while	`while (x != y)`	zero or more iterations

do-while	`do`
	`    y = y - 1;`
	`while (y >= 0);`
		one or more iterations

switch	`switch (s) {`
	`case 1: ++i;   break;`
	`case 2: --i;   break;`
	`.....`
	`default: ++j;`
	`};`
		use `break` to avoid fall-through semantics and default as a last label

break	`break;`	used in `switch` and iteration
continue	`continue;`	used in iterations
declaration	`int i = 7;`	in a block, file, or namespace
try block	`try { ..... }`	see Section 10.4, "Try Blocks," on page 357
labeled	`error: cerr << "ERROR";`	target of `goto`
return	`return x * x * x;`	try for one `return` per function

D.10.1 Expression Statements

In C++, assignment occurs as part of an assignment expression. There is no assignment statement, since it is a form of expression statement:

```
a = b + 1;      //assign (b + 1) to a
++i;            //an expression statement
a + b;          //also a statement - but seemingly useless
```

C++ allows multiple assignments in a single statement:

   a = b = c + 3;   is equivalent to   b = c + 3; a = b;

D.10.2 The Compound Statement

A compound statement in C++ is a series of statements surrounded by braces { }. The chief use of the compound statement is to group statements into an executable unit. The body of a C++ function is always a compound statement. In C, when declarations come at the beginning of a compound statement, the statement is called a block. This rule is relaxed in C++, and declaration statements may occur throughout the statement list. Wherever it is possible to place a statement, it is also possible to place a compound statement.

D.10.3 The `if` and `if-else` Statements

The general form of an `if` statement is:

   if (*condition*)
      statement

If *condition* is `true`, then *statement* is executed; otherwise it is skipped. After the `if` statement has been executed, control passes to the next statement. A condition is an expression or a declaration with initialization that selects flow of control. For a code example, see Section 2.8.3, "The if and if-else Statements," on page 48 (in file if_test.cpp).

The `if-else` statement has the general form

   if (*condition*)
      statement1
   else
      statement2

If *condition* is `true`, then *statement1* is executed and *statement2* is skipped; if *condition* is `false`, then *statement1* is skipped and *statement2* is executed. After the `if-else` statement has been executed, control passes to the next statement. Note that an `else` statement associates with its nearest `if`; this rule prevents the ambiguity of a dangling `else`. For a code example, see Section 2.8.3, "The if and if-else Statements," on page 50 (in file if_test.cpp).

D.10.4 The `while` Statement

The general form of a `while` statement is:

> `while` (*condition*)
>   *statement*

First *condition* is evaluated. If it is `true`, then *statement* is executed and control passes back to the beginning of the `while` loop. The effect of this is that the body of the `while` loop, namely *statement*, is executed repeatedly until *condition* is `false`. At that point control passes to the next statement. The effect of this is that *statement* can be executed zero or more times. For a code example, see Section 2.8.4, "The while Statement," on page 50 (in file while_t.cpp).

D.10.5 The `for` Statement

The general form of a `for` statement is:

> `for` (*for-init-statement*; *condition*; *expression*)
>   *statement*
> *next statement*

First the *for-init-statement* is evaluated, and used to initialize a variable in the loop. Then *condition* is evaluated. If it is true, then *statement* is executed, *expression* is evaluated, and control passes back to the beginning of the `for` loop, except that evaluation of *for-init-statement* is skipped. This iteration continues until *condition* is false, at which point control passes to *next statement*.

The *for-init-statement* can be an expression statement or a simple declaration. Where it is a declaration the declared variable has the scope of the `for` statement. Note that this scope rule has changed from the previous rule that gave such declarations scope outside the enclosing `for` statement.

The `for` statement is iterative, and is typically used with a variable that is incremented or decremented. For a code example, see Section 2.8.5, "The for Statement," on page 52 (in file for_test.cpp).

The comma expressions can be used to initialize more than one variable.

In file forloop.cpp

```
for (factorial = n, i = n - 1; i >= 1; --i)
    factorial *= i;
```

Any or all of the expressions in a for statement can be missing, but the two semicolons must remain. If *for-init-statement* is missing, then no initialization step is performed as part of the for loop. If *expression* is missing, then no incrementation step is performed as part of the for loop. If *condition* is missing, then no testing step is performed as part of the for loop. The special rule for when *condition* is missing is that the test is always *true*. Thus the for loop in the code

```
for (i = 1, sum = 0 ; ; sum += i++)
    cout << sum << endl;
```

is an infinite loop.

The for statement is one common case where a local declaration is used to provide the loop control variable, as in:

```
for (int i = 0; i < N; ++i)
    sum += a[i];            //sum array a[0] + ... + a[N - 1]
```

The semantics are that the int variable i is local to the given loop. In earlier C++ systems, it was considered declared within the surrounding block. This can be confusing, and so it is reasonable to declare all automatic program variables at the heads of blocks.

D.10.6 The do Statement

The general form of a do statement is:

    do
        statement
    while (*condition*);
    next statement

First *statement* is executed, then *condition* is evaluated. If it is true, then control passes back to the beginning of the do statement and the process repeats itself. When the value of *condition* is false, then control passes to *next statement*. For a code example, see Section 2.8.6, "The do Statement," on page 54 (in file do_test.cpp).

D.10.7 The `break` and `continue` Statements

To interrupt the normal flow of control within a loop, the programmer can use the two special statements:

   break;   and   continue;

The `break` statement, in addition to its use in loops, can be used in a `switch` statement. It causes an exit from the innermost enclosing loop or `switch` statement.

The following example illustrates the use of a `break` statement. A test for a negative value is made, and if it is `true`, the `break` statement causes the `for` loop to be exited. Program control jumps to the statement immediately following the loop. For a code example, see Section 2.8.7, "The break and continue Statements," on page 55 (in file for_test.cpp).

The `continue` statement causes the current iteration of a loop to stop and the next iteration of the loop to begin immediately. For a code example, see Section 2.8.7, "The break and continue Statements," on page 55 (in file for_test.cpp).

A `break` statement can occur only inside the body of a `for`, `while`, `do`, or `switch` statement. The `continue` statement can occur only inside the body of a `for`, `while`, or `do` statement.

D.10.8 The `switch` Statement

The `switch` statement is a multiway conditional statement generalizing the `if-else` statement. Its general form is:

   switch (*condition*)
      statement

where *statement* is typically a compound statement containing `case` labels and optionally a `default` label. Typically, a `switch` is composed of many cases, and the condition in parentheses following the keyword `switch` determines which, if any, of the cases are executed.

A `case` label is of the form:

   case *constant integral expression*:

In a `switch` statement, all `case` labels must be unique.

If no `case` label is selected, then control passes to the `default` label, if there is one. No `default` label is required. If no `case` label is selected and there is no `default` label, then the `switch` statement is exited. For a code example, see Section 2.8.8, "The switch Statement," on page 56 (in file switch_t.cpp).

The keywords `case` and `default` cannot occur outside a `switch`.

The Effect of a `switch` Statement

1. Evaluate the integral expression in the parentheses following `switch`.

2. Execute the `case` label that has a constant value that matches the value of the expression found in step 1; if no match is found, execute the `default` label; if there is no `default` label, terminate the `switch`.

3. Terminate the `switch` when a `break` statement is encountered, or by "falling off the end."

A `switch` cannot bypass initialization of a variable unless the entire scope of the variable is bypassed:

```
switch (k) {
case 1:
   int   very_bad = 3; break;
case 2:                       //illegal: bypasses init of very_bad
   .....
}
switch (k) {
case 1:
   {
      int  d = 3; break;
   }
case 2:                       //legal: bypasses scope of d
   .....
}
```

D.10.9 The goto Statement

The `goto` statement is an unconditional branch to an arbitrary labeled statement in the function. It is considered a harmful construct in most accounts of modern programming methodology.

A label is an identifier. By executing a `goto` statement of the form

goto *label*;

control is unconditionally transferred to a labeled statement. Both the `goto` statement and its corresponding labeled statement must be in the body of the same function. For a code example, see Section 2.8.9, "The goto Statement," on page 58 (in file goto_tst.cpp).

A `goto` cannot bypass initialization of a variable, unless the entire scope of the variable is bypassed.

```
if (i < j)
   goto max;          //illegal: bypasses init

int  crazy = 5;

max:
   .....
```

D.10.10 The return Statement

The return statement is used for two purposes. When it is executed, program control is immediately passed back to the calling environment. In addition, if an expression follows the keyword return, the value of the expression is returned to the calling environment as well. This value must be assignment-convertible to the return type of the function-definition header.

A return statement has one of the following two forms:

```
return;
return expression;
```

Some examples are:

```
return;
return 3;
return (a + b);
```

D.10.11 The Declaration Statement

The declaration statement can be placed nearly anywhere in a block. This lifts the C restriction that variable declarations are placed at the head of a block before executable statements. A declaration statement has the form

type variable-name;

Normal block-structure rules apply to a variable so declared. Two examples are:

```
for (int i = 0; i < N; ++i) {    //typical for loop
   a[i] = b[i] * c[i];
   int  k = a[i];                 //k local - possibly inefficient
   .....
}
```

C++ imposes natural restrictions on transferring into blocks passed where declarations occur. These are disallowed, as are declarations that would occur in only one branch of a conditional statement.

D.11 Functions

Special features include the use of function prototypes, overloading, default arguments, and the effects of the keywords `inline`, `friend`, and `virtual`. This section restricts its discussion to basic functions, overloading, call-by-value, default arguments, and inlining. Member functions are discussed in Section D.12.2, "Member Functions," on page 446; friend functions in Section D.12.3, "Friend Functions," on page 446, and virtual functions are covered in Section D.13.6, "Virtual Functions," on page 455. Generic functions are discussed throughout Appendix F, "STL and String Libraries."

In C++, function parameters are call-by-value unless they are declared as reference types.

Function Declaration	C++	Comments

function	`double cube(double x)`
	`{`
	`    return x * x * x;`
	`}`
		parameters are call-by-value; return expression must be assignment-compatible with return type

pure procedure	`void pr_int_sq(int i)`
	`{`
	`    cout << i*i << endl;`
	`}`
		void return type denotes a pure procedure

empty argument list	`void pr_hi()`
	`{`
	`    cout << "HI" << endl;`
	`}`
		can also be `void pr_hi(void)`

reference argument	`void`
	`swap(int& i, int& j)`
	`{`
	`    int t = i;`
	`    i = j; j = t;`
	`}`
		if invoked as `swap(r, s)` r and s exchange values

variable	`int scanf(const char*,...);`	matches any number of arguments

Function Declaration	C++	Comments
inline	`inline cube(int x);`	inline code
default argument	`int power(int x, int n = 2);`	power(4) yields 16 power(4, 3) yields 64
overload	`double power(double x, int n);`	signature is `double, int`

D.11.1 Prototypes

In C++, the prototype form is:

type name(argument-declaration-list) ;

Examples are:

```
double sqrt(double x);                          //in math.h
double stats(const double data[], int size,
             double& max, double& min );
void print(const char* s);
int  printf(char* format, ...);                 //in stdio.h
```

Prototypes make C++ functions type-safe. When functions are called, the actual arguments are assignment-converted to the formal arguments type. With the above `sqrt()` prototype definition, invoking `sqrt()` guarantees that, if feasible, an argument will be converted to type `double`. When variable-length argument lists are needed, the ellipsis symbol is used (...).

D.11.2 Call-by-Reference

Reference declarations allow C++ to have call-by-reference arguments. Let us use this mechanism to write a function, `greater()`, that exchanges two values if the first is greater than the second:

```
int greater(int& a, int& b)
```

Now, if `i` and `j` are `int` variables, then

```
greater(i, j)
```

will use the references to i and j to exchange, if necessary, their two values. In traditional C, this operation must be accomplished using pointers and dereferencing. For a code example, see Section 3.11.2, "Pointer-Based Call-by-Reference," on page 87 (in file call_ref.cpp).

D.11.3 Inline Functions

The keyword inline suggests to the compiler that the function be converted to inline code. This keyword is used for the sake of efficiency, and generally with short functions. It is implicit for member functions that are defined within their classes. A compiler can ignore this directive for a variety of reasons, including that the function is too long. In such cases, the inline function is compiled as an ordinary function. An example is:

```
inline float circum(float rad) { return (pi * 2 * rad); }
```

Inline functions have internal linkage.

D.11.4 Default Arguments

A formal parameter can be given a default argument, but only with contiguous formal parameters that are rightmost in the parameter list. A default value is usually an appropriate constant that occurs frequently when the function is called. The following function illustrates this point.

```
r_sqrd = pow(r);              //return r*r
r_5th  = pow(r, 5);           //return r*r*r*r*r
```

For a code example, see Section 3.5, "Default Arguments," on page 74 (in file def_args.cpp).

D.11.5 Overloading

Overloading is using the same name for multiple meanings of an operator or a function. The meaning selected will depend on the types of the arguments used by the operator or function.

Consider a function that averages the values in an array of double versus one that averages the values in an array of int. Both are conveniently named avg_arr, as shown in the following program.

```
double avg_arr(const int a[], int size)
double avg_arr(const double a[], int size)
```

The function argument type list is called its *signature*. The return type is not a part of the signature, but the order of the arguments is crucial. For a code example, see Section 3.7, "Overloading Functions," on page 76 (in file avg_arr.cpp).

Consider the following overloaded declarations:

```
void   print(int i = 0);             //signature is int
void   print(int i, double x);       //int, double
void   print(double y, int i);       //double,int
```

When the `print()` function is invoked, the compiler matches the actual arguments to the various signatures and picks the best match. In general, there are three possibilities: a best match, an ambiguous match, and no match. Without a best match, the compiler issues an appropriate syntax error.

```
print('A');          //converts and matches int
print(str[]);        //no match, wrong type
print(15, 9);        //ambiguous
print(15, 9.0);      //matches int, double
print();             //matches int by default
```

There are two parts to the signature-matching algorithm. The first part determines a best match for each argument, and the second sees whether there is one function that is a uniquely best match in each argument. This uniquely best match is defined as being a best match on at least one argument, and a "tied-for-best" match on all other arguments.

For a given argument, a best match is always an exact match. An exact match also includes an argument with an outermost `const` or `volatile`. Thus

```
void print(int i);
void print(const int& i);
```

is a redefinition error.

Whichever overloaded function is to be invoked, the invocation argument list must be matched to the declaration parameter list according to the function-selection algorithm.

Overloaded Function-Selection Algorithm

1. Use an exact match if found.

2. Try standard type promotions.

3. Try standard type conversions.

4. Try user-defined conversions.

5. Use a match-to-ellipsis if found.

Standard promotions are better than other standard conversions. These are conversions from `float` to `double`, and from `char`, `short`, or `enum` to `int`. Standard conversions also include pointer conversions.

An exact match is clearly best. Casts can be used to force such a match. The compiler will complain about ambiguous situations.

D.11.6 Type-Safe Linkage for Functions

Linkage rules for non-C++ functions can be specified using a linkage specification. Some examples are:

```
extern "C" atoi(const char* nptr);   //C linkage

extern "C" {                         //C linkage all functions
#include <stdio.h>
}
```

This specification is at file scope, with C and C++ always supported. It is system-dependent if type-safe linkage for other languages is provided. Of a set of overloaded functions with the same number, one at most can be declared to have other than C++ linkage. Class member functions cannot be declared with a linkage specification.

D.12 Classes

Classes are forms of heterogeneous aggregate types. They allow data hiding, inheritance, and member functions as a mechanism to provide user-defined types. An example is:

In file vec3t.h

```
//An implementation of a safe array type dbl_vect

class dbl_vect {
public:
   explicit dbl_vect(int n = 10);            //default constructor
   dbl_vect(const dbl_vect& v);              //copy constructor
   dbl_vect(const double a[], int n);        //init by array
   ~dbl_vect() { delete [] p; }              //destructor
   int  ub() const;                          //upper bound
   int& operator[](int i) const;             //indexing
   dbl_vect&  operator=(const dbl_vect& v);  //assignment
   friend ostream& operator<<(ostream& out, const dbl_vect& v);
private:
   double *p;                                //base pointer
   int  size;                                //number of elements
};
```

The keywords `public`, `private`, and `protected` indicate the access of members that follow. The default for `class` is `private`, and for `struct` is `public`. In the above example, the data members p and size are `private`. This makes them accessible solely to member functions of the same class. For a code example, see Section 4.13, "A Container Class Example: ch_stack," on page 140 (in file ch_stac3.h).

D.12.1 Constructors and Destructors

A constructor is a member function whose name is the same as the class name. It constructs objects of the class type. This involves initialization of data members and also frequently involves free-store allocation using `new`. If a class has a constructor with a void argument list, or a list whose arguments all have defaults, then it can be a base type of an array declaration, where initialization is not explicit. Such a constructor is called the default constructor:

```
dbl_vect::dbl_vect() { ····· }          //default constructor

dbl_vect::dbl_vect(int i = 0) { ····· }  //default constructor
```

A destructor is a member function whose name is the class-name preceded by the tilde character ~. Its usual purpose is to destroy values of the class type. This is typically accomplished using `delete`.

A constructor of the form

type::type(const *type*& x)

is used to copy one *type* value into another according to the following list.

Copy Constructor Use

1. A type variable is initialized by a type value.

2. A type value is passed as an argument in a function.

3. A type value is returned from a function.

This is called the copy constructor, and if not explicitly implemented, it is compiler-generated. The default is member-by-member initialization of value.

Classes with default constructors can have a derived array type. For example,

```
dbl_vect  a[5];
```

is a declaration that uses the empty argument constructor to create an array a of five objects, each of which is a size 10 `dbl_vect`.

A special syntax exists for initializing subelements of objects with constructors. Initializers for structure and class members can be specified in a comma-separated list that follows the constructor parameter list and precedes the code body. An initializer's form is:

member name (expression list)

As in

```
foo::foo(int* t):i(7), x(9.8), z(t)     //initializer list
{ //other executable follows here ····· }
```

When members are themselves classes with constructors, the expression list is matched to the appropriate constructor signature to invoke the correct overloaded constructor. It is not always possible to assign values to members in the body of the constructor. An initializer list is required when a nonstatic member is either a const or a reference. In the class dbl_vect example in the next section, the constructors use an initializer for the member dbl_vect::size.

Constructors cannot be virtual, though destructors can be. Neither is inherited.

Constructors of a single parameter are automatically conversion functions. Consider the following class, whose purpose is to print nonvisible characters with their ASCII designations; for example, the code 07 (octal) is alarm or bel. The automatic creation of a conversion constructor from a single-parameter constructor can be disabled by using the keyword explicit to preface a single-argument constructor. For a code example, see Section 5.11, "Strings Using Reference Semantics," on page 184 (in file string6.cpp).

D.12.2 Member Functions

Member functions are functions declared within a class. As a consequence, they have access to private, protected, and public members of that class. If defined inside the class, they are treated as inline functions and are also treated, when necessary, as overloaded functions. In the class dbl_vect, the member function

```
int  ub() const { return (size - 1); }    //upper bound
```

is defined. In this example, the member function ub is inline, and it has access to the private member size.

Member functions are invoked normally by use of the . or -> operators, as in

```
dbl_vect   a(20), b;            //invoke appropriate constructor
dbl_vect*  ptr_v = &b;
int    uba = a.ub();            //invoke member ub
ubb = ptr_v -> ub();            //invoke member ub
```

Overloaded operator member functions, a special case of member functions, are discussed in Section D.11.5, "Overloading," on page 441.

D.12.3 Friend Functions

The keyword friend is a function specifier. It allows a nonmember function access to the hidden members of the class of which it is a friend. A friend function must be declared inside the class declaration of which it is a friend. It is prefaced by the keyword friend and can appear anywhere in the class. Member functions of one class can be friend functions of another class. In this case, the member function is declared in the friend's class using the scope resolution operator to qualify its function name. If all member functions of one class are friend functions of a second class, this can be specified by writing friend class *class-name*.

The following declarations are typical:

```
class tweedledum {
    .....
    friend int  tweedledee::cheshire();
};

class node {
    .....
    friend class tree;
     //tree member functions have access to node
};
```

In file complexc.cpp

```
class complex {
    .....
    friend complex operator+(complex);
};
```

D.12.4 The this Pointer

The keyword `this` denotes an implicitly declared self-referential pointer. It can be used only in a nonstatic member function. The `this` keyword provides for a built-in, self-referential pointer. It is as if `clock` implicitly declared the private member `clock* const this`. Early C++ systems allowed memory management for objects to be controlled by assignment to the `this` pointer. Such code is obsolete because the `this` pointer is nonmodifiable. For a code example, see Section 6.5, "Unary Operator Overloading," on page 208 (in file clock.cpp).

D.12.5 Operator Overloading

Operator overloading is a special case of function overloading. The keyword `operator` is used. Just as a function, such as `print()`, can be given a variety of meanings that depend on its arguments, so can an operator, such as +, be given additional meanings. This allows infix expressions of both user and built-in types to be written. The precedence and associativity remain fixed.

Operator overloading typically uses either member or friend functions, because both have privileged access. Overloading a unary operator using a member function has an empty argument list because the single operator argument is the implicit argument. For binary operators, member function operator overloading has, as its first argument, the implicitly passed class variable and, as its second argument, the lone argument-list parameter. Friend functions and ordinary functions have both arguments specified in the parameter list.

We expand the dbl_vect class from Section 6.7, "Overloading Assignment and Subscripting Operators," on page 213, to have overloaded operators for addition, assignment, subscripting, and output.

In file dbl_vect_ovl.cpp

```
//Implementation of a safe array type dbl_vect
class dbl_vect {
public:
    .....
    int&  operator[](int i) const;
    dbl_vect&  operator=(const dbl_vect& v);
    friend dbl_vect  operator+(const dbl_vect&, const dbl_vect&);
    friend ostream&  operator<<(ostream& , const dbl_vect&)
private:
    double  *p;              //base pointer
    int  size;               //number of elements
};
```

This class overloads the assignment and subscript operators as member functions. The overloaded operator<<() (put to) is made a friend of dbl_vect so that it may access the private members of dbl_vect. The overloaded operator<<() should always return type ostream so that multiple put to operations may be executed in a single expression. The overloaded binary plus operator is a friend so that conversion operations can be applied to both arguments. Note that the overloaded assignment operator checks for assignment to itself. For a code example, see Section 6.7, "Overloading Assignment and Subscripting Operators," on page 213 (in file dbl_vect2.h).

The ternary conditional operator ?:, the scope resolution operator ::, and the two member operators . and .* cannot be overloaded.

Overloaded postfix autoincrement and autodecrement can be distinguished by defining the postfix overloaded function as having a single unused integer argument, as in:

```
class T {
public:
    //postfix ++ invoked as t.operator++(0);
    void  operator++(int);
    void  operator--(int);
};
```

There is no implied semantic relationship between the postfix and prefix forms.

D.12.6 `static` and `const` Member Functions

An ordinary member function invoked as

```
object.mem(i, j, k);
```

has an explicit argument list i, j, k, and an implicit argument list that contains the members of object. The implicit arguments can be thought of as a list of arguments accessible through the this pointer. In contrast, a static member function cannot access any of the members using the this pointer. A const member function cannot modify its implicit arguments. The following *salary* program illustrates these differences.

In file salary.cpp

```
//Salary calculation using static and constant member functions

#include   <iostream.h>

class salary {
public:
   .....
private:
   int         b_sal;
   int         your_bonus;
   static int  all_bonus;         //declaration
};

int salary::all_bonus = 100;      //declare & define

int main()
{
   salary  w1(1000), w2(2000);
   .....
   salary::reset_all(400);        //also w1.reset_all(400);
}
```

The static member all_bonus requires a file-scope definition. It exists independent of any specific variables of type salary being declared. The static member can also be referred to as:

```
salary::all_bonus
```

The `const` modifier comes between the end of the argument list and the beginning of the code body. It indicates that no data members will have their values changed, making the code more robust. In effect it means that the self-referential pointer is passed as `const salary* const this`.

A `static` member function can be invoked using the scope resolution operator or using a specific object; therefore these are equivalent:

```
salary::reset_all(400);
w1.reset_all(400);
(&w2) -> reset_all(400);
```

While it is legal to invoke a static member function or reference a static data member with the dot operator, as in

```
w1.reset_all(400);
```

it obscures the fact that `reset_all()` is a static member. Scope resolution as in:

```
salary::reset_all(400);
```

is preferred because of clarity. For a code example, see Section 4.10, "static and const Members," on page 135 (in file salary.cpp).

D.12.7 Mutable

The keyword `mutable` allows data members of class variables that have been declared `const` to remain modifiable. This reduces the need to cast away constness. This is a relatively new feature and is not implemented on all C++ compilers. For a code example, see Section 4.10.1, "Mutable," on page 137 (in file mutable.cpp).

D.12.8 Class Design

Occam's razor is a useful design principle. It states that entities should not be multiplied beyond necessity—or beyond completeness, invertibility, orthogonality, consistency, simplicity, efficiency, or expressiveness. Such ideals can be in conflict, and frequently involve trade-offs in arriving at a design.

D.13 Inheritance

Inheritance is the mechanism of deriving a new class from an old one. The existing class can be added to or altered to create the derived class. A class can be derived from an existing class using the form:

   class *class-name*:(public|protected|private)$_{opt}$ *base-name*
   {
      member declarations
   };

As usual, the keyword class can be replaced by the keyword struct, with the usual implication that members are by default public. The keywords public, private, and protected are available as access modifiers for class members. A public member is accessible throughout its scope. A private member is accessible to other member functions within its own class. A protected member is accessible to other member functions within its class and any class immediately derived from it. These access modifiers can be used within a class declaration in any order and with any frequency.

A derived class must have a constructor if its base class lacks a default constructor. Where the base class has constructors requiring arguments, the derived class explicitly invokes the base class constructor in its initializing list. The form of such a constructor is:

   class-name(*arg-list*) : *base-name*$_{opt}$ (*base-class-arg-list*)
   {
      . . . . .
   };

The *base-class-arg-list* is used when invoking the appropriate base class constructor, and is executed before the body of the derived class constructor is executed.

A publicly derived class is a subtype of its base class. A variable of the derived class can in many ways be treated as if it were the base class type. A pointer whose type is pointer to base class can point to objects having the publicly derived class type. A reference to the derived class, when meaningful, may be implicitly converted to a reference to the public base class. It is possible to declare a reference to a base class and initialize it to an object of the publicly derived class.

In the following example, the dbl_vect class from Section 6.7, "Overloading Assignment and Subscripting Operators," on page 213, is used as the base class. The only modification to the base class is to make the private members protected. The following dbl_vect_bnd class is the derived class:

In file vect_bnd.cpp

```cpp
class dbl_vect_bnd : public dbl_vect {
public:
   dbl_vect_bnd(int = 0, int = 9);         //default 10 array
   dbl_vect_bnd(dbl_vect_bnd& v);          //copy constructor
   dbl_vect_bnd(dbl_vect& v);              //conversion constructor
   dbl_vect_bnd(const double a[], int ne, int lb = 0);
   double&  operator[](int) const;
   int  ub() const { return (u_bnd); }
   int  lb() const { return (l_bnd); }
   dbl_vect_bnd& operator=(const dbl_vect_bnd& v);
private:
   int  l_bnd, u_bnd;
};

//default constructor
dbl_vect_bnd::dbl_vect_bnd(int lb, int ub) :
         dbl_vect(ub - lb + 1), l_bnd(lb), u_bnd(ub) { }

//conversion constructor
dbl_vect_bnd::dbl_vect_bnd(dbl_vect& v) :
         dbl_vect(v), l_bnd(0), u_bnd(size - 1) { }

//copy constructor
dbl_vect_bnd::dbl_vect_bnd(dbl_vect_bnd& v) :
         dbl_vect(v), l_bnd(v.l_bnd), u_bnd(v.u_bnd) { }

dbl_vect_bnd::dbl_vect_bnd(const double a[], int n, int lb) :
         dbl_vect(a, n), l_bnd(lb), u_bnd(lb + n) { }
```

In this example, the constructors for the derived class invoke a constructor in the base class, with the argument list following the colon.

D.13.1 Multiple Inheritance

Multiple inheritance allows a class to be derived from more than one base class. The syntax of class headers is extended to allow a list of base classes and their privacy designation. An example is:

```cpp
class shape {
   //class for shape interface
};
```

```
class tview {
   //class implementing text view
};

class tshape:public shape, private tview {
   //adapter of text view to shape view
};
```

In this example, the derived class `tshape` publicly inherits the `shape` base class, an interface, and privately inherits `tview`, an implementation of text view. This pattern of class design is called the *adapter pattern*. It uses multiple inheritance to combine an interface with an implementation; this technique is also known as using a *mixin* class.

In general, the parental relationship between classes is described by the inheritance directed acyclic graph (DAG). The DAG is a graph structure whose nodes are classes and whose directed edges point from base to derived class.

In deriving an identically named member from different classes, ambiguities may arise. These derivations are allowed provided the user does not make an ambiguous reference to such a member.

With multiple inheritance, two base classes can be derived from a common ancestor. If both base classes are used in the ordinary way by their derived class, that class will have two subobjects of the common ancestor. This duplication can be eliminated by using virtual inheritance. For a code example, see Section 9.4, "Virtual Functions," on page 327 (in file shape2.cpp).

D.13.2 Constructor Invocation

The order of execution for initializing constructors in base and member constructors is as follows.

Order of Constructor Execution

1. Base classes are initialized in declaration order.

2. Members are initialized in declaration order.

Virtual base classes are constructed before any of their derived classes, and before any nonvirtual base classes. Their construction order depends on their DAG. It is a depth-first, left-to-right order. Destructors are invoked in the reverse order of the constructors.

D.13.3 Abstract Base Classes

A pure virtual function is a virtual member function whose body is normally undefined. Notationally, it is declared inside the class as follows.

```
virtual function prototype = 0;
```

A class that has at least one pure virtual function is an abstract base class. Variables of an abstract base class cannot exist, but pointers of such a class can be defined and used polymorphically. For a code example, see Section 9.5, "Abstract Base Classes," on page 329 (in file predator.cpp).

A pure virtual destructor must have a definition.

D.13.4 Pointer to Class Member

In C++, a pointer to class member is distinct from a pointer to class. A pointer to class member has type $T::*$, where T is the class name. C++ has two operators that act to dereference a pointer to class member. The pointer to member operators are:

```
.*      and     ->*
```

Think of x.*ptr_mem as first dereferencing the pointer to obtain a member variable and then accessing the member for the designated x. For a code example, see Section 6.11.1, "Pointer to Class Member," on page 224 (in file showhide.cpp).

D.13.5 Run-Time Type Identification

Run-time type identification (RTTI) provides a mechanism for safely determining the type pointed at by a base class pointer at run time. It involves dynamic_cast, an operator on a base class pointer; typeid, an operator for determining the type of an object; and type_info, a structure providing run-time information for the associated type.

The dynamic_cast operator has the form:

```
dynamic_cast< type >( v )
```

where *type* must be a pointer or reference to a class type and *v* must be a corresponding pointer value or reference value. It is used with inherited classes having virtual functions as follows.

```
class Base { ····· };
class Derived : Base { ····· };

void fcn(Derived* ptr)
{
   Base* bptr = dynamic_cast<Base*>(ptr);
}
```

In this example, the cast converts the pointer value `ptr` to a `Base*`. If the conversion is inappropriate, a value of zero is returned or a `bad_cast` exception is thrown. Dynamic casts also work with reference types. Conceptually, the derived type object has a subobject that corresponds to the base type. The conversion replaces the derived type pointer value or reference with an appropriate base type pointer value or reference.

The operator `typeid()` can be applied to a *type-name* or an expression to determine the exact type of the argument. The operator returns a reference to the `class type_info`, which is supplied by the system and is defined in the header file *typeinfo* or *typeinfo.h*. The class `type_info` provides a `name()` member function returning a string that is the type name. It also provides overloaded equality operators. Remember to check the local implementation for the complete class interface. Bad dynamic casts and `typeid` operations can be made to throw the exceptions `bad_cast` and `bad_typeid`, so the user can choose between dealing with the NULL pointer and catching an exception. For a code example, see Section 9.9, "Run-Time Type Identification," on page 342 (in file typeid.cpp).

D.13.6 Virtual Functions

The keyword `virtual` is a function specifier that provides a mechanism for selecting at run time the appropriate member function from among base and derived class functions. It may be used only to modify member function declarations. A virtual function must be executable code. When invoked, its semantics are the same as those of other functions. In a derived class, it can be overridden. The selection of which function to invoke from among a group of overridden virtual functions is dynamic. The typical case is where a base class has a virtual function and derived classes have their versions of this function. A pointer to a base class type can point at either a base class object or a derived class object. The member function to be invoked is selected at run time. It corresponds to the object's type, not the pointer's. In the absence of a derived type member, the base class virtual function is used by default. For a code example, see Section 9.4, "Virtual Functions," on page 327 (in file shape2.cpp).

One reason C++ is so complex is that it has many types of functions and many rule variations that apply to them. At this point, with inheritance and the introduction of virtual functions, we have seen most varieties of function. There are also those functions that are generated by template syntax, and `catch()` handlers that are function-like and are part of the exception mechanism. It is useful to summarize characteristics and rules applying to most of these by category. For example, inlined functions can be member or nonmember functions and can have or not have return types. Inlining forces local linkage.

Function Characteristics				
Function Category	Member	Virtual	Return Type	Special
constructor	yes	no	no	not inherited; default
destructor	yes	yes	no	not inherited; default
assignment	yes	yes	yes	not inherited
-> [] ()	yes	yes	yes	
operator	maybe	yes	yes	
conversion	yes	yes	no	no arguments
new	static	no	void*	
delete	static	no	void*	
inline	maybe	yes	maybe	local linkage
catch	no	no	no	one argument
friend	friend	no	yes	not inherited

D.14 Templates

The keyword `template` is used to implement parameterized types. Rather than repeatedly recoding for each type, the template feature allows instantiation to generate code automatically for each type.

In file stack_p.cpp

```
template <class T>       //parameterize T
class stack {
public:
   stack();
   explicit stack(int s);
   T&   pop();
   void push(T);
   .....
private:
   T*   item;
   int  top;
   int  size;
};

typedef stack<string> str_stack;
str_stack  s(100);       //explicit string stack variable
```

For a code example, see Section 8.1, "Template Class stack," on page 270 (in file stack_t1.cpp).

A template declaration has the form:

template < *template arguments* > *declaration*

and a template argument can be:

class *identifier*
argument declaration

The class *identifier* arguments are instantiated with a type. Other argument declarations are instantiated with constant expressions of a nonfloating type, and can be a function or address of an object with external linkage, as shown in the following code.

In file array.cpp

```
template<class T, int n >
class array_n {
   .....
private:
   T  items[n];                //n explicitly instantiated
   .....
};

array_n<complex, 1000>  w;     //w is an array of complex
```

Member function syntax, when external to the class definition, is as follows.

```
template <class T>
T& stack<T>::pop()
{
    return(item[top--]);
}
```

The class-name used by the scope resolution operator includes the template arguments, and the member function declaration requires the template declaration as a preface to the function declaration.

D.14.1 Template Parameters

The above template can be rewritten with default parameters for both the `int` argument and the type. For example:

```
template<class T = int, int n = 100>
class array_n {
   .....
};
```

The default parameters can be instantiated when declaring variables, or can be omitted, in which case the defaults will be used.

Templates can use the keyword `typename` in place of `class`. For example:

```
template<typename T = double, double* ptr_dbl>
```

This allows the template code to use a pointer to a `double` argument. Ordinary floating-point arguments are not allowed; only pointer and reference to floating-point arguments are allowed.

A template argument can also be a template parameter. For example:

```
template<typename T1, template<class T2> class T3>
```

This allows very sophisticated metatemplates—templates instantiated with templates—to be coded. Libraries such as STL can use such features.

D.14.2 Function Template

Until 1995 compilers allowed ordinary functions to be parameterized using a restricted form of template syntax. Only `class` *identifier* instantiation is allowed. It must occur inside the function argument list.

In file swap.cpp

```
//generic swap
template <class T>
void swap(T& x, T& y)
{
   T  temp;

   temp = x;
   x = y;
   y = temp;
}

//ANSI C++ but unavailable in many current compilers
template <class T, int n>
T foo()
{
  T  temp[n];
  .....
}

foo<char, 20>();         //use char, 20 and call foo
```

A function template is used to construct an appropriate function for any invocation that matches its arguments unambiguously:

```
swap(i, j);              //i j int - okay
swap(c1, c2);            //c1, c2 complex - okay
swap(i, ch);             //i int ch char - illegal
```

The overloading function selection algorithm is as follows.

Overloaded Function Selection Algorithm

1. Exact match with trivial conversions allowed on a nontemplate function.
2. Exact match using a function template.
3. Ordinary argument resolution on a nontemplate function.

In the previous example, an ordinary function declaration whose prototype was

```
void swap(char, char);
```

would have been invoked on `swap(i, ch)`. For a code example, see Section 8.2.1, "Signature Matching and Overloading," on page 274 (in file swap.cpp).

D.14.3 Friends

Template classes can contain friends. A friend function that does not use a template specification is universally a friend of all instantiations of the template class. A friend function that incorporates template arguments is a friend only of its instantiated class:

```
template <class T>
class matrix {
private:
   friend void  foo_bar();                         //universal
   friend dbl_vect<T>  product(dbl_vect<T> v);     //instantiated
   .....
};
```

D.14.4 Static Members

Static members are not universal, but are specific to each instantiation:

```
template <class T>
class foo {
public:
   static int  count;
   .....
};
```

```
foo<int>     a, b;
foo<double>  c;
```

The static variables foo<int>::count and foo<double>::count are distinct. The variables a.count and b.count reference foo<int>::count, but c.count references foo<double>::count. It is preferable to use the form foo<*type*>::count since this makes it clear that the variable referenced is the static variable.

D.14.5 Specialization

When the template code is unsatisfactory for a particular argument type it can be specialized. A template function overloaded by an ordinary function of the same type—that is, one whose list of arguments and return type conform to the template declaration—is a specialization of the template. When the specialization matches the call, then it, rather than code generated from the template, is called.

```
void maxelement<char*>(char*a[],char* &max,int size);
//specialized using strcmp() to return max string
```

This would be a specialization of the previously declared template for template<class T>maxelement(). Class specializations are also possible, as in:

```
class stack<foobar_obj>  { /*specialize for foobar_obj */ };
```

For a code example, see Section 8.2.1, "Signature Matching and Overloading," on page 274 (in file swap.cpp).

D.15 Exceptions

Classically, an exception is an unexpected condition that the program encounters and cannot cope with. An example is floating-point divide by zero. Usually the system aborts the running program.

C++ code is allowed to directly raise an exception in a try block by using the throw expression. The exception will be handled by invoking an appropriate handler selected from a list of handlers found in the handler's try block. A simple example of this is as follows.

In file dbl_vect_ex2.cpp

```
dbl_vect::dbl_vect(int n)
{   //fault tolerant constructor
    try {
        if (n < 1)
            throw (n);
        p = new double[n];
        if (p == 0)
            throw ("FREE STORE EXHAUSTED");
    }
    catch (int n) { ····· }      //catches an incorrect size
    catch (const char* error) { ····· }
                                 //catches free store exhaustion
}
```

Note that new in this example is the traditional new returning zero for an allocation error. C++ systems using exceptions within new can throw an xalloc or bad_alloc exception upon failure. This replaces new returning zero upon failure to allocate. The older-style error handling can be retained by using set_new_handler(0). For a code example, see Section 10.2, "C++ Exceptions," on page 353 (in file dbl_vect4.h).

D.15.1 Throwing Exceptions

Syntactically, throw expressions come in two forms:

throw
throw *expression*

The throw expression raises an exception in a try block. The innermost try block is used to select the catch statement that processes the exception. The throw expression with no argument rethrows the current exception, and is typically used when you want a second handler called from the first handler to further process the exception.

The expression thrown is a static temporary object that persists until exception handling is exited. The expression is caught by a handler that may use this value. An uncaught expression terminates the program.

In file throw_it.cpp

```
void foo()
{
   int  i;
   //will illustrate how an exception is thrown
   i = -15;
   throw i;
}

int main()
{
   try {
      foo();
   }
   catch(int n)
      { cerr << "exception caught\n " << n << endl; }
}
```

The integer value thrown by `throw i` persists until the handler with integer signature `catch(int n)` exits. This value is available for use within the handler as its argument. For a code example, see Section 10.3, "Throwing Exceptions," on page 354 (in file throw1.cpp).

An example of rethrowing an exception is:

```
catch(int n)
{
   .....
   throw;      //rethrown
}
```

Assuming the thrown expression was of integer type, the rethrown exception is the same persistent integer object that is handled by the nearest handler suitable for that type.

D.15.2 Try Blocks

Syntactically, a try block has the form

```
try
```
compound statement
handler list

The try block is the context for deciding which handlers are invoked on a raised exception. The order in which handlers are defined is important, as it determines the order in which a handler for a raised exception of matching type will be tried:

```
try {
    .....
    throw ("SOS");
    .....
    io_condition eof(argv[i]);
    throw (eof);
    .....
}

catch (const char*) { ..... }
catch (io_condition& x) { ..... }
```

Throw Expression Matches the Catch if It Is

1. An exact match.

2. A derived type of the public base class handler type.

3. A thrown object type that is convertible to a pointer type that is the `catch` argument.

It is an error to list handlers in an order that prevents them from being called. An example would be:

```
catch(void*)                //any char* would match
catch(char*)
catch(BaseTypeError&)       //always for DerivedTypeError
catch(DerivedTypeError&)
```

D.15.3 Handlers

Syntactically, a handler has the form

> catch (*formal argument*)
> *compound statement*

The `catch` looks like a function declaration of one argument without a return type.

In file catch.cpp

```
catch (const char* message)
{
   cerr << message << endl;
   exit(1);
}
```

An ellipses signature that matches any argument is allowed. Also, the formal argument can be an abstract declaration, meaning it can have type information without a variable name. For a code example, see Section 10.5, "Handlers," on page 358 (in file catch.cpp).

D.15.4 Exception Specification

Syntactically, an exception specification is part of a function declaration, and has the form

function header `throw` (*type list*)

The *type list* is the list of types that a `throw` expression within the function can have. The function definition and declaration must write out the exception specification identically.

If the list is empty the compiler may assume that no `throw` will be executed by the function, either directly or indirectly.

```
void foo() throw(int, over_flow);
void noex(int i) throw();
```

If an exception specification is left off, then the assumption is that an arbitrary exception can be thrown by such a function. Violations of these specifications are run-time errors. They are caught by the function `unexpected()`.

D.15.5 `terminate()` and `unexpected()`

The system-provided function `terminate()` is called when no handler has been provided to deal with an exception. The `abort()` function is called by default. It immediately terminates the program, returning control to the operating system. Other action can be specified by using `set_terminate()` to provide a handler. These declarations are found in *except* or *except.h*.

The system-provided handler `unexpected()` is called when a function throws an exception that was not in its exception specification list. By default, the `termi-`

nate() function is called. Otherwise, set_unexpected() can be used to provide a handler.

D.15.6 Standard Library Exceptions

The standard library exceptions are derived from the base class exception. Two of the derived classes are logic_error and runtime_error. The logic-error types include bad_cast, out_of_range, and bad_typeid, which are intended to be thrown as indicated by their names. The run-time error types include range_error, overflow_error, and bad_alloc.

The base class defines a virtual function

```
virtual const char* exception::what() const throw();
```

This member function is intended to return a meaningful diagnostic message, and should be defined in each derived class to give more helpful messages. The empty throw specification list indicates the function itself should not throw an exception.

D.16 Caution and Compatibility

C++ is not completely upward compatible with C. In most cases of ordinary use, it is a superset of C. Also, C++ is not a completely stable language design. It is in the process of being standardized. The following sections note features of the language that are problematic.

D.16.1 Nested Class Declarations

The original scoping of nested classes was based on C rules. In effect, nesting was cosmetic, with the inner class globally visible. In C++, the inner class is local to the outer class enclosing it. Accessing such an inner class could require multiple uses of the scope resolution operator.

```
int outer::inner::foo(double w)      //foo is nested
    .....
```

It is also possible to have classes nested inside functions.

D.16.2 Type Compatibilities

In general, C++ is more strongly typed than ANSI C. Some differences are given in the following list.

Type Differences for ANSI C

- Enumerations are distinct types, and enumerators are not explicitly `int`. This means that enumerations must be cast when making assignments from integer types or other enumerations. Enumerations are promotable to integer. (See Section 2.6, "Enumeration Types," on page 41.)

- Any pointer type can be converted to a generic pointer of type `void*`. However, unlike in ANSI C, in C++ a generic pointer is not assignment-compatible with an arbitrary pointer type. This means that C++ requires that generic pointers be cast to an explicit type for assignment to a nongeneric pointer variable. (See Section 3.13, "The Uses of void," on page 93.)

- A character constant in C++ is a `char`, but in ANSI C it is an `int`. The `char` type is distinct from both `signed char` and `unsigned char`. Functions may be overloaded based on the distinctions, and pointers to the three types are not compatible.

D.16.3 Miscellaneous

The old C function syntax, where the argument list is left blank, is replaced in ANSI C by the explicit argument `void`. The signature `foo()` in C is considered equivalent to the use of ellipses, and in C++ is considered equivalent to the empty argument list.

In early C++ systems, the `this` pointer could be modified and used to allocate memory for class objects. Although this use is obsolete, a compiler can continue to allow it. (See Section 4.9, "The this Pointer," on page 132.)

C++ allows declarations to be intermixed with executable statements. ANSI C allows declarations to be at the heads of blocks or in file scope only. However, in C++, `goto`, iteration, and selection statements are not allowed to bypass initialization of variables. This rule differs from ANSI C.

In C++, a global data object must have exactly one definition. Other declarations must use the keyword `extern`. ANSI C allows multiple declarations without the keyword `extern`.

D.17 New Features in C++

Most compilers have complete implementations of templates and exceptions. The behavior of `new` with exceptions implemented is to throw an `xalloc` or `bad_alloc` exception. (See Section 10.9, "Standard Exceptions and Their Uses," on page 362.)

Mechanisms that dynamically determine object type have entered the language. This is called run-time type identification (RTTI). The new operator `typeid()` applies to either a *type-name* or an *expression* and `dynamic_cast<type>(pointer)`, whose effect is either to return zero if the cast fails or to perform the cast. With exceptions in use, the standard library `bad_cast` exception is thrown when a conversion fails. In general, such casts will be allowed in polymorphic class hierarchies. (See Section D.13.5, "Run-Time Type Identification," on page 454.)

Also added are cast conversion operators, `static_cast` and `reinterpret_cast`. (See Section 2.5, "The Traditional Conversions," on page 37.)

Single-argument constructors may be prohibited from being conversion constructors with the use of the keyword `explicit`. (See Section 5.1.3, "Constructors as Conversions," on page 154.)

The keyword `mutable` allows data members of class variables that have been declared `const` to remain modifiable. (See Section 4.10.1, "Mutable," on page 137.)

Two new types, `bool` and `wchar_t`, were added to the simple types. (See Section 2.4, "Simple Types," on page 35.)

The existence of libraries that can lead to name clashes motivated the addition of a namespace scope. (See Section 3.10, "Namespaces," on page 84.) The standard library is encapsulated in the `namespace std`. This library includes the standard container classes, iterators, and algorithms of the STL library.

See system manuals for a detailed description of what is implemented.

Appendix E

Input/Output

This appendix describes input/output in C++ using *iostream.h* and its associated libraries. The software for C++ includes a standard library that contains functions commonly used by the C++ community. The standard input/output library for C, described by the header *stdio.h*, is still available in C++. However, C++ introduces *iostream.h*, which implements its own collection of input/output functions. The header *stream.h* was used on systems before release 2.0, and is still available under many C++ systems.

The stream I/O is described as a set of classes in *iostream.h*. These classes overload the put to and get from operators << and >>. Streams can be associated with files, and examples of file processing using streams are discussed in this section. A lot of file processing requires character-handling macros, which are found in *ctype.h*. These are also discussed here.

In OOP, objects should know how to print themselves, and we have frequently made print() a member function of a class. Notationally, it is also useful to overload << for user-defined ADTs. In this section, we develop output functions for the types card and deck to illustrate these techniques.

E.1 The Output Class `ostream`

Output is inserted into an object of type ostream, declared in the header file *iostream.h*. An operator << is overloaded in this class to perform output conversions from standard types. The overloaded left shift operator is called the *insertion* or *put to* operator. The operator is left associative and returns a value of type ostream&. The standard output ostream corresponding to stdout is cout, and the standard output ostream corresponding to stderr is cerr.

The effect of executing a simple output statement such as

```
cout << "x = " << x << '\n';
```

is to print to the screen a string of four characters, followed by an appropriate representation for the output of x, followed by a new line. The representation depends on which overloaded version of << is invoked.

The class `ostream` contains public members such as:

```
ostream& operator<<(int i);
ostream& operator<<(long i);
ostream& operator<<(double x);
ostream& operator<<(char c);
ostream& operator<<(const char* s);
ostream& put(char c);
ostream& write(const char* p, int n);
ostream& flush();
```

The member function `put()` outputs the character representation of c. The member function `write()` outputs the string of length n pointed at by p. The member function `flush()` forces the stream to be written. Since these are member functions, they can be used as follows.

```
cout.put('A');                      //output A

char*  str = "ABCDEFGHI";
cout.write(str + 2, 3);             //output CDE
cout.flush();                       //write buffered stream
```

E.2 Formatted Output and *iomanip.h*

The put to operator << produces by default the minimum number of characters needed to represent the output. As a consequence, output can be confusing, as seen in the following example.

In file basic_o.cpp

```
int  i = 8, j = 9;

cout << i << j ;                          //confused: prints 89
cout << i << "   " << j;                  //better: prints 8   9
cout << "i= " << i << " j= " << j;        //best: i= 8 j= 9
```

Two schemes that we have used to properly space output are to have strings separating output values, and to use \n and \t to create newlines and tabbing. We can also use manipulators in the stream output to control output formatting.

A manipulator is a value or function that has a special effect on the stream on which it operates. A simple example of a manipulator is `endl`, defined in *iostream.h*. It outputs a newline and flushes the ostream:

```
x = 1;
cout << "x = " << x << endl;
```

This immediately prints the line:

```
x = 1
```

Another manipulator, `flush`, flushes the `ostream`, as in:

```
cout << "x = " << x << flush;
```

This has the almost the same effect as the previous example, but does not advance to a newline.

The manipulators `dec`, `hex`, and `oct` can be used to change integer bases. The default is base 10. The conversion base remains set until it is explicitly changed.

In file manip.cpp

```
//Using different bases in integer I/O
#include  <iostream.h>

int main()
{
   int  i = 10, j = 16, k = 24;
   cout << i << '\t' << j << '\t' << k << endl;
   cout << oct << i << '\t' << j << '\t' << k << endl;
   cout << hex << i << '\t' << j << '\t' << k << endl;
   cout << "Enter 3 integers, e.g. 11 11 12a" << endl;
   cin >> i >> hex >> j >> k;
   cout << dec << i << '\t' << j << '\t' << k << endl;
}
```

The resulting output is:

```
10      16      24
12      20      30
a       10      18
Enter 3 integers, e.g. 11 11 12a
11      17      298
```

The reason the final line of output is 11 followed by 17 is that the second 11 in the input was interpreted as hexadecimal, which is 16 + 1.

The above manipulators are found in *iostream.h*. Other manipulators are found in *iomanip.h*. For example, `setw(int width)` is a manipulator that changes the default field width for the next formatted I/O operation to the value of its argument. This value reverts to the default. The following table briefly lists the standard manipulators, the function of each, and where each is defined.

I/O Manipulators		
Manipulator	Function	File
`endl`	outputs newline and flush	*iostream.h*
`ends`	outputs null in string	*iostream.h*
`flush`	flushes the output	*iostream.h*
`dec`	uses decimal	*iostream.h*
`hex`	uses hexadecimal	*iostream.h*
`oct`	uses octal	*iostream.h*
`ws`	skips white space on input	*iostream.h*
`setw(int)`	sets field width	*iomanip.h*
`setfill(int)`	sets fill character	*iomanip.h*
`setbase(int)`	sets base format	*iomanip.h*
`setprecision(int)`	sets floating-point precision	*iomanip.h*
`setiosflags(long)`	sets format bits	*iomanip.h*
`resetiosflags(long)`	resets format bits	*iomanip.h*

E.3 User-Defined Types: Output

User-defined types have typically been printed by creating a member function print(). Let us use the types card and deck as an example of a simple user-defined type. We write out a set of output routines for displaying cards.

In file pr_card.cpp

```cpp
//card output
#include <iostream.h>

char  pips_symbol[14] = { '?', 'A', '2', '3', '4',
         '5', '6', '7', '8', '9', 'T', 'J', 'Q', 'K' };
char  suit_symbol[4] = { 'c', 'd', 'h', 's' };

enum suit { clubs, diamonds, hearts, spades };

class pips {
public:
   void  assign(int n) { p = n % 13 + 1; }
   void  print() { cout << pips_symbol[p]; }
private:
   int  p;
};

class card {
public:
   suit  s;
   pips  p;
   void  assign(int n)
      { cd = n; s = suit(n / 13); p.assign(n); }
   void  pr_card()
      { p.print(); cout << suit_symbol[s] << " "; }
private:
   int  cd;                  //a cd is from 0 to 51
};
```

```
class deck {
public:
   void   init_deck();
   void   shuffle();
   void   deal(int, int, card*);
   void   pr_deck();
private:
   card d[52];
};

void deck::pr_deck()
{
   for (int i = 0; i < 52; ++i) {
      if (i % 13 == 0)         //13 cards to a line
         cout << endl;
      d[i].pr_card();
   }
}
```

Each card will be printed out in two characters. If d is a variable of type deck, then d.pr_deck() will print out the entire deck, 13 cards to a line.

In keeping with the spirit of OOP, it would also be nice to overload << to accomplish the same aim. The operator << has two arguments, an ostream& and the ADT, and it must produce an ostream&. You want to use a reference to a stream and return a reference to a stream, whenever overloading << or >>, because you do not want to copy a stream object. Let us write these functions for the types card and deck:

In file pr_card2.cpp

```
ostream& operator<<(ostream& out, pips x)
{
    return (out << pips_symbol[x.p]);
}

ostream& operator<<(ostream& out, card cd)
{
   return (out << cd.p << suit_symbol[cd.s] << " " );
}
```

```
cstream& operator<<(ostream& out, deck x)
{
   for (int i = 0; i < 52; ++i) {
      if (i % 13 == 0)        //13 cards to a line
         out << endl;
      out << x.d[i];
   }
   return out;
}
```

The functions that operate on pips and deck need to be friends of the corresponding class because they access private members.

E.4 The Input Class istream

An operator >> is overloaded in istream to perform input conversions to standard types. The overloaded right shift operator is called the *extraction* or *get from* operator. The standard input istream corresponding to stdin is cin.

The effect of executing a simple input statement such as

```
cin >> x >> i;
```

is to read from standard input, normally the keyboard, a value for x and then a value for i. White space is ignored.

The class istream contains public members such as

```
istream& operator>>(int& i);
istream& operator>>(long& i);
istream& operator>>(double& x);
istream& operator>>(char& c);
istream& operator>>(char* s);
istream& get(char& c);
istream& get(char* s, int n, char c = '\n');
istream& getline(char* s, int n, char c = '\n');
istream& read(char* s, int n);
```

The member function get(char& c) inputs the character representation to c, including white space characters. The member function get(char* s, int n, int c = '\n') inputs into the string pointed at by s at most n - 1 characters, up to the specified delimiter character c or an end-of-file (EOF). A terminating zero is placed in the output string. The optionally specified default character acts as a terminator but is not placed in the output string. If not specified, the input is read up to the next newline. The member function `getline()` works like `get(char*, int, char = '\n')`, except that it discards rather than keeps the delimiter character in the designated `istream`. The member function `read(char* s, int n)` inputs into the string pointed at by `s` at most `n` characters. It sets the failbit if an end-of-file is encountered before `n` characters are read. (See Section E.8, "Using Stream States," on page 482.) In systems that have implemented ANSI standard exceptions, the `ios_base::failure` may be thrown.

In file basic_i.cpp

```
cin.get(c);              //one character
cin.get(s, 40);          //length 40 or terminated by '\n'
cin.get(s, 10, '*');     //length 10 or terminated by *
cin.getline(s, 40);      //same as get but '\n' discarded
```

Other useful member functions:

```
int gcount();                            //number of recently extracted chars
istream& ignore(int n=1, int delimeter=EOF);   //skips
int peek();                              //get next character without extraction
istream& putback(char c);    //puts back character
```

When overloading the >> operator to produce input to a user-defined type, the typical form is:

`istream& operator>>(istream& p, `*user-defined-type*`& x)`

If the function needs access to private members of x, it must be made a friend of class x. A major point is to make x a reference parameter so that its value can be modified.

E.5 Files

C systems have `stdin`, `stdout`, and `stderr` as standard files. In addition, systems may define other standard files, such as `stdprn` and `stdaux`. Abstractly, a file may be thought of as a stream of characters that are processed sequentially.

Standard Files			
C	C++	Name	Connected to
stdin	cin	standard input file	keyboard
stdout	cout	standard output file	screen
stderr	cerr	standard error file	screen
stdprn	cprn	standard printer file	printer
stdaux	caux	standard auxiliary file	auxiliary port

The C++ stream input/output ties the first three of these standard files to `cin`, `cout`, and `cerr`, respectively. Typically, C++ ties `cprn` and `caux` to their corresponding standard files `stdprn` and `stdaux`. There is also `clog`, which is a buffered version of `cerr`. Other files can be opened or created by the programmer. We will show how to do this in the context of writing a program that double-spaces an existing file into an existing or new file. The file names will be specified on the command line and passed into `argv`.

File I/O is handled by including *fstream.h*. This contains the classes `ofstream` and `ifstream` for output and input file-stream creation and manipulation. To properly open and manage an `ifstream` or `ofstream` related to a system file, you must first declare it with an appropriate constructor:

```
ifstream();
ifstream(const char*, int = ios::in,
         int prot = filebuf::openprot);
ofstream();
ofstream(const char*, int = ios::out,
         int prot = filebuf::openprot);
```

The constructor of no arguments creates a variable that will later be associated with an input file. The constructor of three arguments takes as its first argument the named file. The second argument specifies the file mode. The third argument is for file protection.

The file-mode arguments are defined as enumerators in class `ios` as shown in the following table.

File Modes	
Argument	**Mode**
`ios::in`	input mode
`ios::app`	append mode
`ios::out`	output mode
`ios::ate`	open and seek to end of file
`ios::nocreate`	open but do not create mode
`ios::trunc`	discard contents and open
`ios::noreplace`	if file exists open fails

Thus the default for an `ifstream` is input mode, and the default for an `ofstream` is output mode. If file opening fails, the stream is put into a bad state. It can be tested with the `!` operator. In libraries built with exceptions, the `failure` exception can be thrown.

Other important member functions found in *fstream.h* include:

```
//opens ifstream file
void open(const char*, int = ios::in,
          int prot = filebuf::openprot);

//opens ofstream file
void open(const char*, int = ios::out,
          int prot = filebuf::openprot);

void close();
```

These functions can be used to open and close appropriate files. If you create a file stream with the default constructor, you would normally use `open()` to associate it with a file. You could then use `close()` to close the file and open another file using the same stream. Additional member functions in other I/O classes allow for a full range of file manipulation.

In file dbl_sp.cpp

```
//A program to double-space a file.
//Usage: executable  f1 f2
//f1 must be present and readable
//f2 must be writable if it exists

#include   <fstream.h>       //includes iostream.h
#include   <stdlib.h>

void double_space(ifstream& f, ofstream& t)
{
   char  c;

   while (f.get(c)) {
      t.put(c);
      if (c == '\n')
         t.put(c);
   }
}

int main(int argc, char** argv)
{
   if (argc != 3) {
      cout << "\nUsage: " << argv[0]
           << "  infile  outfile" << endl;
      exit(1);
   }

   ifstream   f_in(argv[1]);
   ofstream   f_out(argv[2]);

   if (!f_in) {
      cerr << "cannot open " << argv[1] << endl;
      exit(1);
   }
   if (!f_out) {
      cerr << "cannot open " << argv[2] << endl;
      exit(1);
   }
   double_space(f_in, f_out);
}
```

E.6 Using Strings as Streams

The class strstream allows char* strings to be treated as iostreams. When using strstreams, the *strstream.h* library must be included. Newer libraries include *sstream*; this provides both istringstream and ostringstream, which support in-memory IO using the standard library type string.

The istrstream is used when input is from a string, rather than from a stream. The overloaded >> get from operator may be used with istrstream variables. The forms for declaring an istrstream variable are

```
istrstream name (char* s);
istrstream name (char* s, int n);
```

where s is a string to use as input, n is the optional length of the input buffer, and *name* is used instead of cin. If n is not specified, the string must be terminated with a zero. The end-of-string sentinel is treated as an EOF. An example follows.

In file str_strm.cpp

```
char name[15];
int total;
char* scores[4] = { "Dave 2","Ida 5","Jim 4","Ira 8" };

istrstream ist(scores[3]);   //ist uses scores[3]
ist >> name >> total;        //name: Ira , total = 8
```

The ostrstream declarations have the following forms:

```
ostrstream();
ostrstream name(char* s, int n, int mode = ios::out);
```

where s is pointer to buf to receive string, n is the optional size of buffer, and mode specifies whether the data is to be put into an empty buffer (ios::out) or appended to the existing null-terminated string in the buffer (ios::app or ios::ate). If no size is specified, the buffer is dynamically allocated. The ostrstream variable may use the overloaded put to operator << to build the string. The use of ostrstream is particularly useful when you want to construct a single string from information kept in a variety of variables. This technique is used in exception handling to build a single string variable to be used as an argument in a throw(). Our vect example, in Section 10.8, "Example Exception Code," on page 360, uses this technique. In the following example, note that `ost2` must contain an existing null-terminated string in order for the append to work correctly.

```
strstream ost1;
strstream ost2 (charbuf, 1000, ios::app);

ost1 << name << " " << score << endl;
ost2 << address << city << endl << ends;
```

E.7 The Functions and Macros in *ctype.h*

The system provides a standard header file *ctype.h* or *cctype*, which contains a set of functions that are used to test characters and a set of functions that are used to convert characters. These may be implemented as macros or inline functions. This is mentioned here because of its usefulness in C++ input/output. Those functions that only test a character return an `int` value. The argument is type `int`.

ctype.h Function	Nonzero (true) Is Returned if c Is
isalpha(c)	a letter
isupper(c)	an uppercase letter
islower(c)	a lowercase letter
isdigit(c)	a digit
isxdigit(c)	a hexadecimal digit
isspace(c)	a white space character
isalnum(c)	a letter or digit
ispunct(c)	a punctuation character
isgraph(c)	a printing character, except space
isprint(c)	a printable character
iscntrl(c)	a control character
isascii(c)	an ASCII code

Other functions provide for the appropriate conversion of a character value. Note that these functions do not change the value of `c` stored in memory.

ctype.h Conversion Function	Effect
toupper(c)	changes c from lowercase to uppercase
tolower(c)	changes c from uppercase to lowercase
toascii(c)	changes c to ASCII code

The ASCII code functions are usual on ASCII systems.

E.8 Using Stream States

Each stream has an associated state that can be tested. The states on existing systems are:

```
enum io_state { goodbit, eofbit, failbit, badbit };
```

ANSI systems propose the type `ios_base::iostate` to be a bitmask type defining these values. When the nongood values are set by some IO operation, ANSI systems can throw the IO standard exception `ios_base::failure`. Associated with this exception is a member function `what()` returning a `char*` message that gives a reason for the failure.

The values for a particular stream can be tested using the public member functions in the following table.

Stream State Function	What It Returns
int good()	nonzero if not EOF or other error bit set
int eof();	nonzero if istream `eofbit` set
int fail();	nonzero if `failbit`, `badbit` set
int bad();	nonzero if `badbit` set
int rdstate();	returns error state
void clear(int i = 0);	resets error state
int operator!();	return true if `failbit` or `badbit` set
operator void*	return false if `failbit` or `badbit` set

Testing for a stream being in a nongood state can protect a program from hanging up. A stream state of good means that the previous input/output operation worked and the next operation should also. A stream state of EOF means the previous input operation returned an end-of-file condition. A stream state of fail means the previous input/output operation failed, but the stream will be usable once the error bit is cleared. A stream state of bad means the previous input/output operation is invalid, but the stream may be usable once the error condition is corrected.

It is also possible to directly test a stream. It is nonzero if it is in either a good or EOF state:

```
if (cout << x )          //output succeeded
    .....
else
    .....                //output failed
```

The following program counts the number of words coming from the standard input. Normally this would be redirected to use an existing file. It illustrates ideas discussed in this and the last two sections.

In file word_cnt.cpp

```
//The word_cnt program for counting words
//Usage: executable < file
#include   <iostream.h>
#include   <ctype.h>
int   found_next_word();

int main()
{
   int   word_cnt = 0;

   while (found_next_word())
       ++word_cnt;
   cout << "word count is " << word_cnt << endl;
}
```

```
int found_next_word()
{
   char  c;
   int   word_sz = 0;

   cin >> c;
   while (!cin.eof() && !isspace(c)) {
      ++word_sz;
      cin.get(c);
   }
   return word_sz;
}
```

A nonwhite space character is received from the input stream and assigned to c. The while loop tests that adjacent characters are not white space. The loop terminates when either an end-of-file character or a white space character is found. The word size is returned as zero when the only nonwhite space character found is the end-of-file. One last point: The loop cannot be rewritten as

```
while (!cin.eof() && !isspace(c)) {
   ++word_sz;
   cin >> c;
}
```

because this would skip white space.

E.9 Mixing I/O Libraries

We have used *iostream.h* throughout this text. It is perfectly reasonable to want to continue using *stdio.h*. This is the standard in the C community, and it is well understood. Its disadvantage is that it is not type safe. Functions like `printf()` use unchecked variable-length argument lists. Stream I/O requires, as arguments to its functions and overloaded operators, assignment-compatible types. You might also want to mix both forms of I/O. Synchronization problems can occur because the two libraries use different buffering strategies. This can be avoided by calling:

```
ios::sync_with_stdio();
```

In file mix_io.cpp

```cpp
//The mix_io program with syncronized IO
#include <stdio.h>
#include <iostream.h>

unsigned long fact(int n)
{
   unsigned long  f = 1;

   for (int i = 2; i <= n; ++i)
      f *= i;
   return f;
}

int main()
{
   int n;

   ios::sync_with_stdio();

   do {
      cout << "\nEnter n positive or 0 to halt: ";
      scanf("%d", &n);
      printf("\n fact(%d) = %ld", n, fact(n));
   } while (n > 0);
   cout << "\nend of session" << endl;
}
```

Note that for integer values greater than 12, the results will overflow. It is safe to mix `stdio` and `iostream` provided they are not mixed on the same file.

Appendix F

STL and String Libraries

The standard template library (STL) is the C++ standard library providing generic programming for many standard data structures and algorithms. It provides containers, iterators, and algorithms that support a standard for generic programming. We present a brief description emphasizing these three components.

The library is built using templates and is highly orthogonal in design. Components can be used with one another on native and user-provided types through proper instantiation of the various elements of the STL library. Different header files are required depending on the system. Our examples conform to the ANSI standard and are encapsulated in `namespace std`. For a code example, see Section 8.7, "STL," on page 287 (in file stl_cont.cpp).

F.1 Containers

Containers come in two major families: sequence and associative. Sequence containers include vectors, lists, and deques; they are ordered by having a sequence of elements. Associative containers include sets, multisets, maps, and multimaps; they have keys for looking up elements. The map container is a basic associative array and requires that a comparison operation on the stored elements be defined. All varieties of containers share a similar interface.

STL Typical Container Interfaces

- Constructors, including default and copy constructors
- Element access
- Element insertion
- Element deletion
- Destructor
- Iterators

Containers are traversed using iterators. These are pointer-like objects that are available as templates and optimized for use with STL containers. For a code example, see Section 8.8, "Containers," on page 289 (in file stl_deq.cpp).

Container classes are designated as CAN in the table below.

STL Container Definitions	
CAN::value_type	type of value held in the CAN
CAN::reference	reference type to value
CAN::const_reference	const reference
CAN::pointer	pointer to reference type
CAN::iterator	iterator type
CAN::const_iterator	const iterator
CAN::reverse_iterator	reverse iterator
CAN::const_reverse_iterator	const reverse iterator
CAN::difference_type	represents the difference between two CAN::iterator values
CAN::size_type	size of a CAN

All container classes have these definitions available. For example, if we are using the vector container class, then vector<char>::value_type means a character value is stored in the vector container. Such a container could be traversed with a vector<char>::iterator.

Containers allow equality and comparison operators. They also have an extensive list of standard member functions.

STL Container Members	
CAN::CAN()	default constructor
CAN::CAN(c)	copy constructor
c.begin()	beginning location of CAN c
c.end()	ending location of CAN c
c.rbegin()	beginning for a reverse iterator
c.rend()	ending for a reverse iterator
c.size()	number of elements in CAN
c.max_size()	largest possible size
c.empty()	true if the CAN is empty
c.swap(d)	swap two CANs

STL Container Operators	
== != < > <= >=	equality and comparison operators using CAN::value_type

F.1.1 Sequence Containers

The sequence containers are vector, list, and deque. They have a sequence of accessible elements. In many cases the C++ array type can also be treated as a sequence container. For a code example, see Section 8.8.1, "Sequence Containers," on page 290 (in file stl_vect.cpp).

Sequence classes are designated as SEQ in the table below; these are in addition to the already described CAN interface.

STL Sequence Members	
SEQ::SEQ(n, v)	n elements of value v
SEQ::SEQ(b_it, e_it)	starts at b_it and go to e_it - 1
c.insert(w_it, v)	inserts v before w_it
c.insert(w_it, v, n)	inserts n copies of v before w_it
c.insert(w_it, b_it, e_it)	inserts b_it to e_it before w_it
c.erase(w_it)	erases the element at w_it
c.erase(b_it, e_it)	erases b_it to e_it

F.1.2 Associative Containers

The associative containers are set, map, multiset, and multimap. They have key-based accessible elements. These containers have an ordering relation, `Compare`, which is the comparison object for the associative container. For a code example, see Section 8.8.2, "Associative Containers," on page 293 (in file stl_age.cpp).

Associative classes are designated as ASSOC in the table below; these are in addition to the already described CAN interface.

STL Associative Definitions	
ASSOC::key_type	the retrieval key type
ASSOC::key_compare	the comparison object type
ASSOC::value_compare	the type for comparing ASSOC::value_type

The associative containers have several standard constructors for initialization.

STL Associative Constructors	
ASSOC()	default constructor using Compare
ASSOC(cmp)	constructor using cmp as the comparison object
ASSOC(b_it, e_it)	uses element range b_it to e_it using Compare
ASSOC(b_it, e_it, cmp)	uses element range b_it to e_it and cmp as the comparison object

What distinguishes associative constructors from sequence container constructors is the use of a comparison object.

STL Insert and Erase Member Functions	
c.insert(t)	inserts t, if no existing element has the same key as t; returns pair <iterator, bool> with bool being true if t was not present
c.insert(w_it, t)	inserts t with w_it as a starting position for the search; fails on sets and maps if key value is already present; returns position of insertion
c.insert(b_it, e_it)	inserts the elements in this range
c.erase(k)	erases elements whose key value is k, returning the number of erased elements
c.erase(w_it)	erases the pointed-to element
c.erase(b_it, e_it)	erases the range of elements

The insertion works when no element of the same key is already present.

STL Member Functions	
c.find(k)	returns iterator to element having the given key k; otherwise ends
c.count(k)	returns the number of elements with k
c.lower_bound(k)	returns iterator to first element having value greater than or equal to k
c.upper_bound(k)	returns iterator to first element having value greater than k
c.equal_range(k)	returns an iterator pair for lower_bound and upper_bound

F.1.3 Container Adaptors

Container adaptor classes are container classes that modify existing containers to produce different public behaviors based on an existing implementation. Three provided container adaptors are stack, queue, and priority_queue.

The stack can be adapted from vector, list, and deque. It needs an implementation that supports back, push_back, and pop_back operations. This is a last-in-first-out data structure.

STL Adapted stack Functions	
`void push(const value_type& v)`	places v on the stack
`void pop()`	removes the top element of the stack
`value_type& top() const`	returns the top element of the stack
`bool empty() const`	returns `true` if the stack is empty
`size_type size() const`	returns the number of elements in the stack
`operator==` and `operator<`	equality and lexicographically less than

The `queue` can be adapted from `list` or `deque`. It needs an implementation that supports `empty`, `size`, `front`, `back`, `push_back`, and `pop_front` operations. This is a first-in-first-out data structure.

STL Adapted queue Functions	
`void push(const value_type& v)`	places v on the end of the queue
`void pop()`	removes the front element of the queue
`value_type& front() const`	returns the front element of the queue
`value_type& back() const`	returns the back element of the queue
`bool empty() const`	returns `true` if the queue is empty
`size_type size() const`	returns the number of elements in the queue
`operator==` and `operator<`	equality and lexicographically less than

The `priority_queue` can be adapted from `vector` or `deque`. It needs an implementation that supports `empty`, `size`, `front`, `push_back`, and `pop_back` operations. A `priority_queue` also needs a comparison object for its instantiation. The top element is the largest element as defined by the comparison relationship for the `priority_queue`.

STL Adapted priority_queue Functions	
`void push(const value_type& v)`	places v in the `priority_queue`
`void pop()`	removes top element of the `priority_queue`
`value_type& top() const`	returns top element of the `priority_queue`
`bool empty() const`	checks for `priority_queue` empty
`size_type size() const`	shows number of elements in the `priority_queue`

We adapt the `stack` from an underlying `vector` implementation. Notice how the STL ADTs replace our individually designed implementations of these types. For a code example, see Section 8.8.3, "Container Adaptors," on page 296 (in file stl_stak.cpp).

F.2 Iterators

Navigation over containers is by iterator. Iterators can be thought of as an enhanced pointer type. They are templates that are instantiated as to the container class type over which they iterate. There are five iterator types: input, output, forward, bidirectional, and random access (see Section F.2.1, "Iterator Categories," on page 493). Not all iterator types may be available for a given container class. For example, random-access iterators are available for vectors but not maps.

The input and output iterators have the fewest requirements. They can be used for input and output and have special implementations called `istream_iterator` and `ostream_iterator` for these purposes. (See Section F.2.2, "The Istream_iterator," on page 494, and Section F.2.3, "The Ostream_iterator," on page 494.) A forward iterator can do everything an input/output iterator can do and can additionally save a position within a container. A bidirectional iterator can go both forward and backward. A random-access iterator is the most powerful and can access any element in a suitable container, such as a `vector` in constant time. For a code example, see Section 8.9.1, "The istream_iterator and ostream_iterator," on page 297 (in file stl_io.cpp).

F.2.1 Iterator Categories

Input iterators support equality operations, dereferencing, and autoincrement. An iterator that satisfies these conditions can be used for one-pass algorithms that read values of a data structure in one direction. A special case of the input iterator is the `istream_iterator`.

Output iterators support dereferencing restricted to the left-hand side of assignment and autoincrement. An iterator that satisfies these conditions can be used for one-pass algorithms that write values to a data structure in one direction. A special case of the output iterator is the `ostream_iterator`.

Forward iterators support all input/output iterator operations and additionally support unrestricted use of assignment. This allows position within a data structure to be retained from pass to pass. Therefore, general one-directional multipass algorithms can be written with forward iterators.

Bidirectional iterators support all forward iterator operations as well as both autoincrement and autodecrement. Therefore general bidirectional multipass algorithms can be written with bidirectional iterators.

Random-access iterators support all bidirectional iterator operations and also address arithmetic operations such as indexing. In addition, random access iterators support comparison operations. Therefore, algorithms such as quicksort that require efficient random access in linear time can be written with these iterators.

Container classes and algorithms dictate the category of iterator available or needed, so `vector` containers allow random-access iterators, but `lists` do not. Sorting generally requires a random-access iterator, but finding requires only an input iterator.

F.2.2 The `Istream_iterator`

An `istream_iterator` is derived from an `input_iterator` to work specifically with reading from streams. The template for `istream_iterator` is instantiated with a *<type, distance>*. This distance is usually specified by `ptrdiff_t`. As defined in *cstddef* or *stddef.h*, it is an integer type representing the difference between two pointer values. For a code example, see Section 8.9.1, "The istream_iterator and ostream_iterator," on page 297 (in file stl_io.cpp).

F.2.3 The `Ostream_iterator`

An `ostream_iterator` is derived from an `output_iterator` to work specifically with writing to streams. The `ostream_iterator` can be constructed with a `char*` delimiter, in this case "\t". Thus the tab character will be issued to the stream `cout` after each `int` value is written. In this program the iterator `out`, when it is dereferenced, writes the assigned `int` value to `cout`. For a code example, see Section 8.9.1, "The istream_iterator and ostream_iterator," on page 297 (in file stl_io.cpp).

F.2.4 Iterator Adaptors

Iterators can be adapted to provide backward traversal and traversal with insertion. For a code example, see Section 8.9.1, "The istream_iterator and ostream_iterator," on page 297 (in file stl_io.cpp).

STL Iterator Adaptors

- Reverse iterators—reverse the order of iteration

- Insert iterators—insertion takes place instead of the normal overwriting mode

We will briefly list adaptors and their purpose as found in this library.

F.2 ▼ Iterators

- ```
  template<class BidiIter,
     class T, class Ref = T&,
     class Distance = ptrdiff_t>
  class reverse_bidirectional_iterator;
  ```

  This reverses the normal direction of iteration. Use rbegin() and rend() for range.

- ```
  template<class RandAccIter,
     class T, class Ref = T&,
     class Distance = ptrdiff_t>
  class reverse_iterator;
  ```

  This reverses the normal direction of iteration. Use rbegin() and rend() for range.

- ```
  template <class Can>
     class insert_iterator;
  template <class Can, Class Iter>
  insert_iterator<Can>
     inserter(Can& c, Iter p);
  ```

  The insert iterator inserts instead of overwrites. The insertion into c is at position p.

- ```
  template <class Can>
     class front_insert_iterator;
  template <class Can>
  front_insert_iterator<Can>
     front_inserter(Can& c);
  ```

  Front insertion occurs at the front of the container and requires the member push_front().

- ```
  template <class Can>
     class back_insert_iterator;
  template <class Can>
  back_insert_iterator<Can>
     back_inserter(Can& c);
  ```

  Back insertion occurs at the back of the container and requires a push_back() member.
  ```

F.3 Algorithms

The STL algorithms library contains the following four categories.

STL Categories of Algorithms Library

- Sorting algorithms
- Nonmutating sequence algorithms
- Mutating sequence algorithms
- Numerical algorithms

These algorithms generally use iterators to access containers instantiated on a given type. The resulting code can be competitive in efficiency with special-purpose codes.

F.3.1 Sorting Algorithms

Sorting algorithms include general sorting, merges, lexicographic comparison, permutation, binary search, and selected similar operations. These algorithms have versions that use either `operator<()` or a `Compare` object. They often require random-access iterators. Section 8.10.1, "Sorting Algorithms," on page 300.

We present the library prototypes for sorting algorithms.

- ```
  template<class RandAcc>
  void sort(RandAcc b, RandAcc e);
  ```

  This is a quicksort algorithm over the elements in the range b to e. The iterator type RandAcc must be a random-access iterator.

- ```
  template<class RandAcc>
  void stable_sort(RandAcc b, RandAcc e);
  ```

  This is a stable sorting algorithm over the elements in the range b to e. In a stable sort equal elements remain in their relative same position.

- ```
  template<class RandAcc>
  void partial_sort(RandAcc b, RandAcc m, RandAcc e);
  ```

  This is a partial sorting algorithm over the elements in the range b to e. The range b to m is filled with elements sorted up to position m.
  ```

- ```
  template<class InputIter, class RandAcc>
  void partial_sort_copy(InputIter b, InputIter e,
                    RandAcc result_b, RandAcc result_e);
  ```

  This is a partial sorting algorithm over the elements in the range b to e. Elements sorted are taken from the input iterator range and copied to the random-access iterator range. The smaller of the two ranges is used.

- ```
  template<class RandAcc>
  void nth_element(RandAcc b, RandAcc nth, RandAcc e);
  ```

  The nth element is placed in sorted order, with the rest of the elements partitioned by it. For example, if the fifth position is chosen, the four smallest elements are placed to the left of it. The remaining elements are placed to the right of it and will be greater than it.

- ```
  template<class InputIter1, class InputIter2, class OutputIter>
  OutputIter merge(InputIter1 b1, InputIter1 e1, InputIter2 b2,
                    InputIter2 e2, OutputIter result_b);
  ```

  The elements in the range b1 to e1 and b2 to e2 are merged to the starting position result_b.

- ```
  template<class BidiIter>
  void inplace_merge(BidiIter b, BidiIter m, BidiIter e);
  ```

  The elements in the range b to m and m to e are merged in place.

We will use a table to briefly list other algorithms and their purpose as found in this library.

STL Sort Related Library Functions	
binary_search(b, e, t)	true if t is found in b to e
lower_bound(b, e, t)	the first position for placing t while maintaining sorted order
upper_bound(b, e, t)	the last position for placing t while maintaining sorted order
equal_range(b, e, t)	returns an iterator pair for the range where t can be placed maintaining sorted order
push_heap(b, e)	places the location's e element into an already existing heap

STL Sort Related Library Functions	
`pop_heap(b, e)`	swaps the location's e element with its b element and reheaps
`sort_heap(b, e)`	performs a sort on the heap
`make_heap(b, e)`	creates a heap
`next_permutation(b, e)`	produces the next permutation
`prev_permutation(b, e)`	produces the previous permutation
`lexicographical_compare (b1, e1, b2, e2)`	returns `true` if sequence 1 is lexicographically less than sequence 2
`min(t1, t2)`	returns the minimum of `t1` and `t2` that are call-by-reference arguments
`max(t1, t2)`	returns the maximum
`min_element(b, e)`	returns the position of the minimum
`max_element(b, e)`	returns the position of the maximum
`includes(b1, e1, b2, e2)`	returns `true` if the second sequence is a subset of the first sequence
`set_union (b1, e1, b2, e2, r)`	returns the union as an output iterator `r`
`set_intersection (b1, e1, b2, e2, r)`	returns the set intersection as an output iterator `r`
`set_difference (b1, e1, b2, e2, r)`	returns the set difference as an output iterator `r`
`set_symmetric_difference (b1, e1, b2, e2, r)`	returns the set symmetric difference as an output iterator `r`

These algorithms have a form that uses a `Compare` object replacing `operator<()`; for example:

- ```
  template<class RandAcc, class Compare>
  void sort(RandAcc b, RandAcc e, Compare comp);
  ```

  This is a quicksort algorithm over the elements in the range `b` to `e` using `comp` for ordering.
  ```

F.3.2 Nonmutating Sequence Algorithms

Nonmutating algorithms do not modify the contents of the containers they work on. A typical operation is searching a container for a particular element and returning its position. For a code example, see Section 8.10.2, "Nonmutating Sequence Algorithms," on page 301 (in file stl_find.cpp).

We present the library prototypes for nonmutating algorithms.

- ```
  template<class InputIter, Class T>
  InputIter find(InputIter b, InputIter e, const T& t));
  ```

    This finds the position of t in the range b to e.

- ```
  template<class InputIter, Class Predicate>
  InputIter find(InputIter b, InputIter e, Predicate p));
  ```

    This finds the position of the first element that makes the predicate true in the range b to e; otherwise the position e is returned.

- ```
  template<class InputIter, Class Function>
  void for_each(InputIter b, InputIter e, Function f));
  ```

    This applies the function f to each value found in the range b to e.

We will use a table to briefly list other algorithms and their purpose as found in this library.

STL Nonmutating Sequence Library Functions	
next_permutation(b, e)	produces next permutation
prev_permutation(b, e)	produces previous permutation
count(b, e, t, n)	returns to n the count of elements equal to t
count_if(b, e, p, n)	returns to n the count of elements that make predicate p true
adjacent_find(b, e)	returns the first position of adjacent elements that are equal; otherwise returns e
adjacent_find(b, e, binp)	returns the first position of adjacent elements satisfying the binary predicate binp; otherwise returns e
mismatch(b1, e1, b2)	returns an iterator pair indicating the positions where elements do not match from the given sequences starting with b1 and b2
  ```

STL Nonmutating Sequence Library Functions	
mismatch (b1, e1, b2, binp)	as above, with a binary predicate binp used instead of equality
equal(b1, e1, b2)	returns true if the indicated sequences match; otherwise returns false
equal(b1, e1, b2, binp)	as above, with a binary predicate binp used instead of equality
search(b1, e1, b2, e2)	returns an iterator where the second sequence is contained in the first, if it is not e1
search (b1, e1, b2, e2, binp)	as above, with a binary predicate binp used instead of equality

F.3.3 Mutating Sequence Algorithms

Mutating algorithms can modify the contents of the containers they work on. A typical operation is reversing the contents of a container. For a code example, see Section 8.10.3, "Mutating Sequence Algorithms," on page 302 (in file stl_revr.cpp).

We present the library prototypes for mutating algorithms.

- ```
  template<class InputIter, class OutputIter>
  OutputIter copy(InputIter b1, InputIter e1, OutputIter b2);
  ```

  This is a copying algorithm over the elements b1 to e1. The copy is placed starting at b2. The position returned is the end of the copy.

- ```
  template<class BidiIter1, class BidiIter2>
  BidiIter2 copy_backward(BidiIter1 b1, BidiIter1 e1,
                          BidiIter2 b2);
  ```

  This is a copying algorithm over the elements b1 to e1. The copy is placed starting at b2. The copying runs backward from e1 into b2, which are also going backward. The position returned is b2 - (e1 - b1).

- ```
  template<class BidiIter>
  void reverse(BidiIter b, BidiIter e);
  ```

  This reverses in place the elements b to e.
  ```

- ```
  template<class BidiIter, class OutputIter>
  OutputIter reverse_copy(BidiIter b1, BidiIter e1,
                          OutputIter b2);
  ```

  This is a reverse copying algorithm over the elements b1 to e1. The copy in reverse is placed starting at b2. The copying runs backward from e1 into b2, which are also going backward. The position returned is b2 + (e1 - b1).

- ```
  template<class ForwIter>
  ForwardIter unique(ForwIter b, ForwIter e);
  ```

  The adjacent elements in the range b to e are erased. The position returned is the end of the resulting range.

- ```
  template<class ForwIter, class BinaryPred>
  ForwardIter unique(ForwIter b, ForwIter e, BinaryPred bp);
  ```

  The adjacent elements in the range b to e with binary predicate bp satisfied are erased. The position returned is the end of the resulting range.

- ```
  template<class InputIter, class OutputIter>
  OutputIter unique_copy(InputIter b1, InputIter e1,
                         OutputIter b2);

  template<class InputIter, class OutputIter, class BinaryPred>
  OutputIter unique_copy(InputIter b1, InputIter e1,
                         OutputIter b2, BinaryPred bp);
  ```

  The results are copied to b2 with the original range unchanged.

The remaining library functions are described in the following tables.

STL Mutating Sequence Library Functions	
swap(t1, t2)	swaps t1 and t2
iter_swap(b1, b2)	swaps pointed-to locations
swap_range(b1, e1, b2)	swaps elements from b1 to e1 with those starting at b2; returns b2 + (e1 - b1)
transform(b1, e1, b2, op)	using the unary operator op transforms the sequence b1 to e1, placing it at b2; returns the end of the output location

STL Mutating Sequence Library Functions	
`transform(b1, e1, b2, b3, bop)`	uses the binary operator bop on the two sequences starting with b1 and b2 to produce the sequence b3; returns the end of the output location
`replace(b, e, t1, t2)`	replaces in the range b to e the value t1 by t2
`replace_if(b, e, p, t2)`	replaces in the range b to e the elements satisfying the predicate p by t2
`replace_copy(b1, e1, b2, t1, t2)`	copies and replaces into b2 the range b1 to e1, with the value t1 replacing t2
`replace_copy_if(b1, e1, b2, p, t2)`	copies and replaces into b2 the range b1 to e1 with the elements satisfying the predicate p replacing t2
`remove(b, e, t)`	removes elements of value t
`remove_if, remove_copy, remove_copy_if`	similar to `replace` family except that values are removed
`fill(b, e, t)`	assigns t to the range b to e
`fill_n(b, n, t)`	assigns n ts starting at b
`generate(b, e, gen)`	assigns to the range b to e by calling generator gen
`generate_n(b, n, gen)`	assigns n values starting at b using gen
`rotate(b, m, e)`	rotates leftward the elements of the range b to e; element in position i ends up in position $(i + n - m) \% n$, where n is the size of the range, m is the midposition, and b is the first position
`rotate_copy(b1, m, e1, b2)`	as above, but copied to b2 with the original unchanged
`random_shuffle(b, e)`	shuffles the elements

STL Mutating Sequence Library Functions	
random_shuffle(b, e, rand)	shuffles the elements using the supplied random-number generator rand
partition(b, e, p)	partitions the range b to e to have all elements satisfying predicate p placed before those that do not satisfy p
stable_partition(b, e, p)	as above, but preserving relative order

F.3.4 Numerical Algorithms

Numerical algorithms include sums, inner product, and adjacent difference. For a code example, see Section 8.10.4, "Numerical Algorithms," on page 303 (in file stl_numr.cpp).

The library prototypes for numerical algorithms are as follows.

- ```
  template<class InputIter, class T>
  T accumulate(InputIter b, InputIter e, T t);
  ```

  This is a standard accumulation algorithm whose sum is initially t. The successive elements from the range b to e are added to this sum.

- ```
  template<class InputIter, class T, class BinOp>
  T accumulate(InputIter b, InputIter e, T t, BinOp bop);
  ```

  This is an accumulation algorithm whose sum is initially t. The successive elements from the range b to e are summed with sum = bop(sum, element).

We will use a table to briefly list other algorithms and their purpose as found in this library.

STL Numerical Library Functions	
`inner_product(b1, e1, b2, t)`	returns the inner product from the two ranges starting with `b1` and `b2`; this product is initialized to `t`, which is usually zero
`inner_product(b1,e1,b2,t,bop1,bop2)`	returns a generalized inner product using `bop1` to sum and `bop2` to multiply
`partial_sum(b1, e1, b2)`	produces a sequence starting at `b2` that is the partial sum of terms from the range `b1` to `e1`
`partial_sum(b1, e1, b2, bop)`	as above, using `bop` for summation
`adjacent_difference(b1, e1, b2)`	produces a sequence starting at `b2` that is the adjacent difference of terms from the range `b1` to `e1`
`adjacent_difference(b1, e1, b2, bop)`	as above, using `bop` for difference

F.4 Functions

It is useful to have function objects to further leverage the STL library. For example, many of the previous numerical functions had a built-in meaning using + or *, but also had a form in which user-provided binary operators could be passed in as arguments. Defined function objects can be found in *function* or built. Function objects are classes that have `operator()` defined. These are inlined and are compiled to produce efficient object code. For a code example, see Section 8.11, "Functions," on page 305 (in file stl_fucn.cpp).

There are three defined function object classes.

STL Defined Function Object Classes

- Arithmetic objects
- Comparison objects
- Logical objects

We will use tables to briefly list algorithms and their purpose as found in this library.

STL Arithmetic Objects

`template <class T> struct plus<T>`	adds two operands of type T
`template <class T> struct minus<T>`	subtracts two operands of type T
`template <class T> struct times<T>`	multiplies two operands of type T
`template <class T> struct divides<T>`	divides two operands of type T
`template <class T> struct modulus<T>`	modulus for two operands of type T
`template <class T> struct negate<T>`	unary minus for one argument of type T

Arithmetic objects are often used in numerical algorithms, such as `accumulate()`.

STL Comparison Objects

`template <class T> struct equal_to<T>`	equality of two operands of type T
`template <class T> struct not_equal_to<T>`	inequality of two operands of type T
`template <class T> struct greater<T>`	comparison by the greater (>) of two operands of type T
`template <class T> struct less<T>`	comparison by the lesser (<) of two operands of type T
`template <class T> struct greater_equal<T>`	comparison by the greater or equal (>=) of two operands of type T
`template <class T> struct less_equal<T>`	comparison by the lesser or equal (<=) of two operands of type T

The comparison objects are frequently used with sorting algorithms, such as `merge()`.

STL Logical Objects

`template <class T> struct logical_and<T>`	performs logical and (&&) on two operands of type T
`template <class T> struct logical_or<T>`	performs logical or (||) on two operands of type T
`template <class T> struct logical_not<T>`	performs logical negation (!) on a single argument of type T

F.4.1 Function Adaptors

Function adaptors allow for the creation of function objects using adaption. For a code example, see Section 8.12, "Function Adaptors," on page 306 (in file stl_adap.cpp).

STL Function Adaptors

- Negators for negating predicate objects
- Binders for binding a function argument
- Adaptors for pointer to a function

We will use a table to briefly list algorithms and their purpose as found in this library.

STL Function Adaptors	

`template<class Pred>`
`unary_negate<Pred>`
`not1(const Pred& p)`
	returns `!p` where p is a unary predicate

`template<class Pred>`
`binary_negate<Pred>`
`not2(const Pred& p)`
	returns `!p` where p is a binary predicate

`template<class Op, class T>`
`binder1st<Op>bind1st`
`   (const Op& op,const T& t)`
	the binary op has a first argument bound to t; a function object is returned

`template<class Op, class T>`
`binder2nd<Op>bind2nd`
`   (const Op& op,const T& t)`
	the binary op has a second argument bound to t; a function object is returned

`template<class Arg,class T>` `ptr_fun(T (*f)(Arg))`	constructs a `pointer_to_unary_function<Arg, T>`

`template<class Arg1,`
`   class Arg2, class T>`
`ptr_fun(T (*f)(Arg1, Arg2))`
	constructs a `pointer_to_binary_function<Arg,T>`

F.5 Allocators

Allocator objects manage memory for containers. They allow implementations to be tailored to local system conditions while maintaining a portable interface for the container class.

Allocator definitions include: `value_type`, `reference`, `size_type`, `pointer`, and `difference_type`.

We will use a table to briefly list allocator member functions and their purpose as found in this library.

STL Allocator Members	
`allocator();` `~allocator();`	constructor and destructor for allocators
`pointer address(reference r);`	returns the address of r
`pointer allocate(size_type n);`	allocates memory for n objects of `size_type` from free store
`void deallocate(pointer p);`	deallocates memory associated with p
`size_type max_size();`	returns the largest value for `difference_type`; in effect, the largest number of element allocatable to a container

Check your vendor's product for specific system-dependent implementations.

F.6 String Library

C++ provides a string type by including the standard header file *string*. It is the instantiation of a template class `basic_string<T>` with `char`. The string type provides member functions and operators that perform string manipulations, such as concatenation, assignment, or replacement. An example of a program using the string type for simple string manipulation follows.

In file stringt.cpp

```cpp
//String class to rewrite a sentence
#include <iostream>
#include <string>
using namespace std;

int main()
{
    string sentence, words[10];
    int pos = 0, old_pos = 0, nwords, i = 0;

    sentence = "Eskimos have 23 ways to ";
    sentence += "describe snow";

    while (pos < sentence.size()) {
        pos = sentence.find(' ', old_pos);
        words[i++].assign(sentence, old_pos, pos - old_pos);
        cout << words[i - 1] << endl;          //print words
        old_pos = pos + 1;
    }
    nwords = i;
    sentence = "C++ programmers ";
    for (i = 1; i < nwords -1; ++i)
        sentence += words[i] + ' ';
    sentence += "windows";
    cout << sentence << endl;
}
```

The `string` type is used to capture each word from an initial sentence where the words are separated by the space character. The position of the space characters is computed by the `find()` member function. Then the `assign()` member function is used to select a substring from `sentence`. Finally, a new `sentence` is constructed using the overloaded assignment, `operator+=()`, and `operator+()` functions to perform assignments and concatenations.

We will describe the representation for a string of characters. It is also usual to have the instantiation `basic_string<wchar_t>` for a wide string type `wstring`. Other instantiations are possible as well.

String Private Data Members	
char* ptr	for pointing at the initial character
size_t len	for the length of the string
size_t res	for the currently allocated size, or, for an unallocated string, its maximum size

This implementation provides an explicit variable to track the string length; thus string length can be looked up in constant time, which is efficient for many string computations.

F.6.1 Constructors

Strings have seven public constructors, which makes it easy to declare and initialize strings from a wide range of parameters. Two of these provide conversions; namely a constructor on char* and a constructor on vector<char>.

String Constructor Members	
string()	default, creates an empty string
string(const char* p)	conversion constructor from a pointer to char
string(const vector<char>& v)	conversion constructor from the vector container
string(const string& str, size_t pos = 0, size_t n = npos)	copy constructor; npos is usually -1 and indicates no memory was allocated
string(size_t size, capacity cap)	a string of '\0' is constructed of size where capacity is an enumeration type whose enumerator is default_size; otherwise a string of length zero is constructed
string(const char* p, size_t n)	copy n characters where p is the base address
string(char c, size_t n = 1)	construct a string of n cs

These constructors make it quite easy to use the string type initialized from char* pointers, which is the traditional C method for working with strings. Also, many computations are readily handled as a vector of characters. This is also facilitated by the `string` interface.

F.6.2 Member Functions

Strings have some members that overload operators, as described in the next table.

String Overloaded Operator Members	
`string& operator=(const string& s)`	assignment operator
`string& operator=(const char* p)`	assigns a `char*` to a string
`string& operator=(const char c)`	assigns a `char c` to a string
`string& operator+=(const string&s)`	appends string s
`string& operator+=(const char* p)`	appends a `char*` to a string
`string& operator+=(const char c)`	appends a `char c` to a string
`operator vector<char>()const`	converts a string to a vector
`char operator[](size_t pos) const`	returns the character at pos
`char& operator[](size_t pos)`	returns the reference to the character at pos

There is an extensive set of public member functions that let you manipulate strings. In many cases these are overloaded to work with `string`, `char*`, and `char`. We will start by describing `append()`.

- `string& append(const string& s, size_t pos = 0, size_t n=npos);`

    Appends n characters starting at pos from s to the implicit string object.

    ```
    //example s1 "I am " s2 "7 years old"
    s1.append(s2);              // s1 " I am 7 years old"
    s2.append(s1,0,4);          //s2 "7 years old I am"
    ```

- `string& append(const char* p, size_t n);`
  `string& append(const char* p);`
  `string& append(char c, size_t n = 1);`

    In each case a `string` object is constructed using the constructor of the same signature and appended to the implicit `string` object.

- `string& assign(const string& s, size_t pos = 0, size_t n=npos);`

    Assigns n characters starting at pos from s to the implicit string object.

```
//example s1 " I am " s2 "7 years old"
s1.assign(s2);                          // s1 "7 years old"
```

The following signatures with the expected semantics are also overloaded:

```
string& assign(const char* p, size_t n);
string& assign(const char* p);
string& assign(char c, size_t n = 1);
```

- ```
  string& insert(size_t pos1, const string& str, size_t pos2 = 0,
                 size_t n = npos);
  ```

  The insert() function is an overloaded set of definitions that insert a string of characters at a specified position. It inserts n characters taken from str, starting with pos2, into the implicit string at position pos1.

  ```
  //example s1 " I am " s2 " 7 years old"
  s1.insert(2,s2);                        // s1 "I 7 years old am"
  ```

  The following signatures with the expected semantics are also overloaded:

  ```
  string& insert(size_t pos,const char* p, size_t n);
  string& insert(size_t pos, const char* p);
  string& insert(size_t pos, char c, size_t n = 1);
  ```

  The inverse function is remove().

- ```
  string& remove(size_t pos = 0, size_t n = npos);
  ```

  n characters are removed from the implicit string at position pos.

In the following table, we briefly describe further public string member functions.

String Members	
string& replace(pos1, n1, str, pos2 = 0, n2 = npos)	replaces at pos1 for n1 characters, the substring in str at pos2 of n2 characters

string& replace(pos,n,p,n2);
string& replace(pos,n,p);
string& replace(pos,n,c,rep = 1);
	replaces n characters at pos, using a char* p of n2 characters, or a char* p until null, or a character c repeated rep times

char get_at(pos) const;	returns character in position pos
void put_at(pos, c);	places c at position pos

String Members	
`size_t length() const;`	returns the string length
`const char* c_str() const;`	converts `string` to traditional `char*` representation
`const char* data() const;`	returns the base address of the string representation
`void resize(n, c);` `void resize(n);`	resizes the string to length n; the padding character c is used in the first function and the `eos()` character is used in the second
`void reserve(size_t res_arg);` `size_t reserve() const;`	returns the private member `res`; the first function resets this
`size_t copy(p, n, pos = 0) const;`	the implicit string starting at pos is copied into the `char*` p for n characters
`string substr(pos = 0, npos)const;`	a substring of n characters of the implicit string is returned

You can lexicographically compare two strings using `compare()`, a family of overloaded member functions.

- `int compare(const string& str, size_t pos = 0,`
  `           size_t n = npos) const;`

  Compares the implicit string starting at pos for n characters with str. Returns zero if the strings are equal; otherwise returns a positive or negative integer value indicating that the implicit string is greater or less than str lexicographically. The following signatures with the expected semantics are also overloaded:

  `int compare(const char* p, size_t pos, size_t n) const;`
  `int compare(const char* p, size_t pos) const;`
  `int compare(char c, size_t pos, size_t rep = 1) const;`

  Each signature specifies how the explicit string is constructed and then compared to the implicit string.

The final set of member functions perform a find operation. We will discuss one group and then summarize in a table the rest of this group of member functions.

- `size_t find(const string& str, size_t pos = 0) const;`

The string `str` is searched for in the implicit string starting at `pos`. If it is found, the position it is found at is returned; otherwise `npos` is returned, indicating failure.

The following signatures with the expected semantics are also overloaded:

```
size_t find(const char* p, size_t pos, size_t n)const;
size_t find(const char* p, size_t pos= 0) const;
size_t find(char c, size_t pos = 0) const;
```

Each signature specifies how the explicit string is constructed and then searched for in the implicit string. Further functions for finding strings and characters are briefly described in the following table.

String Find Members	

`size_t rfind(str, pos=npos) const;`
`size_t rfind(p, pos, n) const;`
`size_t rfind(p, pos=npos) const;`
`size_t rfind(c, pos=npos) const;`
	like `find()`, but scans the string backward for a first match

`size_t find_first_of`
`        (str, pos = 0) const;`
`size_t find_first_of`
`        (p, pos, n) const;`
`size_t find_first_of`
`        (p, pos = 0) const;`
`size_t find_first_of`
`        (c, pos = 0) const;`
	searches for the first character of any character in the specified pattern, either `str`, `char* p`, or `char c`

`size_t find_last_of`
`        (str, pos = npos) const;`
`size_t find_last_of`
`        (p, pos, n) const;`
`size_t find_last_of`
`        (p, pos= npos) const;`
`size_t find_last_of`
`        (c, pos = npos) const;`
	searches backward for the first character of any character in the specified pattern, either `str`, `char* p`, or `char c`

String Find Members	

`size_t find_first_not_of`
`       (str, pos = 0) const;`
`size_t find_first_not_of`
`       (p, pos, n) const;`
`size_t find_first_not_of`
`       (p, pos = 0) const;`
`size_t find_first_not_of`
`       (c,pos = 0) const;`
	searches for the first character that does not match any character in the specified pattern, either `str`, `char* p`, or `char c`

`size_t find_last_not_of`
`       (str, pos = npos) const;`
`size_t find_last_not_of`
`       (p, pos, n) const;`
`size_t find_last_not_of`
`       (p, pos= npos) const;`
`size_t find_last_not_of`
`       (c,pos = npos) const;`
	searches backward for the first character that does not match any character in the specified pattern, either `str`, `char* p`, or `char c`

F.6.3 Global Operators

The string package contains operator overloadings that provide input/output, concatenation, and comparison operators. These are intuitively understandable and are briefly described in the following table.

String Overloaded Global Operators	
`ostream& operator<<(ostream& o,` `            const string& s);`	output operator
`istream& operator>>(istream& in,` `            string& s);`	input operator
`string operator+(const string& s1,` `            const string& s2);`	concatenates `s1` and `s2`
`bool operator==(const string& s1,` `            const string& s2);`	true if string `s1` and `s2` are lexicographically equal
`<   <=   >   >=   !=`	as expected

The comparison operators and the concatenation `operator+()` are also overloaded with the following four signatures:

```
bool operator==(const char* p, const string& s);
bool operator==(char c, const string& s);
bool operator==(const string& s, const char* p);
bool operator==(const string& s, char c);
```

In effect, a comparison or concatenation of any kind can occur between string and a second argument that is either a string, a character, or a character pointer.

References

Boehm, H., and M. Weiser, "Garbage Collection in an Uncooperative Environment," *Software—Practice and Experience.* September 1988. pp. 807-820.

Booch, G., *Object-Oriented Analysis and Design, Second Edition.* 1995. Reading, Mass.: Addison-Wesley.

Budd, T., *An Introduction to Object-Oriented Programming.* 1991. Reading, Mass.: Addison-Wesley.

Edelson, D., "A Mark and Sweep Collector for C++," in *Proceedings of Principles of Programming Languages.* January 1992.

Edelson, D., and I. Pohl, "A Copying Collector for C++," in *Usenix C++ Conference Proceedings.* 1991. pp. 85-102.

Ellis, M., and B. Stroustrup, *The Annotated C++ Reference Manual.* 1990. Reading, Mass.: Addison-Wesley.

Gamma, E., et al., *Design Patterns: Elements of Reusable Object-Oriented Software.* 1995. Reading, Mass.: Addison-Wesley.

Glass, G., and B. Schuchert, *The STL <Primer>.* 1996. Upper Saddle River, N.J.: Prentice Hall.

Kelley, A., and I. Pohl, *A Book on C, Third Edition.* 1995. Reading, Mass.: Addison-Wesley.

Kernighan, B., and P. Plauger, *The Elements of Programming Style.* 1974. New York: McGraw-Hill.

Kernighan, B., and D. Ritchie, *The C Programming Language, Second Edition.* 1988. Englewood Cliffs, N.J.: Prentice Hall.

Linton, M., J. Vlissides, and P. Calder, "Composing user interfaces with InterViews," IEEE *Computer* v. 22, no. 2, pp. 8-22, 1989.

Lippman, S., *The C++ Primer, Second Edition.* 1991. Reading, Mass.: Addison-Wesley.

Meyers, S., *Effective C++: 50 Specific Ways to Improve your Programs and Designs.* 1992. Reading, Mass.: Addison-Wesley.

Musser, D. and A. Saini, *STL Tutorial and Reference Guide: C++ Programming with the Standard Template Library.* 1996. Reading, Mass.: Addison-Wesley.

Pohl, I., *C++ for C Programmers, Second Edition.* 1994. Reading, Mass.: Addison-Wesley.

Pohl, I., *C++ for Pascal Programmers, Second Edition.* 1995. Reading, Mass.: Addison-Wesley.

Pohl, I. and D. Edelson, "A-Z: C Language Shortcomings," *Computer Languages*, vol. 13, no. 2. 1988. pp. 51-64.

Stroustrup, B., *The C++ Programming Language, Second Edition.* 1991. Reading, Mass.: Addison-Wesley.

Stroustrup, B., *The Design and Evolution of C++.* 1994. Reading, Mass.: Addison-Wesley.

Taligent Inc., *Taligent's Guide to Designing Programs: Well-Mannered Object-Oriented Design in C++.* 1994. Reading, Mass.: Addison-Wesley.

Teale, S., *C++ IO Streams Handbook.* 1993. Reading, Mass.: Addison-Wesley.

Wasserman, A., P. Pircher, and R. Muller, "The Object-Oriented Structured Design Notation for Software Design Representation," IEEE *Computer* v. 23, no. 3, 1990. pp. 50-63.

Index

Symbols

! negation operator, 43, 423
!= not equal operator, 43, 423
% modulus operator, 422
& address operator, 46, 85, 139, 427
& and (bitwise) operator, 46, 426
&& and (logical) operator, 43, 423
() function call operator, 46, 208, 219
() parentheses, 46, 430
* dereferencing or indirection operator, 46, 86, 94, 304, 427, 430
++ autoincrement operator, 47, 208-210, 422, 448
, comma operator, 45, 425
-- autodecrement operator, 47, 208, 422, 448
-> smart pointer operator, 241
-> structure pointer operator, 119, 208, 222
. member operator, 9, 119, 208
.* member object selector operator, 208, 224, 448, 454
/* */ comment pair, 6, 24, 404
// comment, 6, 24, 404
:: scope resolution operator, 121, 125, 208, 410, 412, 414, 429, 446, 448, 450, 466
; semicolon, 431-432
< less than operator, 43, 423
<< left shift operator, 16, 46, 426
<< put to operator, 30, 218, 469-470, 474
<= less than or equal operator, 43, 423
<> angle bracket, 18
= assignment operator, 44, 47
== equal operator, 43, 423
> greater than operator, 43, 423
>= greater than or equal operator, 43, 423
>> get from operator, 30, 218, 475
>> right shift operator, 46, 426
?: conditional expression operator, 45, 208, 420, 425, 448
[] indexing or subscripting operator, 46, 96, 208, 430
\ backslash, 27-28, 407
\" double quote, 28, 407
\' single quote, 28, 407
\0 end-of-string sentinal, 27-28, 161, 371, 407
^ exclusive or (bitwise) operator, 46, 426
^ unary one's complement operator, 426
{} braces, 48, 137, 431-433
| or (bitwise) operator, 46, 426
|| or (logical) operator, 43, 423
~ complement operator, 46
~ destructor, 151
->* pointer to member operator, 208, 224, 454
0 null pointer, 172

A

\a alert, 28, 407
AB_file program, 112
abort(), 359, 465
abstract base class, 16, 328, 340, 454
abstract class, 328
abstract data type, xv, 2, 7, 370, 372
Abstract_Base class, 340
abstraction, 372
acc_mod program, 343
access, 124, 144
access keywords
    private, 123-124, 144, 316, 444, 446, 451
    protected, 144, 316, 444, 446, 451
    public, 123, 145, 316-317, 444, 446, 451
accessor function, 145, 157

Index

`accumulate()` (STL), 20, 248, 287-288, 303-304, 503
Actor, 1
ad hoc polymorphism, 199, 374
Ada, 370, 375, 383
adapter pattern, 453
adaptor (STL)
    container, 295
    function, 306
    iterator, 298
`add_term()`, 182
add3 program, 71
`add3()`, 72
address operator &, 46, 85, 139, 427
`address()` (STL), 507
`adjacent_difference()` (STL), 504
`adjacent_find()` (STL), 499
ADT, xv, 2, 7, 370, 372
    binary tree, 321
    clock, 208, 211, 231
    complex, 8-12, 125
    list, 171, 257-258
    matrix, 176, 206, 220, 276
    point, 121-124, 132-133, 156
    polynomial, 178, 216-217
    shape, 16, 327
    stack, 17, 140, 142, 144, 157, 160, 256, 270
    string, 100, 161, 185, 252
    student, 13-14, 316
    template binary search tree, 283
    template stack, 17, 270
    template vector, 277
    vector, 167, 170, 206, 213, 230, 246, 278, 356
alert \a, 28, 407

ALGOL, 383
algorithm (STL), 19, 287, 299, 487, 496
    mutating sequence, 302
    nonmutating sequence, 301
    numerical, 303
    sorting, 300
alias, 89
`allocate()` (STL), 507
allocator object (STL), 507
ancestor, 337
and (bitwise) operator &, 46, 426
AND (Fortran), 399
and (logical) operator &&, 43, 423
angle bracket <>, 18
anonymous enumeration, 42
anonymous namespace, 85
anonymous structure, 119
anonymous union, 138, 187, 415
ANSI C++, xvii
`append()`, 510
aprint program, 96
`area()`, 17
argument, 70
    default, 74, 441
    explicit, 134
    implicit, 134, 212
    return, 403
    template, 276, 457
arithmetic expression, 42, 422
arithmetic object (STL), 305
array, 65, 85, 95, 168, 401
    bounds, 167
    dynamic, 168
    element, 96
    index, 168
    initialization, 97, 102
    multidimensional, 101, 176
    passing to function, 99

    pointer to, 97
    subscript, 96
    two-dimensional, 176
array program, 458
array_tm program, 277
assert library, 103, 114, 351
`assert()`, 34
assertion, 102, 351-352, 403
`assign()`, 162, 186, 510-511
`assign_array` class, 277
assignment, 424, 433
    multiple, 30, 215, 222, 424
    pointer, 320
assignment operator =, 44, 47
assignment-compatible conversion, 70
associative container (STL), 487, 490
associativity, 43, 208, 391
`auto`, 80, 416
autodecrement operator --, 47, 208, 422, 448
autoincrement operator ++, 47, 208-210, 422, 448
automatic variables, 80
`average()`, 72
avg_arr program, 76
`avg_arr()`, 76
avg3 program, 72

B

\b backspace, 28, 407
`back()` (STL), 295, 492
`back_inserter()` (STL), 495
backslash \, 27-28, 407
backspace \b, 28, 407
Backus, J., xv, 2
`bad()`, 482
`bad_alloc`, 363

▼ Index   521

bad_alloc(), 430, 468
bad_cast, 342, 363, 455
bad_cast program, 363
bad_typeid, 342, 455
bandwagon effect, 370, 376
Base class, 341
base class, 13, 22, 315
basic_i program, 476
basic_o program, 470
begin() (STL), 20, 290, 489
bell program, 66
bellmult program, 67
BidiIter() (STL), 500
bidirectional iterator (STL), 493
binary operator overloading, 211
binary_search() (STL), 497
bind1st() (STL), 506
bind2nd() (STL), 306, 506
bisect(), 263
bit field, 139
bit manipulation operator, 46, 426
black box principle, 145, 372-374
block, 48, 78-80
    exit, 160, 188, 355
    scope, 79, 409
    structure, 31, 393, 431
bnode class, 283, 321
bool, 35, 44, 371, 414-415, 417, 423-424
braces {}, 48, 137, 431-433
break, 54, 432, 436-437
bubble program, 367
built-in type, 419, 447

C

C, 369-370, 375
c_str(), 512

call-by-reference, 87, 89, 400, 440
call-by-value, 31, 67, 87, 152, 159, 393, 439
call_ref program, 87
card class, 128, 473
carriage return \r, 28, 407
case, 57, 432, 436-437
CASE (Fortran), 398
CASE tools, 379
cast, 38, 155, 229, 417-419
    down, 341
cast conversion operator, 468
casts
    const_cast, 137, 418-419
    dynamic_cast, 418, 454, 468
    mutable, 137, 450, 468
    reinterpret_cast, 418-419
    static_cast, 418-419
    typeid, 341-342, 454-455, 468
catch, 352, 354, 357-358, 456, 464
catch handler, 358, 464
catch program, 358, 465
caux, 477
cctype library, 481
cerr, 30, 477
ch_stack class, 140, 142, 144, 157, 160
ch_stack program, 140-141, 157, 159-160
char, 34-35, 414, 467
CHARACTER (Fortran), 397
character constant, 407
checks library, 352
cin, 30, 475, 477
circle class, 16
circle(), 82
class, xv, 2, 7, 95, 117, 124, 316, 444, 451, 457
    abstract, 328
    abstract base, 16

base, 13, 22, 315, 451, 453
container, 17, 19, 245, 321, 378, 494
data member, 145
derived, 13, 317, 451, 453
friends, 251
global, 130
handler, 184
hierarchy, 13, 22, 327, 379
initialization, 9, 151-153
iterator (STL), 19, 382
mixin, 453
nested, 126, 411, 466
scope, 125, 409
template, 275
type, 415
virtual base, 338, 453
classes
    Abstract_Base, 340
    assign_array, 277
    Base, 341
    bnode, 283, 321
    card, 128, 473
    ch_stack, 140, 142, 144, 157, 160
    circle, 16
    clock, 208, 211, 231
    complex, 8, 10, 125
    convert_it, 309
    dbl_vect, 167, 206, 213, 230
    dbl_vect_error, 356
    dbl_vect_iterator, 237
    deck, 129, 474
    deque, 148
    Derived, 341
    empty, 330
    fox, 330
    fruit, 118
    functor, 166
    gen_tree, 284, 322
    grad_student, 14, 317
    grass, 330

classes (cont'd)
  iterator, 258
  list, 257
  listelem, 258
  living, 329
  matrix, 176, 206, 220, 276
  mod_int, 152
  my_string, 161, 185, 252
  pair_vect, 170
  pcard, 139
  pers_data, 187
  person, 137
  pips, 128, 473
  point, 118, 121-124, 132-133, 156
  polynomial, 178, 217
  pr_char, 154
  rabbit, 330
  rational, 202, 218
  rectangle, 16
  safe_char_stack, 335
  safe_stack, 336
  salary, 135
  set, 197
  shape, 16, 327
  slist, 171
  slistelem, 171
  smart_ptr_vect, 241
  square, 17
  stack, 17, 256, 270
  str, 131
  str_obj, 185, 252
  string_iterator, 253
  student, 14, 316
  suit, 150
  t_ptr, 223
  triple, 223
  type_info, 455
  vector, 246, 278
  word, 139
clear(), 482
client, 3, 8, 16, 199, 351, 364, 372
clock class, 208, 211, 231
clock program, 208, 211, 231
clog, 477
CLOS, 384
close(), 478
Clu, 1
cnt_char(), 159
COBOL, 370, 383
code reuse, 13, 315
coerce program, 276
coerce(), 276
coercion, 37, 374
comma expression, 425
comma operator ,, 45, 425
command program, 113
comment //, 6, 24, 404
comment pair /* */, 6, 24, 404
comp(), 284, 323
compare object (STL), 496
compare(), 512
comparison object (STL), 293, 305, 490, 492, 505
comparison operator (STL), 488
compatibility, 466
compiler, 468
complement operator ~, 46
completeness, 378
COMPLEX (Fortran), 397
complex class, 8, 10, 125
complex library, 3, 34, 85
complex program, 8, 10-11, 125, 447
complexity, 4, 383
compound statement, 48, 433
concat(), 162
conditional expression operator ?:, 45, 208, 420, 425, 448
const, 40, 82, 101, 133-134, 137, 145, 154, 157, 408-409, 416, 418, 449-450, 468
const member function, 133
const-correctness, 134
const_cast, 137, 418-419
constant, 26
  character, 407
  enumeration, 408, 413
  floating-point, 406-407
  long, 406
  string, 407
  unsigned, 406
constructor, 9-10, 151-152, 318, 444, 446
  conversion, 154, 189, 419, 446
  copy, 159, 163, 186, 189, 445
  default, 153, 444
  explicit, 154, 168, 189, 278, 446
  initialization, 188, 453
  initializer, 154, 445
  invocation, 453
  order, 338
container (STL), 287-289, 487-488
  adaptor, 295, 491
  associative, 288, 293
  deque, 288-290, 295
  list, 288, 290, 295
  map, 288, 293
  members, 290, 489
  multimap, 288, 293
  multiset, 288, 293
  priority_queue, 295
  queue, 295
  sequence, 288, 290
  set, 288, 293
  stack, 295
  vector, 288, 290, 295
container class, 17, 19, 245, 321, 378, 494
continue, 54, 432, 436
conversion, 199, 318
  ADT, 200
  assignment-compatible, 70

▼ Index 523

cast operators, 468
constructor, 154, 189, 419, 446
  explicit, 38, 200, 417-418
  function, 154
  implicit, 38, 155, 417-418
  narrowing, 38, 43
  rules, 422
  traditional, 37
  trivial, 230
  widening, 38, 43
convert(), 309
convert_it class, 309
Conway's "Game of Life", 329
copy constructor, 159, 163, 186, 189, 445
copy program, 272-273
copy(), 272-273, 302, 512
copy() (STL), 302-303, 500
copy_backward() (STL), 303, 500
count() (STL), 491, 499
count_if() (STL), 499
cout, 30, 477
cprn, 477
CRC notecard, 379
cstddef library, 297, 494
cstdio library, 30
cstring library, 94, 100, 109, 161
ctype library, 469, 481-482
cubes program, 111

D

DAG, 337, 453
dangling else, 434
data hiding, 2-3, 7, 21, 123, 145-146, 372
data member, 444
data(), 512
dbl_sp program, 479
dbl_vect class, 167, 206, 213, 230
dbl_vect program, 167, 213, 353, 360
dbl_vect_error class, 356
dbl_vect_iterator class, 237
deal(), 129
deallocate() (STL), 507
deallocation, 9, 151
dec, 472
deck class, 129, 474
declaration, 25, 36, 403
  global, 412
  statement, 409-410, 438, 467
  template, 457
declarations, 37
  const, 40, 82, 101, 133-134, 137, 145, 154, 157, 408-409, 416, 418, 449-450, 468
  typedef, 120, 409, 413, 416
  volatile, 230, 416
deep copy semantics, 164
def_args program, 74
default, 57, 432, 436-437
default argument, 74, 441
default constructor, 153, 444
deferred method, 328
#define, 77, 96, 409
definition, 36
del(), 172
dele(), 333
delete, 104, 151, 160, 208, 226, 228, 427-429, 445
demotion, 38
deque (STL), 487, 489, 491-492
deque class, 148
deque program, 290

dereferencing or indirection operator *, 46, 86, 94, 304, 427, 430
Derived class, 341
derived class, 13
deriving, 23, 315, 451
design, 339, 378, 382
destructor, 9, 151, 160, 188, 444, 446
diagrams, 379
directed acyclic graph(DAG), 337, 453
directive, 403, 408
dissections
  add3, 72
  dynarray, 106
  matrix, 221
  my_string, 163
  operator+(), 12
  operator=(), 215
  order, 88
  print() and release(), 173
  rational, 203
  salary, 136
  showhide, 225
  stl_vect, 291
divide-and-conquer, 248
do, 53, 55, 432, 435
DO (Fortran), 398
do_test program, 54
double, 34-35, 414
double quote \", 28, 407
double underscore, 405
double_space(), 479
doubly linked list, 257
downcast, 341
dynamic data structure, 86
dynamic storage allocation, 9
dynamic_cast, 341, 418, 454, 468
dynarray program, 105

E

Eiffel, 1, 384
element of array, 96
`element()`, 177
ellipsis, 358, 465
Ellis, M., 375
`else`, 49, 432-433
ELSE (Fortran), 398
empty class, 330
empty parameter list, 70
`empty()` (STL), 290, 295, 489, 492
encapsulation, 3, 7, 21, 125, 372, 376
`end()` (STL), 20, 290-291, 489
end-of-string sentinel \0, 27-28, 161, 371, 407
`endl`, 31, 472
`ends`, 472
`enum`, 41, 408
enum_tst program, 42
enumeration, 41, 411, 467
  anonymous, 42
  constant, 408, 413
  type, 41
EOF, 475, 482
`eof()`, 482
equal operator ==, 43, 423
`equal()` (STL), 500
`equal_range()` (STL), 491, 497
equality operator (STL), 488
equality operators, 43, 423
`erase()` (STL), 292, 294, 489, 491
error condition, 351
except library, 359
except program, 362
exception, 20, 342, 351, 455
  handler, 20, 358, 461, 464
  specification, 359, 465
exception library, 363
exceptions
  `catch`, 352, 354, 357-358, 456, 464
  `throw`, 352, 354-355, 358-359, 462, 465
  `try`, 355, 357-358, 432, 463
exclusive or (bitwise) operator ^, 46, 426
`explicit`, 154, 168, 189, 278, 446
explicit argument, 134
explicit conversion, 38, 200, 418
expression, 42
  address, 427
  arithmetic, 42, 422
  assignment, 47, 424, 433
  bit manipulation, 46, 426
  comma, 425
  conversion, 37
  equality, 43, 423
  evaluation, 423
  indirection, 427
  infix, 207
  logical, 423
  mixed, 37
  relational, 423
  statement, 433
  throw, 462
extensibility, 7, 23, 376-377
`extern`, 81, 413, 416, 467
extraction, 475

F

\f formfeed, 28, 407
f(), 83
`fact()`, 485
`fail()`, 482
`false`, 44, 415, 423
fault-tolerant, 365
figures
  CRC Card, 380
  IDE Design Template, 382
  Inheritance Structure, 15
  Multiple Inheritance, 338
  Philosopher's Chairs, 377
  Pointer Declarations, 90
  Polymorphic Genie, 269
  Polynomial Prepend, 180
  Quicksort Partitioning, 250
  Singly Linked List, 172
  Wasserman-Pircher Diagram, 381
file, 477
file modes, 478
file scope, 78, 84, 130, 409, 443
`fill()` (STL), 502
finalization, 9, 384
`find()`, 285, 322, 508, 513
`find()` (STL), 301, 491, 499
`find_first_not_of()`, 514
`find_first_of()`, 513
`find_last_not_of()`, 514
`find_last_of()`, 513
`find_zero()`, 262
`first_element()`, 170
`float`, 35, 414
float library, 35
floating-point constant, 406-407
flow of control, 423
`flush`, 472
`flush()`, 470
`for`, 51, 55, 245, 410, 432, 434-435
`for_each()` (STL), 499
for_test program, 52, 55

forloop program, 435
formal parameter, 67, 94
formfeed \f, 28, 407
FORTRAN 77, xvii, 2
Fortran 90, xvii, 2, 7, 393
Fortran keywords
    AND, 399
    CASE, 398
    CHARACTER, 397
    COMPLEX, 397
    DO, 398
    ELSE, 398
    FUNCTION, 396, 400
    GO TO, 398
    IF, 398
    INTEGER, 397
    LOGICAL, 397
    NOT, 399
    OR, 399
    PROCEDURE, 400
    PROGRAM, 394
    REAL, 397
    RETURN, 398
    SAVE, 400
    TYPE, 396
    WHILE, 398
forward iterator (STL), 493
found_next_word(), 484
fox class, 330
free store, 9, 104, 151, 157, 226, 427-428
friend, 11, 185, 204, 207, 211-212, 229, 275, 439, 446, 460
front() (STL), 295, 492
front_inserter() (STL), 495
fruit class, 118
fstream, 63
fstream library, 63, 401, 477-478
function, 65, 403
    accessor, 145, 157
    adaptor (STL), 306, 506
    argument, 70
    call, 430

call operator (), 46, 208, 219
call-by-reference, 87, 89, 400, 440
call-by-value, 31, 67, 87, 152, 159, 393, 439
characteristics, 456
const member, 133
conversion, 154
declaration, 439
default argument, 74, 441
definition, 34, 66
exit, 161, 188
friend, 11, 185, 204, 207, 211-212, 229, 275, 439, 446, 460
header, 66
inline, 40-41, 77, 121-122, 413, 439, 441, 446
invocation, 66
member, 11, 118, 121, 420, 446
mutator, 145, 157
nested, 355
object (STL), 304, 504
overloading, 76, 274, 325-326, 441, 467
overridden, 455
overridden virtual, 325
parameter, 67, 70, 94
passing array to, 99
prototype, 70, 72, 409, 440
pure virtual, 16, 328, 454
scope, 409
selection, 201
signature, 15, 442
signature matching, 77, 230, 274, 442
static member, 133, 276
STL, 304, 504
syntax, 467
template, 272, 459

virtual, 324, 327, 439, 453-455
FUNCTION (Fortran), 396, 400
function library (STL), 304-305, 504
functions
    abort(), 359, 465
    add_term(), 182
    add3(), 72
    append(), 510
    area(), 17
    assert(), 34
    assign(), 162, 186, 510-511
    average(), 72
    avg_arr(), 76
    bad(), 482
    bad_alloc(), 430, 468
    bisect(), 263
    c_str(), 512
    circle(), 82
    clear(), 482
    close(), 478
    cnt_char(), 159
    coerce(), 276
    comp(), 284, 323
    compare(), 512
    concat(), 162
    convert(), 309
    copy(), 272-273, 302, 512
    data(), 512
    deal(), 129
    del(), 172
    dele(), 333
    double_space(), 479
    element(), 177
    eof(), 482
    f(), 83
    fact(), 485
    fail(), 482
    find(), 285, 322, 508, 513
    find_first_not_of(), 514
    find_first_of(), 513

functions (cont'd)
  find_last_not_of(), 514
  find_last_of(), 513
  find_zero(), 262
  first_element(), 170
  flush(), 470
  found_next_word(), 484
  gcd(), 32, 110, 395
  get(), 476
  get_at(), 511
  getline(), 476
  good(), 482
  greater(), 92
  heap_exhausted(), 229
  how_many(), 126
  init(), 19, 271, 333
  init_deck(), 129
  insert(), 285, 322, 511
  isalnum(), 481
  isalpha(), 481
  isascii(), 481
  iscntrl(), 481
  isdigit(), 481
  isgraph(), 481
  islower(), 481
  isprint(), 481
  ispunct(), 481
  isspace(), 254, 481
  isupper(), 481
  isxdigit(), 481
  length(), 512
  main(), 34, 66, 403
  max(), 79
  maxelement(), 309, 461
  memcpy(), 114, 255
  mpy(), 206
  name(), 455
  next(), 331-332
  open(), 478
  operator, 247, 253, 259
  operator double(), 201
  operator new(), 429
  operator(), 220, 238
  operator*(), 212
  operator+(), 11, 211, 216, 508
  operator++(), 210, 259, 264
  operator+=(), 221, 508
  operator->(), 223
  operator<<(), 219, 448, 474-475
  operator=(), 215, 218, 221, 229, 280
  operator>>(), 247
  operator[](), 214, 279
  operator-(), 211
  order(), 87, 90-91, 103
  partition(), 249, 282
  place_min(), 103
  plot(), 75, 166
  plus(), 122, 183
  pr_deck(), 474
  prepend(), 172
  print(), 11, 19, 93, 173, 286-287, 299, 306, 319, 323-324
  printf(), 71
  push_front(), 260
  put(), 470
  put_at(), 511
  quicksort(), 248-249, 281
  rdstate(), 482
  read(), 476
  release(), 173, 261
  replace(), 511
  reserve(), 512
  reset(), 231
  resetiosflags(), 472
  resize(), 512
  rest_of(), 183
  reverse(), 18, 179, 271
  rfind(), 513
  ring(), 66-67
  search(), 371
  second_element(), 170
  set_new_handler(), 430, 462
  set_terminate(), 359, 465
  set_unexpected(), 359, 466
  setbase(), 472
  setfill(), 472
  setiosflags(), 472
  setprecision(), 472
  setw(), 472
  shuffle(), 129
  sqr_or_power(), 74
  strcmp(), 100-101
  strcpy(), 100-101, 164
  streq(), 109
  strlen(), 100-101, 110
  sub_str(), 188
  substr(), 512
  successor(), 254
  sum(), 99, 289
  sum_of_squares(), 68
  sums(), 329
  swap(), 238, 251, 274-275, 459
  terminate(), 358-359, 465
  throw(), 480
  tick(), 209
  toascii(), 482
  tolower(), 482
  toupper(), 482
  unexpected(), 359, 465
  update(), 333
  word(), 254
  write(), 470
  xalloc(), 468
functor class, 166

G

garbage collection, 184, 384
gcd program, 31-32, 394-395
`gcd()`, 32, 110, 395
`gen_tree` class, 284, 322
`generate()` (STL), 502
`generate_n()` (STL), 502
generic pointer, 94, 254, 283, 321, 415, 417, 467
generic programming, 269, 274
genstack program, 256
gentree program, 283, 286, 321, 323
get from operator >>, 30, 218, 475
`get()`, 476
`get_at()`, 511
`getline()`, 476
global, 81
    class, 130
    data object, 467
    declaration, 412
    function, 403
    scope, 409
GO TO (Fortran), 398
`good()`, 482
goto, 58, 431-432, 437, 467
goto_tst program, 58
`grad_student` class, 14, 317
`grass` class, 330
greater than operator >, 43, 423
greater than or equal operator >=, 43, 423
`greater()`, 92

H

handler, 20, 352, 358, 456, 461, 464
    class, 184

HASA relationship, 170, 339, 380
`heap_exhausted()`, 229
hello program, 5-6
`hex`, 472
hidden member, 204
hierarchy, 13, 22, 379
higher dimensional array, 176
Hoare, A., 248
how_many program, 126
`how_many()`, 126

I

I/O library, 30, 469
I/O manipulators, 472
ICON, 378
identifier, 26, 396, 405
`if`, 48, 410, 420, 432-433
IF (Fortran), 398
if-else, 48, 433-434
if_test program, 48-50
ifstream, 478
implementation inheritance, 321
implicit argument, 134, 212
implicit conversion, 38, 155, 417-418
`#include`, 408
`includes()` (STL), 498
inclusion, 374
indexing or subscripting operator [], 46, 96, 208, 430
infix expression, 207
inheritance, 2-3, 13, 22, 373
    implementation, 321
    interface, 317
    multiple, 336, 339, 452
    public, 14
    single, 339
    template, 334
    virtual, 337
`init()`, 19, 271, 333

`init_deck()`, 129
initialization, 36, 83, 97, 444
    array, 97, 102
    class, 9, 151-153
    constructor, 188, 453
    memberwise, 159
initializer list, 154, 445
`inline`, 40-41, 77, 121-122, 413, 439, 441, 446
inline program, 77
`inner_product()` (STL), 303-304, 504
inorder, 347
`inplace_merge()` (STL), 497
input, 30, 469
    iterator (STL), 296, 493
`insert()`, 285, 322, 511
`insert()` (STL), 292, 294, 489, 491
`inserter()` (STL), 495
insertion, 469
instantiation, 18, 269, 275, 460
`int`, 34-35, 414
INTEGER (Fortran), 397
interface, 145
interface inheritance, 317
InterViews, 373
invertibility, 378
io program, 30
iomanip library, 470, 472
iostream, xvii
iostream library, xvii, 6, 30, 34, 85, 253, 338, 403, 469, 471-472, 484
ISA relationship, 317, 321, 339, 380
`isalnum()`, 481
`isalpha()`, 481
`isascii()`, 481
`iscntrl()`, 481
`isdigit()`, 481
`isgraph()`, 481
`islower()`, 481

isprint(), 481
ispunct(), 481
isspace(), 254, 481
istream, 475
Istream_iterator (STL), 494
isupper(), 481
isxdigit(), 481
iter_swap() (STL), 501
iterator, 245, 247, 251, 257, 467
iterator (STL), 287-288, 296, 487, 493-494
   adaptor, 298, 494
   bidirectional, 296-297
   class, 19, 382
   forward, 296-297
   input, 296
   istream, 297-298
   ostream, 297-298
   output, 296
   random access, 296-297
iterator class, 258
iterator library (STL), 299

J

Java, 1

K

Kelley, A., xvi, 248
kernel language, 23, 65
key-based element (STL), 293
keywords, 25, 405
   auto, 80, 416
   bool, 35, 44, 371, 414-415, 417, 423-424
   break, 54, 432, 436-437
   case, 57, 432, 436-437
   catch, 352, 354, 357-358, 456, 464
   char, 34-35, 414, 467
   class, 117, 124, 316, 444, 451, 457

   const, 40, 82, 101, 133-134, 137, 145, 154, 157, 408-409, 416, 418, 449-450, 468
   const_cast, 137, 418-419
   continue, 54, 432, 436
   default, 57, 432, 436-437
   delete, 104, 151, 160, 208, 226, 228, 427-429, 445
   do, 53, 55, 432, 435
   double, 34-35, 414
   dynamic_cast, 341, 418, 454, 468
   else, 49, 432-433
   enum, 41, 408
   explicit, 154, 168, 189, 278, 446
   extern, 81, 413, 416, 467
   false, 44, 415, 423
   float, 35, 414
   for, 51, 55, 245, 410, 432, 434-435
   friend, 11, 185, 204, 207, 211-212, 229, 275, 439, 446, 460
   goto, 58, 431-432, 437, 467
   if, 48, 410, 420, 432-433
   if-else, 48, 433-434
   inline, 40-41, 77, 121-122, 413, 439, 441, 446
   int, 34-35, 414
   long, 34-35, 414
   long double, 414
   mutable, 137, 450, 468
   namespace, 6, 30, 83-84, 411-412
   new, 104, 151, 189, 208, 226, 427-430, 468
   operator, 11, 207

   private, 123-124, 144, 316, 444, 446, 451
   protected, 144, 316, 444, 446, 451
   public, 123, 145, 316-317, 444, 446, 451
   record, 95
   register, 80, 416
   reinterpret_cast, 418-419
   return, 68, 152, 432, 438
   short, 34-35, 414
   signed, 34
   signed char, 467
   sizeof, 35, 46, 208, 421
   static, 81-82, 130, 133, 137-138, 187, 376, 416, 449-450, 460
   static_cast, 418-419
   struct, 117-120, 124, 142, 316, 415, 444, 451
   switch, 54, 56, 410, 432, 436-437
   template, 17, 269-270, 456
   this, 132, 134, 229, 376, 447, 449, 467
   throw, 352, 354-355, 358-359, 462, 465
   true, 44, 415, 423
   try, 355, 357-358, 432, 463
   typedef, 120, 409, 413, 416
   typeid, 341-342, 454-455, 468
   union, 137, 139, 187
   unsigned, 34-35, 414
   using, 6, 84, 412
   virtual, 324, 327, 439, 453-455
   void, 93, 439, 467
   void*, 94, 254, 283, 321, 415, 417, 467

volatile, 230, 416
wchar_t, 34-35, 414
while, 50, 53, 55, 420, 432, 434

L

label, 58, 437
left shift operator <<, 16, 46, 426
length(), 512
less than operator <, 43, 423
less than or equal operator <=, 43, 423
lexicographical_compare() (STL), 498
libraries
    assert, 103, 114, 351
    cctype, 481
    checks, 352
    complex, 3, 34, 85
    cstddef, 297, 494
    cstdio, 30
    cstring, 94, 100, 109, 161
    ctype, 469, 481
    except, 359
    exception, 363
    float, 35
    fstream, 63, 401, 477-478
    function (STL), 304-305, 504
    iomanip, 470, 472
    iostream, xvii, 6, 30, 34, 85, 253, 338, 403, 469, 471-472, 484
    iterator (STL), 299
    limits, 35
    math, 382
    new, 227-228, 429-430
    numeric (STL), 288, 503
    signal, 352
    stddef, 94, 297, 494
    stdio, 30, 63, 71, 371, 469, 484
    stdlib, 147, 160, 227
    stream, 469
    string, 6, 94, 100, 161, 312, 371, 382
    strstream, 480
    time, 194
    type_info, 342, 455
library mixing, 484
LIKEA relationship, 321, 380
limits library, 35
linkage, 84, 443
linked list, 177
LISP, 1, 184, 370
list (STL), 487, 489, 491-492
list class, 257
list program, 257-258, 260, 264
listelem class, 258
lists
    Automatic Expression Conversion, 417
    Automatic Expression Conversion x op y, 37
    Benefits of Using a Derived Class, 318
    Black Box for the Client, 372
    Black Box for the Manufacturer, 372
    C++ Program Organization, 34, 403
    Call-by-reference Using Pointers, 88
    Copy Constructor Use, 163, 445
    Design Patterns in This Text, 383
    Effect of a switch, 57, 437
    Elements of a Design Pattern, 383
    Function Use in C++, 343
    List Operations, 172
    OOD Design Methodology, 316
    OOP Design Methodology, 13, 373
    OOP Language Has, 369
    Order of Constructor Execution, 338, 453
    Overloaded Function Selection Algorithm, 201, 275, 443, 460
    Some Differences Between C++ and Pascal, 33, 396
    Some Functions in the Library, 100
    STL Categories of Algorithms Library, 299, 496
    STL Defined Function Object Classes, 504
    STL Function Adaptors, 306, 506
    STL Iterator Adaptors, 298, 494
    STL Typical Container Interfaces, 288, 488
    Throw Expression Matches the Catch If It Is, 464
    Throw Expression Matches the Catch if It Is, 357
    Type Differences for ANSI C, 467
    Types of Polymorphism, 374
literal, 26
living class, 329
local scope, 40, 78
location, 85
logical, 423
LOGICAL (Fortran), 397
logical objects (STL), 305
logical operators, 43-44, 423
long, 34-35, 414
long constant, 406

`long double`, 414
loop, 54
`lower_bound()` (STL), 491, 497
lval program, 427
lvalue, 47, 168, 177, 230, 409, 424

M

machine addresses, 85
macro expansion, 77
`main()`, 34, 66, 403
`make_heap()` (STL), 498
manip program, 471
manipulator, 6, 31, 471
manufacturer, 102, 199, 351, 364, 372
map (STL), 487, 490
math library, 382
`matrix` class, 176, 206, 220, 276
matrix program, 176, 206, 220
`max()`, 79
`max()` (STL), 498
`max_element()` (STL), 498
`max_size()` (STL), 290, 489, 507
`maxelement()`, 309, 461
member, 95, 170
    data, 444
    function, 11, 118, 121, 420, 446
    hidden, 204
member object selector operator .*, 208, 224, 448, 454
member operator ., 9, 119, 208
memberwise copy, 187
memberwise initialization, 159
memcopy program, 255
`memcpy()`, 114, 255
memory location, 85

memory management
    delete, 104, 151, 160, 208, 226, 228, 427–429, 445
    new, 104, 151, 189, 208, 226, 427–430, 468
memory register, 80
`merge()` (STL), 497
merge-sort, 181
message, 7, 326
method, 7, 326
MI, 339
mi_to_k program, 39–40
`min()` (STL), 498
`min_element()` (STL), 498
`mismatch()` (STL), 499–500
mix_io program, 485
mixed expression, 37
mixin class, 453
mixing libraries, 484
mixing types, 43
`mod_int` class, 152
Modula-2, 370, 375
Modula-3, 375
modulo program, 152
modulus operator %, 422
Monte Carlo calculation, 128
month program, 256
`mpy()`, 206
multidimensional array, 101, 176
multifile program, 84, 413
multiline comment, 404
multimap (STL), 487, 490
multiple assignment, 30, 215, 222, 424
multiple inheritance, 336, 339, 452
multiset (STL), 487, 490
`mutable`, 137, 450, 468
mutable program, 137
mutator function, 145, 157
`my_string` class, 161, 185, 252

N

\n newline, 28, 407, 471
`name()`, 455
namespac program, 85
namespace
    anonymous, 85
    scope, 84, 270, 409
`namespace`, 6, 30, 83–84, 411–412
narrowing, 38, 43
native type, 23, 155, 199
need to know style, 125
negation operator !, 43, 423
nested class, 126, 411, 466
nested function, 355
nested program, 127
new, 104, 151, 189, 208, 226, 427–430, 468
new library, 227–228, 429–430
new_hdlr program, 229
newline \n, 28, 407, 471
newtyp program, 414
`next()`, 331–332
`next_permutation()` (STL), 498–499
nonmutating algorithm (STL), 499
NOT (Fortran), 399
not equal operator !=, 43, 423
`not1()` (STL), 506
`not2()` (STL), 506
`nth_element()` (STL), 497
null character \0, 27–28, 161, 371, 407
null pointer 0, 172
null statement, 48
numeric library (STL), 288, 503

O

object, xvi, 3, 9, 21, 122, 145, 151
object-oriented programming, xv, 1-2, 21, 369
Occam's razor, 378
oct, 472
ofstream, 478
one-dimensional array, 167
OOP, xv, 1-2, 21, 369
open(), 478
operator, 28, 420
   assignment overloading, 213
   associativity, 43, 208, 391, 420
   binary overloading, 211
   bit manipulation, 46, 426
   bit shift, 30
   equality, 43, 423
   logical, 43-44, 423
   overloading, 199, 207, 229, 447
   precedence, 43, 208, 391, 420
   relational, 43, 423
   subscript overloading, 213
   unary overloading, 208
`operator`, 11, 207, 247, 253, 259
`operator double()`, 201
`operator new()`, 429
`operator()`, 220, 238
`operator*()`, 212
`operator+()`, 11, 211, 216, 508
`operator++()`, 210, 259, 264
`operator+=()`, 221, 508
`operator->()`, 223
`operator<() `(STL), 295
`operator<<()`, 219, 448, 474-475
`operator=()`, 215, 218, 221, 229, 280
`operator==()` (STL), 295
`operator>>()`, 247
`operator[]()`, 214, 279
`operator-()`, 211
operators
   address &, 46, 85, 139, 427
   and (bitwise) &, 46, 426
   and (logical) &&, 43, 423
   assignment =, 44, 47
   autodecrement --, 47, 208, 422, 448
   autoincrement ++, 47, 208-210, 422, 448
   comma ,, 45, 425
   complement ~, 46
   conditional expression ?:, 45, 208, 420, 425, 448
   delete, 104, 151, 160, 208, 226, 228, 427-429, 445
   dereferencing or indirection *, 46, 86, 94, 304, 427, 430
   equal ==, 43, 423
   exclusive or (bitwise) ^, 46, 426
   function call (), 46, 208, 219
   get from >>, 30, 218, 475
   greater than >, 43, 423
   greater than or equal >=, 43, 423
   indexing or subscripting [], 46, 96, 208, 430
   left shift <<, 16, 46, 426
   less than <, 43, 423
   less than or equal <=, 43, 423
   member ., 9, 119, 208
   member object selector .*, 208, 224, 448, 454
   modulus %, 422
   `mutable`, 137, 450, 468
   negation !, 43, 423
   new, 104, 151, 189, 208, 226, 427-430, 468
   not equal !=, 43, 423
   or (bitwise) |, 46, 426
   or (logical) ||, 43, 423
   pointer to member ->*, 208, 224, 454
   put to <<, 30, 218, 469-470, 474
   right shift >>, 46, 426
   scope resolution ::, 121, 125, 208, 410, 412, 414, 429, 446, 448, 450, 466
   `sizeof`, 35, 46, 208, 421
   smart pointer ->, 241
   structure pointer ->, 119, 208, 222
   `typeid`, 341-342, 454-455, 468
   unary one's complement ^, 426
or (bitwise) operator |, 46, 426
OR (Fortran), 399
or (logical) operator ||, 43, 423
order program, 90-91, 103
`order()`, 87, 90-91, 103
orthogonality, 309, 379
ostream, 469
Ostream_iterator (STL), 494
out of bounds, 167
out of free store, 228
output, 30, 469
   iterator (STL), 296, 493
   user-defined, 473
over_new program, 228

overloading, 10, 374
  assignment, 213-214
  constructor, 153
  function, 76, 274, 325-326, 441, 467
  I/O operators, 218
  indexing, 219
  new, 428
  new and delete, 226
  operator, 199, 207, 229, 447
  operator, 11, 207
  subscript, 213-214
  template function, 461
override, 317, 324-325, 455

P

pair_vect class, 170
pairvect program, 170
parameter, 70
  formal, 67, 94
  template, 309
parametric polymorphism, 17, 269-270, 374, 456
parentheses (), 46, 430
partial_sort() (STL), 496
partial_sort_copy() (STL), 497
partial_sum() (STL), 504
partition(), 249, 282
partition() (STL), 503
Pascal, 370, 375, 384
pcard class, 139
pers_data class, 187
person class, 137
pips class, 128, 473
PL/1, 370, 383
place_min(), 103
placement, 227
Platonism, 377
plot(), 75, 166
plus(), 122, 183
Pohl, I., xvi, 248

point class, 118, 121-124, 132-133, 156
point program, 121, 123-124, 132
pointer, 65, 85, 95, 320
  arithmetic, 98
  array, 97
  assignment, 320
  generic, 94, 254, 283, 321, 415, 417, 467
  null 0, 172
  operators, 222
  self-referential, 132, 447
  this, 132, 134, 229, 376, 447, 449, 467
  to class member, 224
  type, 65
  universal constant, 406
pointer to member operator ->*, 208, 224, 454
poker program, 128
poly program, 178, 217
polymorphism, 15, 334, 340, 374, 376
  ad hoc, 199, 374
  parametric, 17, 269, 374
  pure, 315, 324, 374
polynomial class, 178, 217
pop() (STL), 295, 492
pop_heap() (STL), 498
postcondition, 102, 351
postfix, 47, 422
pr_card program, 473-474
pr_char class, 154
pr_deck(), 474
precedence, 43, 208, 391
precondition, 102, 351
predator program, 329
prefix, 47, 422
preorder, 348
prepend(), 172
preprocessor, 6, 34, 403, 408
  #define, 77, 96, 409
  #include, 408

prev_permutation() (STL), 498-499
print(), 11, 19, 93, 173, 286-287, 299, 306, 319, 323-324
printabl program, 154
printf(), 71
priority_queue (STL), 491-492
private, 123-124, 144, 316, 444, 446, 451
PROCEDURE (Fortran), 400
prog program, 413
program
  correctness, 102, 351
  multifile, 413
  structure, 31, 393
PROGRAM (Fortran), 394
programs
  AB_file, 112
  acc_mod, 343
  add3, 71
  aprint, 96
  array, 458
  array_tm, 277
  avg_arr, 76
  avg3, 72
  bad_cast, 363
  basic_i, 476
  basic_o, 470
  bell, 66
  bellmult, 67
  bubble, 367
  call_ref, 87
  catch, 358, 465
  ch_stack, 140-141, 157, 159-160
  clock, 208, 211, 231
  coerce, 276
  command, 113
  complex, 8, 10-11, 125
  complexc, 447
  copy, 272-273
  cubes, 111
  dbl_sp, 479
  dbl_vect, 167, 213, 353, 360

def_args, 74
deque, 290
do_test, 54
dynarray, 105
enum_tst, 42
except, 362
for_test, 52, 55
forloop, 435
gcd, 31-32, 394-395
genstack, 256
gentree, 283, 286, 321, 323
goto_tst, 58
hello, 5-6
how_many, 126
if_test, 48-50
inline, 77
io, 30
list, 257-258, 260, 264
lval, 427
manip, 471
matrix, 176, 206, 220
memcopy, 255
mi_to_k, 39-40
mix_io, 485
modulo, 152
month, 256
mutable, 137
namespac, 85
nested, 127
new_hdlr, 229
newtyp, 414
order, 90-91, 103
over_new, 228
pairvect, 170
point, 121, 123-124, 132
poker, 128
poly, 178, 217-218
pr_card, 473-474
predator, 329
printabl, 154
prog, 413
quicksort, 281
rational, 202, 218
root, 75
salary, 135, 449

scope, 411
scope_t, 79
set, 139
shape, 16, 327
showhide, 224
sim_call, 92
slist, 171, 173-174
stack, 21
stack_p, 457
stack_t, 270-271, 335-336
stat_count, 112
stat_tst, 83
stcast, 419
stl_adap, 306
stl_age, 293
stl_cont, 287
stl_deq, 289
stl_find, 301
stl_fucn, 305
stl_iadp, 298
stl_io, 297
stl_list, 19, 287
stl_numr, 303
stl_revr, 302
stl_sort, 300
stl_stak, 296, 493
stl_vect, 290
str_func, 101
str_strm, 480
string, 161, 165, 184, 252-254, 508
student, 13, 316-319
sum_arr, 95, 98-99
sum_sq, 68-69
sum_sq_dbl, 70
swap, 274, 459
switch_t, 56
throw, 354-355
throw_it, 463
tracking, 187
triple, 223
tstack, 17
typeid, 342
union, 138
vect, 444
vect_bnd, 452

vect_ex, 462
vect_it, 278, 280
vect_ovl, 448
vectacum, 248
vector, 246-247
vectsort, 249
virt_err, 326
virt_sel, 325
voidcast, 93
weekend, 138
while_t, 50
word_cnt, 483
promotion, 38
`protected`, 144, 316, 444, 446, 451
prototype, 440
pseudotype, 370
`ptr_fun()` (STL), 506
`public`, 123, 145, 316-317, 444, 446, 451
public inheritance, 14
punctuator, 28
pure polymorphism, 315, 324, 374
pure virtual function, 16, 328, 454
`push()` (STL), 295, 492
`push_front()`, 260
`push_heap()` (STL), 497
put to operator <<, 30, 218, 469-470, 474
`put()`, 470
`put_at()`, 511

Q

queue (STL), 491-492
quicksort program, 281
`quicksort()`, 248-249, 281

R

\r carriage return, 28, 407
`rabbit` class, 330
random-access iterator (STL), 493-494

random_shuffle() (STL), 502-503
rational class, 202, 218
rational program, 202, 218
rbegin() (STL), 290, 489
rdstate(), 482
read(), 476
REAL (Fortran), 397
record, 95
rectangle class, 16
recursion, 281, 400
reference
    counting, 184
    declaration, 89
    semantics, 184
    type, 439
    variable, 85
register, 80, 416
reinterpret_cast, 418-419
relational expression, 423
relational operators, 43
release(), 173, 261
remove() (STL), 502
remove_copy() (STL), 502
remove_copy_if() (STL), 502
remove_if() (STL), 502
rend() (STL), 290, 489
replace(), 511
replace() (STL), 502
replace_copy() (STL), 502
replace_copy_if() (STL), 502
replace_if() (STL), 502
reserve(), 512
reset(), 231
resetiosflags(), 472
resize(), 512
rest_of(), 183
rethrow, 354-355, 463
return, 68, 152, 432, 438
RETURN (Fortran), 398
return argument, 403
return type, 67
reuse, 334, 373, 384
reverse(), 18, 179, 271
reverse() (STL), 302
reverse_copy() (STL), 501
revision process, 16
rfind(), 513
right shift operator >>, 46, 426
ring(), 66-67
Ritchie, D., 1
root program, 75
rotate() (STL), 502
rotate_copy() (STL), 502
run-time type identification (RTTI), 341, 363, 454, 468

S

safe dynamic array, 168
safe_char_stack class, 335
safe_stack class, 336
salary class, 135
salary program, 135, 449
SAVE (Fortran), 400
scope, 42, 78, 83, 85, 409, 412
    block, 79, 409
    class, 125, 409
    file, 78, 84, 130, 409, 443
    function, 409
    global, 409
    local, 40, 78
    namespace, 84, 270, 409
scope program, 411
scope resolution operator ::, 121, 125, 208, 410, 412, 414, 429, 446, 448, 450, 466
scope_t program, 79
search(), 371
search() (STL), 500
second_element(), 170
selection statement, 467
self-referential pointer, 132, 447
self-referential structure, 171
semicolon, 431-432
semicolon terminator, 47
sequence algorithm (STL), 500
sequence container (STL), 487, 489
set (STL), 487, 490
set class, 197
set program, 139
set_difference() (STL), 498
set_intersection() (STL), 498
set_new_handler(), 430, 462
set_symmetric_difference() (STL), 498
set_terminate(), 359, 465
set_unexpected(), 359, 466
set_union() (STL), 498
setbase(), 472
setfill(), 472
setiosflags(), 472
setprecision(), 472
setw(), 472
shallow copy, 160, 164, 187
shape class, 16, 327
shape program, 16, 327
short, 34-35, 414
short-circuit evaluation, 44, 423
showhide program, 224
shuffle(), 129
SI, 339
side effect, 48, 431
signal library, 352
signature, 15
signature matching, 77, 230, 274, 442
signed, 34

signed char, 467
sim_call program, 92
simple data type, 34, 397
simple derived type, 415
Simula 67, 1, 328, 370, 378
single inheritance, 339
single quote \', 28, 407
size() (STL), 290, 295, 489, 492
sizeof, 35, 46, 208, 421
slist class, 171
slist program, 171, 173-174
slistelem class, 171
Smalltalk, 1, 7, 184, 370, 384
smart pointer operator ->, 241
smart_ptr_vect class, 241
SNOBOL, 378
sort(), 20
sort() (STL), 288, 300, 496, 498
sort_heap() (STL), 498
sorting algorithm (STL), 496
special character, 407
specialization, 284
sqr_or_power(), 74
square class, 17
stable_partition() (STL), 503
stable_sort() (STL), 496
stack (STL), 491
stack class, 17, 256, 270
stack program, 21
stack_p program, 457
stack_t program, 270-271, 335-336
stat_count program, 112
stat_tst program, 83
statement, 47, 398
   compound, 48, 433
   declaration, 409-410, 438, 467
   expression, 42, 433

labeled, 58, 437
null, 48
return, 438
selection, 467
terminator, 431
terminator ;, 47
statements
   break, 54, 432, 436-437
   case, 57, 432, 436-437
   continue, 54, 432, 436
   default, 57, 432, 436-437
   do, 53, 55, 432, 435
   else, 49, 432-433
   for, 51, 55, 245, 410, 432, 434-435
   goto, 58, 431-432, 437, 467
   if, 48, 410, 420, 432-433
   if-else, 48, 433-434
   return, 68, 152, 432, 438
   switch, 54, 56, 410, 432, 436-437
   while, 50, 53, 55, 420, 432, 434
static, 81-82, 130, 133, 137-138, 187, 376, 416, 449-450, 460
static member, 130, 133, 276
static_cast, 418-419
stcast program, 419
stddef library, 94, 297, 494
stdio library, 30, 63, 71, 371, 469, 484
stdlib library, 147, 160, 227
stepwise refinement, 65
STL, 19, 269, 287
   adapted priority_queue, 492
   adapted queue function, 295, 492
   adapted stack function, 295, 492

algorithm, 19, 287, 299, 487, 496
algorithms library, 299, 496
allocator object, 507
arithmetic object, 305, 505
associative constructor, 294, 490
associative container, 288, 293, 487, 490
associative definition, 293, 490
bidirectional iterator, 296-297
comparison object, 293, 305, 490, 492, 505
comparison operator, 488
container, 287-289, 487
container adaptor, 295, 491
container definition, 289, 488
container member, 290, 489
container operator, 489
deque, 288-290, 295, 487, 489, 491-492
equality operator, 488
forward iterator, 296-297
function, 304, 504
function adaptor, 306, 506
function object, 304-305, 504
input iterator, 296
insert and erase, 294, 491
istream_iterator, 297-298, 494
iterator, 287-288, 296, 487, 493-494
   adaptor, 298, 494
   bidirectional, 493
   forward, 493

STL (cont'd)
    input, 493
    output, 493
    random-access, 493–494
  key, 293
  list, 288, 290, 295, 487, 489, 491–492
  list container, 288
  logical objects, 305, 505
  map, 288, 293, 487, 490
  member function, 491
  multimap, 288, 293, 487, 490
  multiset, 288, 293, 487, 490
  mutating sequence algorithm, 302, 500
  nonmutating algorithm, 499
  nonmutating sequence algorithm, 301
  numerical algorithm, 303
  ostream_iterator, 297–298, 494
  output iterator, 296
  priority_queue, 295, 491–492
  queue, 295, 491–492
  random access iterator, 296–297
  reverse_bidirectional_iterator, 495
  reverse_iterator, 495
  sequence container, 288, 290, 487
  sequence member, 292, 489
  set, 288, 293, 487, 490
  sort library function, 497
  sorting algorithm, 300, 496
  stack, 295, 491
  vector, 288, 290, 295, 487, 489, 491–492

STL functions
  accumulate(), 20, 248, 287–288, 303–304, 503
  address(), 507
  adjacent_difference(), 504
  adjacent_find(), 499
  allocate(), 507
  back(), 295, 492
  back_inserter(), 495
  begin(), 20, 290, 489
  BidiIter(), 500
  binary_search(), 497
  bind1st(), 506
  bind2nd(), 306, 506
  copy(), 302–303, 500
  copy_backward(), 303, 500
  count(), 491, 499
  count_if(), 499
  deallocate(), 507
  empty(), 290, 295, 489, 492
  end(), 20, 290–291, 489
  equal(), 500
  equal_range(), 491, 497
  erase(), 292, 294, 489, 491
  fill(), 502
  find(), 301, 491, 499
  for_each(), 499
  front(), 295, 492
  front_inserter(), 495
  generate(), 502
  generate_n(), 502
  includes(), 498
  inner_product(), 303–304, 504
  inplace_merge(), 497
  insert(), 292, 294, 489, 491
  inserter(), 495
  iter_swap(), 501
  lexicographical_compare(), 498
  lower_bound(), 491, 497
  make_heap(), 498
  max(), 498
  max_element(), 498
  max_size(), 290, 489, 507
  merge(), 497
  min(), 498
  min_element(), 498
  mismatch(), 499–500
  next_permutation(), 498–499
  not1(), 506
  not2(), 506
  nth_element(), 497
  operator<(), 295
  operator==(), 295
  partial_sort(), 496
  partial_sort_copy(), 497
  partial_sum(), 504
  partition(), 503
  pop(), 295, 492
  pop_heap(), 498
  prev_permutation(), 498–499
  ptr_fun(), 506
  push(), 295, 492
  push_heap(), 497
  random_shuffle(), 502–503
  rbegin(), 290, 489
  remove(), 502
  remove_copy(), 502
  remove_copy_if(), 502
  remove_if(), 502
  rend(), 290, 489
  replace(), 502
  replace_copy(), 502
  replace_copy_if(), 502
  replace_if(), 502
  reverse(), 302

reverse_copy(), 501
rotate(), 502
rotate_copy(), 502
search(), 500
set_difference(), 498
set_intersection(), 498
set_symmetric_difference(), 498
set_union(), 498
size(), 290, 295, 489, 492
sort(), 20, 288, 300, 496, 498
sort_heap(), 498
stable_partition(), 503
stable_sort(), 496
swap(), 290, 489, 501
swap_range(), 501
top(), 295, 492
transform(), 501-502
unique(), 501
unique_copy(), 501
upper_bound(), 491, 497
stl_adap program, 306
stl_age program, 293
stl_cont program, 287
stl_deq program, 289
stl_find program, 301
stl_fucn program, 305
stl_iadp program, 298
stl_io program, 297
stl_list program, 19, 287
stl_numr program, 303
stl_revr program, 302
stl_sort program, 300
stl_stak program, 296, 493
stl_vect program, 290
storage class, 78, 416
storage types
  auto, 80, 416
  extern, 81, 413, 416, 467
  register, 80, 416
  static, 81-82, 130, 133, 137-138, 187, 376, 416, 449-450, 460
str class, 131
str_func program, 101
str_obj class, 185, 252
str_strm program, 480
strcmp(), 100-101
strcpy(), 100-101, 164
stream library, 469
stream states, 482
streams
  caux, 477
  cerr, 30, 477
  cin, 30, 475, 477
  clog, 477
  cout, 30, 469, 477
  cprn, 477
streq(), 109
string, 85, 507
  ADT, 100, 161, 252
  constant, 407
  constructor, 509
  data member, 509
  find member, 513
  function member, 511
  global operator, 514
  literal, 26-27
  member function, 510
  overloaded operator, 510
  reference semantics, 184
  type, 161, 371
string library, 6, 94, 100, 161, 312, 371, 382
string program, 161, 165, 184, 252-254, 508
string_iterator class, 253
strlen(), 100-101, 110
Stroustrup, B., xv, 1, 117, 375
strstream library, 480
struct, 117-120, 124, 142, 316, 415, 444, 451
structure, 95
  anonymous, 119
  block, 31, 393
  member, 118
  program, 31, 393
structure pointer operator ->, 119, 208, 222
student class, 14, 316
student program, 13, 316-319
style
  divide-and-conquer, 248
  need to know, 125
  polymorphic, 369
sub_str(), 188
substr(), 512
subtype, 318, 340, 451
successor(), 254
suit class, 150
sum(), 99, 289
sum_arr program, 95, 98-99
sum_of_squares(), 68
sum_sq program, 68-69
sum_sq_dbl program, 70
sums(), 329
swap program, 274, 459
swap(), 238, 251, 274-275, 459
swap() (STL), 290, 489, 501
swap_range() (STL), 501
switch, 54, 56, 410, 432, 436-437
switch_t program, 56
symbol, 29
symbolic constant, 96

T

t_ptr class, 223
tab \t, 28, 407, 471
tables
    Arithmetic Expressions, 422
    Assignment Expressions, 425
    Autoincrement and Autodecrement, 422
    Bitwise Operators, 46, 426
    C++ Relational, Equality, and Logical Operators, 43
    Casts, 419
    Character Literals, 28, 407
    Constant Examples, 406
    Container Operators, 489
    ctype.h Functions, 481–482
    delete Operator, 428
    Enumeration Constants, 408
    Examples of Declarations of Arrays, 102
    Expressions in Pascal and C++, 399
    File Modes, 478
    Floating-Point Constant Examples, 407
    Function Characteristics, 456
    Function Declaration, 439
    Fundamental Data Types, 35, 414
    I/O Manipulators, 472
    Identifier Examples, 405
    Keywords, 25, 405
    Language Complexity, 375
    new Operator, 427
    Operator Precedence and Associativity, 391, 420
    Procedures and Functions in Pascal and C++, 400
    Relational, Equality, and Logical Operators, 423
    Standard Files, 477
    Statement Comparisons, 398
    Statements, 432
    Statements in Pascal and C++, 398
    STL Adapted priority_queue Functions, 492
    STL Adapted queue Functions, 295, 492
    STL Adapted stack Functions, 295, 492
    STL Allocator Members, 507
    STL Arithmetic Objects, 505
    STL Associative Constructors, 294, 490
    STL Associative Definitions, 293, 490
    STL Comparison Objects, 505
    STL Container Definitions, 289, 488
    STL Container Members, 290, 489
    STL Function Adaptors, 506
    STL Function Objects, 305
    STL Insert and Erase Member Functions, 294, 491
    STL Logical Objects, 505
    STL Member Functions, 491
    STL Mutating Sequence Library Functions, 501
    STL Nonmutating Sequence Library Functions, 499
    STL Numerical Library Functions, 504
    STL Sequence Members, 292, 489
    STL Sort Related Library Functions, 497
    Storage Class, 416
    Stream State Function, 482
    String Constant Examples, 408
    String Constructor Members, 509
    String Find Members, 513
    String Members, 511
    String Overloaded Global Operators, 514
    String Overloaded Operator Members, 510
    String Private Data Members, 509
    Structured Types in Pascal and C++, 401
    Summing Elements of an Array, 99
    Trivial Conversions, 230
    Typedefs, 409
    Types, 415
    Using the const Keyword, 408
tag name, 41, 119
template, 269, 334
    argument, 276, 457
    declaration, 457
    function, 272, 459
    library (STL), 19, 269, 287
    methodology, 324
    parameter, 309
    specialization, 461

`template`, 17, 269-270, 456
`terminate()`, 358-359, 465
terminator statement, 431
`this`, 132, 134, 229, 376, 447, 449, 467
`throw`, 352, 354-355, 358-359, 462, 465
throw expression, 354, 462
throw program, 354-355
`throw()`, 480
throw_it program, 463
`tick()`, 209
time library, 194
`toascii()`, 482
tokens, 24, 404
`tolower()`, 482
tools, 379
`top()` (STL), 295, 492
`toupper()`, 482
tracking program, 187
traditional conversion, 37
`transform()` (STL), 501-502
`triple` class, 223
triple program, 223
trivial conversion, 230
`true`, 44, 415, 423
`try`, 355, 357-358, 432, 463
try block, 20, 357
tstack program, 17
two-dimensional array, 176
type, 40
    built-in, 419, 447
    checking, 70
    class, 415
    compatibility, 467
    declaration, 25, 403
    derived, 415
    enumeration, 41, 467
    extensibility, 7, 23, 376-377

generic pointer, 94, 254, 283, 321, 415, 417, 467
instantiation, 18, 269, 275, 460
mixed, 43
native, 7, 23, 155, 199
pointer, 65
reference, 439
return, 67
safety, 78, 376, 440
simple, 34, 397
string, 85, 161, 371, 507
tag name, 41, 119
user-defined, 199, 444, 473
TYPE (Fortran), 396
`type_info` class, 455
type_info library, 342, 455
`typedef`, 120, 409, 413, 416
`typeid`, 341-342, 454-455, 468
typeid program, 342
types
    `bool`, 35, 44, 371, 414-415, 417, 423-424
    `char`, 34-35, 414, 467
    `class`, 117, 124, 316, 444, 451, 457
    `double`, 34-35, 414
    `enum`, 41, 408
    `float`, 35, 414
    `int`, 34-35, 414
    `long`, 34-35, 414
    `long double`, 414
    `short`, 34-35, 414
    `signed`, 34
    `signed char`, 467
    `struct`, 117-120, 124, 142, 316, 415, 444, 451
    `template`, 17, 269-270, 456
    `union`, 137, 139, 187
    `unsigned`, 34-35, 414
    `void`, 93, 439, 467

`void*`, 94, 283, 321, 415, 417, 467
`wchar_t`, 34-35, 414

U

unary one's complement operator ^, 426
unary operator overloading, 208
unconditional branch, 58
underscore, 405
`unexpected()`, 359, 465
union
    anonymous, 138, 187, 415
    initializer, 137
    member, 137
`union`, 137, 139, 187
union program, 138
`unique()` (STL), 501
`unique_copy()` (STL), 501
universal pointer constant, 406
UNIX, 1
`unsigned`, 34-35, 414
unsigned constant, 406
`update()`, 333
`upper_bound()` (STL), 491, 497
user-defined output, 473
user-defined type, 199, 444, 473
`using`, 6, 84, 412

V

\v vertical tab, 28, 407
variable, 409
    global, 81
    reference, 85
vect program, 444
vect_bnd program, 452
vect_ex program, 462
vect_it program, 278, 280
vect_ovl program, 448
vectacum program, 248

vector (STL), 487, 489, 491–492
vector class, 246, 278
vector program, 246–247
vectsort program, 249
vertical tab \v, 28, 407
virt_err program, 326
virt_sel program, 325
virtual
    base class, 338, 453
    inheritance, 337
virtual, 324, 327, 439, 453–455
visibility, 83, 117, 318
visitation, 245
void, 93, 439, 467
void*, 94, 254, 283, 321, 415, 417, 467
voidcast program, 93
volatile, 230, 416

W

Wasserman-Pircher diagram, 379
wchar_t, 34–35, 414
website, xvii
weekend program, 138
while, 50, 53, 55, 420, 432, 434
WHILE (Fortran), 398
while_t program, 50
white space, 27, 29, 407
widening, 38, 43
width of bit field, 139
Wirth Pascal, 396
word class, 139
word(), 254
word_cnt program, 483
write(), 470
ws, 472

X

xalloc(), 468

Z

zero, 27–28, 161, 371, 407
zero null pointer, 172

About the Author

Ira Pohl, Ph.D., is a professor of Computer Science at the University of California, Santa Cruz. He has over 25 years of experience as a software methodologist. His teaching and research interests are in the areas of artificial intelligence and programming languages. He has lectured at Berkeley, Stanford, the Vrije University in Amsterdam, the Courant Institute, Edinburgh University in Scotland, and Auckland University in New Zealand.

Ira Pohl is the coauthor, with Al Kelley, of a series of books published by Addison Wesley Longman and Benjamin Cummings on the C programming language: *A Book on C: An Introduction to Programming in C*, *C by Dissection*, and *Turbo C: The Essentials of C Programming*. He is also the author of *C++ for C Programmers*, *C++ for Pascal Programmers*, *Turbo C++*, *Object Oriented Programming Using C++*, and *C++ Distilled*, all Addison Wesley Longman or Benjamin Cummings publications. His first book, *The Nature of Computation: An Introduction to Computer Science* (Computer Science Press, 1981), coauthored with Alan Shaw, was a pioneering text on computer science. When not programming, he enjoys riding bicycles in Aptos, California, with his wife Debra and daughter Laura.

Photo by Todd Tsukushi

C++ Distilled
A Concise ANSI/ISO Reference and Style Guide
Ira Pohl, University of California, Santa Cruz

In *C++ Distilled*, veteran teacher and programmer Dr. Ira Pohl condenses 700 pages of proposed ANSI standard into a concise road map to C++. Selecting the most important and commonly used language elements, Dr. Pohl provides syntax, semantics, and examples, as well as style tips that he has distilled from more than two decades of experience. *C++ Distilled* is a handy reference to the most recent additions to the language, many of which have yet to be covered in existing C++ books. All source code from the book is available via the World Wide Web.

224 pages • Paperback • ISBN 0-201-69587-1
http://www.aw.com/cseng/authors/pohl/drp/drp.html

Object-Oriented Programming Using C++
Second Edition
Ira Pohl, University of California, Santa Cruz

Object-Oriented Programming Using C++, Second Edition provides the experienced programmer with a clear and thorough introduction to the object-oriented paradigm using ANSI C++. Each chapter introduces you to specific C++ language features that support object-oriented programming concepts, including the most recent additions to the language such as STL, namespaces, RTTI, and the bool type. The book illustrates concepts by example, providing full working programs right from the start. All source code from the book is available via the World Wide Web.

576 pages • Paperback • ISBN 0-201-89550-1
http://www.aw.com/cseng/authors/pohl/opus2e/opus2e.html

C++ For C Programmers
Second Edition
Ira Pohl, University of California, Santa Cruz

C++ For C Programmers, Second Edition makes the move to C++ fast and easy for C Programmers. By building on your knowledge of C, the book's extensive exercises and frequent language comparisons teach you C++ concepts quickly and demonstrate the language's powerful object-oriented features. The author uses his trademark "dissection" technique for illustrating the underlying structure of programs and the program design tradeoffs made. Based on the proposed ANSI C++ standard, the book covers many of the newest features including templates and exception handling.

384 pages • Paperback • ISBN 0-8053-3159-X
http://www.aw.com/cseng/authors/pohl/CPPFPROG/CPPFPROG.html